THE REVOLUTION OF ROBERT KENNEDY

THE
REVOLUTION
OF ROBERT
KENNEDY

■ ■ ■

FROM POWER TO
PROTEST AFTER JFK

JOHN R. BOHRER

BLOOMSBURY PRESS

NEW YORK · LONDON · OXFORD · NEW DELHI · SYDNEY

Bloomsbury Press
An imprint of Bloomsbury Publishing Plc

1385 Broadway	50 Bedford Square
New York	London
NY 10018	WC1B 3DP
USA	UK

www.bloomsbury.com

BLOOMSBURY and the Diana logo are trademarks of Bloomsbury Publishing Plc.

First published 2017

ISBN: HB: 978-1-60819-964-8
        ePub: 978-1-60819-982-2

LIBRARY OF CONGRESS CATALOGING-IN-PUBLICATION DATA

Names: Bohrer, John R., author.
Title: The revolution of Robert Kennedy: from power
to protest after JFK / John R. Bohrer.
Description: New York: Bloomsbury USA, 2017. | Includes
bibliographical references and index.
Identifiers: LCCN 2016059042 | ISBN 9781608199648 (hardcover: alk. paper)
Subjects: LCSH: Kennedy, Robert F., 1925–1968. | Presidential candidates—
United States—Biography. | Legislators—United States—Biography. |
Cabinet officers—United States—Biography. | United States—Politics and
government—1963–1969. | United States. Congress. Senate—Biography.
Classification: LCC E840.8.K4 B64 2017 | DDC 973.922092 [B]—dc23
LC record available at https://lccn.loc.gov/2016059042

2 4 6 8 10 9 7 5 3 1

Typeset by Westchester Publishing Services
Printed and bound in the U.S.A. by Berryville Graphics Inc., Berryville, Virginia

To find out more about our authors and books visit www.bloomsbury.com.
Here you will find extracts, author interviews, details of forthcoming events,
and the option to sign up for our newsletters.

Bloomsbury books may be purchased for business or promotional use.
For information on bulk purchases please contact Macmillan Corporate
and Premium Sales Department at specialmarkets@macmillan.com.

For all my JB's . . .

CONTENTS

INTRODUCTION

Memorial

December 18, 1963

IN HIS DARKEST MOMENT, Robert Kennedy defined change.

"We are a young country," he wrote on December 18, 1963, four weeks after his brother, the President, was assassinated. "We are growing and expanding until it appears that this planet will no longer contain us. We have problems now that people fifty, even ten years ago, would not have dreamed would have to be faced."

Bobby was writing the foreword to a memorial edition of John F. Kennedy's book *Profiles in Courage*—something he would not have dreamed of facing four weeks earlier. In an instant, he had lost his brother, his boss, and his security. The mingling loyalties to family and country had made life before "simple," he would say. Now it was racked by uncertainty. The presidency belonged to Lyndon Baines Johnson, a man whose morals and judgment he questioned, and whose insatiable appetite for political domination convinced Bobby that the name Kennedy would mean little in a few short months. The attorney general warned friends to act fast and get what they wanted, for their political power would soon expire.

Bobby himself was unsure of what he wanted. With each passing day, pressure mounted for him to decide how to use what he had inherited. So many had put their faith in a future with JFK at the helm. People now looked to Bobby for action—some for direction, most just for comfort in their grief.

This reaction would have seemed strange just a few weeks earlier. Many liberals did not trust the President's younger brother and chief political strategist. They thought he put elections before principles and were disgusted by his battering style on behalf of Communist-hunting and crime-fighting Senate committees in the 1950s. "Robert was perceived as a tough guy, insensitive, cruel, vindictive, clannish, summed up in a word which he never shook off . . . ruthless," the Yale law professor Alexander Bickel would write.[1] He was so polarizing that civil rights managed to cut against him both ways: demonstrators picketed him for lacking urgency and segregationists accused him of cramming court orders down their throats.[2] In the weeks leading up to the assassination, Bobby felt he was becoming so politically toxic that he spoke with his brother about resigning before the reelection campaign. Recounting the conversation in 1964, he said, "What was costing us was the great dislike for me in the South particularly, but in certain other [areas]" as well, and that the blame for enforcing desegregation rulings in what had been reliably Democratic states like Alabama and Mississippi "had changed from just *me* in '62 and '63 to both of *us*—'the Kennedy brothers.'" Bobby couldn't even go off to manage the campaign as he did in 1960, he told the President, "because then they would have thought I was still in there, still important." When Bobby suggested they say he was leaving "to make speeches," JFK insisted he stay on to avoid the appearance of wavering. "It was an unnecessary burden, in my judgment," Bobby recalled.[3] At a gathering of Justice Department aides for the attorney general's thirty-eighth birthday on November 20, two of his assistants left with the impression he was "depressed that night" and about to resign.[4] Less than forty-eight hours later, the President was dead.

That mood was nothing compared to the lows Bobby would experience after JFK's assassination. But the tragedy also elevated him in ways he wouldn't have expected. In time, "ruthless" Robert Kennedy would become the redoubt of a young decade's ideals. There were people who wanted to hope, to recapture the excitement, and believe that the New Frontier President Kennedy spoke of was not behind them.

This idea was slow to dawn on Bobby as the cold crept in, the days became shorter, and the sleepless nights stretched on. He would later say that he thought about the future in that month to the point where the only decision he could make was "to stop thinking about it."[5] Yet in those lost days, he wrote the truest expression of who he was and what he lived for.

On December 18, the day they renamed New York's Idlewild Airport for JFK and Congress authorized putting his face on money,[6] tributes to the late president were piling up. The *Profiles in Courage* memorial edition was one of them, and a rumor had made its way to the publisher that Bobby might write the foreword. If not Bobby, the book's editor gently suggested, "how about Sandburg?"[7] Carl Sandburg, the poet and biographer of Lincoln, was ancient—nearly eighty-six years old. Bobby had just turned thirty-eight. It was up to him.

And so the attorney general sat alone in his Justice Department office—"this enormous mausoleum," as a reporter once described it[8]—with ceilings so high he could lob a football. Children's drawings clung from pieces of tape to the walnut-paneled walls, as dreadful thoughts of the future crowded that terribly empty space. He sent questions to JFK's top aide and their father's office, looking for a quote from a speech, or wondering about Jack's illnesses—*his suffering*—as a young man.[9] Bobby ignored his speechwriter's recommendations[10] and put the draft down entirely in his own hand. He wrote the word **Courage** in bold, underlined text at the top of the first sheet of ruled paper. Hardly any revisions were necessary.

He wrote how President Kennedy had suffered greatly in his forty-six years. A bad stomach. A bad back. Long spells in hospitals. "At least half of the days that he spent on this earth were days of intense physical pain." Bobby remembered their 1951 trip around the world, to Okinawa, where Jack's fever reached 106 degrees. "They didn't think he would live," he wrote. "But during all this time, I never heard him complain. I never heard him say anything which would indicate that he felt God had dealt with him unjustly."

Kennedys didn't cry. They did not wear their pain for all to see. They were not halted midsentence by emotion or have eyes welled with tears. They were not given a sleeping pill and heard through the door, crying, "Why God?"

In the four weeks between his brother's death and writing the foreword, Robert Kennedy had done all these things, no matter how much he willed himself not to. He didn't just feel pain—he emitted it. "Desolation," scribbled Edwin Lahey, the smoky old newsman who was granted the first interview days before Bobby's writing. Lahey had watched him since he first arrived in Washington as one of Senator Joe McCarthy's tenacious boy prosecutors, determined to root out Communism and win absolute victory in the clean-cut 1950s. A dozen years on, the youthful face was creased with experience and "crushed" by despair. To see Robert Kennedy was to feel his pain.

This was not how Jack Kennedy would be seen, as Bobby wrote in the foreword: "Those who knew him well would know he was suffering only because his face was a little whiter, the lines around his eyes were a little deeper, his words a little sharper. Those who did not know him well detected nothing. He didn't complain about his problem so why should I complain about mine—that is how one always felt."[11]

Kennedys didn't cry. This was the family mantra and hard-hearted edict of their father, ruthless entrepreneur and ambassador to the Court of St. James, Joseph P. Kennedy, who pounded into his children this unmatched toughness and stubborn refusal of defeat. But few understood the deeper meaning: that Kennedys didn't cry so that others might not cry, too. As their mother, Rose, would write, "What he really meant was that there was to be *no self-pity*, and no burdening of others with any personal misfortunes by making a commotion about them. He knew that for almost everyone life is likely to hold many knocks and bruises, and that people had better get used to that idea at an early age."[12]

Robert Kennedy's entire life had led to a bruise he could not forget, a pain that fell drop by "drop upon the heart," in the words of a Greek poem he would months later discover. Bobby had to cope with change. Sudden, unwanted, stunning change. It was a time to be brave, a time to have courage. In his memorial foreword, he quoted a passage from his brother's inaugural, beginning with the part just before the eternal "Let the word go forth . . . the torch has been passed to a new generation . . ."

"We dare not forget today that we are the heirs of that first revolution."[13]

In the years that followed, Robert Kennedy underwent his own revolution, recasting him in his time and beyond into a glimpse of a leader still longed for. He had been as rough as JFK had been smooth, and his transition was at many times rocky. He searched for power in traditional means and, when he found himself incapable, used his dissenting voice to exert what influence he could. His actions and gestures, from someone who had been so clearly wounded by the world, brought hope to those who needed healing, even across political divides. These years tell the story of how he dreamed and plotted, where he failed and succeeded—but ultimately, how he handled change and tried to send it forth. By 1966, he would find his revolution was catching and watch it sweep across his life and cross currents with a generation, to the extent that a person who had walked the secret corridors of power would at last claim membership among the world's youth. "This world demands the qualities of youth," he would say, "not a time of life but a state of mind." For Robert Kennedy understood that a true revolution takes a leader young enough to change with the times.[14]

THOUGH NOT A politician in the traditional sense, Bobby was the most political of the Kennedys in November 1963. Unlike his two brothers, he had never run for office—a difference that freed him from the burden of having to be liked by all. He became the Kennedy most closely identified with the cold, calculating compromises beneath every successful campaign.

Campaigns had consumed most of his adult life. He missed his law school graduation to return to Massachusetts to run Jack's 1952 Senate campaign.[15] He put his future aside or altered its course every time Jack Kennedy's political career required. He joined Adlai Stevenson on the road in 1956 to learn the workings of a presidential operation,[16] and his ruthless reputation only grew as he took his brother's ambition nationwide. "Gentlemen, I don't give a damn if the state and county organizations survive after November," he told a meeting of New York reform Democrats in 1960. "And I don't care if *you* survive. I want to elect John F. Kennedy."[17]

Ask anyone why Bobby was appointed attorney general in 1961 at the age of thirty-five, and they would say because his brother was elected president.

But few would observe what was equally true: that JFK would never have been elected president had Bobby not delivered the unpopular decisions the candidate didn't want to sully himself with. Every negative thing about Jack was put on Bobby. From the right, from the left—he was the bogeyman. One anonymous politician remarked to a columnist how "both always told it to me straight. The difference was that Jack spoon-fed it to you while Bobby barked it at you."[18] As U.S. senator, Jack was the one who met with favor seekers, smiling and nodding as they made impossible demands in his Senate Office Building suite. Then he would send them down to Bobby's office in the basement, where little brother's stone face said no.[19]

As evident as the routine was, many refused to accept the truth, even as Jack moved to the White House and Bobby went from the basement to the Justice Department. *Bobby Kennedy did it to me* was Washington-speak for *The President would* never *do this to me. The President would have given me what I wanted.* It was the role Bobby played. Political columnist Drew Pearson wrote that Bobby was "one of the most devoted brothers in American history . . . He took the knocks, let his brother get the praise."[20] Bobby was the "fall guy," another wrote. "Absorbing the blows so that his brother would remain untouched."[21] He didn't cry about it. He just took it.

"You won't have any trouble finding my enemies," he told a reporter in 1962. "They're all over town."[22]

And just as he did with the favor seekers, Bobby was often the one telling his brother the things he did not want to hear. Bobby was a critical voice in the Kennedy administration—advising, pushing, and often challenging the President's thinking. His unimpeachable loyalty allowed him to do this without raising a single question about his motives, his ambition, his angle. To spur was his role, his father's rationale for putting him at the head of a powerful executive department, making them the closest two relatives—let alone siblings— in the line of succession since Woodrow Wilson's treasury secretary married the president's daughter.

"I think there was an advantage in our relationship," Bobby said in February 1964, "because my motivation really could never be questioned. There wasn't anything to be gained by me, and I wasn't running for any office, so I didn't have any political future that I was attempting to work for or help."[23]

He was willing to make this trade-off because his relationship with his brother gave his life meaning. "No one telephoned the President more often than his brother Bob did," JFK's personal secretary Evelyn Lincoln later wrote, "and it was a rare day when Bob did not come to see him at least once."[24]

Bobby had a superhuman devotion. Even while he was up all hours running the 1960 West Virginia campaign, he still made it to mass on Sunday mornings.[25] "Jack works as hard as any mortal man can," Joseph Kennedy said. "Bobby goes a little further."[26] This was the legend, born in part from words attributed to the Ambassador: *He hates like me.* The infamous anecdote has never been pinned down and was most likely never said,[27] rising out of the ether, typifying how others felt Bobby came into being. It was wrong, though, because if anything gave Bobby Kennedy his toughness, it was being on his own.

He was born eight years after Jack and seven years before Teddy. "So there he was," his mother wrote, "with two older brothers and one very much younger, none of whom was much use to him as boyhood pals, playmates."[28] He attended more schools than he could remember, and his coming of age was punctuated by international upheaval, war, and the loss or impairment of three older siblings between 1941 and 1948. It was along this tragic and lonely path that he discovered strength within himself—a tremendous fight. He lettered in football at Harvard despite his smaller stature, was the first brother to marry, and fathered the first Kennedy grandchild. He quickly plunged all of his energies and devotion into his family. "Bobby's a tough one," the Ambassador told a reporter in 1957. "He'll keep the Kennedys together, you can bet."[29] He didn't have to stand as tall as his brothers had because he was the one they leaned on. And therefore he could be as ruthless as he had to.

"I don't think about the future," he said in 1962. "If you start thinking about doing something else, you have a tendency to change. You start preparing for it—you can't help it. During the campaign I rarely considered doing anything in government. I thought I might travel. I thought of going back to Harvard after Election Day to study history. You can't let it change you. If you begin changing, you've got to get out."[30]

Now change had come for him.

Newscasts offered glimpses of his sorrow in those first weeks after the assassination, short reports on his activities. Journalists cheered him on, speculating over when—not if—he would emerge. The *New York Times* reported that at the time of his writing the foreword "the possibility of his resigning was rumored." The *New York Herald Tribune* quoted one of his closest associates: "Bob is in a state of shock. He's been wounded in combat. He has to recover, and only then can he really make a decision." Other people who knew him well spoke of Johnson's pleas for him to stay, but that a political bid in Massachusetts "seems inevitable." The *New York Daily News* had close associates saying he would stay attorney general through the passage of the civil rights bill—a JFK proposal that President Johnson advocated as a tribute—but that he would be gone by the November election, lest he hurt LBJ's chances in the South. And some—"those closest to the Attorney General"—believed he would seek the vice presidential nomination.[31] To many, this notion seemed absurd. To Bobby, it seemed his duty.

WHEN HE WAS still a senator, Jack had once told a reporter, "Just as I went into politics because Joe died, if anything happened to me tomorrow, my brother Bobby would run for my seat in the Senate. And if Bobby died, Teddy would take over for him."[32]

Though he was confused and conflicted, Robert Kennedy undertook a bid for the vice presidency, which became vacant with Lyndon Johnson's ascension and would remain that way—as it had during the nearly four years Harry Truman inherited from FDR—until a successor could be elected in the next general election. Recent tradition dictated that Johnson would have most, if not all, of the influence over who his running mate should be. But the final decision would be made by the delegates to the summer's Democratic National Convention, nine months away. Bobby had the difficult task of swaying the delegates and the near-impossible mission of convincing the President. His actions and thinking were occasionally out in the open, but most often in secret, with some of its aspects hidden to close aides, unknown or misunderstood. Ultimately, he decided against carrying out his final and what would have been his most dramatic play to join the Johnson ticket—to resign his office as attorney general and wage a full-out campaign to stampede the convention. Whatever his reason for going so far down the path and then abruptly stepping off it, the fact remains that he had made such preparations. And the reason he did can be found within the memorial foreword he wrote in December 1963, where he quoted "one of the President's favorite authors," Lord Tweedsmuir, who wrote, "Politics is still the greatest and most honorable adventure."

Bobby added, "It has been fashionable in many places to look down on politics, on those in Government." He had done so himself, saying after the 1952 Senate race, "Politicians do nothing but hold meetings." By December 1963, he understood what politics could mean: "Government is where the decisions will be made affecting not only all our destinies, but the future of our children born and unborn." He remembered talking with his brother during the Cuban missile crisis about their being killed in nuclear annihilation, writing that what the President feared most was the fate of the world's children. "They would never have been given a chance to make a decision, to vote in an election, to run for office, to lead a revolution, to determine their own destinies."[33]

This was his inheritance—one he knew he had to pass on. And so when speaking to young people anywhere in the world, he would return to the theme.

"A revolution is now in progress," he said on New York college campuses in 1965. "It is a revolution for individual dignity . . . for economic freedom . . . for social reform and political freedom, for internal justice and international independence."

"This revolution," he would say, "is directed against *us*—against the one third of the world that diets while others starve; against a nation that buys eight million new cars a year while most of the world goes without shoes . . ."[34]

To students in Peru, Robert Kennedy—who had recently been among the most powerful men on the planet—advised that it was their "responsibility" to lead a revolution. "A revolution which will be peaceful if we are wise enough; humane if we care enough; successful if we are fortunate enough. But a revolution will come whether we will it or not. We can affect its character, we cannot alter its inevitability."[35]

Robert Kennedy's exile from political power had sharpened his awareness of change and heightened his ability to embrace it. He was one of the comfortable, yet afflicted. A member of the establishment who understood how powerless the old order was against people and an idea whose time had come.

Robert Kennedy occupied both sides of the coin in the middle of the 1960s. He became the old and the new—architect of a war and its chief critic; master of the backroom politics and defender of street protest; able to evoke nostalgia and hope for the future—for he stood and spoke like the Kennedy who had led the country into the decade, but wore the hair of someone who looked like he had actually learned from it. He was an authority figure and troublemaker, chiding abusive lawmen and executives in committee hearings, rallying to the side of farmworkers on the picket line, and railing against oppressive governments in foreign countries. He crusaded for mental health, education, an end to the ghettos, and, ultimately, an end to a war. He spoke of revolutions across society, inevitable but threatening only that which was wrong. Revolutions were cathartic, corrective experiences, as evidenced by the one he underwent himself. Through it all, he dared not forget that he and his adopted generation of young people were, too, the heirs of that first revolution.

This is how Robert Kennedy came to define change, and find his way forward through the valley of his life. "What happens to the country, to the world," he wrote on that lonely December day, "depends on what we do with what others have left us."[36]

BOOK I

THE NEW
FRONTIER BEHIND

THE FUTURE QUESTION

November 1963–January 1964

THE POOLSIDE TELEPHONE RANG at Hickory Hill, Bobby Kennedy's Virginia manor house across the Chain Bridge from Washington, piercing what had been a quiet, unseasonably warm November afternoon. The extension was one of many secure lines that ran through his property, installed by the Signal Corps. It was a testament to his power and place in his brother's administration—to be within a digit's reach at all times. On November 22, 1963, Bobby was having a swim and a tuna fish sandwich because it was Friday and he was Catholic. The telephone at the foot of the pool delivered words that burst into his life, never to exit: "The President's been shot."

Jack's condition was bad, inconclusive, and Bobby went from the pool to his bedroom to dress, intending to go to his brother's side in Dallas at once. Then the extension in the upstairs study rang and he learned that the trip would not be necessary.[1]

Bobby had expressed shock by the swimming pool, clapping his hand to his mouth, speechless.[2] He cried out when the official word came. And then, passing by the framed pictures in Hickory Hill's hallways—photographs of his father, his deceased siblings, his wife, his young children—he seemed to find a well of calm within himself. His lunch guests had gone to the television set in the living room, searching for news. Bob came down the stairs and poked his head in. "He died," he said softly.

Robert Kennedy spent the next hours wandering the grassy slopes around his house, going from telephone to telephone, speaking with family and friends, consoling them and assigning tasks: there was an office to turn over, people to collect, a funeral to plan . . . He saw to it that the White House changed the locks on the President's personal and medical files, for reasons only he knew.[3] He spoke with his brother's successor, Lyndon Baines Johnson, who sought his attorney general's legal opinion on whether he should be sworn in immediately or wait until landing in Washington. Bobby said it didn't matter. Johnson's secretary asked for the wording of the oath of office, and Bobby started to read it over the phone to her, but his voice trembled repeating the words he had last heard on a bright, cold day some three years earlier. His deputy Nicholas Katzenbach took over.[4]

Still, the encounter showed just how tough Bob Kennedy truly was, and how tough Lyndon Johnson must have seen him to be. Johnson wanted Bobby's approval for a ceremonial swearing-in not just as attorney general, but as leader of the Kennedy family. And Bobby showed him he was tough enough to discuss it while the blood still cooled in his brother's veins.

Bobby spoke to many others that afternoon. Comforted them. Asked questions. Gave answers. Of all the words he spoke, the most revealing were the ones he spoke to himself. As he moved between the phone calls, Bobby Kennedy said to himself simply, "There's been so much hate."[5]

Family had defined Robert Kennedy's public service, and now he believed the public was through with his family. He even blamed them in the hours after the assassination.

He paced the lawn behind Hickory Hill, while his press aide, Ed Guthman, loyally paced at his side. Bobby vented that through all the anger directed toward the Kennedys, he never thought a horror like this would happen, and if it did, "I thought it would be me." He told Guthman, "There's been so much bitterness and hatred, and so many people who might have said something have remained silent—" and the sound drained from his throat before he could finish. It was one of the few times in his life that Bobby would verbally direct his anger for his brother's death, and it was toward the words of opponents, the silence of friends—a toxic political discourse.

Guthman tried to comfort him, saying maybe it would bring people together.

"No," Bob said slowly, "this will make it worse."[6]

Two days after President Kennedy's funeral, Jack Rosenthal, Guthman's assistant in the Justice Department press office, was walking to his desk when he caught a glimpse of the attorney general. Rosenthal was shocked to see him back in the office so soon and slightly relieved his boss hadn't noticed him. Rosenthal was only twenty-eight years old. He simply didn't know what he would say to him. Then Guthman summoned Rosenthal to his office.

There was the attorney general—"Bob," as the men and women who worked on his staff called him—a week over thirty-eight, five days into his grief, the color drained from his face. He looked awful. He held out that morning's copy of the *Wall Street Journal*. Smack in the middle of the front page was a story detailing Washington's embrace of President Johnson—glowing reviews all, with the exception of one complaint, that of a "Kennedy appointee at the

Justice Department," who said, "It's pretty hard to identify with a Texas wheeler-dealer."[7] The attorney general wanted to know who in the department would say such a stupid thing to a reporter.

"You know," Guthman said to Rosenthal, "you talk to the *Wall Street Journal* reporter every day. Could you call him up and ask him who that was?" Rosenthal knew it'd be a lot to ask, but, given the circumstances, said he would try.

Rosenthal got hold of his friend at the *Journal* and asked about the source.

"Well, I'm really embarrassed to tell you this, Jack," he said, "but it was *you*."

Rosenthal's friend didn't have a byline on the story, but contributed to its reporting, and Jack had all but forgotten that, the day before, the friend had asked for Jack's opinion of Lyndon Johnson. Jack replied, "It's pretty hard to identify with his shit-kick style."

Since *shit-kick* couldn't be printed in the *Wall Street Journal* in 1963, the reporter changed the phrase to "Texas wheeler-dealer"—which Rosenthal would have objected to, had he been asked, but there was nothing he could do now. He went back into the office to face the music.

"Oh, thank God," Bob replied—he was worried an assistant attorney general was behind the quote. He knew that it was only a matter of time before Johnson ferreted out the source, and that it was a lot better if it was the junior press officer. Nothing was ever spoken of the incident again, but even decades later Rosenthal couldn't help but wonder, "*Why did he care?*"

What the concern showed was how even in the days after the assassination, when he was racked by exhaustion and despair, Robert Kennedy was thinking about where he stood with President Johnson.[8] It showed that in those days of aching grief Robert Kennedy was thinking about his future. Robert Kennedy was thinking about politics.

LATER THAT AFTERNOON, Johnson summoned Kennedy to the Oval Office to clear up what a White House staff memo called "several points of misunderstanding." Bobby had 'misunderstood' why the plane in Dallas couldn't take off until Johnson was sworn in, and Bobby had 'misunderstood' how Jacqueline Kennedy had been made into a prop at Johnson's side, and Bobby had 'misunderstood' why President Kennedy's furniture was moved, and Bobby had misunderstood, *period*. The memo concluded, "The Attorney General has the feeling the President doesn't deal directly . . . The arts of the Hill are not his arts." Johnson tried to put Bobby's mind at ease, explaining why he moved into the Oval Office so swiftly, how he had treated Jackie on the plane back to Washington. "People around you are saying things about me," Johnson told him. "I won't let people around me say anything about your people, and don't let any of your people say anything about me." They were done within twelve minutes.[9]

Bobby later said of the conversation, "I didn't get into an argument about it . . . I didn't know quite what to say."[10]

That night, at President Johnson's address before a joint session of Congress, the *New York Times* described Bobby's slight figure sitting among the other cabinet members as "the most moving sight in the House chamber."[11]

Kennedy wasn't ready to discuss his future yet or at least didn't attempt to with his dear friend and former aide John Seigenthaler. Seigenthaler took heart at how Bob "was still functional" in those first days after the assassination, how he made dark, wry jokes about the absurd and strange new world he occupied.

"Come on in," he said the night of the burial, "somebody shot my brother and we're watching his funeral on television."[12]

He and Ethel had invited their usual mix of Justice Department officials and newspapermen, serving Bloody Marys and putting up a front of light banter. His joking did not hide that he was on the verge of a breakdown. Some feared that he would follow his grief away from public life and abruptly resign his office. "We need you, you know," one former aide told Bobby.

"Yeah, I know, but I don't have the heart for it right now."[13]

Nor did he have the heart to spend Thanksgiving at Hyannis Port, the summer home on Cape Cod where, in the past, the Kennedys had planned and celebrated so often. "It was something he could not quite do," Bobby's mother, Rose, later wrote. "He had reached a state, I suppose, of almost insupportable emotional shock." Instead, he chose a week of recuperation in Florida, where Treasury Secretary C. Douglas Dillon lent the Robert Kennedys his house on Hobe Sound. There, he walked the beach and thought. His feelings came out, Pierre Salinger remembered, in "really vicious games" of touch football, "knocking people down."[14] He was angry. He was hurt. He wanted to resign.

ON THE DAY he returned from Florida,[15] Bobby spent two hours talking to Clark Clifford about what he would do next, another of the contrasts the attorney general faced after Dallas. Clifford was Washington's Democratic wise man and had handled the Kennedys' White House transition in late 1960. He had even tried to get Bobby off the hook for the cabinet position that his father insisted he take. The Kennedy brothers let Clifford go down to Palm Beach to explain to the Ambassador in person why Bobby shouldn't be the attorney general. Ambassador Kennedy listened politely, thanked Clifford for sharing his views, then told him forcefully but without malice, *"Bobby is going to be attorney general."*[16] And so he was.

Now, three years later, a stroke had taken Joseph Kennedy's ability to speak, Jack was dead, and President Johnson told Clifford, "Clark, you're *my* transition expert now." The fixer was ordered to talk the attorney general into keeping his post.[17]

"I have just finished a two-hour session with Bobby," an exhausted-sounding Clifford told President Johnson on the evening of December 4, "and first I want to say, he's going to stay . . . We, we really had it out and we covered it all. And I think there are some arguments that he found unanswerable, and I'm just authorized to say now that he's going to stay."[18]

This was not what Bobby wanted, for he knew as well as his enemies that he was "just another lawyer" now. "Bobby Kennedy is out," Teamsters president Jimmy Hoffa told his membership—a crude, but accurate observation from the corrupt union chief whom Bobby was closing in on after years of pursuit.[19] Ironically, the organization helping Bobby put Hoffa away—the Federal Bureau of Investigation—was the first to echo Hoffa's sentiment. FBI Director J. Edgar Hoover welcomed the end of Bobby's power. The director had been in his post since before the attorney general was born, and though the bureau was nominally under the umbrella of the Justice Department, Hoover had grown accustomed to an open-door policy with the Oval Office. But that changed in the Kennedy administration. Bobby had Hoover report to *him* and even installed a direct line to the director's desk so he wouldn't get a secretary when he called.

That line was dead when Bobby returned from Florida, and when an aide brought up the FBI's insubordination, he smiled back wryly and said, "Those people don't work for us anymore." Whenever Hoover and Kennedy spoke after Dallas, and the times were few, their interactions were insignificant. Bobby had to go to President Johnson to make requests of his subordinate. "As I've said before," he told LBJ that July, "it's quite difficult for me . . . I have no dealings with the FBI anymore. It's a very difficult situation." Johnson did nothing—even feigned ignorance. Bobby later said of this time that given the President's lack of support for him, "If I had just been appointed attorney general, I would have resigned." But he felt that "it would be considered that I was getting out for a different reason, so that wouldn't do any good, and I was going to accept that relationship through the year—and then I'd get out."[20]

His friend Dean Markham warned him in a letter a week after Dallas, "The entire country is on your side. If you should make any hasty decision to resign, this attitude could boomerang. The reaction would be that if you can't play the game under your rules you will take your ball and go home." So he stayed, merely to keep up appearances. He ordered a late Christmas present for each of his top aides: gold cuff links bearing the Department of Justice seal and inscribed *1961–1963*, as if his term as attorney general had already come to an end.[21]

His life included one grim task after another. On the night that he promised Clifford he would stay, he took Jackie and Teddy to Arlington National Cemetery, eerily calm after another day of mourners passing in endless procession. Silent in the glow of the eternal flame, Bobby watched the reburial of President Kennedy's babies alongside their father. An infant son, Patrick, had died a mere fifteen weeks before. A baby girl was stillborn in the summer of 1956 while Jack was sailing in the Mediterranean. It was Bobby at Jackie's bedside when she awoke. It was Bobby who told her. It was Bobby who comforted her.[22]

And it was Bobby who, upon Jackie's return from Dallas, sat with her behind the gray curtains of the ambulance to Bethesda Naval Hospital, next to the box with the remains of her husband—his brother—as she unburdened herself of "the full horror" of what had happened in the motorcade. Bobby listened in silence for twenty minutes. He knew Jackie needed to tell him, tell *someone*. "I didn't think about whether I wanted to hear it or not," he said later.

The relationship was not one-sided. Jackie gave to Bobby, too, as someone who felt the loss as deeply as he did and indulged his grief. She was the one he turned to the night of the funeral, shortly before Jack's first midnight in the ground, and nodded when he asked, "Should we go visit our friend?"[23]

Bobby would go to the grave more than anyone else. Living out at Hickory Hill, he had to pass his brother's final resting place on his way to and from work, but he would most often go at night, after the crowds had been locked out, when it was just him bathed in the orange light of the eternal flame. A columnist quoted a friend, "In times of great trouble, Bobby instinctively felt he ought to be in physical range of his brother's call." Robert Kennedy was the only one the President trusted to give him direct answers—as another columnist put it in 1962, "the brother to whom the President could talk as though to himself."[24] Bobby would go to the grave often, to be near him. He would go there with nothing but his own thoughts, as though he were talking to himself.

Ethel would tell a reporter months later, "Bobby never thought about himself—or his own life. So when the President died—well, it was like part of Bobby died, too."[25]

Ethel, ever chipper, ever trusting in God's will, kept him strong, kept him in the world. She was the candle in the window, guiding him home past the marker of death in his path. "Without her," a friend said in 1964, "Bobby might have gone off the deep end . . ."[26]

THE DAY AFTER the children's reburial, Bobby flew to Boston to incorporate the John F. Kennedy Memorial Library. On the flight back aboard the *Caroline*, he asked Arthur Schlesinger whether he should go for the vice presidency. It was December 5, less than two weeks after the assassination. The vice president's chair would be vacant for another thirteen months, as a constitutional remedy to replace one was only in its early stages. The choice of the next vice president rested with President Johnson, but could be heavily influenced by Democratic Party leaders. In the years before reforms turned the delegate selection process over to primary and caucus elections, insiders decided who had the power at the national nominating convention. The assassination's impact on the 1964 race was considered almost immediately. The *New York Times*' Warren Weaver filed a story from Washington on the day JFK was killed, appearing in the next day's paper, speculating over Bobby's role going forward.[27] He and Johnson might not have seen eye to eye, but the name Kennedy still meant something.

"My first reaction was negative," Schlesinger recorded in his journal about Bobby's suggestion of the vice presidency, "though, when he asked me why, I found it hard to give clear reasons." Schlesinger felt it might seem "a little too artificial and calculated," and that he needed to develop his own political base. "Bobby added that he did not like the idea of taking a job which was really based on the premise of waiting around for someone to die."[28]

He asked Schlesinger what he thought he should do. Schlesinger suggested staying on as attorney general "for an appropriate period," then softening his image with a few years of working on civil rights or juvenile delinquency. "This would help erase the national impression that he was a demonic prosecutor," Schlesinger thought. He suggested buying the liberal *New York Post*, whose owner, Dorothy Schiff, had tried to sell the paper to Jack only months earlier as a post–White House hobby.[29] Then in 1966, depending on where Bobby moved, he could either run for governor of Massachusetts or New York.

Bobby said Teddy had suggested the Alliance for Progress, the Kennedy administration's initiative to improve relations with Latin America. Schlesinger remembered the President's idea of putting Bobby in charge both of the Alliance and Latin American political affairs under the auspices of the State Department. The idea was one Bobby liked.

As they talked, Schlesinger showed him letters from leading thinkers Isaiah Berlin and Reinhold Niebuhr reacting to the death of his brother. Bobby read and wiped tears from his eyes—the first time Schlesinger saw him lose his composure.[30] It was not to be the last.

Schlesinger told him that Labor Secretary Willard Wirtz, who had been for Adlai Stevenson at the 1960 Democratic convention and a believer in "ruthless Robert Kennedy," said a few days before, "I am very high on him—and you know how much that means, since you know how far back I started." Bobby "seemed pleased," Schlesinger recorded in his journal, "and said that he would get in touch with Bill so that they could concert their plans and strategies."[31]

Days later, *New York Post* columnist James Wechsler placed a single line in his column: "Bobby Kennedy is beginning to schedule conversations with political associates over his own future."[32]

The first press interview Bobby did after the assassination went to Edwin A. Lahey, the chain-smoking, blunt-spoken veteran correspondent of the *Chicago Daily News*. Lahey first got to know Bob Kennedy's determined cool years earlier on the Senate Rackets Committee, when the boy prosecutor dressed down hardened labor leaders, throwing questions like punches. Lahey looked at the kid again now, behind a desk in his calm and cavernous Justice Department office. Bobby was still young, the newspaperman wrote, only there was this "desolation . . . written all over [his] boyish face." When Lahey entered, Bobby was on the telephone with his father, long distance. Despite his stroke, Joseph Kennedy could still listen and feel disappointment when his children didn't call. So Bobby and his siblings each had their assigned days to phone and lift their father's spirits.[33] Bobby spoke into the receiver and heard nothing back. "Outwardly," Lahey wrote, "Bob Kennedy seems crushed beyond hope, mentally, spiritually, and physically. He puts on a bright bit of banter for an occasional visitor and seems to act at times like the chief legal officer of the United States." Gently, Lahey became the first reporter to ask him the future question—*What will you do?*—and the first to get the reply that Robert Kennedy would give over and over again that year.

"I just don't know . . .

"I suppose I'll stay here until the civil rights bill gets through Congress," Bobby said of the legislation his brother had proposed and put him in charge of. "After that, I don't know." Lahey asked about the vice presidency. RFK returned a blank look. This, too, would become a familiar dance. Bobby said he wasn't considering it and that he had seen the job and knew it too well to want it. A speculative bid for Massachusetts governor seemed far-fetched, too. He just didn't know—publicly or privately. Bobby remarked to a friend, "I don't know whether I'll stay, or whether I want to go on the ticket in '64, or anything, until I know whether I think Johnson can be President of the United States and follow through with the Kennedy program. I'm not going to make my judgment on anything other than that. It's too early for me to even think about '64, because I don't know whether I want to have any part of these people. I don't know how they're going to be, running this country. And if they don't fulfill and follow out my brother's program, I don't want to have anything to do with them."[34]

Soon after, the columnist Murray Kempton would write, "In December Robert Kennedy said to an old friend from the papers that he had to find a goal for the first time in his life because, for as long as he could remember, he had had no goal that was not his brother's."[35]

ON DECEMBER 13, Schlesinger and JFK aide Richard Goodwin, who had started as a speechwriter on the campaign and was now at the State Department, met with Bobby in his tomblike Justice Department office. So many things about the room were still the same: the furniture was just as it was, the children's drawings taped to the walls. Yet the phone didn't ring the way it had before Dallas. And though visitors continued to stop by, they seemed duller. They were all little tells, journalist Hugh Sidey wrote, "that the power had passed."[36]

Bobby had brought Schlesinger and Goodwin in to talk about what they would do next. His idea of the Alliance for Progress was already vanishing, as Johnson was giving a key Latin America appointment to Thomas Mann, an Eisenhower-era colonialist whom Johnson privately called "the nut-cutter." Under Secretary of State Averell Harriman told Schlesinger that Mann's designation would reverse the direction of President Kennedy's progressive Latin American policy, and that he was willing to resign over it. Bobby had been hoping Johnson would hold off on the appointment, in deference to President Kennedy's memory.[37] But he was wrong, and now they had to figure out what to do—not just about this incident, but in a broader sense.

"I don't want to see Averell Harriman get hurt, or anyone else," Bob told Schlesinger and Goodwin. "Harriman's got his faults. I've got my faults. We've all got faults. The important thing for us to do now is to stick together. Our power will last for just eleven months. It will disappear the day of the election. What we have to do is to use that power in these months to the best permanent advantage." Schlesinger said the vice presidency was the best way to achieve that. Bobby seemed to agree but said that wasn't important at the moment. Schlesinger would remember him imploring them, "We must all stay in touch and not let them pick us off one by one." Goodwin recalled Bobby twice saying, "The secret is collective action." They had to concert the efforts of the hundreds of New Frontiersmen in government. "We're important to Johnson. I'm the most important because my name happens to be Kennedy. But we're all important. I haven't thought it through yet, but we are." Bobby stood next to his desk, next to the telephone connected to the White House that no longer rang, his hands tense at his sides. "Sure, I've lost a brother," he said, keeping his head down. "Other people lose wives—" and his voice broke off while he struggled to maintain his composure.

"But that's not what's important. What's important is what we were trying to do for this country. We got a good start." Schlesinger recorded him saying, "The thing is we worked hard to get where we are, and we can't let it all go to waste. My brother barely had a chance to get started—and there is so much now to be done—for the Negroes and the unemployed and the schoolkids and everyone else who is not getting a decent break in our society. This is what counts. The new fellow doesn't get this. He knows all about politics and nothing about human beings . . . I haven't talked to him yet. I don't feel mentally or physically prepared to do so yet. When I talk to him, I am ready to be tough about what we must have . . . There are a lot of people in this town. They didn't come here just to work for John Kennedy, an individual, but for ideas, things we wanted to do. It's one thing if you've got personal reasons for leaving, like you may want to leave, Arthur. But I don't think people should run off . . . After November fifth we'll all be dead. We won't matter a damn. A lot of people could scramble around now, get themselves positions of power and influence. I could do that. But that's not important. What's important is what we can get done. Remember, after November fifth we're all done. We won't be wanted or needed."[38]

Just before the meeting broke up, Goodwin showed Bob a poll in the paper that said "naming Robert Kennedy for Vice President could tear the Democrats apart." More than a third of pro-Johnson Southerners told the pollster that they would vote against a ticket with Bobby on it. Among nonblack Northerners, more than half were against him. Among non-Catholics, three-to-one against. At the same time, the poll found the opposite reaction in black neighborhoods. A fifty-eight-year-old mechanic in the Bedford-Stuyvesant section of Brooklyn was quoted: "Mr. Kennedy's picture is on my wall. It hurts to look at it now . . . I'd go for Robert. He is a fine man."

Bobby fixed his eyes on the newspaper, studying it. Without looking up, he replied flatly, "Well, Johnson's already got the Negroes . . ." And then again, as if to himself: ". . . But he's already got the Negroes."[39]

The next day, with the Mann appointment imminent, Schlesinger asked Bobby if he wanted to make his views plain to President Johnson. Bobby chose not to.

"As you say," Schlesinger wrote him, "it promises to be a long, hard winter."[40]

WITHOUT PUBLICLY VOICING his concern, there was little Bobby could do. Children were a salve. RFK kept a commitment made before the assassination to give a Christmas party for hundreds of underprivileged Washington, D.C., children at the Justice Department building. Forty tons of crushed ice were brought in and spread to make a roadway for two mule-drawn sleighs. Members of the Washington Redskins, dressed as Santa's helpers, lifted the children to and from the carriages, singing "Jingle Bells." Barney Ross, JFK's PT-109 crewmate, played Santa Claus. A woman dressed as a fairy handed out little dolls to girls, while lawyers, dressed as tigers, bears, and donkeys, handed out miniature footballs to boys. The children rode the elevator up to the attorney general's fifth-floor office, and Bobby greeted them, smiled, tousled hair, squeezed hands, and laughed. "How are you? . . . Merry Christmas . . . Nice to see you."

A small child stepped out in front of him and shouted, "Your brother's dead!"

The room froze. The child realized he had done something wrong and began to cry.

Bobby bent down and took him into his arms.

"That's all right . . ." he said softly. "I have another."

The pain didn't matter there, for there was ice cream and popcorn and candy canes. Carol Channing sang "Hello, Dolly!" and the Smothers Brothers did a comedy routine. The wire reporter couldn't tell how many Kennedy children were mixed in the bunch save for little Mary Kerry, who hugged her father. RFK smiled—a moment captured in a wire service photo that appeared in a Chicago paper with the caption "Good to See Our Man Smile Again." All around them, the office was festooned with Christmas decorations and pictures of John F. Kennedy in action—at a news conference, inspecting a ship, campaigning. They bore his quotations. At the end, Bob thanked his staff for throwing the party and said to the children, "Have a merry Christmas, have a happy Christmas. I hope you will think back on this day and the act of love and kindness shown here today. And I hope you will return it to others, your teachers, your friends, your mothers and fathers."[41]

The day after the Christmas party, Bobby was with Jackie and her two children, shopping on Worth Avenue in Palm Beach, two Secret Service agents in tow. He was expected at the dedication and renaming of New York City's Idlewild Airport after JFK, but instead left to spend the holiday with his family at a secluded cabin in Aspen, Colorado. Before leaving, a visitor told him it was good that he was taking the time off, and Bob replied, "You're the ninth person to tell me that today. What's everybody plotting here, a palace coup?" But they wanted him to get away, for himself. He looked battered, hollowed out, shrunken from his pain. So he went to Aspen, where he skied hard and got a deep tan, though not deep enough to conceal the dark circles under his eyes. He told friends the skiing had done a lot to clear his head. Life before Dallas, he would later say, "was simple. Now it's much more complex. For six weeks after my brother's death I thought about it, and I didn't come to any conclusion, so I decided to stop thinking about it for a while and just finish out my term as attorney general."[42]

IN EARLY JANUARY, the National Security Council, of which Bobby was still a member, convened for a meeting at the White House to discuss an escalating situation in Southeast Asia. A few months earlier, Great Britain had relinquished control over Malaysia, creating a rival power to Indonesia and its nationalist dictator, Sukarno. In retaliation, a mob of Indonesians stormed the British embassy in Jakarta, while Sukarno vowed to smash the new country, disputed its borders, and sent bands of guerrilla raiders into its territories. Deadly battles with British security forces ensued. This left President Johnson at an impasse. The United States sent aid to Indonesia as a bulwark against Communism and to protect $500 million in American oil properties. Yet the U.S. could not appear to sanction Sukarno's aggression—and could possibly be obligated by treaty with the British Commonwealth to defend Malaysia. Johnson either had to cut off Indonesia's aid and lose an ally; keep it going and appear weak; or find an alternative solution.[43]

Attorney General Kennedy, unsure of his place, had said nothing in the NSC meeting. His silences, so loud in these months, always invited others to speculate. Everyone saw it written on his face because his face resembled the one that they no longer saw: JFK's. And then President Johnson looked down the long mahogany table and said to Bobby, "General, what do you think?"

Bobby appeared surprised by the question. Then he smiled and said that it would be difficult to continue aiding Indonesia and not appear to be sponsoring the guerrillas. If immediate action was necessary—and he questioned whether any action was—the United States needed to be forthright about its displeasure with Sukarno. Secretary of State Dean Rusk spoke favorably of cutting off the aid, yet reminded the men that with Indonesia's population of a hundred million, more was at stake there than in the hot conflict of Vietnam. Bobby started asking questions: Did they have to act just yet? Could they sit tight for another two weeks and wait?

It was a pivotal moment for Bobby, one extended to him by Lyndon Johnson. Other members at the table turned toward Bobby and listened, glad to have the man they knew back. National Security Adviser McGeorge Bundy said that Congress would soon be demanding answers and proposed that Bobby go to Asia and handle Sukarno personally. Sending Bobby made perfect sense. Sukarno would relish the prestige of a high-profile emissary, and could use it to escape the mess he had made. He and Bobby had also negotiated before. Sukarno's flamboyant behavior disturbed Bobby; reports about the prostitutes that the United States had provided him were just becoming public. Nonetheless, the two had a strange mutual respect. "I like people with flame in their eyes," Sukarno said. Still, Bobby was cagey and said he would rather not go. His friends insisted—for his own sake, if not public service.[44]

Whatever Robert Kennedy thought when he left that meeting, the morning after he met with *New York Times* reporter Anthony Lewis to say on the record that he would remain as attorney general through the November election. The journalists who saw him over the next few days would write that he seemed like his old self. The pale, subdued man who had haunted the capital for a month emerged relaxed and thinking frankly—not sorrowfully—about his future. *Newsweek* noted the change in his appearance: "He had taken in his belt a notch or two, and his tie was funeral black," but "he looked tanned and fit and energetic as ever." The *Times* ran a front-page, three-column headline: "Bobby Kennedy Defeats Despair." He told them he wanted to help the civil rights legislation get through Congress, and that he would decide what to do after that. "I could go teach," he said. "I could run for office in Massachusetts. Or I could go into business or private life." Yet he promised that even if he left government service, "I'm sure I will return to it sometime in the future."[45]

INDEPENDENT OF THE media blitz, a *Washington Post* reporter on the diplomatic beat learned of the proposed Indonesia trip, and a front-page story trumpeted RFK's return "to the White House limelight" for "the same foreign trouble-shooting assignments that the late President Kennedy charged his brother with." This rubbed President Johnson the wrong way. He had not yet signed off on the trip and resented the leak, which he blamed the attorney general for. LBJ sent Bobby anyway, but McGeorge Bundy later said the President wrongly "felt that he had been maneuvered into approving by staff people who weren't thinking about the Johnson interest." Bobby conferred with the President at the White House the day before leaving and was charged with obtaining a cease-fire and bringing the parties to the negotiating table. If successful, he would travel to England and convince the British to go along with it.[46]

The two weeks were a blur—a diplomatic race around the world. Ethel, a light staff, and a few favorite reporters came along for the Asian capital-hopping. Bobby said he would stress the importance of the U.S.-Indonesian relationship. "The purpose of my discussion is to see if this controversy

cannot be taken out of the jungle, out of warfare, and put around the conference table. I did not come with a solution—this is an Asian problem to be
decided by people in this part of the world, not by the United States."[47]

The first stop was Tokyo, where he began his talks with Sukarno. The
general entered with his peci cap and chest full of medals and asked Bobby,
"Did you come here to threaten me?"

"No," Bobby said, "I've come to help get you out of trouble."[48]

Bobby's "disarming directness" rattled some of the American diplomats, a
member of the U.S. national security staff said. Bobby told the Malaysians
that Sukarno thought they were British puppets and told Sukarno that Malaysians thought he was a land-grabbing dictator. Bobby told both sides they
could have a war if they wanted it, but that they ought to try talking first. "On
several occasions, the more proper types who sat in with him were appalled
at Mr. Kennedy's frankness in talking to these people," an unidentified U.S.
official told the *New York Times*, "but he has a way of dealing with people as
equals, talking neither up nor down to them." Within ten days, the attorney
general was able to say that his mission was fulfilled: a cease-fire was in place,
and there was agreement on talks. The *Saturday Evening Post* wrote that "diplomatic circles [had] sniffed that he would accomplish nothing," while the *New
York Post* editorial board said the trip had more to do with "the highly publicized coolness between" him and the President, and "we would have preferred
that he be allowed to stay at home to mind the store." Now he had persuaded
Sukarno to halt Indonesia's guerrilla raids and got the two sides talking.
Though nothing would be solved between Indonesia and Malaysia for some
time, diplomat Bobby "had performed a minor miracle" wrote *Newsweek*.[49]

This frank, fast-moving diplomacy spanned Southeast Asia—from Tokyo to
Manila to Kuala Lumpur to Jakarta and Bangkok—capped off by a fourteen-
hour flight to London. Even with this schedule, grief and politics dogged
him. Aboard the plane, Bobby fought off sleep by responding to telegrams
and letters of condolence that had amassed over weeks. The first question he
got in Tokyo was about the vice presidency. "I have decided not to decide,"
he said. The American embassy had been flooded with pleas for him to return
to Japan's Waseda University, where he had been screamed at and denounced
in a 1962 visit. Someone had even cut the power to the hall to try to prevent
the President's brother from speaking.

But this time, the students wanted to see him—and for *him* to see *them*
and the depth of their grief.[50]

"He was not only President of one nation," Bobby told a solemn audience
of thousands, spilling out of the hall, "he was president of young people
around the world. If President Kennedy's life and death are to mean anything,
we young people must work harder for a better life for all the people in the

world." He sought out U.S. servicemen in South Korea—"to take this opportunity to see American soldiers serving in this part of the world." When he asked
to visit six observation posts near the demilitarized zone, the commanding
officer told him it would be difficult. "Why is it difficult, General?" Bobby
asked. And suddenly, it wasn't. RFK spent the night with the troops in Korea
three miles behind the lines, and then traveled out to a cold and frozen hill
overlooking the demilitarized zone, reportedly within sight of Communist
guns. He wore a suit with his black tie under a dark overcoat among the American and Korean soldiers in their fatigues. They ate breakfast in the mess hall
and attended mass together, Bobby shaking hands all along the way. He went
on to Manila, where nearly two thousand Filipinos met him and Ethel at the
airport. He handed out PT-109 tie clasps and acknowledged the students'
applause. "This reception was something more than just a reception for a
citizen of the United States," *Newsweek* wrote, "something more than a reception for a Kennedy. It is a reception for the ideals and beliefs for which President Kennedy lived and died."[51]

In Manila, he spoke to another rapturous group of students, who crowded
around and pulled at his clothes, pawing at him for a touch. When it was
over, Bobby got into his car, his blue eyes welled with tears. "It wasn't really
for me," he said. "It was for him."

A friend seated next to him said, "You've got to do it for him now."

Bobby sat quietly for what seemed like half a minute and gently nodded.[52]

Of his trip abroad, he would say, "I hadn't wanted to go on that trip, but
afterwards, I was glad I had."[53]

The British were worried that RFK was selling out the Malaysians to his
chum Sukarno, and the State Department informed Kennedy that several
British papers had written "Sukarno may have tried to mesmerize the Attorney
General," resulting in his pulling support for the British interests in the
region. As the plane taxied, he joked to the American reporters in his party,
"Suppose I get off carrying a sign that says, *'I just sold Singapore and I'm
glad!'* " Bobby visited with British prime minister Sir Alec Douglas-Home at
Chequers, the PM's official country residence, and asked for an official news
blackout to visit the grave of his sister Kathleen, who had died in a plane
crash many years earlier. In London, Bobby met again with the PM and other
officials at 10 Downing Street. He gave Foreign Secretary Rab Butler his sharply
critical opinion of Britain's colonial minister Duncan Sandys. Butler went
white with rage, telling Kennedy he could not speak about one of his secretaries
in such a way. Yet Bobby did, and when he saw Sandys the next day, he diffused
the situation with a smile, saying, "Mr. Sandys, you're about as popular in the
East as I am in Alabama." It had been a lively trip. When their plane unexpectedly stopped for refueling at an air base in Évreux, France, Bobby, Ethel, and

members of the press piled into cars to go have drinks at a café. The French townspeople stood mouths agape as President Kennedy's brother passed by. Philip Scheffler from CBS bought a stack of berets in a department store and put one on Bob's head. It was a good time. As they landed in Washington that evening, Ethel said quietly, "This is the worst part. To go back to Washington and not find Jack waiting for him."[54]

In fact, no president waited for him. Johnson was bitter over the way Kennedy's trip had turned out, feeling he had been suckered into raising Bobby's profile as the capital gamed who the next vice president would be. The President appeared unappreciative and uninterested in Bobby's findings, having him brief in the presence of ranking members of the Senate Foreign Relations and Armed Services committees. The message was clear: Bobby's Oval Office privileges were revoked. The attorney general was left bitter over the assignment.[55]

IN THE EARLY winter, his brother's men such as Arthur Schlesinger and speechwriter Ted Sorensen began leaving the administration. Bob told an interviewer, "I'm not in the same position they are. It's much harder for them. They have been in jobs where their whole responsibility is serving just one man. You cannot expect them to change the man." But Bobby's position was different: he was responsible for an entire department. "A month can go by before I need to take a problem to the White House. After all, even my brother never asked me about the Lands Division," one of the many provinces in the Justice Department. "I have the National Security Council and the Youth Commission and a good many other things to keep me busy and I can do them all without ever needing to go into the White House. I am different from the others. If I go—" he stopped and searched for the word. "If I should, uh, *desert*, that would be harmful . . . And then I'm selfish. I want to sit here and watch what my brother was trying to do and see how it turns out for this year, anyway. What is different now and what makes me sad is that I see a problem or someone tells me about a problem and I can't do anything about it. There was this time when if people had something and couldn't see my brother, they could always see me, and I could pick up the phone and call him." The mistakes "might have happened with us anyway, but it's strange to think that you can't just pick up the phone."[56]

That disconnect was perhaps why Bobby doubted he could ever "commit myself to any individual again."[57] Certainly not Johnson.

It was around this time—this realization—when John Seigenthaler saw the pall return: "The black plague was on him." Bobby had lost weight since November—"always close to the bone anyway," another observed, but he now appeared frightening. "His jaw had a sunken, hangdog look. His collars swam about his neck. His wide shirt cuffs gave his hands and wrists a skeletal appearance." His eyes were glazed, new wrinkles beneath them. And the gray that might once have made his hair look lighter and younger now told a different story. "He seems to have aged so in the last couple of months," his personal secretary, Angie Novello, said in one of her rare public comments. Seigenthaler went to see him at the office and couldn't help but be blunt: "I told him he looked like hell. He said he felt fine. I said he can't feel fine and look terrible. He said he couldn't sleep." Seigenthaler thought Bob regretted saying that—"the only time I ever talked to him when I thought he was holding back." Seigenthaler decided not to press him, and they sat there silently while Bob caught up on his messages. Journalist Peter Lisagor wrote that Bobby sometimes had a "monosyllabic curtness" in the months after the assassination. Angie said the Indonesia trip "helped him get away from himself, but deep down he's just covering up his real feelings." The silences spoke. A Justice Department aide said, "Every now and then Bobby will sort of go blank for a minute. You can tell what he's thinking about." Seigenthaler noticed that it was not just the conversation that was different: the pain seemed to be physically crippling—that "almost when he got up to walk that it hurt to get up to walk." It was as if everything he did was "through that sort of haze or pain that he felt." Another interviewer who observed Bob that winter wrote, "He sits just where he did in November."[58] He seemed to lose his drive, Peter Maas wrote. "Time no longer seems to have quite the same urgency for him."

And other times, the mask fell completely. Maas reported one such occasion in the *Saturday Evening Post*, when he asked about John Kennedy's legacy.

"You have to put it all together," Bobby replied. "I suppose the Cuban missile crisis was the single most important moment. But that was not all of it . . ." and his voice fell away, halted—lost—in the emotion of what he wanted to say. He started again. "He brought a new spirit to the land. He made politics something that a young person wanted to get into—" and again, an abrupt silence. He went on. "What we did didn't always turn out to be the right thing, but we tried. I'm selfish enough to think that in the long run we will be supported by history."[59]

"To some," one reporter wrote after interviewing him, "he appeared to be a man on the verge of breakdown."[60]

2

A JOB FOR BOBBY

January 1964–March 1964

ON JANUARY 6, 1964, Assistant Attorney General John Douglas tore a sheet of paper from a legal pad, sat down at a typewriter, and tapped out four single-spaced paragraphs with messy cross-outs and notes. Douglas didn't have to do this. He was the head of the Justice Department's Civil Division, the son of Illinois's three-term U.S. senator, had letterhead and a battery of secretaries and attorneys to dictate correspondence to. Only Douglas wanted to keep this memo strictly between himself and its recipient: Attorney General Robert Kennedy.

Douglas was providing Bobby with details on election law in the New Hampshire and Oregon presidential primaries, the pertinent sections underlined in blue pen. The memo emphasized that New Hampshire's March 10 primary was "<u>for both president *and* vice president</u>," *vice president* underlined twice with an arrow next to it. "There are to be separate columns on the ballot for the two offices," it said. "Write-ins are explicitly permitted." Douglas signed his memo atop the page with four words: "Bob: Think about this."[1]

Douglas said years later that Kennedy never acknowledged the memo, but he clearly reviewed it, as the long yellow lined paper, archived in the attorney general's files, bares his scribbled *RK* initials. The memo came during an important week for Bobby. It was written the day before the National Security Council meeting in which Johnson first displayed confidence in him, asking for his view on Indonesia. The next morning, Bobby told the *New York Times* he would remain in the cabinet. An hour after that, he went home to Hickory Hill for a secret lunch with Peter J. Crotty, the Democratic boss of Buffalo, New York.[2]

As chairman of the Erie County Democratic Committee, Crotty controlled the machine in what was then the fifteenth-largest metropolitan area in the United States. He held sway over a sizable portion of New York's delegation to the 1964 Democratic National Convention, in the days when power brokers— not primaries—ruled. Crotty had been close with the Kennedys back to 1960 as one of the New York bosses who put the state in JFK's column. An associate later described him as a typical machine boss but a liberal at heart and extremely loyal to Jack Kennedy.[3] In other words, he was Bob Kennedy's kind of Democrat, a most welcome guest at his home, and an important political asset.

When Arthur Schlesinger doubted RFK's ability to shoehorn his way onto Johnson's ticket that December, Bobby told Schlesinger that he underestimated "the Kennedy relationship to the big city machines," naming Democratic bosses Richard Daley in Chicago, Bill Green in Philadelphia, Charlie Buckley in the Bronx—and Peter Crotty in Buffalo. Not long after their lunch, while Bobby was overseas on his diplomatic mission, Crotty suddenly announced his endorsement of RFK for vice president, pledging the full weight of his organization to the effort. He was the first major leader to make such an announcement, telling the *New York Times* that Bobby would "help the ticket sweep the big cities of the Northeast, of Pennsylvania, Ohio, Illinois and California"—the battleground states of the 1960 election. He said he hoped that Buffalo's decision would inspire other organizations to act. Kennedy intimates denied that Bobby approved of Crotty's action, and Crotty claimed that he had not spoken to Bobby about the vice presidency at all. And while that could be true, the men's lunch less than a week before Bobby left, documented in his desk diary, was never reported and apparently unknown to even his close political associates.[4]

In mid-February, two weeks after the endorsement, Crotty sent Bobby a letter telling him of the positive reaction Crotty had received from "from all over the country." He wrote, "The point I am trying to make simply is this. I think that it is not too early to take more affirmative action. I realize full well that the ultimate choice rests with President Johnson. But in a large sense he is only an instrument. He is going to be guided by the realities of politics." Crotty's letter indicates that Bobby might have discouraged him from making the endorsement or disapproved of it afterward. "I cannot agree with the notion that the choice of the vice president is left to presidential nominee except within very circumscribed limits," telling Bobby that every nominee in recent history was picked because of politics. "Why shouldn't some effort be made to release the sentiment for RFK which undoubtedly exists around the country?" Crotty wrote. "I am of the opinion that if the President is not made aware of your rank and file support as early as possible, he might well go to Senator Humphrey. I don't have to tell you that nobody gets anything unless he works for it." Bobby didn't write down his reply, instead asking Teddy to talk with Crotty.[5]

The Buffalo endorsement had come on the eve of New York Democrats' massive fund-raising dinner and state committee meeting. There, Crotty

hoped to set off a wave of endorsements by putting the largest state delegation to the '64 convention in Bobby's column. Hundreds of Democrats packed
the halls of New York City's Americana Hotel, trading gossip about Crotty's
push to make Bobby VP. Crotty claimed other county leaders were with him,
but Kenneth O'Donnell and Larry O'Brien, JFK's political lieutenants who
stayed on in the Johnson White House, put the word out to other New York
bosses not to hop on board. O'Donnell believed that time—not pressure—
might improve relations between LBJ and RFK. So the leaders followed the
advice and the state committee took no formal action. Yet the sentiment for
Bobby that needed "release," as Crotty put it, was undeniably there. The *Daily
News'* City Hall columnist wrote that the movement toward Bobby was real.
"New York State, the boys ruefully concede, could wind up with a runaway
convention delegation."[6]

The Kennedy camp was split. On one side were the official Kennedy men
like "the Irish Mafia" of O'Donnell and O'Brien, or the intellectuals like
Schlesinger and Ted Sorensen, quoted in the newspapers and made famous
by their columnists. And then there were the other Kennedy operatives . . .
the ones on the edges, without the glory, who took on the thankless job of
winning.

PAUL CORBIN WAS gruff, swarthy, and had a gravelly voice that lingered
like a bad taste. Among the few people who liked him, and the many, many who
hated him, one thing about Corbin was undeniable: the guy was loyal. "You
could tell him to go out and jump off a bridge for you," said the assistant to
Kennedy brother-in-law Stephen E. Smith, "and he'd do it." Smith liked to
joke that one of Corbin's many important responsibilities in the Kennedy
administration was walking Brumus, Bobby's shaggy giant Newfoundland
dog.[7] Yet Corbin was also notoriously brash and single-minded, with a knack
for making enemies and a checkered past that allowed those enemies to
marginalize him.

Corbin was born Paul Kobrinsky in Winnipeg, Canada, and came to the
United States in the 1930s, taking odd jobs until he found work as a union
organizer. He made his way through several unions over the next few years—
jobs that associated him with suspected Communist Party members. In
1943 when Corbin was twenty-nine, he became a naturalized citizen and
entered the Marine Corps. After his discharge, he continued as a union organizer and public relations man, which eventually landed him in Wisconsin.
He would later say he was a flag salesman after the war, describing it as good
business until the implosion of McCarthyism and "the bottom dropped out
of the flag market." What he didn't say was that he contributed to that

nationalist boom by spending some of that time working on Senator Joseph McCarthy's Wisconsin staff. In 1951, McCarthy requested the FBI do a back-ground check on Corbin, only to call back four days later and say, according to a bureau memo, "that he had found that Corbin was all right and that he did not want the name check, and that he would rather not have any record made that he had requested it." The investigation, which McCarthy never received, "reflected that Corbin has been a Communist Party member since 1939" and was "still an active member as of 1949 or 1950."[8]

Corbin's Communist past hung over the rest of his career. He was working for a Democratic congressman in April of 1959 when his boss confronted him with a report on his associations, including a picture of him with two known Communists in 1946. According to the FBI, Corbin broke down in tears and resigned on the spot. He had just finished organizing a fund-raising dinner that attracted presidential hopeful John F. Kennedy to Janesville.[9]

A year later, Wisconsin was holding the first contested Democratic primary for the 1960 nomination, with JFK facing Senator Hubert Humphrey from neighboring Minnesota. Wisconsin Democratic state chairman Patrick J. Lucey told Bobby Kennedy that he should hire Corbin to organize the Seventh Congressional District. The two first met in Bobby's hotel room when Bobby was washing up and Corbin barged in to tell the campaign manager that he was making him late for another meeting. "Don't you ever talk to me that way," Bob said. "I can see why people don't like you. You weren't my choice. If I had my way, I wouldn't hire you. I just made this as a gesture to Pat Lucey; we couldn't afford to fight a state chairman." But the incorrigible Corbin didn't back down and told his boss that he never liked people from Massachusetts. The two would get along perfectly.

Bob came to trust Corbin's political judgment and admire his dogged-ness during the primary. Corbin went from small town to small town, orga-nizing Kennedy supporters outside the Democratic label. He would bypass the politicians by going straight to the local Catholic priest and asking him to recommend someone who was a Republican and a Protestant—three or four names were all he needed. Corbin wanted surrogates who challenged the preconceived notions of who Kennedy's supporters were. Helen Keyes, a devout Catholic from Cambridge, Massachusetts, assigned to work with him, later recalled that whenever they encountered anti-Catholic bigotry, Corbin would proclaim, "Well, this lady's a Baptist from Boston, and *she's* for Kennedy." (Corbin and his wife would later convert to Catholicism, with Bobby and Ethel as their godparents.) When all was said and done, Corbin had set up about two local committees per day, and Wisconsin's Seventh District went for Kennedy.[10]

From there, Corbin followed the campaign to West Virginia for the primary, and upstate New York for the general election. He continued to specialize in bypassing the local Democrats where they were inept, setting up independent committees. Bobby knew that his special aide would be stepping on a lot of toes, as Corbin later recalled his firm instructions upon taking the New York assignment. "Don't take any calls from anybody from Washington," Bobby said. "Don't talk to anybody from Washington. If they happen to catch you sometime, just say, 'Yes, yes, yes.' But keep going. I want you to call me continuously, keep in touch with me. You'll have a clear line." Within a week, ticked-off Democratic leaders were calling JFK's Washington headquarters about some son of a bitch named Corbin touring the state trashing the party regulars on behalf of the Kennedys. But Corbin followed Bobby's instructions and kept on doing what he had to. Bob, as promised, let Corbin take all the heat. And Corbin did. After all, he would have jumped off a bridge for him if he told him to.

Corbin took an assignment on Bobby's staff after the election, working out of the Democratic National Committee until they could find him a job in the new administration—except Corbin's Communist past precluded that. On January 11, 1961, an aide to Robert Kennedy asked the FBI to investigate Corbin before he received a government position. The attorney general–designate, the resulting FBI memo said, "wanted the results of this investigation delivered to him personally." It determined that Corbin could not be approved for a security clearance. Yet later, when he became a target of the House Committee on Un-American Activities, Bobby selectively leaked portions of the FBI report to show the charges of Communism were false.[11] The loyalty extended both ways.

Since Corbin was ineligible for a government position, Bobby asked the Democratic National Committee to hire him, and Corbin did what political fixers do: he waited for the next campaign. A notorious gossip, Corbin was always on the lookout for inside dope. He would spend hours over at the Justice Department, just sitting around on the off chance Bobby had some time to talk. On the days when Steve Smith was at the DNC's Washington headquarters, Corbin popped in and out so frequently, Smith's assistant recalled she "had to throw him out of the office a million times." Corbin was also tough and acted as if he had nothing to lose, while many DNC employees were restrained and insecure. And so, Paul often got his way—and more enemies.[12]

Those enemies included many among the Kennedy set. "Why do you like Paul Corbin?" a loyal New Frontiersman once asked Bobby.

"You, too?" he replied. The aide asked what Bobby meant, and he said, "Nobody likes Paul Corbin."

"Well, why do you like Paul Corbin?"

"Well, he gets so much work out of me."[13]

Some who were close to Bobby—John Seigenthaler, Walter Sheridan, and a few others—liked Corbin a great deal. John F. Kennedy, however, did not. Even Bobby acknowledged that while Corbin "was extremely loyal to me," he was only "somewhat loyal to President Kennedy." Corbin felt mistreated by JFK's inner circle—the ballyhooed "Irish Mafia," whom he always referred to as just "the Mafia." He resented the Mafia for living large during the campaign, flying in jets and staying at nice hotels while he was scraping by, sometimes so broke he couldn't afford a pack of smokes. From their very first meeting, Corbin wanted to fight Kenny O'Donnell, the Mafia's top man, which Bobby advised against "because he does push-ups and he'll make mincemeat out of you." O'Donnell met Bobby at Harvard, where they were roommates on the football squad. They remained a unit for the next decade and a half, fighting Jack's political battles, and it appears Corbin tried to tear them apart.

Shortly before the assassination, Corbin went to Bobby and gave him a list of the people working for JFK that he alleged were embezzling money from the reelection campaign and greasing the wheels of federal government for cash. According to Walter Sheridan, Corbin's list included O'Donnell and Dick Maguire, treasurer of the Democratic National Committee. Corbin told Sheridan that a lot of donations Maguire received never got where they were supposed to, and that Corbin had affidavits to prove it. "Bob Kennedy believed him," Sheridan later said, and Corbin would claim that Bobby promised to take it up with the President when he returned from Dallas. RFK was not the only person Corbin went to: he had earlier asked columnist and Jack Kennedy's classmate Charles Bartlett to relay the information, which Bartlett said he did to no result. According to Seigenthaler, Bobby was upset with Corbin at the time of the assassination—perhaps over this—until he asked Seigenthaler how Corbin was doing the night after Dallas. Seigenthaler told Bob how Paul had broken down to him, deeply sobbing over the President's death. RFK seemed moved. The next time Bobby and Corbin spoke, the Mafia's alleged bribes came up and Bob dismissed it, saying, "Forget it. We don't have 1600 Pennsylvania Avenue anymore." Bartlett said Corbin quoted Bobby as saying, "Lyndon wouldn't believe me," yet later, RFK would cite Corbin's investigations of graft at the DNC when defending him to Johnson.[14]

As Democrats began picking up the pieces in 1964, Peter Crotty and the Erie County Democrats' endorsement of Bobby for vice president registered in the right place: New Hampshire. The state's top Democrat, Governor John W. King, was aiming to pass a controversial sweepstakes referendum on the day of the March 10 presidential primary vote, and his advisers were concerned that a sleepy Democratic contest during a competitive Republican one would lead to their defeat. New Hampshire voters had the option to register their preference for vice president on their ballots, and King's strategists had been contemplating how to gin up a primary as early as two weeks after JFK's death. The morning after Crotty's endorsement in late January, William Dunfey, a Granite State political operative and JFK's coordinator for New England in 1960, wrote a memo to Governor King highlighting Bobby's support from Democrats in Buffalo. Dunfey estimated that a RFK write-in movement could boost Democratic turnout by thirty thousand votes. No one had qualified for the vice presidential ballot, and by the end of the week, prominent Democrats from New Hampshire's biggest cities launched an effort to write in Bobby's name. Publicly, Governor King remained neutral, and a poll of New Hampshire Democrats found that 85 percent supported RFK for vice president.[15] By those accounts, the "write in Robert Kennedy" campaign was a localized, grassroots movement. And yet it involved Bobby Kennedy's most loyal—and least discreet—political operative.

It's unclear when exactly Paul Corbin got involved with the vice presidential effort, but he was said to be working with Peter Crotty in lobbying for Bobby at the New York Democratic state committee meeting and dinner in January, which might account for their failure. At DNC headquarters, Corbin had kept a map of New York State on his wall with red and blue flags pinned in each county—blue flags for the party leaders he liked, red flags for ones he would get rid of. Most were red. "He used to just torture these people," one leader recalled.[16] While he was useful for counting votes, the rumor of his presence was certainly counterproductive.

Next, Corbin went to New Hampshire, connecting with a Manchester public relations man and Democratic activist named Robert B. Shaine in early February. Through Shaine, Corbin purchased billboards and advertisements. Shaine remembers their budget was about $23,000—all raised from volunteers. While the amount was steep, Corbin had proven himself adept at fund-raising before. He had jingled money out of Republican pockets to bring JFK to Janesville in 1959 and, in sealed interviews conducted after President Kennedy's death, complained of having had to raise his own money to organize in Wisconsin and New York. Corbin never said anything in these interviews about money in the West Virginia primary, but his FBI file noted that on at least one occasion, when he had had too much to drink at a party, Corbin bragged that he swung West Virginia for Kennedy by handing out $10 bills—a completely plausible scenario, given how the state was awash in Joseph Kennedy's money. The Kennedy family fortune apparently did not bankroll the 1964 New Hampshire effort, since the man who then oversaw the fortune, Steve Smith, visited the state in February and privately told Corbin and Shaine to knock it off. Smith, too, was wise enough to distance himself from

Corbin, and this meeting could have come because Lyndon Johnson was growing suspicious.[17]

Because word traveled fast of the gravelly voiced, blunt-spoken Kennedy aide in the hamlets of New Hampshire. *Time* magazine later reported that Corbin had showed up and started throwing around the phrase "*Bobby says . . .*" As one Kennedy hand put it, hiding Corbin in New Hampshire was "like trying to conceal Mount Everest in Manhattan Island." Johnson was already on alert as Bobby was being coy with the press, opting not to comment on his prospects. A week after his return from Indonesia, he appeared on NBC's *Today* show and tried to explain why he couldn't say yes or no to the vice presidency yet. "It's a bit like a woman if you ask her, 'If so-and-so would ask you to marry him, then would you marry him?' I haven't been asked, and I want to really decide my own future, later on, not try to make up my mind now."[18]

On February 10, Johnson asked Cliff Carter, his longtime aide recently installed at the Democratic National Committee, about "this damn Corbin." Carter had only been at the committee for a month, but from what he could tell, Corbin didn't listen to anyone, not even Chairman John Bailey, a Kennedy holdover. As the President understood it, Ken O'Donnell had talked to Bobby about Corbin, "and Bobby said they just couldn't fire him, that—just, out of the question."

After a long pause in which Johnson breathed heavily into the receiver, Carter said in a low voice, "He's working against us, and I'm afraid—from what I have heard about him, he could well be a source of embarrassment to us. I don't know how." Johnson chewed over this report and asked after the expenses of the committee. He wanted an audit of the DNC within three weeks.

Then the President asked, "How much Corbin make?"

"This I don't know, sir."

"Do you know what he's supposed to do?"

"Uh, run errands for the attorney general," Carter said. "He just takes off and *goes*. He's on his own on an expense account. This is the best I can ascertain. He had gone up two weeks ago to this New York, big Democratic dinner they had up there, and I was told he was up there, I didn't see him. I understood he went on from there to, well, he met with county chairmen the next morning trying to sell them on Pete Crotty's resolution. And he went on to New Hampshire from there."

"Who told you that?"

"Uh, one of the national committeemen from New Hampshire told me that he came up there and, uh, Dick Maguire and couple of them told me that he'd worked these county chairmen over—New York county chairmen—over the next morning."

Johnson wanted to know if Dick Maguire and O'Donnell were against Corbin, and Carter said they were. As party treasurer, Maguire was emphatic that Corbin had to go.[19]

Late the next afternoon, President Johnson met with Bobby and a handful of top aides in the Oval Office about moving civil rights legislation forward in the Senate. After the meeting, Johnson told Bobby to fire Corbin from the DNC. The President said it was part of his taking "extreme precautions to show my friendship for all of President Kennedy's hierarchy" by not favoring one particular vice presidential hopeful. He said that among the many displays of "confidence" he had shown for the contenders, he had sent Bobby to Indonesia. But for the committee to pay Corbin while he drummed up support for him was unfair.[20] Bobby remembered the President saying, "I know he's been up in New Hampshire. I've received reports that he's been around New Hampshire. He's got to get out of there."

"Well, why don't you find out?" Bobby said. "I didn't know he'd been in New Hampshire."[21]

So LBJ continued his investigation the next day, asking Chairman Bailey to "come over here tomorrow and bring this fellow Corbin's record with you . . . everything you have on him and what he does and . . . and so on and so forth . . . He's been up to New York State Committee and up to New Hampshire."

"He has?" said Bailey.

"Yeah. And I want his travel record—just see where he's been going, what he's been doing."

"All right, now what—"

"What do you know about him?" Johnson asked, looking for dirt.

"Got an hour?" Bailey said jokingly.

He told the President how Corbin had worked "under [the attorney general's] directions" during the campaign, and how he had been "given Corbin and told that he was to work [at the DNC], and shortly thereafter there were some problems with the Un-American Activities Committee, and, which there were some contentions that sometime or another he had Communist leanings and there was considerable communications and considerable amount of a file on this"—they even gave him a lie detector test. "I have all those records here if you'd like them."

"Yeah, I do want 'em," said Johnson.

"All right."

"And if you don't mind," the President continued, "I wish you'd call him in and talk to him and ask him if he's been up in the vice presidential campaign in New York or New Hampshire, if he's talked to anybody up there about it, because we're getting criticisms that we've had a man from the committee up there running the attorney general for vice president."

"Well, he isn't here now," Bailey said. "Last I'd heard, they told me he went to Wisconsin, but I don't—I'll check, he isn't in the office today, but I'll check with his secretary and find out when he comes."

Johnson said all right and asked Bailey again to bring Corbin's files and travel records.[22] The President was collecting evidence. Later that day, he asked Cliff Carter to talk to the New Hampshire committeeman again and "have a recorder on when you do." Carter said he got the information about the New York dinner from DNC treasurer Dick Maguire—whom Corbin accused of graft—and the New Hampshire committeeman still complained about Corbin's running wild in his state.[23] However, the President was ultimately unable to locate any information definitively linking Corbin's antics to Bobby.

While RFK might have been unaware at the time or remained willfully ignorant of Corbin's presence in New Hampshire, it is far more likely that he successfully stonewalled about what he knew to foes and friends alike. Bobby's denials were steadfast from his initial confrontation with Johnson in February, to the controversy's emergence in the press in March, and even for posterity in May, in a sealed interview conducted for the Kennedy Library Oral History project. "Actually, Paul Corbin had never been up to New Hampshire,"[24] Bobby claimed, well after it had been established, publicized, and personally relayed to him that Corbin had been *all over* New Hampshire.

Bobby also omitted from his sealed interview that he had been personally involved in New Hampshire's primary—before and especially after Johnson confronted him. In the week preceding the meeting with Johnson, Bobby had been talking to Corbin's friend Charles Bartlett. Just hours before Kennedy and Johnson first discussed Corbin, Bartlett called to cancel a lunch meeting and left a message recorded by Bobby's secretary: "In the meantime [Charlie] wanted you to know that a Richard J. Beaulieu, Windom Rd., Derry [New Hampshire], filed at the last minute for alternate delegate. Charlie says there was no publicity on it."[25] It was an awful lot of information for someone with no clue about what was happening there.

Then after meeting with the President, Bobby called Bernie Boutin, a New Hampshire contact during the 1960 campaign, perhaps to learn more about what Corbin had done. Bobby met with Boutin in person the following week, and what they discussed is clear from the message Boutin left shortly after, which Bobby's secretary relayed: "He has been in touch with New Hampshire and everything is in operation. There's no problem; he thinks they will be able to take care of everything." William Dunfey, the New Hampshire operative who initially suggested the RFK write-in campaign to Governor King, later said that he and Boutin pushed Corbin out of the state. Dunfey was never sure, but was under the impression that Corbin was up there on Bobby's orders.[26]

Ever the brash interloper, Corbin lit a fire under the Democratic regulars—and aggravated them enough to get their act together. It was the same thankless job he had done on Bobby's behalf for JFK in 1960. And it mobilized votes.

RFK remained in regular contact with Boutin and other New Hampshire figures right up until the March 10 primary. Whether he sent him or not, by that time he knew that Paul Corbin had been up there. Yet his multiple disavowals are no surprise given their relationship during the 1960 campaign. As Bobby's close friend and colleague Walter Sheridan said, "Bob trusted [Corbin] implicitly and yet would disown him, you know? 'Paul *who*?'" It was an easy con for Bobby to sell when he had the vaunted Irish Mafia at his disposal. The *New York Times* wrote later that year, "Mr. Corbin was not regarded as an important enough figure to have been given the assignment of organizing such an effort, had it been deliberate on Mr. Kennedy's part."[27] Even those close to Bobby believed Corbin was a rogue operative—which is exactly what Bobby always wanted people to believe.

Lyndon Johnson had his own version of his meeting with Bobby about Corbin. The President recorded his conversation with Cliff Carter, Ken O'Donnell, and Dick Maguire immediately after speaking to Bobby and likely bent the truth in his telling, too. According to Johnson's version, Bobby said that Corbin "reports to Ken O'Donnell and I told him to take his orders from Ken O'Donnell, and Ken O'Donnell gives him his orders"—Johnsonian disinformation meant to draw out what, if anything, O'Donnell knew, since he knew O'Donnell and Corbin were enemies and believed Kenny was a Bobby spy. Johnson remembered Bobby telling him that Corbin had "had difficulties in his life" and that he had served President Kennedy well. The President said he had no problem with Corbin working at Justice, and Kennedy said Corbin's record wouldn't allow for that—the Communist rap. Johnson told them that Bobby said, "The President liked the work he did."

"I know it, Bobby, but *I* am President, and *I* don't like what he's doing and I don't want to be held responsible for it and therefore I don't want him."

Bobby said, "Well, Ken O'Donnell doesn't like him."

Johnson replied, "Well, I haven't found anybody over there that *does* like him."

Bobby insisted that that wasn't true, that Chairman Bailey and Steve Smith trusted Corbin, and that "he hasn't been given a fair hearing." Johnson promised to give him a fair deal, but insisted Corbin had to cooperate.

"Everybody that plays here plays on the team," the President said.[28]

Bobby remembered Johnson saying, "I don't want to have anybody up there [in New Hampshire], I don't want anybody working over there that's interested—well, do you understand?"

Finally, Bobby replied, "You're not talking—I don't want to talk to you like that. And you could find out—you could ask Paul Corbin."[29]

In Johnson's version, tears got in Bobby's eyes "and he said he's sorry that I sent him to Indonesia only on account of wanting to show confidence in him." Johnson insisted, "No, I didn't say that at all. I said I was glad to show confidence in you by sending you there." Bobby started out of the room, got about halfway to the door, and again said he didn't think Corbin had gotten a fair hearing. Johnson also said that Bobby told him the man was worth his weight because "he's uncovered four or five contractors' corruption over there [at the Democratic National Committee], and that's the reason that he's had him—" and the Oval Office recording system's tape cut out.[30]

"It was a bitter, mean conversation," Bobby later said. "It was the meanest tone that I've heard." Paul Corbin left his job at the DNC. Ed Guthman remembered RFK standing at his window that evening, staring silently for four or five minutes. Then he collected papers, put them in his briefcase, and said, "I'll tell you one thing, this relationship can't last much longer."[31]

THE SUSPICIONS LINGERED in the Johnson camp. Ken O'Donnell, hearing Johnson's side of the story, told the President "my two bits" about Corbin: "First, this fella is absolutely no good, and I can say on the other hand, Bob's got a complete blind spot on him." Jack Valenti wondered if O'Donnell's vehemence against Corbin was just an act—spreading "a false scent across the trail" for O'Donnell's own promotion of Kennedy's candidacy. O'Donnell advocated for Bobby in his own way, saying to people in the White House that if the President and Bobby only spent more time together, they would grow closer. O'Donnell claimed that Bobby was more and more impressed with Johnson, especially for his devotion to the civil rights bill.[32]

The President was too enraged to cut Bobby's man any slack, saying he would not seek a full term if he had to be disrespected like this. "I'll give up the damn thing [before allowing Corbin to stay]," Johnson said aloud in his office the next day. "I'll quit it first. I don't want it that much." He felt manipulated by the Kennedy loyalists. He told John Bailey that he'd kept him on as DNC chairman, sent Bobby to Indonesia, and given their man Pierre Salinger all kinds of power. Johnson didn't resent being pushed around; what he resented was *the appearance* of being pushed around. "I don't give a damn about Corbin. Why do I care about a thousand dollars a month?" referring to his DNC salary. "Let him have it." But he insisted Bobby put a stop to whatever the troublemaker was up to. "If we've got to hide him, well, hide him, but don't let him go around doing what he's doing."[33]

Tension inside the Justice Department made things even worse.

Days after the Corbin affair, on the evening of February 17, Johnson chief of staff Walter Jenkins and Bill Moyers summoned assistant FBI director Deke DeLoach to the White House. Director Hoover's trusted aide arrived just ahead of the night courier, who was delivering a hefty file from the Justice Department: their dossier on Dr. Martin Luther King Jr. As Hoover's FBI hunted for connections between the civil rights leader and Communists, Bobby had approved wiretaps of King's home and office in October 1963. The office wiretap led to the FBI's planting listening devices in King's hotel room on January 5, capturing what appeared to be the married minister having sex with multiple women. Hoover prepared transcripts and copies of the recordings for release and informed members of Congress on January 29, in what he later assured Attorney General Kennedy was "off-the-record" testimony.[34]

Burke Marshall, assistant attorney general and Bobby's liaison to the civil rights community, had sent the King file over, telling Jenkins that the FBI was going to leak derogatory stories about King to undermine the civil rights bill. Marshall wanted the White House to know exactly what the FBI had. According to an FBI memo prepared by DeLoach, Jenkins told him that Bobby, "who desperately wants to become Vice President," was trying to undermine the FBI's relationship with the President. Moyers told DeLoach that he suspected Bobby would personally leak the information to embarrass Johnson for keeping up "political footsie" with King after learning of his Communist ties. DeLoach told Jenkins and Moyers that the Kennedys were the ones who would suffer the fallout—having "shielded King for a long time," and that Bobby knew everything, too, since he had signed the order to have King wiretapped. DeLoach encouraged Jenkins and Moyers to return the files to Justice right away, which they did.

When DeLoach informed Hoover of this Kennedy plot against the bureau, the director scrawled on a memo that Kennedy's Justice Department "is trying to poison the W.H. [White House] about [the] FBI." Hoover was still smarting from rumors that the Kennedys—namely, Bobby—wanted to retire him. And so the bureau worked to keep Bobby from ever regaining his power, throwing logs on the fire of Johnson's suspicion. Hoover began sending Johnson secret messages through DeLoach that Bobby was secretly employing spies and assisting journalists to sabotage the President. Johnson not only accepted the information, he further utilized the bureau to mine for intelligence on fellow Democratic Party members and civil rights leaders, turning the FBI into what historian Taylor Branch called his "politically loyal detective agency."[35]

There were many reports of friction between Bobby and Hoover, but as Guthman wrote, "Bob had little difficulty in determining whether a report was fact or gossip" since O'Donnell and O'Brien were still in the West Wing.[36] A few weeks later, Guthman met with DeLoach and confronted him about the FBI's treatment of the attorney general since President Kennedy's death. The FBI had not only circumvented RFK's office, Guthman said, they were hearing stories about the secret messages to the President. DeLoach denied it and told Hoover about the meeting.

Hoover then took Guthman's complaint to Johnson as more evidence of Kennedy spies inside the White House.[37]

To Hoover, even the most powerful in Washington were interlopers, foolishly thinking they could control his bureau. Sitting in the Oval Office with President Richard Nixon seven years later, the director bragged that he made Johnson believe his attorney general "would try to steal the nomination . . . That's what got me in bad with Bobby."[38]

JOHNSON HAD ENOUGH to fear already. In mid-February, RFK made his first political appearance since his brother's death: remarks at Washington's Mayflower Hotel before seven hundred members of the United Auto Workers. It was going to be a lot of handshakes and few words. His speech was essentially a bow and a nod—no more than three minutes. Only he didn't need to say anything at all. The audience was in a trance, almost instinctually drawn toward him. The men in the room swarmed and Bobby couldn't move, enveloped by big shoulders in dark suits, palms slapping his back, rough hands thrust into his chest for a grip. The scene was inconceivable just a few months earlier, before Dallas, when he was a political liability, not a savior. Now he need only walk into a room to find hundreds pouring out their feelings toward the martyred president, desperate to release their sorrow and turn it into action.[39]

This was a new experience for Bob. He had worked hundreds of rooms for his brother over the years. He had been the man with the ear of the President, someone it paid to get close to. That type of power had vanished, and yet their desire to reach out and touch him was like never before. Bobby knew that they weren't reaching for him—they were still reaching for Jack. The power Bobby had known was gone, this new power in its stead. And as much as he had never wanted this power, he could *feel* it.[40]

The national polls told him of his transformation. Gallup showed he was the rank and file's choice for vice president, far ahead of two-time presidential nominee Adlai Stevenson, 37 percent to 25 percent.[41] Dallas had turned a thirty-eight-year-old who had never run for public office into an elder statesman of the party—an elder statesman at odds with the President. A runaway convention was in the making.

Which is why the President of the United States cared so much about a no-name hack like Paul Corbin. Because, as Johnson said, if an employee of the Democratic National Committee was allowed to campaign for Bobby in New Hampshire without repercussions, it would appear as if the President either approved of the action or couldn't quash it. Other party leaders would have joined the Kennedy bandwagon—the national movement that Peter Crotty hoped to inspire. And while Corbin might not have been the best operative to put forward in New Hampshire, he was willing, he was capable, and he had done this kind of work before.

Corbin's presence in New Hampshire was nothing more than a test of Johnson's power. And for a time, Johnson had won.

THEN THE DAM broke. With party regulars Bernie Boutin and William Dunfey in charge, New Hampshire's Democratic establishment fully embraced the Draft Bobby for Vice President movement. Discarding his publicly neutral stance, Governor King endorsed RFK less than two weeks before the primary. "What I say is, I'm going to write in the name of President Johnson, and Robert Kennedy for vice president, and I recommend that you follow my example." The idea was a hit with voters, and an easily identifiable ploy for King's struggling sweepstakes referendum.[42] This was the strange dichotomy of Bobby's support: raw emotion on one hand, and political self-interest on the other.

"Almost every day," Guthman would remember, "brought a visit or phone calls from politicians friendly to Bob, urging him to give some indication that he would accept the vice presidential nomination if it was offered." They wanted him on the ballot to boost their tickets, to wield his power for their benefit. Governor King's gain was Johnson's loss—the endorsement was embarrassing to the President. The *Concord Daily Monitor* editorialized, "It is possible that the size of the write-in vote for the Attorney General for Vice President might equal or exceed President Johnson, especially if it is combined with votes for Kennedy for President, of which there will be some."[43]

Furthermore, the *Boston Globe* noted that Bobby made no attempt to halt the write-in train for another week, until after it had a head of steam. As speculation grew, RFK asked Ken O'Donnell at the White House if he should put out a statement. O'Donnell said not to do anything. Then Bobby worried it was getting out of hand, and O'Donnell put together something for the papers just five days before the primary.

The Attorney General has said that the choice of the Democratic nominee for vice-president will be made, and it should be made, by the Democratic Convention in August, guided by the wishes of President Johnson and that President Johnson should be free to select his own running mate. The Attorney General, therefore, wishes to discourage any efforts on his behalf in New Hampshire or elsewhere.[44]

Bobby barely edited the statement, Ed Guthman would recall, except to strike a line through one sentence: "~~The Attorney General is not seeking the nomination for Vice President.~~"[45]

All the statement indicated was that Bobby was keeping up appearances. Corbin dropped off the map, and Shaine, who had earlier boasted of working with Corbin, changed his tune, saying he hardly knew the rogue Kennedy aide. Governor King said the write-in movement was "the product of spontaneous combustion" and claimed to be helpless, likening his position to trying to stop a forest fire in minutes. *Newsweek* editor Ben Bradlee remarked privately to Jack Valenti, "My God, if there's one state in the union other than Massachusetts that these [Kennedy] people know well—and I'm not saying this in any critical way at all—it's New Hampshire. They know that. They know the people to call to say, 'Look, absolutely not.' And they just didn't make those calls! . . . A couple of phone calls to the right people would've stopped that thing in a minute."[46]

LBJ cast himself as the helpless victim, lamenting to House Speaker John McCormack, "Bobby's running for vice president up in New Hampshire, and that's causing us a lot of embarrassment. They've got an advertising agency hired"—naming Corbin's man Robert Shaine—"and they're trying to get more votes up there than I get. I can't do anything so then won't anybody write in my name 'cause they assume I'm going to be president. They've got a big movement going there. So you know how those things are, you faced them before." In 1962, Speaker McCormack's nephew had been in line for Massachusetts' open Senate seat until the Kennedys got behind Teddy. McCormack agreed and told Johnson how the Kennedys were trying to juice the vote for Bobby in the Massachusetts primary, too.

"A lot of peculiar things happening, Mr. Speaker," Johnson said. "A *lot* of peculiar things."[47]

At his next press conference, the President was forced to do what he had threatened to quit over—he praised Bobby as he was being shoved down his throat. Johnson said the attorney general "has established a very fine record of public service," as had all of those mentioned for the number two spot.[48]

But the praise faded with the camera flashes. Johnson was certain that

Bobby had gotten the ball rolling on the stories of money, sex, and power around Johnson's former aide Bobby Baker—"Little Lyndon" in the newspapers. Baker's scandals were old news by then, but the President thought his attorney general was working up other ways to tarnish him. "He's up having lunch today with the *Wall Street Journal*," the President said in a self-recorded phone call on March 9, the day before the New Hampshire primary. LBJ said Bobby and the *Journal* were getting together "a big article" on Johnson's family's television-station holdings—multimillion-dollar gains ill-gotten through connections with federal regulators. "And I found out pretty definite that's where the Baker thing started." As usual, Johnson had accurate intelligence as to Bobby's whereabouts: a lunch was indeed scheduled with the *Wall Street Journal* in RFK's desk diary that day. And while the *Journal* soon ran articles chronicling the Johnsons' wealth and how Lady Bird had built a television empire, there was no damning scoop about manipulating broadcast licenses.[49] Still, the President was rattled, and unsure of what to do next.

On the eve of primary day, Johnson recounted to his close friend Edwin Weisl all that Bobby and Corbin and New Hampshire Democrats had done behind LBJ's back. "And I don't know how we ought to treat it—I guess just ignore it," the President said. Weisl told him he didn't think it meant anything. Johnson said, "Well, it'll mean a lot in publicity because it already fills the papers here." He talked about an editorial in the *Washington Star* "saying the Kennedy name is magic and this means he'll be swept in." Johnson told Weisl that a fellow had come in and told him that the *Star*, *Newsweek*, and the *New York Times* "just sit inside the office"—the attorney general's office—"all the time." The informant, the President recounted, "said he went in the other day and one of them said, 'You can use *this* part of the story in New Hampshire, and you can use the other part in New Hampshire,' and he, he—they were directing it all right from there."[50]

Johnson press aide George Reedy would later say the President had a deep desire for control, and an irrational fear of Bobby. "He wanted [the press] to use *his* adjectives in describing *his* actions, and when they did not do so, he decided they were in the pay of Bobby Kennedy, toward whom he was virtually paranoid."[51]

That night, Bill Moyers read Johnson an article in *Newsweek* about tensions over Corbin and the write-in effort for Kennedy in New Hampshire. "Well, I think that's all right," Johnson said softly. "I think it makes Bobby look bad instead of us." They speculated over where leaks about the Johnson-Kennedy relationship were coming from within the White House, suspecting Ken O'Donnell. "Ask Ken in the morning," Johnson said. "Get him to write down his answer. Because they're quotin' him, aren't they?"

"Yes, sir," Moyers said. "Well, it's really on. It's really a campaign."

The President told his aide to expect a bumpy start. "Well, he'll sweep, but I think that we'll just ride it out," Johnson said. "Just take a little time and he'll make an ass of himself. That's what [J. Edgar] Hoover says he'll do."

"I think that's true," Moyers said. "I still think that while he does have an organization, there's just a lot of people in this country who in 1960, they stole things from that, uh, want to see that family out." Moyers fanned the flames of the race LBJ lost, while the President stewed over Bobby's lack of fealty to him and toyed with firing him.

"I don't see how he can have much self-respect sitting in the Justice Department and doing stuff like this. I think in a matter of time, probably after the convention, that he'll be bound to have to run off and cry."

"Mr. President, he was trained by Jesuits," Moyers said, "and Jesuits have a funny philosophy. I mean, it's an effective one, but you know, 'If you're not for me, you're against me' and 'The means justify the end.' So, he has a very simple ethic. *Black is black; white is white.* Black is if you're against me. White is if you're for me."

"Well, but we could ask him to resign tomorrow," the President said.

The question dangled in the air before Moyers said calmly, "But that wouldn't do any good though."

"I don't know," LBJ said. "He'd be pretty lonesome without that, that, all his people around him, and without that power."

Moyers cautioned him about what Bobby was capable of: "I think then he'd probably get out and really generate a fight, whereas, a little bit, he doesn't think right now he has to." Moyers stopped. "Well, I think you could beat him. I'm sure you could. I think these Northern liberals are with him on this civil rights bill. Although all, though? I don't think so."

"Yeah," Johnson said. "I think that's what we've got to have him on—civil rights. And when he gets through with that, why . . . if we ever get through with it."[52]

The President had chosen not to fire Bobby, his biggest rival for the party's leadership, on the day of the New Hampshire primary. He had other means of defense. New Hampshire Democratic leaders jump-started an effort to write in the President's name on the top of the ticket—in part to save him from embarrassment, in part to drum up even more support for their referendum. In a twisted way, Johnson became Kennedy's running mate. The state party bought ads and printed palm cards with Bobby's picture on them. They instructed local leaders to write in Johnson when turning out to support Kennedy.[53]

The hubbub over Bobby was ultimately to Johnson's advantage: expectations for the President were exceptionally low. "There appears to be little doubt," the *Boston Globe*'s political editor wrote on the eve of the primary, "that Kennedy will get a large write-in, most likely larger than the President's."[54]

Fate again stepped in on Johnson's side. On the Republican side of the New Hampshire primary, Henry Cabot Lodge—Richard Nixon's running mate in 1960, whom JFK made ambassador to South Vietnam—stunned the leading candidates, Barry Goldwater and Nelson Rockefeller, by winning a write-in victory all the way from his post in Saigon. Lodge's feat completely overshadowed the Democratic race. When the votes were tallied, Johnson led with 29,317 to Bobby's 25,094.[55] And Governor King's sweepstakes referendum passed.

QUIETLY, THE DEMOCRATIC contest moved on to Paul Corbin's home state of Wisconsin, where a Draft Kennedy group had mysteriously popped up. The organizer, who had close ties to the state's Democratic national committeeman Pat Lucey, fit the description of Corbin's favorite kind of committee leader in his denial to the press: "Who's Corbin? I'm not even a Democrat."

Corbin remained elusive. He was said to have attended a news conference given by Wisconsin governor John Reynolds and dined at the executive mansion in Madison, though no reporter could pin Corbin's whereabouts down.[56]

The bigger story was completely out of sight: that Bobby was secretly conferring with Governor Reynolds and Lucey as the Wisconsin primary drew near. Phone logs show multiple calls between the Wisconsin Democratic leaders and Kennedy. Reynolds even met with Bobby in his office twice, including the day after the New Hampshire primary.[57] None of it was ever reported, and no one was able to tie Bobby to the campaign that intended to sweep him to the vice presidency.

But Corbin was left exposed. On March 11, the day after the New Hampshire primary, the New York Times published a front-page story revealing that the White House had forced him from the DNC for supporting Bobby in New Hampshire. The paper wrote that Bobby had personally called Corbin about the allegation that he had gone up to New Hampshire, and that Corbin had sworn to him he hadn't. Nevertheless, "Mr. Kennedy has been embarrassed by Mr. Corbin's zeal," the Times reported, "and has sought to assure the President that he has given it no support." The Washington Post followed up, writing, "The Attorney General is amused when it is suggested that he had Corbin work for him in New Hampshire. Why should he assign Corbin when he could call on some of the most brilliant politicians in the country to take on the chore?"[58]

Because Paul Corbin was one of the most loyal men Bobby Kennedy had, and Bobby was loyal to him. When Corbin called the Justice Department as these front-page stories were landing on his head, phone logs show the attorney general took his call. It is still unknown what exactly their conversation yielded, but the situation in Wisconsin clearly changed over the next few days. The organizers of the Draft Kennedy group had claimed that they were about voters expressing their preference and would "not be stopped." Then they turned on a dime and disbanded.[59]

It is also documented that Corbin was looking to Bobby for guidance a week later on March 19, when he left a phone message with the attorney general's secretary, asking if he should attend a dinner or not.[60]

WISCONSIN WAS THE tipping point, spilling private disagreements between Bobby and the President out into public view. It was a chance to rehash the Johnson-Kennedy history: the fight over the vice presidency in 1960, when Bobby tried to rescind the offer after it had been made—their deep dislike of each other during the Kennedy administration, how Johnson regretted sending Bobby to Indonesia, and now the battle over the vice presidency. The White House press secretary had to deny reports that the two had "stopped speaking" altogether.[61]

And so, two days after the New Hampshire primary, Bobby made it known publicly. "I have the highest regard for him," the attorney general said of Johnson to a group of visiting Pennsylvania grade-schoolers with reporters looking on. "Our relations are friendly. They always have been . . . I have read these reports about a feud. There is no substance to these reports." For his part, Johnson soon appeared before the press and dismissed the "newspaper talk"—"I take his word that he has done nothing to encourage those efforts."[62]

One of the visiting youngsters asked Bobby who he thought was going to be Johnson's running mate.

"Teddy," he quipped.

Then came the future question—*What will you do next?*—which even with children Bobby could not escape.

He told them he just didn't know. "Scary, isn't it?"[63]

3

SEEING GHOSTS

March 1964–June 1964

LOYALTY BROUGHT BOBBY OUT. Loyalty, and the Irish.

After personal appeals from Pennsylvania's Democratic boss, former governor Dave Lawrence—a man who "was awfully good to us in 1960," as Bobby would say—RFK agreed to address Scranton's Friendly Sons of St. Patrick dinner in his first major speech since Dallas.[1]

He had been preparing for this day. On March 3, a week before the New Hampshire primary, the attorney general secretly began taking public-speaking lessons in New York City. His teacher was a woman named Maxeda von Hesse, whose mother, Elisabeth, had been Eleanor Roosevelt's speech coach when she was first lady. Maxeda von Hesse was a vintage character—a gray-haired, middle-aged Republican who "weighs more than she should," she would write a year later. Most of her clients were men, including New York's Republican governor, Nelson Rockefeller, though she tutored members of both parties as long as they were paying top dollar and weren't running against each other. Politicians "need results fast, and there's less margin for increasing their skills gradually," she wrote in 1965. "When I accept a student, I work with his total personality, his gestures, stance, timing, walk, and delivery. We highlight a mannerism which might become a political asset, such as Roosevelt's cigarette holder and Kennedy's jabbing forefinger." Von Hesse had studied a film reel of Bobby speaking in January, and after a get-to-know-you meeting, the attorney general paid nearly $2,200 for twelve hours of instruction.[2]

Throughout the spring, Bobby would take the shuttle up to her studios on the east side of Manhattan, sometimes coinciding with other business, sometimes not—as was his lesson the day before his Scranton trip.[3] The speech was to end with a poem, a sad Irish lament upon the death of a leader.

> *Your troubles are all over,*
> *you're at rest with God on high,*

But we are slaves, and we're orphans, Owen!
—why did you die?

We're sheep without a shepherd,
when the snow shuts out the sky—
Oh! why did you leave us, Owen?
Why did you die?[4]

When Ed Guthman saw it in the draft, he cut it and told Bob, "You'll never get through it. You don't have to put yourself through that."

Bobby replied, "I've been practicing. I've been practicing in front of a mirror. I can't get through it yet—but I will."[5]

When the *Caroline* landed in Scranton that rainy St. Patrick's afternoon, a crowd of three thousand flooded the tarmac as he disembarked. Local and state police struggled to clear a path through the sea of outstretched hands. Young girls cried hysterically, "I touched him! I touched him!" Bobby was oddly calm, one observer noted—"the least excited person in the gathering"— asking the police not to worry about him. The crush continued as he climbed into his car, with people toppling on, plunging their hands through the window opening for his touch. Bobby obliged while a *Scranton Times* reporter heard him repeatedly caution the FBI agent behind the wheel not to hit anyone.[6]

As soon as Bobby had agreed to speak before the Friendly Sons, invitations from the outlying areas flooded in, and so a short visit ballooned into a multiple-stop, seven-hour affair. After a day of frenzied events, Bobby arrived at Scranton's Casey Hotel for the speech. A handful of local college students burst into the ballroom bearing three-foot-square placards declaring LET'S KEEP THE JOHNSON-KENNEDY TEAM IN 1964 and YOUTH WANTS TO KNOW: WILL YOU TAKE VP BOB? They marched around the hall and were escorted out to applause. Bobby showed little interest in the demonstration, except to say, "I appreciate it, but I think it's out of place." He also said he did not welcome write-in votes in the Pennsylvania Democratic primary, yet in his speech, the only diversion from his prepared remarks was a joke that when St. Patrick freed his annual twelve Irish souls from the pits of hell, "some of them must have been released just before the primary in New Hampshire last week." Columnists Rowland Evans and Bob Novak reported that Washington's "hard-boiled Democratic leaders were startled" at this "tumultuous reception," finding it "of the caliber of greetings given a presidential candidate or even a popular incumbent President." Bobby seemed dazed by it, as a *Scranton Times* reporter wrote, "When he commented that he had not made up his mind about the vice presidency, he was looking beyond the newsmen, not to try and present a diversionary answer, but seemingly searching in a sea of faces for something he had lost."[7]

His speech was serious, centered on civil rights and how their progress as Irishmen was "chilled by the tragic irony that it has not been progress for everyone . . . There are Americans who, as the Irish did, still face discrimination in employment—sometimes open, sometimes hidden . . . It is toward concern for these issues—and vigorous participation on the side of freedom— that our Irish heritage must impel us. If we are true to this heritage, we cannot stand aside."[8]

A local reporter noticed the change in Bobby's speaking manner, how when he had seen him in the past, he would waggle a finger and build a section to a climax, much like his brother had done. "His presentation last night was more matter-of-fact." Bobby was stiff. He made no gestures during the speech and showed emotion only once, when he read the poem. His voice lowered and his reading pace quickened as he came to the words that everyone knew applied to his brother: " 'Sheep without a shepherd, when the snow shuts out the sky—Oh, why did you leave us, Owen? Why did you die?' " It was the only time that night that the raucous ballroom stood utterly still and silent, gripping the thousand men and waiters and reporters, one wrote, "in a silence which showed they knew what was in his heart." When he finished, he closed his folder and whispered, "Thank you," and a standing ovation crossed the room. Bobby met them with a pinched smile. An observer noted how he moved between the outstretched hands as he left the ballroom: his shoulders "slightly hunched and leaning slightly forward much in the manner of walk of the late President."[9] It was as if they had seen a ghost.

John F. Kennedy, in Robert's form, permeated American politics. A consensus was building that the tribute at the Democratic convention that summer would set off a stampede to put Bobby on the ticket. The Gallup Poll showed his continued rise as the rank-and-file choice for vice president: 47 percent in April, after 37 in March and 34 in January. Statewide polls conducted privately by candidates running for governor and senator across the country said the same thing. It was around this time, Guthman wrote years later, that Bobby "allowed himself to drift into" an "unannounced, restrained" campaign for the vice presidency.[10] Yet this hindsight characterization—"restrained"— was either a stretch of definition or revisionist history, for the lengths Bobby soon went to in forcing Johnson's hand reveal just how badly he wanted it.

THE ARCHITECT OF Bobby's vice presidential campaign was Fred Dutton, a West Coast operative who Kennedy would later describe as "the best political brain in America." Dutton quietly earned his keep in New Frontier

Washington by bridging rival factions. He had been an infantryman in World War II, spent four months in a German prison camp, and later returned to military service as an officer in Korea. He got his start as an attorney at a Southern California utility company and began dabbling in politics—his true passion—writing columns for the *Los Angeles Times*. Dutton's work on Adlai Stevenson's 1956 presidential campaign got him noticed by Pat Brown, the state's ambitious attorney general, who recruited him to run his 1958 bid for governor. After they won, Brown made him his executive secretary. Fred was brilliant and original in his thinking, so much so that it seemed to make Brown uncomfortable. Jesse Unruh, the top Democrat in the California State Assembly and the governor's chief political antagonist, thought Dutton's only fault was that he overlooked nothing and was too needling in his advice. The Kennedys scouted Dutton for their campaign at the 1960 Los Angeles convention, and Dutton went to the Washington headquarters, where he worked closely with Bob. He expected to follow him to the Justice Department in the new administration, but was instead sent to the White House as special assistant to the President, the only top staffer with state government or executive office experience. His job was managing the cabinet and keeping the peace between the Sorensen-Goodwin-Schlesinger intellectual clique and the hard-boiled O'Donnell-O'Brien Irish Mafia.[11] In this sense, he was a low-key version of Robert Kennedy—a hybrid mind for politics and policy who smoothed rough edges in the West Wing.

In January 1961, Dutton had a cramped office in the West Wing and was sleeping with his twenty-one-year-old administrative assistant, Nancy Hogan, despite being married with two kids. The affair was documented in a government dossier on Dutton, after a nun at Nancy's alma mater, Manhattanville College, tipped off the FBI. White House liaison Courtney Evans informed Kenny O'Donnell, who "expressed amazement that we had uncovered this information," an FBI memo said. O'Donnell told the bureau that he had taken the matter to JFK, and that "under the President's direction . . . the romantic affair has been terminated." On the day the memo was sent, March 3, Nancy and Fred spent the night in his room at the Willard Hotel one last time before breaking it off. "Three months later, I told him I was pregnant," Nancy would recall, "and I'm not going to see Bobby Baker," Lyndon Johnson's former Senate aide who procured abortions for Washington's elite during the early sixties.[12]

On the day their baby was born in secret in late November 1961, Dutton accepted a job as assistant secretary for congressional relations at the State Department. The change was a coincidence. No one in the White House knew Nancy was pregnant, thanks to the shape of her hips. She took a two-week vacation and returned to working in Fred's office, leaving the baby with a nursery in Maryland Mondays through Fridays. Dutton remained married and the FBI didn't become aware of the child until another background check years later.[13]

Fred remained friendly with Bobby for the rest of the Kennedy administration, and when Dallas made the vice presidency look like RFK's only viable option for national power, Dutton's political brain went to work. Within weeks of the assassination, he sent Bobby a memo on the history of vice presidential nominations. While he condensed nearly every one from 1800 to 1956 into a single paragraph or two, Fred spent pages detailing how Teddy Roosevelt and Harry Truman unexpectedly seized the vice presidential nominations at their parties' conventions in 1900 and 1944. It was no coincidence that both men ended up presidents themselves, he wrote. Dutton also pointed out that in years when the incumbent president had ascended from the vice presidency and then tried to handpick his running mate—years like 1964—the incumbents "have not generally been able to work their will on the number two spot."[14]

Dutton spent the next few months organizing the JFK memorial library's oral history project, often meeting with Bobby.[15] Then, in early April, he began to plot RFK's course to the vice presidency on his State Department letterhead.

Dutton saw problems in the rampant speculation about Bobby's vice presidential campaign. He thought a "substantive" angle was needed to improve his chances. He knew Bobby's strengths and that he would benefit through multiple and open interactions with young people. "Overall, what I am really suggesting," he wrote in an April 3, 1964, memo, "is not only fuller harnassing [sic] of your potential impact with the rising generation (over half of the people on this globe are under 26), but a way to infuse new spirit in much of the rest of American society."[16] In broad terms, Dutton suggested blocking out time for visits to high schools in nearby cities, primarily ones with poor and minority students, and occasionally middle class groups.

Meeting with Dutton on April 21, Bobby asked for some specific steps to implement this plan, and so Dutton authored a follow-up memo, outlining a series of "low-keyed and personalized" trips with as little staff as possible. The week of April 27, Bobby should go to a high school in D.C.—as he often did—with a similar appearance at an urban high school in Baltimore. The week of May 4, to a "mixed" high school or college in New York or Jersey City, combined with whatever other business he had. On May 11, he should make a major speech in Chicago, possibly visit the U.S. Attorney's Office, and definitely call on powerful Mayor Richard J. Daley. Dutton recommended a trip to West Virginia, then a stop in North Carolina, making sure to see Governor Terry Sanford, a potential ally in the South. The week of May 25, to Philadelphia or Pittsburgh. Dutton suggested a trip to Southern California immediately after its presidential primary in early June, and then a ten-day trip abroad within the next month, perhaps to Sweden, with stops at Soviet universities, then maybe India or East Africa before returning home. "Going abroad will project your influence into student groups throughout the world," Dutton wrote. "In a domestic sense, it would provide excellent news copy while still implicitly demonstrating your staying 'cool' during the increasing political speculation as we near the Convention period."[17]

Almost immediately, Bobby Kennedy did or planned to do all of these things. He received speaking invitations at the rate of thirty to forty a week, so following Dutton's itinerary was simply a matter of saying yes. And while he did not always adhere to Dutton's exact order, his appearances tracked awfully close. He even plotted a foreign trip—to Germany instead of Sweden, and universities in Communist Poland instead of the Soviet Union—putting Dutton in charge of obtaining visas through his State Department position. The only trip in Dutton's plan that Bobby did not make was to North Carolina—except unsealed documents reveal that one was scheduled for almost exactly the time Dutton prescribed. An FBI memorandum in RFK's file reveals that the local bureau office made plans for his security and travel to Duke University, while preparing for an impromptu visit to Governor Sanford's office. The trip was canceled the day before, while all its details made their way back to Washington and Director Hoover—and likely the White House. Dutton would continue writing memos into the summer, suggesting Bobby's travel and activities. In one instance, he encouraged him to go to Los Angeles "in a private capacity" to attend a U.S.-Soviet track meet where he could confer with Southern California's Democratic boss Jesse Unruh. Bobby took that trip, too.[18]

Dutton's suggestions were not the only appearances Bobby made at the time: he was still attorney general and he was still fund-raising for the Kennedy memorial library. Yet the fact remains that Dutton's advice—specifically relating to the vice presidency—was not only heard; it was taken.

THE LEGACY OF John F. Kennedy was wrapped in civil rights, the great domestic battle in the last year of his presidency. Bobby was once asked why he and his brother had waited until 1963 to introduce a civil rights law. Simple politics, he said: it had no chance of passing in 1962, and they didn't feel like wasting political capital until they could get results. That time came late in the spring of 1963, after months of agitation, violence, and assassination. Through it all, RFK had urged caution. He was slow to find the urgency—or the issue itself. He hadn't been terribly conscious of race as a child. "I know it's the worst thing in the world to say that some of your best friends are Negroes," he said privately in 1964, "but as I was growing up, I suppose two out of my four best friends were Negroes." Bobby's ignorance of racial strife was partly the product of his racial privilege, but more so his family's great wealth. He could not easily identify with the daily chores that people of any color faced. He never felt the need to carry his own money or house keys or pocket combs, which he used and discarded multiple times per day. He even once nearly doubled up on a New York City subway turnstile because he didn't know he had to insert a token. In those ways, Robert Kennedy was out of touch with regular citizens. Nor did he understand the racial problem the way he ulti- mately would, one of his closest aides would say, until it registered on a moral level. "There was a right and wrong thing, and then I think the more he became exposed to it, the more he actually felt it and felt identified with them."[19]

As peaceful protests were met with increasing violence in May of 1963, Bobby read an essay on the Negro experience in the *New Yorker* and invited its author, James Baldwin, for breakfast at Hickory Hill. But Baldwin's plane was late and they only had time for a brief conversation, so Bob suggested they reconvene in New York City the next day at his father's Park Avenue apart- ment. He suggested Baldwin invite other Negro voices who ought to be heard. It was an experiment of sorts—a meeting with celebrities, intellec- tuals, and activists below the leadership ranks of the civil rights movement, whom the White House typically dealt with. RFK hoped for suggestions on what they thought the government should be doing.

Yet that was not what he heard from the luminaries gathered in the expen- sive apartment. One young man stood out: the Congress of Racial Equality's twenty-four-year-old New Orleans chairman, Jerome Smith. Smith, who had been beaten in the Freedom Rides that had caused the White House head- aches, began the meeting by telling Bobby, "Mr. Kennedy, I want you to understand I don't care anything about you or your brother." Smith said that after their failure to support civil rights demonstrators, just being in the same room with a Kennedy made him want to vomit. Bobby tried to rebut, to give examples of what the administration had done, but young Smith kept interrupting.

"Just let me say something," Bobby said.

Smith replied, "Okay, but this time say something that means something. So far you haven't said a thing." Bobby ran through his list of accomplish- ments. It moved no one. Baldwin egged Smith on, asking if he would fight for his country in war. "Never! Never!" shouted Smith.

Bobby snapped. "How can you say that?" And the young man said it again.

They did this for three hours. Anger, all on the surface. Bobby heard no solutions. "They didn't want to talk about doing anything," he said the next day, "they don't know the facts. They just wanted to shout." He was particularly troubled by how Smith said he would not fight for his country. "Imagine anyone saying that," he told Guthman. And then his anger softened. "I guess if I were in his shoes, if I had gone through what he's gone through, I might feel differently about this country." The more Bobby was exposed to the anguish and urgency of youth, the less the statistics and programs he spoke of mattered.[20]

The Park Avenue unpleasantness almost immediately leaked to the press, and Baldwin basked in the notoriety of assembling a "secret meeting" for the attorney general and humiliating him.[21] But Bobby didn't let his pride overtake the lesson he learned that day. Over the course of the next year, the word *insult* crept into his talks about civil rights. "A motel will serve a Communist or a narcotics pusher but the Negro is refused," he told an audience in Georgia in May 1964. "Yet we ask the Negro to perform many services for the United States. Six Negroes have been killed recently in Vietnam. Yet if one of their families buried their loved one in Arlington Cemetery and started home to Alabama, the mother would not know the motel to use, what restaurant, what restroom for her children. Yet her husband was killed for all of us. It is a continuous insult."[22] The rage he encountered on Park Avenue that day was the product of a continuous insult inflicted upon the Negro by society. The insult was what mattered. The insult was *all* that mattered. Bobby came to understand that. And in the coming years, he would not make Negro leaders come to him on Park Avenue. In fact, he would go to them.

BOBBY HAD BEEN President Kennedy's point man on Capitol Hill for the civil rights bill and continued in that role for President Johnson. Throughout the spring of 1964, he huddled in strategy sessions with Majority Leader Mike Mansfield; the bill's Senate floor manager, Hubert Humphrey; and White House liaison Lawrence O'Brien. He trekked to Minority Leader Everett Dirksen's office in search of language that could work for the Republican caucus and overwhelm the Southern Democrats' filibuster. By mid-May, the negotiations with Dirksen secured a deal that could obtain a two-thirds majority in the Senate—enough votes to close debate. One angry Republican senator denounced Bobby's involvement: "[The attorney general] may be running the Democratic Party; he may be the next vice president, but I didn't know he was running the Republican conference, too." Senator Richard Russell of Georgia, master of parliamentary procedure and leader of the Southern

Democrats, argued that Bobby's involvement constituted a violation of the separation of powers. Shortly before the vote, Russell mischievously filed an amendment to name the legislation the "Dirksen-Humphrey-Kennedy Bill."[23]

Yet Bobby did not see the civil rights bill as simply directed at the South. In April, he said, "Passage would give us some time to act on these other problems, particularly in the North." He had long warned of the danger of racial tensions above the Mason-Dixon Line, where there were no WHITES ONLY signs but only because none were necessary. "In the North," Bobby said that May, "I think you have had de facto segregation, which in some areas is bad or even more extreme than in the South," and that people in "those communities, including my own state of Massachusetts, concentrated on what was happening in Birmingham, Alabama, or Jackson, Mississippi, and didn't look at what was needed to be done in our own home, our own town, our own city." Bobby said that these factors—ten years after the Supreme Court's landmark *Brown v. Board of Education* school desegregation decision—had led "to the idea that there hasn't been progress." The ultimate solution was not about the actions of the federal government, he said. "What it rests with, really, is a truly major effort at the local level to deal with the problem—Negroes and whites working together, within the structure of the law, obedience to the law, and respect for the law. If we don't do that, if we don't have that kind of cooperation, I don't care whether it's Georgia or Massachusetts, Mississippi or Illinois, you are not going to find a solution."[24]

The broader answer was to do something about poverty. Like civil rights, the legislative package dubbed the War on Poverty was a top priority for President Johnson. For Bobby, it was a tribute to his late brother, whom he called "totally committed" to "involving the national administration to a greater extent than ever before."[25] That April of 1964, Bobby took to Capitol Hill in support of antipoverty legislation, testifying before a House subcommittee. One member, a Nebraska Republican, fretted over the government's trampling the "pioneer spirit of many of our people."

RFK replied directly, "Have you ever told a coal miner in West Virginia or Kentucky that what he needs is individual initiative to go out to get a job where there isn't any?"[26]

A few weeks later, Bobby went to those mountains of West Virginia, down to the isolated hollows far from the national gaze. He arrived in Charleston early, to look over a jobs-training program for poverty-stricken areas, and then to Dry Creek Hollow, where he met an out-of-work coal miner named Greenie Mullins, who had eight children, just like he did at the time. Mullins told the attorney general, "We loved your brother. That was a dirty trick they did on him." They patted each other on the shoulder, quiet and knowing, not needing to say anything else. A young single mother of six showed Bobby into her family's decaying two-room shack. He took one of her daughters, a four-year-old with cerebral palsy, into his lap. He talked with the girl in a soft voice and clipped his PT-109 tie clasp to her worn dress. "These are our people," he was heard to say. "If we can't break into this cycle, it will never end."[27] Over and over, families told him how they cut his brother's picture out of magazines and newspapers and tacked them to the walls in their homes. One such portrait was handed to him by a person who had almost nothing to give . . . a token of their shared mourning. Bobby took it back to the car and placed it on the dash, Jack's face staring back at him.

A reporter in the car asked, "This has been a hard day for you, hasn't it?"

Bobby paused and said, "That's a difficult question to answer." He then took the picture of his brother and gently turned it over.[28]

PART OF ACHIEVING progress on civil rights was selling federal action to Southerners, and in May, Bobby made his first trips to Dixie since his brother had died there. In Prince Edward County, Virginia, local authorities closed the public schools in 1959 rather than integrate. Its Negro children were deprived of an education until friends of the Kennedy administration privately raised the funds to open the Free Schools. The children, who came from families with no money to spare, had saved $99.64 in pennies to donate to the Kennedy library, which Bobby accepted in bags tied with red, white, and blue bows. He told the children how his brother had been "concerned about your failure to get an education and talked about it frequently" and presented large checks from teachers' unions in California and Washington State to continue funding their schools. After, he went to nearby Hampden-Sydney, a college exclusively for white men, where a crowded, steamy auditorium waited. One student brandished a Confederate flag, and the audience hissed when an official appeared onstage. Then the attorney general came out, delivered a brief, lighthearted introduction, and opened the assembly to questions.[29]

Someone asked if he had any hopes for his "pet" civil rights bill to pass. He said he did, even with all the dozens of possible revisions.[30]

"I don't understand your opposition" to integration, Bobby said, encouraging them to go to the Free Schools and "see the children put their hands over their hearts and swear allegiance to America the Beautiful."

Another student asked him why it wasn't "involuntary servitude" to make a whites-only proprietor serve someone he didn't want to. RFK replied that the bill didn't require this, only that the basis could not merely be race. A student reporter felt Kennedy's tone varied between warm and friendly, to one that "showed his hardness and steel." He turned their questions around on them, asking them to justify their way of life instead of him justifying the civil rights bill. A student accused him of political pandering, saying that President Kennedy had only come out for civil rights to gain votes. Bobby told them that it was quite the opposite: it actually cost them votes—not only in the South but in the North, too. Yet he said this was their problem to deal with, and if it was left untended to, it would pass on to the next generation. Hampden-Sydney being a campus of young men, the students also wanted to know about the budding war in Vietnam, and he told them that further American involvement depended on the determination and desire of the South Vietnamese people.[31] Despite all the friction, he got a standing ovation when the program ended.

A columnist for the college newspaper wrote, "Perhaps the most obvious result of Mr. Kennedy's visit was that everyone, whether in agreement with his political views or not, couldn't wait to get in line and shake the famous man's hand." A group of shrieking young women even stopped the Kennedy motorcade at Longwood, Hampden-Sydney's sister school, also for whites only.[32]

Two weeks later, at West Georgia College, a small state school sixty miles west of Atlanta near the Alabama border, Bobby dedicated an interfaith chapel named for his brother and held a forty-minute Q&A with students in the school auditorium. The young people's blunt questions reflected the Southern rhetoric they were inundated with, and Bobby, a reporter wrote, came back "direct and rough-edge, never tangential or slippery." First they wanted to know about his future—the question he never answered. Then came the subject of civil rights.[33] Alabama governor George Wallace was making strong showings in Northern Democratic presidential primaries—protest votes against the civil rights bill—and someone asked what its effect would be.

"I don't think it is helpful to the passage of the legislation," he said, but it wouldn't stop it. Nor was it an honest debate. "If the bill did what Governor Wallace says it would, I'd be against the bill. If people are not dressed well, if they don't pay their bills," then the public-accommodations section would not affect them. "It means if a place is open to the general public, it has to treat all of the public equally." As for Northern Democrats backing an Alabama segregationist, Bobby replied, "I am not surprised, really, at Governor Wallace's votes in Indiana and Wisconsin. First, there is always an 'anti' vote of twenty to twenty-five percent. They will vote against anything. Second, a kind of revolt is going on. Massachusetts and New York were very upset a year ago . . . They were concentrating on how awful it was in the South. And then they found out they had trouble in Boston, New York, Baltimore, and Chicago . . . It's disturbing their lives. They want the Negroes to be quiet, but the Negroes are not going to be quiet." He told them, "This is a revolution going on in connection with civil rights and the Negroes. And people don't like to have their lives changed."[34]

Bobby reminded them of the men—Negro men—dying in Vietnam, "killed for all of us."[35] Then he asked a question that the *Atlanta Constitution*'s political correspondent wrote "most politicians wouldn't ask" in a segregated theater: Bobby asked whites to put themselves on the same level as Negroes.

"How would any of us like it if we were in that situation?"

A ripple went through the audience. A silent moment passed before applause "so solid," the correspondent wrote, "it was startling." Another veteran Southern newspaperman turned to him and said, "That was one of the most thrilling moments I can remember." He wrote that the applause "meant that while many students probably would disagree with him, they respected his frankness." Bobby just looked out upon the audience, stunned. Asked if he was surprised by his reception in Carrollton, he replied, "Frankly, I was."[36]

These messages were not tailored exclusively to students in the South. He was also going to colleges in decidedly Northern and metropolitan areas such as Newark and Teaneck, New Jersey, and saying the same things. Don Irwin of the *Los Angeles Times* recognized a pattern in Bobby's appearances: the best ones were before student groups. "He feels he has a particular rapport with Americans who have come of age since the start of World War II. When— and if—he makes his political move, it will be to that generation that he will look for the muscle that wins campaigns."[37] Fred Dutton's strategy was evident—and a success.

President Johnson was not having it. That month, he was quoted second-hand in Rowland Evans and Robert Novak's nationally syndicated column: "If they try to push Bobby Kennedy down my throat for vice president, I'll tell them to nominate him for the *presidency* and leave me out of it"—a remark much like the ones he was making in private. Evans and Novak saw no real organized movement to make Bobby vice president, as "John F. Kennedy's old lieutenants around the country have no stomach for battling the new President in behalf of the old President's brother." Johnson could take "any white American male as his running mate" if the Republican Party was as divided as it appeared to be going into the fall. Yet, an old Texas friend assured them, "If the occasion demands it, Johnson will take Bobby Kennedy, Sargent Shriver, and at least one Kennedy sister on the ticket with him."[38]

"I would think about it," Bobby told the *Boston Globe* about the vice presidency—a change from his public stance a few months earlier. To the *New York Times*, he shared his desire for change after spending his entire professional career as a prosecutor. "I'm tired of chasing people. I want to go on now to something else." He knew this before the assassination, he said, learning by his years in the White House that law enforcement was not his passion. Bobby felt too much had been said about the vice presidency already, and he had no interest in furthering it. He saw no reason for Johnson and him to discuss it. "What could he say?" Bobby asked. "And obviously I can say nothing."[39] In private, Bobby was cynical about the vice presidency, telling John Bartlow Martin in his sealed oral history interview on May 14 that the Kennedys' Democratic network around the country "worries" LBJ "because the one thing Lyndon Johnson doesn't want is me as vice president, and he's concerned about whether he is going to be forced into that . . . I think he's hysterical about how he's going to try to avoid having me or having to ask me. That's what he spends most of his time on, from what I understand: figuring out how he's going to avoid me." Bobby debated what he should do, saying he was trying to make up his mind. "I think it's a great problem, of course, if I stayed as vice president and was forced on him. It would be an unpleasant relationship, number one. Number two, I would lose all ability to ever take any independent positions on matters. Lyndon Johnson has explained quite clearly that it's not the Democratic Party anymore; it's an all-American party. The businessmen like it. All the people who were opposed to the President like it. I don't like it much." Bobby was also considering getting "out of government" or an "independent base," like running for the U.S. Senate, that could give him more flexibility. He knew how strong Johnson was. "The fact is that he's able to eat people up, even people who are considered rather strong figures." The vice presidency was no place to hold the line on the Kennedy legacy. "I don't think you can have any influence. Lyndon Johnson didn't have any influence." Bobby said that Secretary McNamara suggested he and Johnson could get along if he was willing to "kiss his behind all the time." Though Bobby told Martin he believed he could get the vice presidency, he doubted he was capable of the flattery it required. Moreover, he said for him to try to do anything quietly on his own would be "a disloyal operation." Martin argued that the "Kennedy constituency" could not be ignored, but Bobby pointed out that Johnson was already ignoring it in his policies toward Latin America, "not doing anything for the Alliance for Progress, and he's not paying proper attention to Panama or Brazil . . ." Then, Bobby hit on something.

"If I was in the United States Senate, I would have raised a fuss about Panama."

So what? Martin said. He would be one of a hundred senators.

"Yeah, but I'm not just a senator. I'm a senator from New York and I'm head of the Kennedy wing of the Democratic Party."[40]

* * *

MASSACHUSETTS WAS NEVER really in the cards. Earlier that spring, Bobby stepped up to the microphone at Fenway Park in Boston's Back Bay before a capacity crowd. The Red Sox's owner, Tom Yawkey, was giving the opening day's proceeds to the JFK memorial library, and Bobby and Teddy were invited onto the field to address the stadium over the public address system. "I want to thank all the Redskins—er, Red *Sox*," Bobby squeaked. The ballpark erupted in laughter at Bobby's inadvertently referring to D.C.'s football team on New England baseball's hallowed ground. Bobby just grinned. "That's what happens from living in Washington so long."[41]

There was no room for another Kennedy in Massachusetts anyway. Teddy was running for his first Senate term that fall, and they were both backing Governor Endicott Peabody, a Democrat, for reelection. In a local radio interview, Teddy suggested Bobby might be President Johnson's running mate. "Of course, his home is Massachusetts," Teddy added. "If it's to be a political career, I'm confident that this is the place where he would run for a political office."[42]

The brothers were elected as Massachusetts delegates to the Democratic National Convention in the April primary, Teddy from Boston and Bobby from Cape Cod. When the final tallies were released, Teddy came out far ahead of every other Democrat in the statewide vote. The *Boston Globe* labeled it "embarrassing" that Bobby trailed his baby brother by 22 percent. They dubbed Ted "the indisputable leader" of Bay State Democrats. Bobby and Ethel didn't even bother to vote—they were out of state on election day.[43] If Massachusetts held Bobby's interest, he barely showed it.

While one of Teddy's aides prepared a memo weighing the pros and cons of running there against running in New York, Bobby ruled out Massachusetts early on. "That never made much sense really," he told a reporter in June. "Teddy's there. He's a senator. He's identified with the state. He's organized it. For me to come in there now would have been difficult. I don't want to interfere." Then Bobby smiled and said, "Anyway, I'd be a carpetbagger there."[44]

It was Jean Kennedy's husband, Steve Smith, who pushed Bobby into New York. Smith was supposed to spend 1964 reelecting President Kennedy while his brothers-in-law were busy running the country. In 1963, he was organizing the campaign in several large states, including New York. "Steve's here to sew up '68 for Bobby Kennedy," a New York pol had joked in March of 1963. Then Dallas changed their plans. But by January 1964, Smith was back to organizing a campaign in New York: Robert Kennedy for Senate. Smith began at the dedication of JFK High School in Bethpage, Long Island, where he spoke with Nassau County Democratic chairman Jack English about running Bobby in the fall. Jack English was a guy they could trust, the kind who still wore his PT-109 tie clip to the Johnson White House. Smith picked English to be one of the leaders in laying the groundwork, while he spent the winter and spring months quietly touring the state, gauging Bobby's chances.[45]

In early May 1964, "friends" of the attorney general tipped off the *Washington Post* that they were exploring a Senate bid on his behalf. Incumbent Republican senator Kenneth Keating was so worried about the nomination of conservative Barry Goldwater that he was tempted to retire rather than run on a Goldwater-led ticket. Bobby could establish residency at his father's apartment and make a play. "The idea is to groom the younger brother . . . for the White House eight years from now, when he will be 47 years old," the *Post* said.[46]

Most Democrats met the news with goodwill. State party chairman William McKeon said, "Our own sources indicate he has substantial strength in every part of New York State." Three-term New York City mayor Robert Wagner was more circumspect: "If Robert Kennedy wants to run, he should be given every consideration." The papers were aghast. The *New York Times* editorialized, "There is nothing illegal about the possible nomination of Robert F. Kennedy of Massachusetts as Senator from New York, but there is plenty that is cynical about it." They said Kennedy was choosing New York "as a convenient launching-pad for the political ambitions of himself and others." *Newsday* decried the "cynicism" and said, "We can do without dynastic succession in New York State."[47]

Again, anonymous "friends" of the attorney general alerted the *New York Times* that he would be making a decision within a few weeks, as he thought it was unfair to freeze the field of would-be Keating challengers until late in the process. His visits to New York–area college campuses, prescribed by Fred Dutton, gave local press and students a chance to pepper him with questions. In Newark, New Jersey, students hailed Bobby as "Senator." One asked if it was a good idea for a party to eliminate an opponent by running a popular candidate from another state against him. "I wouldn't advocate that. I don't think it's practical. It's better to get good people in the state to run against the opponent. That's what the Democratic Party does—generally."[48] At both stops, RFK confined his formal remarks to words about the John F. Kennedy Memorial Library and then opened the floor to questions. Asked about the New York Senate race, he said, "I have no plans at present other than being attorney general."

When pressed if that was an absolute denial, he turned to the newspapermen. "Don't interpret that."[49]

The reporters wanted to know if he felt it was ethical to run from New York as an out-of-state resident.

"That's what the law says."[50]

They asked how many years of his life he had spent in New York.

"About ten years," he said.[51]

Rose Kennedy noticed the reports and helped her son pad his résumé. Her secretary privately informed the attorney general, "There is a period of 15 or 16 years of residence in New York and not ten as quoted in the papers."[52]

The metropolitan trip also included a swing up to 161st Street, to the Concourse Plaza Hotel, where Bobby endorsed Congressman Charles A. Buckley, boss of the Bronx, for reelection in a hotly contested primary against a reform Democrat. This was anathema to liberals and good-government types who had been chipping away at Buckley's political fiefdom for years and were finally on the cusp of ousting him. Buckley was old, in failing health, and seemed destined to be the last of his borough's Irish power brokers. Only Buckley had something the future couldn't touch: Bobby's loyalty. He had been *awfully* good to them in 1960. "If we had to select," Bobby said that night, "the three or four men most responsible for President Kennedy's being President, Charlie Buckley would be one of them." Washington columnist Marquis Childs judged from afar that Kennedy was endorsing Buckley to help his Senate or vice presidential ambitions at the expense of JFK's alleged promise to New York liberals that Buckley would step aside after a final term in 1962. "I'm hopeful he will have thirty years more in Congress," Bobby declared.[53]

And Buckley was loyal right back. "He'd make a darn good man on the ticket," he told the pack of reporters about Bobby.

For Senate or vice president?

"I mean for either position."[54]

Bobby's short visit to New York had awoken his enemies' dormant hatred for him. Reform liberals were disgusted with his endorsement of Buckley, as was the *Times* editorial board. Prominent liberal Gore Vidal announced in an interview, "I'm engaged in a campaign to keep him out of New York State and, hopefully, out of the White House, which he somehow thinks is his rightful home. A good many people assume Bobby's like Jack, but there's a great difference between them. He's a rather sinister figure, really. Cynical, fanatic, simplistic, excessively zealous, unmerciful. His temperament is all wrong for the presidency. If the people vote for him because he's Caroline's uncle, God help us!" The *Los Angeles Times*' political columnist expounded that RFK's supposed interest in New York and Massachusetts was "just another piece of fluff pumped out as part of the 'don't know' charade." Ruthless Bobby was angling for the vice presidency, getting local leaders to turn up the heat on LBJ. The Republicans were on the warpath, too, with the state Senate majority leader casting Bobby as "a Back Bay carpetbagger" who "knows as much about the needs and the problems and the aspirations of our people as one of the Beatles." Even some organization Democratic leaders acknowledged that Bobby-facilitated Senate hearings on organized crime had alienated Italian

American voters, while his investigations of Hoffa and the Teamsters had upset union members.[55] To many, Bobby was the most unforgiving, punishing, single-willed man in American politics.

This was the legend, born in part from words attributed to Joseph Kennedy: "Bobby is as hard as nails. *He hates like me.*" The first line of the infamous anecdote can be traced to a fawning biography before Jack's 1960 campaign, but the second—"hates like me"—is likely untrue.[56] Yet it endured because it so easily explained how Bobby learned to be so ruthless, through the example of his cutthroat father. Only Bobby did not inherit his toughness from anyone. If anything, he gained his toughness from being on his own.

One of the union men Bobby put away was Teamsters president Dave Beck, convicted of tax evasion and embezzlement. "But to me," Bobby told a reporter in March of 1964, "Beck's attitude toward his son was his worst sin." He had "mothered" his boy, RFK said, "never allowed him to go out alone, insisted on ordering all the meals, selected all his friends, even though the younger Beck was a grown man . . . Beck had destroyed his son . . . made him a jelly-fish." Bobby, on the other hand, explained that he was largely left to himself as a child: "I was the seventh of nine children, and when you come from that far down, you have to struggle to survive."[57] From his earliest years, Bobby had a desire to be a part of something—*family.*

Family was just a twenty-minute drive from the Justice Department to McLean, where the walls of Hickory Hill were decorated with memories of happy times. "My father once said that if we wanted to retire, all we had to do was put David in the movies," he told *Chicago Daily News* bureau chief Peter Lisagor during a midday visit with the children. He called Mary Kerry "Kerry Merry" and challenged the kids to do flips off the diving board. JFK's Caroline and John were usually milling about with the light-haired children.

Lisagor told Bobby, "I don't see why you'd want to fool around with politics with a family like that."

He smiled. "I agree."[58]

Jacqueline said her children thought of Hickory Hill "as their own home. Anything that comes up involving a father, like father's day at school, I always mention Bobby's name. Caroline shows him her report cards. She makes drawings at school marked 'To Uncle Bobby.' We used to think that if anything happened to us, we'd want to leave the children with Ethel and Bobby. But we always felt they had their own big responsibilities. Now I want them to be part of that family."[59]

Bobby noted Caroline was sensitive and "doesn't let people get close to her." She still carried memories of her father, he said, so he felt she needed special attention. William Manchester would write, "She had something of that remote look which was so pronounced in Robert Kennedy during those months."

"She's my pal," Bobby said of Caroline, who often clung to her uncle.[60]

As for John John, Bobby called him "a rogue." Jackie said, "Jack made John the mischievous, independent boy he is. Bobby is keeping that alive." A reporter recalled seeing Bobby walking down the corridor of the Justice Department with the child on his shoulders, swinging him down and around like a pinwheel, then back up and around his neck again—John squealing with delight all the while. Bobby brought him into meetings, nudging him to introduce himself. Then it was off to the next appointment. "Let's go, John, we've got many things to attend to." On one occasion, the three-year-old was curious to see the FBI's guns, so a special agent arranged for a demonstration at the Indoor Range. They let John "fire a couple of shots with the revolver," a bureau memo said, and gave him the target paper as a souvenir. RFK asked if Director Hoover was in, and they went up for a visit. The Director showed the child around his office, explaining various items. "Little John was particularly interested in the model airplanes and missiles," the memo reported, "and the Director promised the boy that he would send one of the model missiles over to his Uncle Robert this afternoon so that he could give it to him."[61]

Bobby thought of Jack all the time. He was forced to: in his work, driving by Arlington Cemetery, the commemorations and anniversaries and requests on his calendar. He dropped in on Jackie when their spirits needed lifting. She gave him a book, Edith Hamilton's *The Greek Way*, and he lost himself in its pages about ancient society, democracy, and philosophy in Greece, scribbling down tokens of wisdom—"All things are to be examined and called into question. There are no limits set to thought." He found comfort in stories of just men, and unjust endings. "Wisdom cannot be bought," Hamilton's book said. "The idea is repeated again and again with only slight variations in the imagery," she wrote, invoking the poet Aeschylus:

> God, whose law it is that he who learns must suffer. And even in our sleep pain that cannot forget, falls drop by drop upon the heart, and in our own despite, against our will, comes wisdom to us by the awful grace of God.[62]

Bobby would recall that passage from memory years later in Indianapolis, before a stunned crowd on the night Martin Luther King Jr. met his unjust end. He changed the word *despite* to *despair*, but not the meaning.

Bobby was so busy with grief. Nearly every day had some reason to go mourn and remember, like pain falling drop by drop upon his heart. He had still to find his wisdom—what he should do. But as Bobby said to Lisagor and many others, "Sorrow is a form of self-pity . . . and we have to go on."[63]

Ethel kept him grounded. Their friend Dave Hackett said that after mourning "she went back to a normal routine" and pulled Bobby out of the past by example. His wife kept him in the present, and the children reminded him of the future.[64]

BOBBY THREW A party for union leaders at Hickory Hill on May 18, which a friendly labor columnist covered in detail. For many, it was their first invitation to the society destination of New Frontier Washington—a snub that registered. But the presence of Jacqueline and the kids softened these hard men, as Bobby teased them about an extension just put on the house. "We had it built with union labor, so it's expensive, but it's kosher." Joe Curran of the National Maritime Union approached Bobby and asked him about the Senate. Bobby smiled at the union chief—there was history there. Nearly thirty years earlier, then–Maritime Commission chairman Joseph Kennedy severely punished some of Curran's union seamen for a work stoppage. Curran vowed he was "going to get Kennedy's scalp," but Joe got the best of him. Bobby acknowledged that he had heard some things about New York and asked Curran for his advice. Curran said labor would be with him. Dave Dubinsky of the Ladies' Garment Workers' Union believed the same. Jack Potofsky of the Amalgamated Clothing Workers union disagreed. Some of the men there felt strongly that RFK was interested in the Senate post above all others, even the vice presidency.[65]

In New York, supporters were talking up the early results of a Senate poll, making its way into the papers. Bobby told reporters that it wasn't him polling and he didn't know who was.[66]

"There is no poll," he said flatly on June 7.[67]

However, in Robert Kennedy's papers is a polling memo dated June 7 and addressed to Steve Smith and Ted Kennedy, dissecting Bobby's potential Senate bid. The vast majority of New Yorkers said the carpetbagger issue made no difference to them, and RFK was doing "spectacular" in head-to-head matchups with Senator Keating. Whether or not Bobby knew about the poll at the time of his denials, the results arrived at his office later that week.[68]

Touring Syracuse on Justice Department business in early June, Bobby ordered the car to stop when they passed the students of Cathedral Academy— hundreds of screaming young girls. Later police were escorting him to his car when he broke away to greet hundreds more standing across the street. The *Syracuse Post-Standard* estimated that some ten thousand people saw him that day. "Every time he goes to New York, including the latest trip, speculation grows that he is about to announce his candidacy. His aides, however, believe that a decision one way or another is still some weeks away." One of RFK's New York emissaries told columnist Murray Kempton, "There's been a tremendous change in him just over the last three weeks. There isn't that hollow look in the eyes, and the talk just doesn't turn automatically back to his brother the way it did a little while ago."[69]

By this time, Bob was so familiar with the "future" question that he answered it without hesitation, before it was even asked. "I haven't made up my mind yet," he cut off one stuttering reporter. Though as his self-imposed New York deadline loomed, RFK denied reports that he was making his announcement. "I just don't know," he told a *Times* reporter over the telephone. "My decision, when made, will involve personal, family, and political considerations because it represents what I will want to do with the rest of my life."[70]

Washington columnist Jack Anderson reported on June 10 "from three aides in a position to know . . . Kennedy notified the President of his desire to resign as attorney general after the civil rights vote" to run for the Senate. Labor insider Victor Riesel also reported the item, sourcing "intimate friends of Mr. Johnson." The *Times* editorial board replied, "We hope that Mr. Kennedy will resist the temptation thus to capitalize on the magic of his family name."[71]

They were wrong—at least for a time. Just as they were going to press, Bobby had something else in mind.

4

DISTRACTIONS

June 1964–July 1964

A LOT OF BOBBY KENNEDY'S life had become about distraction. Finding something other than his grief to do or think about: Malaysia, civil rights, the JFK library, New York, and, most seriously, the vice presidency. One reporter who observed him through all this wrote in June that sorrow had "literally staggered him for five months."[1] Then, events took some of these precious distractions away from him, and one by one changed the course of national politics.

That first week of June, Senator Barry Goldwater all but clinched the Republican nomination in the California primary, providing Johnson with an opponent whose views on nuclear weapons and civil rights were so repugnant to the Northeast, the President could pick any running mate he liked. Days later, the civil rights bill obtained cloture in the Senate, ensuring its passage. Bobby went over to the White House to celebrate, and upon entering the Oval Office, President Johnson exclaimed, "Hello, hero!"

"Wasn't that good?" RFK replied.[2]

Only not for him. With another piece of the Kennedy agenda set in place, another distraction was gone. Goldwater's impending nomination foretold Bobby's complete loss of power, of the past finally being put behind him. He mused openly to reporters what life would be like away from the action. He thought he might want "to go away . . . To live in another country and teach. I'd like to go to England and write a book," he said, though "not about the President"—President Kennedy—"there have been so many of those." In front of another reporter, he scanned a Washington newspaper with columnists speculating about his future. "Nothing new in those," he said with mock detachment, as he loosened his tie and unbuttoned his shirt collar. "I guess they have to write about something every day." He listened to the possibilities, including running a newspaper—the fantasy he would buy the *New York Post*, perhaps. Yet he admitted that all the talk of the future, of England or business or academia, amounted to distraction—"just an easy way to get these things off my mind." He knew where he belonged. "I have this feeling that I'm going to end up in government. These things have a way of solving themselves . . . all of a sudden everything is obvious and right."[3]

He wanted to serve. He wanted to go where he was needed. A reporter once asked him if he was troubled that he hadn't served in combat, and Bobby said no.

"But," the reporter wrote, "he didn't sound as if he had yet convinced himself."[4]

A NEW ENVOY was needed in war-torn South Vietnam, where American servicemen were bleeding and dying in military operations that spring. Washington was ready to replace Ambassador Henry Cabot Lodge Jr., whom Johnson never much trusted. Lodge's upset victory in New Hampshire's Republican primary that March had marked the beginning of the end of his tenure, though he insisted to the *Boston Globe* that he was focused on the importance of his assignment, even as a potential president. He recalled what President Kennedy had told him upon his acceptance of the job in Saigon: "Vietnam takes more of my time than any other problem in the world."[5]

Bobby, too, spent a great deal of time on Vietnam, attending meetings and absorbing documents from Defense, State, and the CIA. He kept a Vietcong rifle in his office as a trophy, or perhaps as a reminder of the conflict that had ramped up from 948 American military advisers posted to over 16,000 in the last two years of his brother's presidency. In late May 1964, Bobby publicly admitted before an audience of New Jersey college students that the situation had worsened, though he remained certain that the South Vietnamese allies of the United States would defeat the Communists in the north. The primary concern, he said, had to be convincing the Vietnamese people that America was there to protect them—that America *cared*.[6]

It was difficult for Bobby to put it so directly to President Johnson. After discussing the civil rights bill in a May 28 phone call, the attorney general had repeatedly tripped over his words to get to the other thing on his mind: a political solution in Vietnam:

"I have not been involved intimately with the, on the Southeast Asia, Vietnam—just those two National Security Council meetings," he said. "Bob McNamara, about five or six days ago, had a talk with me and asked me to come over and went through it . . . I think that there's a lot of people around such as [Treasury Secretary] Douglas Dillon and some others who, whether they're involved in making the decisions or not, they frequently—based on experience and some judgment—have some good ideas in some of these matters." Bobby suggested that the President "utilize some of those brains and talent" displayed in the 1962 missile crisis to "make sure that there is a full discussion" about the fundamental questions of the conflict.

"I, if I can be quite frank about it," Bobby stammered, "I, based on my two meetings with the—the National Security Council meeting—I thought that there was too much—which I said to Bob McNamara—that there was too much emphasis, really, on the military aspects of it. That and, I would think that that war will never be won militarily, but where it's gonna be won, really, is the political war." Bobby told Johnson that "the best talent, of course, is over at the Pentagon because you have Bob McNamara, but that same kind of talent really has to be applied to doing what needs to be done politically in that country." The United States needed county-by-county political organizations in Vietnam to focus on domestic needs, since the broader military operations meant little to the Vietnamese people, "as you point out frequently," Bobby reminded the President. He said military action "obviously will have to be taken, but unless the political action is taken concurrently, in my judgment, I just don't think it can be successful."

Bobby's words were scattered but his point got across. The political element was missing in the war, and the political element was necessary for victory, which he badly wanted, for his country and for his brother.

"I think that that's good thinking," Johnson said slowly, "and that's not any different from the way I have felt about it."

Bobby interjected a reassuring "No, no."

Johnson said he agreed that people were hesitant to bring their ideas before the President, and told Bobby, "I have been trying to stimulate and encourage political thinking . . . One of our basic problems there is the ambassador." Johnson said Lodge was an unwilling and ineffective manager and that the situation needed to change. "We're not ready to have a declaration of war or a war by executive order. We're trying every way we can to soup up what we've got and stabilize it, and to find some way to call upon people to help us preserve the peace and have some diplomatic programs, political programs, instead of just sending out twenty extra planes." He said Secretary of State Rusk wanted to bring civilian leadership to the people of Vietnam, give them some hope, and send the Canadians to Hanoi to show that we don't want to be the power in that part of the world, only "to get 'em to leave these other folks [the South Vietnamese] alone." Johnson told Bobby he wanted him "to get in" with the planning of programs and worried that they were hemorrhaging support in the Senate. "Our thinking is very much the same," the President told his attorney general, wishing again that he would get involved.

"I'd be glad to. I'd be glad to," Bobby said quickly.

"I think it's the most hottest thing we've got on our hands and the most potentially dangerous."

"Yes," Bobby stammered, "I didn't want to, uh, you know, uh, put myself in there. I'd be, I'd be—"

"Oh, you put yourself in everything that you've ever been doing. Just forget that stuff—now, I've told you that about three times." Johnson laid it on extra thick: "You're *wanted*, and *needed*, and we *care*, and we *must* have all the capacity we have and all the experience," he said in a rapid-fire staccato. He told Bobby to act as he had under President Kennedy, and that "you're needed more than you were, so just handle it that way. I wouldn't say that if I didn't mean that and I don't need to say it. I just could say, 'Much obliged and thank you,' if I didn't want it. I sincerely want it . . . They're never going to separate us as far as I'm concerned."

"Thank you," Bobby said softly.

"And if my people ever contribute to it, why, I'll get rid of any one of them if we can put the finger on 'em"—an unmistakable reference to Paul Corbin.

"Speaking frankly about it, when I talked to Bob McNamara five or six days ago," Bobby said, "he didn't feel at that time that there really had been any coordination. He's getting his job done, as he always does. But as far as getting the political program and what needs to be done—it wasn't being done at that time." Bobby told Johnson, "I think that the group that met on Cuba and some of these other people in government, as you know, are smart people. Perhaps if they can be brought together and just go through some of these matters to see if somebody has an original idea . . . it could be helpful in stimulating some of this thought."

Johnson assured him that Secretary of State Dean Rusk, some of the generals, and the Vietnam task force were going to meet with Ambassador Lodge in a week to talk these issues through. The President was quite optimistic about it.[7]

Bobby thanked him and they hung up. He did not share the President's rosy outlook, nor faith in the individuals he was trusting. Lodge was on his way out. Bobby found Rusk too belligerent for a diplomat. Cuba had taught him that generals had a natural inclination toward military solutions.

No one was fixing America's political problem in Vietnam.

Two weeks later, on June 11, Robert Kennedy paid an afternoon visit to Clark Clifford's office. It was a peculiar meeting simply because Bobby rarely, if ever, went to see him. He wanted to tell Clifford in person about a handwritten letter he had just sent to the White House. "Dear Mr. President," it said. "I just wanted to make sure you understood that if you wished me to go to Viet Nam in any capacity I would be glad to go. It is obviously the most important problem facing the United States and if you felt I could help I am at your service." Bobby wrote that he understood the "complications" of his going, but that if the President felt it was the right thing, they could work it out. "In any case I wished you to know my feelings on the matter." He signed, "Respectfully, Bob."[8]

And so there RFK was in Clifford's office, telling him about it. "Bobby was hardly in the habit of seeking Clifford's advice," wrote Jeff Shesol, who interviewed Clifford toward the end of his life. "When Bobby told Clifford his offer was not a political ploy, he obviously meant the message for President Johnson."[9]

It may never be known what exactly drove Bob Kennedy to volunteer for service in Vietnam. Less than a week before he sent his letter, McGeorge Bundy dictated a memo to the President, suggesting multiple candidates to replace Lodge, including Bobby. "I come back to this suggestion, although I know you have thought it wild in the past, for two reasons: the first is that the Attorney General has tremendous appeal to younger people and to non-Americans all around the world. He would give a picture of idealism and peace-seeking which our case will badly need, especially if we have to move to stronger measures. I have heard it said that he would take this challenge with some relish, but I have never talked to him about it myself."[10]

In fact, none of Bobby's close friends or confidants would ever recall seriously discussing it with him. He told Arthur Schlesinger on June 9 that he believed "the situation in Vietnam may get worse and become a serious political liability to the administration," but said nothing about volunteering to go there to fix it, which he did two days later. He told John Seigenthaler only that he thought it would be terribly difficult for the children. Ted Sorensen would later wonder if it was Bobby's way of staying in public life while getting out of Washington—to provide himself with another distraction.[11]

Clifford later wrote that it was "an utterly sincere act" from a deeply depressed man, wondering if some "guilt" was mixed in over his brother's commitment of troops. Clifford relayed the message to the White House,[12] and the President called his attorney general that evening.

"I just wanted you to know that the nicest thing happened to me since I've been here was your note and I appreciate it—"

"Oh, thank you," Bobby eked out under Johnson's stream of words.

"—so very much and I can't think of letting you do that, but you've got to help me with who we do get, and we got to get him pretty soon, and we'll talk about it in the next few hours. But I think we're in better shape than we've ever been, when that letter come in, I wanted you to know I'd sleep better tonight."

"Thank you very much, Mr. President."

"I appreciate it more than you'll ever know."

"Oh, that's very nice."

"And you're a great, great guy or you wouldn't write that kind of letter."

"Thank you very much," Bobby said.

"Good-bye."[13]

Johnson could not possibly let Bobby go, for three reasons he outlined to James "Scotty" Reston of the *New York Times*:

1. To keep him at Justice for the civil rights law's implementation.
2. For how it would look politically—sending his top opponent in the party into a war zone.
3. And, God forbid, if he was killed.[14]

The country couldn't stand to lose another Kennedy, the President told Jack Valenti. "I would be accusing myself for the rest of my life if something happened to him out there . . . I couldn't live with that."[15]

Yet LBJ was genuinely touched by the offer. He would keep the letter close by. A reporter spotted it on his desk more than a month later. Even when news of the exchange leaked, it did not create a rift in the relationship. The President not only denied a feud to Reston; he said he was talking to the attorney general more than any other member of the cabinet, save McNamara or Rusk.[16]

Bobby, too, was at peace with the decision. Schlesinger found him relieved that Johnson did not accept his offer.[17] Rather, it seemed to be an offering of trust on his part—a sign of utter fealty, of Bobby's willingness to do anything required to be a part of the President's team.

Yet their private conversations and notes reveal how far apart they were, even then, on Vietnam. Johnson and Bobby had very different ideas of how to improve the situation, especially with regard to the type of ambassador that was needed. Shortly before calling Bobby to turn him down, the President talked over his predicament with his old friend and mentor Senator Richard Russell of Georgia. "We're just doing fine except for this damn Vietnam thing," LBJ said. Johnson didn't want a tweed-suited Foreign Service officer; he wanted a man in uniform. He thought maybe General Westmoreland could be both the military commander and top diplomat in the country, whereas Bobby believed it had to be "somebody that's had that political experience," suggesting North Carolina governor Terry Sanford. Johnson ultimately selected General Maxwell Taylor, ex-chairman of the Joint Chiefs of Staff, for reasons he explained to Secretary McNamara: "Taylor can give us the cover that we need with the country and with the Republicans and with the Congress . . . We need somebody to give us cover with the opinion boards," he said. "I don't know how to do that. That worries me. You see Bobby's instinctive reaction: '*Political job; not a military job.*'" But the President worried about damaging leaks from the State Department, especially before the election. "It's all going to be a military operation," he said. "The only man I really know that's got—that's not regarded as a warmonger, that's got a bunch of stars and got standing, is Taylor."[18] Johnson was giving lip service to diplomacy, but his faith was in the uniform—that military force was most important to victory.

Bobby was the opposite, standing firmly in favor of the military action in public while pushing political reform in private. He thought Vietnamese president Ngo Dinh Diem had been a "corrupt and a bad leader" whom the United States was better off without, but regretted deposing him—and had argued against it at the time—because of the message it sent to other countries. "It's a bad policy to get into for us to run a coup out there and replace somebody we don't like with somebody we do because it would just make every other country nervous as can be that we were running coups in and out," he said that spring.[19] While he expressed his doubts about an expanded military campaign with Johnson, the attorney general was unflinching with the Soviets.

Over lunch with Anatoly Dobrynin in early July, the Soviet ambassador to the United States asked RFK about Vietnam. "I said that we didn't want to fight in Vietnam," Bob wrote in a memo-to-file, and "if the choice came to attacking North Vietnam or leaving in defeat that we would attack North Vietnam, that this was a question of principle to us, that, as he and I had discussed on previous occasions, there were certain matters from which a country could not retreat and that it should be understood by the other powers that one of them as far as the United States was concerned was South Vietnam. We had given our word that we were going to stay there. That word had originally been given by President Dwight D. Eisenhower, that it had been reaffirmed by President Kennedy, and reaffirmed again by President Johnson. Our national prestige and position throughout the world was at stake and so we had to remain there. And this was unsatisfactory, I agreed, but, we shouldn't be pushed too much because this was a very difficult situation for the United States."[20] Still, he understood insurgencies well enough to know that a military effort could never lead to victory. Political reforms were the key. Unfortunately, the only political prospects on Johnson's mind were his own. The President's broad design was to stall diplomacy and let the war idle through the election year. Taylor's appointment gave him the political cover he desired—political cover he would extend after a summer skirmish on the Gulf of Tonkin, setting the course for massive escalation.

AT HICKORY HILL, Bobby huddled with his brother Ted under the oak trees, a child's swing next to them, and discussed what he should do next.

Bobby was headed for Europe: speeches in Germany and an unofficial trip to Communist Poland. On the night of June 19, the civil rights bill formally passed the Senate, and Teddy boarded a small plane bound for the Massachusetts Democratic Party's state convention in Springfield. Nearing the destination, the plane descended too quickly in a dense fog and crash-landed in an apple orchard, killing the pilot on impact, breaking Teddy's back, and mortally wounding one of his aides. Two other passengers, Senator Birch Bayh of Indiana and his wife, Marvella, were buckled in the back and suffered relatively minor injuries. Bayh pulled Teddy's broken body from the wreckage and called for help.[21]

Bobby was at the Cape for the night, where a number of Kennedys were gathered for a summer weekend. He was in bed when word arrived. He and sister Jean raced across the state to Teddy's side, not knowing how bad his injuries were, or if he'd even be alive when they got there. They entered the hospital through a crush of reporters and policemen. Teddy was veiled in an oxygen tent—he had pierced a lung and was struggling to breathe. A nurse directed Bobby to wait in the X-ray department, where he sat alone and stared at the floor. It was happening again. "I have never seen anyone look so dejected, so sad," one nurse said.[22]

Bobby and Teddy shared a unique bond—not just as the last surviving brothers, but as links to an icon. Journalists would often write about how Bobby's mannerisms were Jack's—"the same short wave of the hand, brief nod, half smile." His self-reflections, another wrote, had "the same candor and almost amused detachment that his brother had in talking about himself." The only other person who received this treatment was Teddy, as one reporter described his haunting "extended forefinger, jabbing in emphasis" during a speech, noting "the delivery, a little too rapid, as JFK's also had been before he attained the confidence of the presidency." They were two developing men, cloaked in the shadow of greatness and yet beaming with promise because of it. Being younger and more wholesome, Ted had it easier. Bob even envied him for being "more gregarious, more outgoing, less reserved." Their bond was tighter than ever. As one Kennedy described it, "The relationship between Teddy and Bob has become far deeper the last six months. Teddy has become to him now what Bob was to Jack. They're like crossed fingers. They talk every morning, and every night, wherever they are."[23]

Once again, there was grim business to attend to. Bobby telephoned the family of the pilot to extend their grief and consoled the wife of Teddy's aide as her husband slipped away. Johnson phoned from the West Coast. Bobby sounded tired, stunned. "Any way in the world I can help, I'm just as close as bones," the President told his attorney general.[24] Even he pitied his longtime adversary in this hour.

Aides arrived from Washington to see how Ted and also the attorney general were doing. Bobby wanted to go for a walk, and when he emerged from the hospital, people hung close by, at first. Autograph-hunting children on bikes and curious townspeople could sense that he wanted to be left alone, so they let him and Walter Sheridan, a Bobby loyalist who had worked the Hoffa case, pass into a local park across from the hospital, as they watched from its edge. Bob sat down on the grass in exhaustion. He spent an hour lying there, tugging at the blades, rumpling his suit. He said little, until suddenly, looking up at the great blue sky, he said, "Somebody up there doesn't like me." Then he asked Sheridan if he should go for the Senate or the vice presidency. It was the first time Bob had asked him about that. Sheridan said the vice presidency, and even though Bob wasn't talking much that day, he seemed to agree.[25] He rose, put his jacket under his arm, and walked through the group of people looking to tell him "I'm sorry," to touch him, for him to autograph money. He couldn't really recall the previous twelve hours, he told the columnist Jimmy Breslin. Bobby took his sisters, Teddy's wife, Joan, and Steve Smith into a small wood-paneled coffee shop. People watched him there, too. Breslin saw how they talked easily, "and no one lapsed into silence or let the face show what was inside." Bobby had a bowl of vegetable soup and went up to the counter for a Coke. Breslin asked, "Is it ever going to end for you people?"

"I guess the only reason we've survived is that there are too many of us. There are more of us than there is trouble." Bobby put his glass down and looked at the counter. "I was just thinking before. If my mother did not have any more children after her first four, she would have nothing now. My brothers Joe and Jack are dead and Kathleen is dead and Rosemary is in the nursing home. She would be left with nothing if she only had four."

"How is your mother?"

He nodded.

"Does your father know?"

He said, "I just spoke to him." Bobby sounded grim. He and Breslin talked a bit about 1960, New York, and other things, Bobby letting his mind wander around for a while.[26] He was clearly unwell. Nearby, at the Massachusetts state Democratic convention, JFK aide Dave Powers told the delegates that the attorney general had wanted to accept the nomination for his brother, but physicians advised him against it because of the strain put upon him by the accident. The news that Ted wasn't paralyzed and would not require an operation brought color back to Bobby's face. He took Joan back to the Cape on Saturday afternoon.[27] Ted's crash rushed the thought back to the front of his mind: he had to take care of the family.

When Bobby returned to Washington, he drafted a short statement and told Ed Guthman to release it:[28] ". . . to end speculation, I wish to state that I will not be a candidate for United States senator from New York."[29]

Guthman couldn't tell exactly what Bob was thinking, except that he "seemed governed by emotion rather than calculation" in those hours. He could have removed himself from the vice presidential field, too, Ed thought, but for whatever reason he did not.[30]

The reporter Peter Lisagor shadowed Bobby that day and asked if he felt relieved.

"No," he said, pausing. "I may think I made a mistake five years from now."

The events were quickly overtaken by the disappearance of three young civil rights workers in the belly of Mississippi. Two of them were Jewish boys from the North. Bobby met with their families and spent the day on the investigation, working closely with the White House. Soon, their burned-out station wagon was discovered, smoldering in the woods. They were idealistic youths, taking part in a voter registration drive called Freedom Summer. Now they had died for it. Bobby postponed his departure for Europe.[31]

The NAACP was having its annual convention in Washington that week and organized a march on the Justice Department to demand increased federal protection for the remaining Freedom Summer organizers. Bobby met with their leadership in his office for an hour and a half. He was told how some Negroes felt abandoned, and how, feeling such a way, they would easily turn to violence. Bobby could only listen—he did not have much hope to offer. They went downstairs, and for ten minutes he stood on the steps of the Justice Department, watching the protesters march by silently, two by two. He told them that they had been sending in more agents but was hamstrung on what could be done legally. The marchers applauded weakly. Many were outraged by his comments. Legal scholars even signed an open letter to him, chiding that the government could do a lot more—starting with deploying federal troops.[32]

But that was not the approach that Bobby, or the President, wanted. The civil rights bill was days away from becoming law, one year after President Kennedy introduced it. They were making progress at a painfully steady pace, and this was its price. "Unpleasant as these events may be," Bobby soon said of the three murdered men, "they are a sign of the change America is undergoing."[33] Or, as the Greek poet might say, wisdom "through the awful grace of God."

And so there he stood after the march, with nothing to give but his sympathy. Bobby shook hands with about a hundred of the marchers, until he was approached by a woman and her small children. It was the family of Medgar Evers, the Mississippi civil rights leader gunned down in front of his home on the night JFK called for a civil rights bill. Bobby looked into the eyes of

Evers's widow, Myrlie, who knew so deeply pain that falls drop by drop upon the heart.

"God bless you," Bobby said to Myrlie.

"God bless you," she replied.

He left for the airport, headed to Berlin.[34]

"GO TO GERMANY, go to Berlin . . ." Those were the words of advice President Kennedy said he would have for his successor. Upon leaving the city a year earlier, less than five months before his demise, John Kennedy told those who were with him that he would leave a note for the next president that urged "in a moment of discouragement or despair . . . go to Germany, go to Berlin," and see the courage of the people there, living in freedom behind the wall, the Brandenburg Gate, the embodiment of the Iron Curtain.

It was Fred Dutton's idea for Bobby to go abroad, to show international good feeling toward him, and how his name was a symbol of freedom to the world. They chose an invitation to the Brandenburg Gate for a renaming of the plaza after JFK, one of the truly great tributes to his name. Dutton began planning the day after he sent the second vice presidential strategy memo in April, with the Poland leg added in early June, also the fruits of his planning. Wearing his State Department hat, he called up the Polish embassy and said that the Kennedys wanted to go see Cracow as private tourists. Dutton was in charge of the organizing and put together the list for visas.[35]

In mid-June, Bobby called Johnson seeking his blessing for the trip. "This is the first I've heard of it," the President lied. He was aware of Bobby's every movement and had been scheming to stop him from going to Europe since late April. In the phone call, Bobby said he wouldn't go if the President didn't think it was helpful. "You just use your own judgment and I'll ride with it," Johnson said. He hung up and worried aloud that Bobby would say the President had sent him to Warsaw, but on the other hand, he didn't want word to get out that he said *not* to go.[36]

RFK was an unofficial visitor, but it was not a typical tourist's trip. Memorandums from the State Department and speech drafts came in from journalist and onetime JFK speechwriter Joseph Kraft, Arthur Schlesinger, and even one from Walt Rostow, chairman of the State Department's Policy Planning Council. Schlesinger appended a note to one of his drafts: "Personally, I think you would be best advised to throw all the drafts away and write the speech yourself. I know that this may sound drastic, but I agree with Fred Dutton that you have to get more of yourself into your speeches." And so, after Jack Rosenthal compiled the ideas into a rough draft, Bob scribbled his own version on the back of an envelope during the flight over.[37]

A rambling crew accompanied him. Ethel and some of the children were already vacationing in Europe. Dutton's mistress and assistant Nancy went along, as did national reporters and photographers, trailing the fast-paced Kennedys from tarmac to tarmac. A Justice Department aide advised guests to take a triple ration of vitamin tablets. Ethel told them, "If you don't come back from this trip with circles under your eyes down to your chin, you haven't worked hard enough for your country." They put in eighteen-hour days with Bobby's three-pronged approach: visit historical and religious landmarks to learn the place's history; talk with state officials to learn its present; and talk with students and young people to learn its future.[38]

Upon arrival in Frankfurt, they took a helicopter to the U.S. Army's Fried-berg armored-tactics training area, where Bobby wore a helmet and rode in a tank that occasionally stopped to fire a volley of blank shells. A left-of-center German newspaper observed Bobby as he inspected the American troops: "When seen at a distance of five meters, Kennedy looks like a film star. But not so from a short distance . . . His eyes are those of an old man. His gait is somewhat stooped." The paper noted how he took an extra-long time in shaking hands with a black officer, as if to say to the people who would see the photograph, "Why can't you meet him in as friendly a manner?"[39]

Riding through West Berlin in an open limousine, Bobby retraced much of the route his brother had taken a year earlier in a scene that was eerily similar. Three hundred thousand Germans lined the streets to see him, with seventy thousand at the dedication of John F. Kennedy Platz. Bobby's speech was translated almost sentence by sentence, his recalling his brother's advice to the next president: "In a moment of discouragement or despair . . . go to Germany, go to Berlin." Standing before a sea of uplifted, predominately young faces, Bobby said, "I see again what he meant because I look out at all of you. I know what he meant when he surveyed the wall of shame and measured it against your courage and said, 'Ich bin ein Berliner.'"

A chant, "Kenn-e-dee, Kenn-e-dee," rolled across the square, just as it had when Jack spoke there, except this time it transformed into a chant of "Bob-bee, Bob-bee."

Concluding his Platz speech, he spoke to "the coming generation" about the rapidly changing world order. "The older leaders of established states cannot hope to speak effectively to the young, impatient, rebellious men of the developing states." He encouraged them to change their countries, to move the world, for as President Kennedy said in the beginning, the work would not be done in a single lifetime—including his. "I have come to under-stand," Bobby told students at the Free University in Berlin, "that the hope President Kennedy kindled is not dead but alive. It is not a memory, but a living force. The torch still burns, and because it does, there remains a chance for all of us. The chance to light up the tomorrows, and to brighten the future."[40] Among these young people, he knew it was.

He addressed a mass audience of students at Heidelberg University, his speech transmitted to several auditoriums. But the speeches weren't what interested him. They were short, stiff—public speaking was still unnatural to him. He most enjoyed the question-and-answer portions with the students—any students—a bold and opinionated lot. It was as if he were a young Senate investigator again, at a desk in a hearing room, sparring with witnesses. He quoted Theodore Roosevelt—"Our country calls not for the life of ease but for the life of strenuous endeavor"—a line he would later revisit, modify, and make his own in South Africa. He brought the Greeks with him as well, noting, "The English and German words *idiot* both come from the Greek for a person who did not participate in public affairs." Through an interpreter, a student asked him about America's plans for Vietnam, and Bobby got defensive: "If we pull out of South Vietnam," he said, "what makes you think we would stay in Germany? What makes you think we would stay in Berlin? Those American troops in Vietnam would like to be home . . . it is not nice to be shot at. But they fight for you. When they are killed, they are killed also for you."[41]

Bobby could spar this way in West Germany, where people were free to dissent. He had doubts about the state of discourse in Communist Poland, where his party would go next as "private" tourists.

THE EMBRACE IN Poland was surprising. Communist officials barred advance reports of the trip in the state-run media. But Western radio stations beamed in his travel itinerary, and the handful of European editions of the *New York Times* and *Herald Tribune* that reached Warsaw carried small items about the visit. Word of "Kennedy's brother" spread through sidewalk cafés. Curious Poles began discreetly approaching foreigners seeking news about the rumored visitor. Then he arrived and crowds materialized everywhere he went, as if drawn to a magnet. Bobby spotted the first group held back behind barricades by the airport, and he stopped his car and went out to walk the line and shake hands, smiling. Men and women threw bouquets—roses and carnations, the flower Poles brought to greet relatives. They broke into a chant of "Sto Lat" (One hundred years), a song of congratulations, a song that would follow him throughout the country over the next three days. Through an embassy interpreter, he asked, "How many of you have got relatives in the United States?" Over fifty hands shot up. "President Kennedy, my brother, had a special affection for the Poles. You have contributed so much to the United States—your relatives who went there—that whatever we have done has been because of people like that who came to us." In other places, the well-wishers grew so thick, his car could not move until he shook more hands. Hundreds gathered outside his hotel in downtown Warsaw—onlookers hanging out of every window—to see him step out of his limousine. Before he could get inside, three men and a woman each pulled him in for a traditional kiss.[42]

On his first morning, a Sunday, Bobby and his family walked to St. John's Cathedral for mass. At first, only five or six people were outside the sleepy hotel; within a block, the crowd had grown to a hundred. By the time they reached the cathedral five blocks later, they were surrounded by two thousand, shouting Bobby's name and reaching for his hand. Inside, another four thousand attended the service in the summer heat, and when mass let out, the market square was dangerously full, with Bobby at the center of the standstill. This was one of those moments the *Times* correspondent would later write about, "when it was doubtful whether all members of the American party would emerge uninjured from the surging crowds." A police captain sent for a motorcycle escort, but only Bobby and Ethel could disperse the people. The Polish authorities did not give the Kennedys open cars, possibly to hide them, so they climbed onto the roofs of closed ones and gave the people what they came to see. Most did not speak English, but they cheered everything Bobby said anyway. A woman in the crowd spoke for them, shouting in stilted rhythm, "We all want to say how much we all love you and all Kennedys, and we have a special love and friendship for the Kennedy family." The crowd then joined her in shouting, "Long live Kennedy." Again he asked how many had relatives in the United States. "When I get home, I'll bring them your greetings." And then the family sang an improvised ballad, "When *Polish* Eyes Are Smiling." It was magic, the people, the love and friendship. Young Poles in suspenders and slacks jumped onto the trunk of his car as it slowly rolled past, and Kennedy waved off the police who moved in toward them.[43] A voice called out, "Are you going to run for president?"

"Maybe if you would all come over to the United States and vote for me."[44]

The American ambassador, John Moors Cabot, leaned out of the car, tapped one of the reporters on the shoulder, and said, "Would you mind telling the attorney general that the roof of the car is sagging badly?" ("We had an awful time fixing it," Cabot later said.) The Kennedys' trip back took at least an hour and became a *Look* magazine cover: Bobby in a black suit, standing over a sea of glowing faces, holding a woman's stray shoe.

"This is the way we always come home from mass," he joked.[45]

When Bobby arrived in Cracow, the students took him from his car and raised him on their shoulders. He met with hostile groups of Communist leaders, intellectuals, and students and received their questions. "These," a reporter observed, "he answered in the manner that perhaps most vividly sets him apart from President Kennedy—that is, with brutal candor, unadorned by elegance of phrase."[46]

One student, Hieronim Kubiak, thirty years old and head of the Polish Student Union in Cracow, bluntly posed a question that would receive worldwide attention: "We always greatly respected President Kennedy, and we are very interested in your version of his death. We hope you will forgive us for asking such a direct question, but we really would like your view."

Bobby became deadly serious. "It is a proper question which deserves an answer," he said.

He had grappled with it himself. In the flurry of action in the hours and days after the assassination, he sought answers, an explanation. At some point, though, it seemed no longer to matter.

And so he told the students, "I believe it was done by a man with the name of Oswald, who was a misfit in society, who lived in the United States and was dissatisfied with our government and our way of life, who took up Communism and went to the Soviet Union. He was dissatisfied there. He came back to the United States and was antisocial and felt that the only way to take out his strong feelings against life and society was by killing the President of the United States. There is no question that he did it on his own and by himself. He was not a member of a right-wing organization. He was a confessed Communist, but even the Communists would not have anything to do with him."

An aide commented to a reporter, "That is the first time I've ever heard him mention Oswald."

"I don't care if it was done by one person or ten. But I don't believe in all these complex theories."

The audience was struck silent, some weeping for the memory Bobby evoked. Among the choked-up onlookers was the mayor of Cracow. He asked the attorney general if he wished to announce his candidacy for president with them.

Bobby paused for a moment. "No, I don't think I'll run for president of the United States—I think I'll run for mayor of Cracow."

"And you would win," the mayor said back to him.

They all laughed.[47]

Bobby could let himself laugh there, far from Washington and its haunting reminders. Even in a supposedly hostile country, he was surrounded by people who adored what his brother had meant and, thereby, adored him. After the university tour, thousands of Poles gathered in the central square on ten minutes' notice, bringing the city center to a literal halt. Bobby and his children stood atop their Soviet-made Volga while the people sang "Sto Lat."

"Now we will sing something for you," Bobby said, beaming. "We're not sure what we will sing, but anyway we'll sing." And "Polish Eyes" it was.[48]

The country had stopped for a man whom state officials refused to acknowledge, and its leaders were aghast. The Polish government had granted the Kennedys' visa applications expecting a sedate, friendly visit. They tried to put him on sightseeing tours and indoor conferences, even evacuated an orphanage just before he arrived—anything to keep the people away from him. Bobby caught on quickly and was annoyed. After two days of ignoring his visit, state media finally mentioned his presence, briefly. One Polish newspaper, *Warsaw Life*, accused the Kennedys of manufacturing a spectacle with their car-surfing, asking, "Do they travel this way through American city streets?" The newspaper *Polityka* criticized Bobby for "divorcing himself from the norms of public life and of tourist behavior." The authorities dismissed the trip as a mere ruse for the vice presidential nomination. A few high-ranking officials finally agreed to meet with the Kennedys, hiding their appointment behind an informal dinner at the U.S. ambassador's home. Ethel snubbed the gathering, claiming to be ill, but was later seen out on the town with newspaper reporters.[49]

Several government cabinet ministers had to fight their way past a thousand starstruck Poles at the gates of the American embassy.[50] They felt Bobby was encouraging these people to follow him around with his impromptu performances. They became more furious when he arrived an hour late to their dinner and kept them waiting even longer so he could he shake more hands.

"Now, Mr. Kennedy, you've addressed the crowd outside," said Jozef Winiewicz, vice minister of foreign affairs and former ambassador to the United States, "why don't you get on this table and address us?" Bobby had just announced a surprise trip to the six-hundred-year-old Pauline monastery in Czestochowa, the holiest Roman Catholic shrine in Poland, where he would meet with Cardinal Stefan Wyszyński, spiritual leader to the country's Catholics. The Polish government regarded the cardinal as its principal political adversary, and he usually turned away prominent Westerners—often for his own good—including Jack and Ted Kennedy on earlier visits. Relations between the Church and the government had recently worsened, and Vice Minister Winiewicz was sent to the dinner that night to inform Bobby that he would "seriously damage" their countries' relationship if he continued the street parades and met with the cardinal.[51]

In what Bobby privately described as a "somewhat strained" discussion, he agreed to limit the impromptu rallies but kept his meeting with the cardinal.[52] "He was very agitated that I had been talking frequently to groups of people," Bobby recorded in his notes about Vice Minister Winiewicz. "For example, he was very upset that I had stopped at a market that morning and had shaken hands with several hundred persons. One old lady had given me a loaf of bread and this bothered him greatly, partly because I was given the bread and partly because his cook was there."

Another official would tell Bobby that 99 percent of the Polish people were uninterested in the things he was hearing on the streets. Vice Minister Winiewicz said "that the leaders of Poland never spoke to the people." Bobby suggested that maybe this was what was wrong with Polish leaders, revealing "that shattering candor" a friend had once described as "so frightening—and so useful."[53]

Bobby later wrote that Winiewicz "suggested that since I had come to Poland as a 'visitor' that my actions were unwelcome and unwise." Just after Winiewicz finished lecturing him, Bobby continued, "a waitress came to my place, handed me a religious medal and kissed me. Winiewicz's reaction was to ask: 'Is she a Pole?'"[54]

Three hours had passed from the time Bobby went inside the ambassador's house, and still a massive crowd waited. Despite his promises, Bobby climbed onto the roof of a nearby car and gave his speech on the connection between them. "Now, let's get some sleep." Leaving, he told a reporter, "I am delighted and moved by the reception of the people. I wish the reception were as warm from the government."[55]

They drove three hours to Czestochowa, finally ascending the hill to the monastery. The gates were engulfed by a thousand souls, enthusiastic but orderly, taking direction from white-frocked monks. The Pauline fathers shepherded Bobby through the people, so young, he would remember thinking. He spoke to them through interpreters, wanting them to know that while there were five hundred thousand Poles in Cracow, there were seven hundred thousand in New York and a million in Chicago, and that President Kennedy owed his election to the vote of Poles in America, that their people had made his brother great. An old woman kept pace behind his car for six blocks until Bobby spotted her. "Look at that face!" he said. She looked up at him with glowing eyes as he reached out to her. She took his hand and smiled, pulled it in, and kissed it.[56]

Kennedy met with the cardinal at the monastery, alone save for another priest there to interpret. Bobby would not publicly reveal what they discussed, casting it as too delicate, but privately he recorded, "The Cardinal said that our visit to Czestochowa and our attendance at Mass made a big difference for them. He said the church was having a difficult time and he foresaw more difficult days ahead." He told Bobby that "the government had lost touch with the people," and that things would only get worse. He said, Bobby remembered, that "the best thing that had happened to the Catholic church in Poland was that it had been deprived of its wealth. This had brought the priests and bishops much closer to the people. The government officials . . .

have become the capitalists and the church has become the proletariat . . . He said the outpouring for us was a manifestation of the Poles' protest against the government, their religious feeling and their basic desires."[57]

Bobby privately told journalist Joseph Kraft that he had commented to the cardinal how, throughout Poland, he had seen so many older people, and yet in Czestochowa, they were so young. The youth around the monastery—it was astounding to him.

"That's right," the cardinal said to him. "The Communists took away from us all our lands, and that is what established us with the young people. Now they all come and they like to work with us." The persecution sent a message to the youth of Poland: not that the monks in Czestochowa were the opposition, but that they were the *hope*.

"It was part of the radicalization of Robert Kennedy," Kraft would remember years later.[58]

Bobby would write that the cardinal told him they had to be careful their work did not appear "to be against the government outwardly. Rather, he believed the church should have its own program—appear to be positive and to avoid open conflict." Bobby was in awe. "He talked as though he expected to be jailed again. Without question, he is the most impressive Catholic clergyman I have ever met." Those wanting a better future saw someone who had suffered and persisted and decided to cast their lot with his. Bobby would also remember the cardinal's power over the Communist officials. Of all their disruptive behavior, Bobby wrote, the "trip to Czestochowa appeared to displease the Polish government more than anything else we did."[59]

After meeting with the cardinal, Bobby walked through a crowd of two thousand, and he got atop a car and gave his speech about Poland and the United States. As the cars descended the hill—with the Kennedy family on the roof—the crowd of young people and children ran alongside them.[60]

No government official was present at the airport for Bobby's departure. But the American journalists there suspected the authorities had sent the small band of pro-government demonstrators—the first of the trip—who showed up carrying banners demanding U.S. recognition for Poland's western frontier and denouncing the armament of West Germany. Bobby treated them just as he had treated every other Pole who crossed his path: he walked up and shook their hands. The banner carriers were left in a daze, the perfect coda to his trip. In a farewell speech to the Polish people, Bobby spoke of a peaceful world and what it required of them.

"Just because we cannot see clearly the end of the road, that is no reason for not setting out on the essential journey. On the contrary, great change dominates the world, and unless we move with change, we will become its victims."[61]

"In three days," the *New York Times'* correspondent wrote, "he ripped to shreds the elaborate web of carefully articulated relationships that the United States and Poland have spun in the last eight years." It was well understood that despite their Soviet-bloc government, the people of Poland were pro-Western, and that the United States took a softer tone toward them because of it. Yet RFK humiliated his hosts. "The Attorney General had no intention of playing by these rules, and, when local authorities tried to force him into line, he struck back ruthlessly," *Times* correspondent Arthur Olsen observed.

"I wouldn't be my grandfather's grandson if I didn't," Bobby replied, invoking turn-of-the-century Boston mayor John "Honey Fitz" Fitzgerald.[62]

Bobby would talk about this experience with President Johnson after his return. "Well, you know it just makes you feel so good" in comparison with the daily political problems they faced, Bobby said to Johnson. "You go to a country like Poland that's been hearing bad things . . . for twenty years about the United States, and to have the people as enthusiastic about our country as they are?" Bobby figured they must be upset in Moscow, likening it to "Khrushchev's brother" or some high-ranking Communist official being cheered in the streets of America. "I just think that it's a damn inspiring thing for the United States." Bobby told the President that he should go to Eastern Europe or the Soviet Union after the election. "I just think it'd make a hell of a difference," he said.[63]

5

LOYALTY ABOVE ALL

July 1964–August 1964

BOBBY KENNEDY SOAKED NAKED in a bathtub, sipping a highball as a magazine journalist sat off to the side. It was an open secret what he wanted.

The attorney general was chasing the vice presidency, something he would only hint at with vague and often cryptic comments in multiple national magazine profiles he cooperated with before leaving for Germany and Poland. "I want to get away for a while," he mused to one. "If there is something important that has to be done, of course I'll do it." He still cared about service. "[Look at] General Taylor going to Vietnam," Bobby said. "If he cared about personal comfort, he wouldn't be going, after all he's done for his country. So it's foolish to say that something might not come up. My main interest is to stay in government and continue the things we started. But right now my feeling is that I probably shouldn't be around here."[1]

Bobby was terribly vulnerable in these interviews, literally naked for one, bringing the reporter into the bathroom at Hickory Hill while he bathed, doubting there was anything worthwhile to write about his future. "I'm not the kind of guy who can talk about myself," he said, "and I don't want to go on the couch."[2]

June had been a pivotal month in his relationship with the President. As an unidentified White House aide told columnist Marguerite Higgins, "In the past three weeks the attorney general and President Johnson saw more of each other than in the past three years . . . The attorney general has begun to admit—by his actions and behavior—that Lyndon Johnson is a good president. He is giving the President his due." The aide said, "The biggest bar to the vice presidency for the attorney general has been the lack of rapport between the two men. That lack is being overcome. But whether the two can preserve this new rapport remains to be seen."[3]

Despite all their history—and all common sense—a tenderness developed in their relationship. It was, for a time, easy to believe that RFK was being tested, and that he was acquitting himself well. Even the pugilistic newspaperman Drew Pearson admitted that "the tousle-headed little dynamo" had "gone out of his way to consult with the man he once terribly resented." It had to be said: Bobby was "very much in the running for vice president."[4]

Friendly journalists framed him as humbled. They quoted comments about the coming years that made him seem wounded, or coy. And though he was, the reporters knew what he was really talking about—what he really wanted. No one dared to give his words their full weight . . . No one, until Ben Bradlee.

JFK's Harvard classmate and *Newsweek*'s Washington bureau chief, Benjamin C. Bradlee had accompanied Bobby on a trip to Kansas City in mid-June, during which they had a candid conversation about his future.[5] Unlike the other interviewers, Bradlee had been wise to the lengths Bobby was going to in his quest for the vice presidency, all the way back to Paul Corbin in New Hampshire. He did not mince words: "Kennedy himself obviously wants the job, but not without reservations and not to the exclusion of other jobs. He understands without bitterness why President Johnson might actually prefer someone else."

And then Bradlee began to present Bobby's words back to him—and the world—in a spectacularly damaging fashion.

"Actually, I should think I'd be the last man in the world he would want," RFK told him, "because my name is Kennedy, because he wants a Johnson administration with no Kennedys in it, because we travel different paths, because I suppose some businessmen would object, and because I'd cost them a few votes in the South . . . I don't think as many as some say, but some."

Then why, Bradlee asked, was he still so talked about?

"Because most of the major political leaders in the North want me," Bobby said with no trace of embarrassment for being the bosses' choice. "All of them, really. And that's about all I've got going for me."

At another point, Kennedy spoke deliberately, deadly serious about what he truly wanted. "I'd like to harness all the energy and effort and incentive and imagination that was attracted to government by President Kennedy. I don't want any of that to die. It's important that the striving for excellence continue, that there be an end to mediocrity. The torch really has passed to a new generation. People are still looking for all that idealism. It permeated young people all over the globe. And I became sort of a symbol, not just as an individual. If I could figure out some course for me that would keep all that alive and utilize it for the country, that's what I'd do."[6]

The issue hit newsstands on June 29 and immediately stirred trouble for its sensational quotes. Columnists pounced on Bobby for implying that he was essential—*"a symbol?"*—to holding the Democratic Party together. The pressure campaign was a blatant insult to President Johnson, they wrote, and an insult to the office of the presidency. Kennedy allies responded that Bradlee took no notes during the six hours he spent with Bob, and that though the attorney general never went off the record, they believed that any quotes attributed to him were to be submitted for review prior to publication. Bobby's comment about his relationship with "the party bosses in the North" got the most attention. It was the second question at the President's next news conference, a topic he did not wish to discuss.[7]

As soon as Bobby was back from Poland, he telephoned Johnson—"Mr. President"—to explain what had happened. He said that he had spoken with Bradlee "about all of these matters quite frankly and openly as I always have. And I never thought that he was going to quote me and take things out of context." Bobby explained how each quote came about. "He said, 'Do you think anybody's for you?' And I said I worked for a long time in political campaigns so I know a lot of those leaders in the North ... He didn't take notes, so he couldn't possibly get the quote correctly." Bobby said he told Bradlee that he thought the President wanted to have his own administration after January, and "he would like to have it on his own, so I wouldn't think that he would like to have a Kennedy directly associated with it—if I were he, I'd feel that way."

Johnson said it was all "quite unfortunate," but he understood what the press aimed to do: drive a story that "some of the extremists backing Kennedy are challenging Johnson—"

"Of course nobody's doing that," Bobby assured him, as the President rolled on.

"They're going to try to get us fighting. I hope we don't have to," Johnson said, half a wish and half a threat. Bobby said that he had done interviews like the one with Bradlee for seven months and no one had ever quoted him like that. "Let's forget it," Johnson told him. "There are too few left in the family, and let's, let's hold together as much as we can."[8]

But Johnson's true feelings emerged that evening in the East Room of the White House, where he signed the civil rights bill into law. Bobby was seated in front of the nation's top congressmen, civil rights and labor leaders, and was the first man on his feet as Johnson strode in toward the desk. A battery of over seventy-five ceremonial pens stood at attention for Johnson to use and hand out as souvenirs. Republican leader Everett Dirksen got the first. The second went to Senator Hubert Humphrey of Minnesota, Bobby's chief rival for the vice presidency. Humphrey had been a national figure in the party since his civil rights speech at the 1948 convention and was JFK's opponent in the 1960 primaries. "You look mighty healthy to me," Humphrey said as LBJ recalled his heart attack of exactly nine years earlier. Bobby stayed off toward the back of the dignitaries encircling the President, looking lost, speaking to no one. Johnson handed pens to other congressmen, who slowly filed away, and then more pens to civilian leaders, including Martin Luther King Jr., whom LBJ crooked around to shake hands with. As King came up from the President's embrace, he had an unobstructed view of Bobby's face, staring ahead, his expression blank. King later told others he was struck by the sadness in those blue eyes. Labor leader Roy Reuther spotted the attorney general standing there meekly and helped clear a path.

"Let's bring him forward," Reuther shouted. "Bobby?"

Just then, Johnson spotted FBI director Hoover "Hello, Edgar!" LBJ said. "Glad to see ya." Hoover's FBI had secretly terrorized Dr. King, sending his wife recordings of him having sex with another woman and a letter suggesting he kill himself. Johnson handed Hoover a pen. "You deserve several of those."

Robert Kennedy was no ordinary dignitary in that room. He had shepherded the civil rights bill through hearings and legislative negotiations for thirteen months, ever since his brother had called for its passage. Yet he received no special or even warm recognition on this day of triumph. As if he were any other person, President Johnson counted off four pens for him and his Justice Department deputies. "Got any more now?"

"Can you give me one for Mrs. Kennedy?" Bobby asked. Johnson gave him an extra two, and Bobby nodded and silently walked away.[9] He knew the damage had been done.

"Lyndon Johnson was very upset about the *Newsweek* article," RFK wrote in a memo-to-file one week later. "I guess he spoke to everybody—Kenny, Bob McNamara, many others—about it, how disturbed he was. Relationship up to that time was improving, but that made it very difficult all the way around. Ben Bradlee had said that he would clear the quotes and just never did so. But I should never have trusted him anyway."[10]

Bobby attempted to mend the wounds, to subjugate himself when addressing a meeting of U.S. Attorneys at the Department of Justice, praising the President's leadership and mimicking what the anonymous White House aide had told the columnist. "There is a confidence in him and in his judgment," he said, "and the people have followed him." The next day, Johnson and Bobby appeared for another event in the East Room, walking in together. Bobby placed his hand collegially on the President's arm, as if to say that they could do this, that they could be partners.[11]

In private, there were doubts. Johnson was deeply paranoid, misjudging RFK's positioning himself for the vice presidency as an all-out offensive— perhaps even for the presidential nomination itself. Bobby, too, had severe misgivings about Johnson's capacities, the sticking point always coming back to Vietnam.

In a phone call that started off about typical Justice Department matters,

Bobby tried to swing the conversation to political efforts that might stabilize Southeast Asia as General Maxwell Taylor took over as ambassador. "The problems of Laos and Vietnam are so intertwined," Kennedy said, "to have a central authority out there could be very meaningful, because what they do in Vietnam is going to affect Laos, and what the people do in Laos affects those in Vietnam." Johnson listened and quickly ended the conversation.[12]

Bobby wrote to himself the following day, "My impression is that he's really not greatly interested in these foreign affairs matters. I go back to that meeting that we had several months ago where the Cabinet meeting spent an hour and thirty minutes or so on economy within the government and then we had a National Security Council meeting on overflights in Cuba and what would happen if an American plane was shot down by the Cubans and only five minutes were spent there. None of the questions were raised that would ordinarily be raised by President Kennedy at those kind of meetings, searching for analytical questions which people would have to come up with the answers to. In fact, in my judgment, in many of these meetings we don't get really to the heart of the problem."[13]

Winning the war had taken a back seat for the President. He was concerned with his election and his election alone. It was mid-July and Johnson could see the hurdles between himself and victory. The first was the Democratic convention in Atlantic City, and LBJ did not like where the bar was set. Originally, JFK was to be honored on the first day, a Monday, with a film and memorial speeches. "But after seeing an effecting [sic] 20-minute documentary film of President Kennedy," columnist Mary McGrory wrote on July 22, a month before the convention, "the planners decided to change the memorial observances into the final day, Thursday." The fear was that showing the film at the outset "might start an emotional stampede" to nominate Bobby, so better to move the tribute to the final day, which also happened to be Johnson's birthday. There would be an awkward transition from funereal drapes to birthday cake, but there would be no room for a revolt.[14]

Within hours of the column's publication, Johnson was on the phone with his man at the DNC, Cliff Carter. "Somebody leaked out our plan here to Mary McGrory . . . who do you reckon that was?"[15]

The power of JFK's memory was a potent one, so powerful it transformed Bobby from ruthless hatchet man to president-in-waiting. In May, the White House had commissioned a private nationwide survey on the vice presidency after Johnson grew concerned about all the public polling showing Bobby in the lead. They claimed the survey found Bobby behind Senator Humphrey by two points and felt reassured in their direction. The President even called Humphrey to share the good news. As July came, the White House started to worry that Bobby thought he stood a chance, and Johnson told friends that he was merely trying to help his depressed attorney general get back into circulation—not to rally his hopes.

But the public wanted him, too, and the President felt the reins of the Democratic electorate bucking against his grip. Johnson would later refer to the "tidal wave" washing over him, "letters and memos about how great a Vice President Bobby would be." Another large private poll told him Bobby was the best vote-getter. Johnson learned that big-city leaders were backing Kennedy, but thankfully not to the point where they would force him upon the President—at least, not yet . . . Johnson clung to precious little pieces of data, like moderates' and businessmen's opposition to Bobby. By late July, the attorney general was polling at 35 percent to Humphrey's 16, with various other candidates trailing far behind. Johnson knew these numbers well. Once, in a news conference that summer, the President dug in his pockets looking for a paper and accidentally pulled out the latest Gallup Poll. He barely glanced at it but could recite its results perfectly—he knew the polls by heart.[16]

There could only be one explanation for why Bobby Kennedy went from political liability on the verge of resigning in November 1963 to the person most desired to be put a heartbeat from the presidency: Jack Kennedy's ghost. And this was the only way Johnson could suffer defeat even with a resounding victory over the flawed Goldwater. To see JFK's memory carry Bobby through at the convention, and then to have a Kennedy over his shoulder into the fall and the next four years . . . the victory would not be *his*. He could not allow that to happen. Moving the memorial film was not enough.

Johnson faced daily reminders of the prolonged mourning whenever he opened a newspaper. "I think it's sad," Bobby said to the press on July 22 after visiting the display of his brother's mementos in Chicago, part of the John F. Kennedy Memorial Library fund-raising drive. Mayor Richard J. Daley—the most prominent of Bobby's "Northern leaders"—threw a reception for the library, drawing over four hundred Illinois politicians, civic boosters, and donors. Bobby wore a black necktie—he had only worn black ties since Dallas—as he and Ethel toured the exhibit with the Daleys. Evocative pictures arrived over the wire—one of Bobby solemnly looking at his brother's White House desk, another of him standing before his empty rocking chair.[17]

Robert Kennedy truly became the symbol he said he was to Ben Bradlee, the symbol he regretted calling himself but felt deeply within. The public could feel it, too, and that was distressing enough for Lyndon Johnson. But if that feeling was shared by Richard J. Daley—who would be one of the most powerful men at the 1964 Democratic National Convention—then Johnson had to act.

The President told his old friend Texas governor John Connally about waking up in the middle of the night, not being able to sleep, thinking about what he would do if Bobby was running for vice president. "Joe Rauh and Martin Luther King and folks that normally run with that crowd are leading it. Humphrey is trying his best to put an end to it, but he hadn't had much luck with them." They were trying to split the party—to stir up trouble with the Southern delegations. Johnson then descended into theories about the coordination of recent rioting in the cities—"a Texas oil millionaire, messin' around in Harlem . . . ," sightings of folks with walkie-talkies and helmets, so "somebody's financing them big." Then Johnson came back to Bobby and the convention. "Now, I have about come to the conclusion that it is just as positive as we're sitting here that he is going to force a roll call on his name for this place or the other place"—the presidency or the vice presidency.

"Mmm," Connally sounded.

"I think probably the vice presidency at the moment. He will have some people in every delegation that have been friendly, or some way or other, and he'll be in touch with them. And they're going to have an emotional thing with this film, and Ms. Kennedy and all of them. Then he's going to really make the pitch. Now, most of my advisers here think I ought to call him in now, a month ahead of time, so I can get word to all the leaders and tell them how I feel. And if they don't want me, why, it's all right, they can just take him because he will have the nomination if I don't have it."[18]

Cliff Carter and Dick Maguire at the Democratic National Committee had just sent LBJ's personal aide Walter Jenkins a memo urging the President to get it over with and tell Bobby he would not be the running mate. Johnson turned to intermediary Clark Clifford to draft talking points for a conversation, ideas for what he could say.[19]

To Connally, Johnson said he would ask Bobby to come over in the next week and "say to him that I have given a lot of thought to this and in view of the polls and the problems in the Midwest and the problems in the border states—not the South particularly, because he knows that, and I don't want him to use that as an issue on me, that I just signed up Mississippi against him . . . It just seems to me like I ought to tell him that I'm not going to recommend to the delegation that they take him. He will want to argue about it, and they say he is very much against Humphrey. He told Clark Clifford that he would consider that a great insult to his brother's memory—'Humphrey ran against him,' and all that kind of stuff. So, I would tell him that, and my guess is— some of them think that he might decide not to do anything about it, but most of them"—Johnson's advisers—"think that he was determined, that he wants this job, and he will do anything in the world he can to get it, and if by causing a fight, he thinks that he can probably make me throw the election and he wouldn't—he'd like to see me a defeated man like Stevenson."

Connally: "Mmhmm."

"And that's one reason he's not unhappy about what's happening in the South," with the unrest over civil rights and the move toward Goldwater. Johnson lamented that he could never control Daley's Illinois, Lawrence's Pennsylvania, or the other convention delegations "owned by them"—the Kennedys. The President felt Bobby had no respect for him, saw him as a usurper. "And when this fella looks at me, he looks at me like he's gonna look a hole through me, like I'm a spy or something—Bobby." Johnson was unsure of his course, of how to knock RFK out and keep him out—or if he even could. "Now, my present intention although I don't see—I think if we just go down, start fighting, maybe the prestige of the office would carry us through, but I think it'd be like Daley says. Daley says, 'Please don't do it. Wait till you get up there. Let's in committee—executive committee—come in and tell him. And don't you take the blame in knocking him off because you can't take the South on and the Kennedys on and the North on, too, and get 'em all mad at ya, and let us do it up there.' Clark Clifford and others say here that if I do that, it'll be too late, that they'll be in charge up there. That they're running every day and that I've got to tell him now, and if I can't stop it from the cabinet, then he'd probably resign and then we'll just have to see which one could win. I have the office but I don't have much to fight with." There were just too many demands on the President. He was too busy governing to campaign—just like in 1960, when they took it from him, getting one step ahead with the bosses before the convention. Then Bobby tried to knock Johnson off the ticket altogether.

Connally reassured his friend. "Of course, I feel very strongly about it . . . I think if you have to take on Bobby in a goddamn fight, then let's take him on . . . I think you'll whoop him in a standstill. It won't even be close. I don't think he'll make the fight. And I damn sure agree that you ought not give him running room between now and August. I agree with Clark Clifford. I just think you ought to just tell him now, and if he wants to do something about it, sure he's got thirty days, but then you got thirty days, too . . . I'd rather fight with him between now and August than the next four years."[20]

The decision was made. That was what Johnson would do.

THE FOLLOWING MONDAY, July 27, Johnson invited Bobby to come to the White House—Tuesday, if he could—to talk over "some other matters." Bobby said okay and hung up the telephone. "He's going to tell me I'm not going to be vice president," he said to Ed Guthman. "I wondered when he'd get around to it."[21]

Bobby was not out yet, though.

He immediately placed a call to Steve Smith, phone logs show, then to columnist Joseph Alsop, and then to Smith again. Forty minutes after his first conversation with the President setting their meeting for Tuesday, Bobby called the White House back and said he had forgotten that he had a Kennedy library meeting in New York City, and that he would prefer to push their meeting to Wednesday. Johnson allowed it, and Bobby took the shuttle to New York the next morning.[22]

Bobby really did have an appointment in the city that day—a board meeting at the Four Seasons that doubled as a celebration of Jacqueline Kennedy's thirty-fifth birthday. However, he abruptly scheduled another meeting for eleven thirty A.M. at the Hotel Carlyle, this time with Louis Harris, JFK's pollster in the 1960 campaign. Harris had become influential in New York City politics during the Kennedy administration, coordinating with Mayor Robert Wagner Jr., and would have been a valuable person to discuss a possible Senate bid with.

But the Senate was not on Bobby's mind that day—at least, Harris did not mention their discussing it when he told the story to Alex Rose.[23]

Rose was a Warsaw-born labor leader and the vice chairman of New York's Liberal Party, a make-or-break political force for state Democrats. Rose was also influential within the liberal circles who saw Bobby as President Kennedy's cutthroat, McCarthyite little brother and he was much happier under President Lyndon Johnson. "After President Kennedy was assassinated," a friend of Bobby's later said, "there were certain people who went out of their way to be unkind to Bob because they thought he had no power left. One of those people was Alex Rose."[24] When Lou Harris told Rose later that week about his conversation with Bobby, Rose promptly relayed the information to the President, who recorded the phone call.

Rose said that Bobby told Harris "he had come to the conclusion that he wants to run for the vice presidency, that he is needed and developed a whole theory that he's in a position to take care of the so-called 'low-income Catholics backlash.'" Kennedy and his allies, Rose said, had "made up their mind that now that the South was lost, he's got to help elect you on the same basis he elected his brother"—winning the Northeast and everywhere else. Except they believed that Johnson was inexperienced working with the big-city leaders, and Rose said Bobby had rationalized "that he has the organizational ability and he will provide you with all the organizational strength . . . And then he developed a theory that as it stands right now, you are not sufficiently prepared for the national campaign, and he began to compare with the conditions the way they existed four years ago when his brother was campaigning for the nomination . . . and then he said he was going to go down and see you about it and tell you that."[25]

A week earlier, Bobby had questioned the President about the campaign, saying he needed to get started since they were just "dead in August" of 1960, picking out television spots and plotting strategy. Bobby talked more about his experience managing Jack's campaign and said he didn't know what Johnson was planning. The President told him about a few conversations he had been having, but nothing in detail. Most of their conversation was about how Johnson was hearing that civil rights was putting the South "almost beyond our reach." The President mentioned that Lou Harris had just completed a round of polling there, and it may explain why Bobby wanted to speak with Harris, of all people, about the President's thinking.[26]

RFK's plan to seize the vice presidential nomination had a final element, one he apparently didn't mention in his conversation with Harris: he would take the job as campaign manager on the condition that the President accept his resignation as attorney general.

Bobby insisted that the nation's top law enforcement officer could not play a role in party politics, and evidence suggests that he was ready to resign immediately. The very day Johnson called to schedule a meeting—July 27— Guthman and his assistant, Jack Rosenthal, were preparing a draft speech for the President to deliver upon accepting Bobby's resignation. It appears Rosenthal didn't even know the intent of what he was working on, describing it as a "vague" assignment in a note at the top of the draft.[27]

If Johnson agreed, Bobby would have left the Justice Department to run the campaign full-time. He would have spent the month of August openly coordinating with state and county Democratic organizations directly on the President's behalf. Every skeptical Democrat in the country would have talked to him, worked with him, and, to their surprise, maybe even gotten along with him. Add that factor to the emotional outpouring sure to come at the convention, and Bobby might well have been swept to the vice presidential nomination.

And so, the night before he was to meet with President Johnson, Bobby attended a small birthday party for Jackie at the Four Seasons Hotel, the specter of another campaign hanging over them. McGeorge Bundy came up to attend—something he would regret. Bobby had been talking to Bundy about vice presidential politics for months. The day after the New Hampshire primary, Bobby sent Bundy a wire story on a New York "Draft Kennedy" group with a handwritten note: "Mac, You political genius—now what do I do?"[28] That night, both Bob and Jackie pressed Bundy for inside information on Johnson's deliberations. Bundy played dumb, worried that if he told them,

Bobby might start his candidacy then and there. "I couldn't, you know, tip [the President's] hand," Bundy recalled years later, "because if that led to an immediate announcement of active candidacy, I would be . . ." and he trailed off.

Bundy was a New Frontiersman, a loyal and trusted aide to President Kennedy. Yet he served the office, not the man. Bobby believed that his loyalty to the dead president should outweigh his loyalty to the living one—especially when it came to politics.

Bundy disagreed, though he pocketed small loyalties for Bobby, playing a bit part to further their interests when President Johnson interrogated Bundy the next morning. He held his tongue on some of the harsher things Bob and Jackie had to say about LBJ. ("What people say after three drinks in a time of great sorrow is peddled much too rapidly most of the time," Bundy said years later, hiding what he knew even then.)[29] He was, however, quick to reveal other things, as President Johnson's secret telephone recordings show.

"Does he know what this meeting is about, in your judgment?" Johnson asked.

"He guesses," Bundy said. "Yes. That I do know . . . And he knows, he really does know, and neither Bob [McNamara] or I in separate conversations have, have corrected him. He knows which way your mind is tending."

"Does he find fault with it?" the President asked.

"Well," Bundy said, "he wants that job . . . I don't think he finds fault with your right to have a view. I think he just plain wants it." Then Bundy stammered over what Bob might say when Johnson finally told him. "I think he honestly doesn't know what his reaction is going to be. Just having watched him over the last nine months, I think in a matter of this kind, I wouldn't, I would try not to ask him for, for full comment in the first flush." Bundy suggested Johnson should tell him who he was going to pick, thinking maybe it would help—a sign of respect. Johnson said no, that it would leak. Bundy then delicately told him of "a finite chance that an attack would be mounted on whoever" he did eventually choose.

This was no surprise, Johnson said. "Kenny [O'Donnell] said the other night that it had to be this"—take Bob as vice president—"or a big blowup."[30] It was just then being reported that Kenny was taking Teddy's place in the Massachusetts delegation to the convention, the likely floor manager for Kennedy delegates if Bobby made a stand. Within the hour, the President would learn of a *Boston Globe* story that, despite previous reports, Jackie Kennedy was also interested in going to Atlantic City. "He's got the lady thinking about going to the convention," Johnson groused to Clark Clifford the morning of his meeting with Bobby.[31]

Bundy had told Johnson that, yes, the Kennedy people were talking about the convention, but he didn't believe a floor fight would actually happen. "That might be psychological warfare," he said.[32]

If it was, it was working.

THEIR MEETING WAS awkward to start. Bobby entered the Oval Office just after one o'clock, and while Johnson usually took visitors to sit on the couch, this time he sat behind the presidential desk, with Bobby in a chair beside it. The President looked away from him, then down at his desk, and began talking—*reading*, to be more precise, from a statement that Clark Clifford had prepared for him on his decision, as if he were a judge presiding in a courtroom and Bobby were sitting in the dock, being arraigned.

For three minutes, he read.

"I have concluded, for a number of reasons, that it would be inadvisable for you to be the Democratic candidate for vice president in this year's election," Johnson said.[33, 34] He told Bob that he had the obligation to make a decision based on what was best for the country, the party and for himself, and that he hoped Bobby would understand the factors of the decision. He repeatedly invoked President Kennedy to say that he was only making the same calculations Bobby's brother had made, four years earlier.

It was a hell of a way to begin a conversation. Bobby calmly listened. They started to talk. Though Bobby saw from the buttons on the President's recording system that he was being taped, nearly fifty-three years later after the meeting, no recording has emerged. What is presently known comes from notes that RFK and those he spoke to left behind, and what Johnson would recount to aides in recorded phone calls that began immediately after Bobby left his office. "I feel like this is not the time for you," Johnson said he told Bobby, "if you have ambitions to lead the country, to go after this spot—President Kennedy always wondered how I could endure it, he said, it must be very frustrating." Johnson continued to talk about 1960 and how "I more or less wanted to retire from the Senate. I certainly did. I felt like I ought to do what is good for my country and good for my party and good for my state. And I thought the Democrat much more preferable than Nixon and that's why I did it." Johnson told Bobby the vice presidency was no rose garden. "I found it very frustrating to sit there and not be able to do anything in the Senate; sit in the cabinet and not have any employees under your jurisdiction; and I don't think that anybody recognized how I felt except for President Kennedy." JFK had said to Johnson that he felt sorry for him, Johnson told Bobby. "I think that there's much that you can do that will make yourself better understood and better prepared for any responsibilities or ambitions you may have than just hearing the roll call in the

Senate." On another call, LBJ said he told Bobby, "I don't think that you'd be very happy [in the vice presidency]—though I'm not in charge of your happiness—presiding over situations in the Senate you couldn't do a damn thing about."[35]

Bobby asked who Johnson had decided on, and he said he hadn't yet. The President asked if Bobby would like to stay on as attorney general after November and Bobby said no.[36]

They discussed the position of campaign manager. Bobby would claim that Johnson brought it up, according to notes taken by Ed Guthman after hearing RFK's side.[37] Johnson said otherwise.

While Clark Clifford's initial talking points memo advised, "The Attorney General has an unequalled talent for the management of a campaign," the script he provided Johnson to literally read at the start of the meeting did not ask Bobby to be his campaign manager. In fact, Johnson grew hot with anger when presented with Bobby's assertion in the days following the meeting, and said it was Bobby who interrupted *him* and offered to run the campaign. Johnson told him that he would be glad for his help in "any way that you desire," to which he claimed Bobby replied, "'Well, I would have to resign if I became a campaign director.'" Johnson disagreed and rattled off the names of all the politically active attorneys general in the previous forty years. LBJ said he told Bobby that he could carry on with his duties while he made speeches and gave suggestions "and kind of have you be familiar with every-body that's working for the ticket." Johnson said that they left the meeting without a decision, and that Bobby then went to the press and garnered head-lines like "Johnson Is Said to Have Asked Kennedy to Manage Campaign," and columns about the Democrats' disarray—only to say he didn't want to be campaign manager anyway. "Puts up a straw man and then knocks it down," Johnson exclaimed.[38]

But Bobby's indecisiveness about his role in the campaign was merely a symptom of his unease with Johnson. As Bundy had warned, there was no telling how he would react. And it may have been that RFK thought he wanted to be vice president right up until the moment when he actually had to discuss it with Johnson, face to face.

The meeting began under the cloud of mistrust with Johnson secretly taping Bobby on the Oval Office recording system. "I saw the buttons on while I was sitting talking to him," Bobby memorialized in his private account of the meeting one week later. The President then offended him while praising the staff Bobby had built at Justice: fine, competent men—unlike Johnson's own, who weren't worth a damn . . . "He said he could really not count on his own people," Bobby recalled. "I was shocked to hear him being so critical to me of people who had been so loyal to him."[39]

After the meeting, Bobby went to the office of Joseph Kraft, who remembered how Bobby was "upset by the general toughness and harshness that he felt he saw in Johnson." Bobby told Kraft that Johnson had said, "You know, none of the people that work for me are any good." "Bob was astonished," Kraft later said, "that Johnson would say that to him—*Bob Kennedy*—about the people that had worked for Johnson for so long."[40]

In May, when Bobby was talking with John Bartlow Martin about how the Senate would be a better future for him, he said of Johnson, "I think his reaction on a lot of things is correct, but I think he's got this other side of him in his relationship with human beings which makes it very difficult." Bobby called the President "mean, bitter, vicious—an animal in many ways"—a contrast to JFK, who was a "gentleman and a human being."[41] Johnson felt his loyalty to President Kennedy had given him the right to Bobby's. But in Bobby's eyes, the President didn't know what loyalty was.

Faced with how Johnson operated, how he treated people, and how he treated him in that meeting, Bobby knew this was wrong. "Just as much as anything else, it convinced me that I could not have worked closely with him," he would write for posterity.

Letting go was a hard thing for Bobby to do. He swallowed deeply during the meeting—enough for Johnson to notice his unease. For the most part, he kept his emotions in check. "He seemed to have expected what happened," Johnson told Clifford afterward, "cherished the kind of hope . . . He wasn't combative in any way." Johnson asked Bobby how he wanted to announce this, and Bob said he would like to think about that. Johnson said one way of going about it would be to tell one person and that "it would be all over the place in five minutes." Bobby said again that he wanted to think about it. Bobby brought up some of the trouble spots in the campaign—first and foremost, the Bobby Baker gifts scandal, saying that it looked problematic and could hurt them. Johnson denied having any contact with Baker after leaving the Senate. Kennedy would recall that he said they had to make a decision about how to proceed on the scandal, and they should get an outside opinion from Washington power lawyer and Johnson's 1960 campaign manager, James Rowe.[42] Johnson wanted Clark Clifford to be the one to handle it—badly enough that he called him immediately after the meeting and asked him to act on it. During that call Johnson also told Clifford to plant the idea in Bobby's head that Johnson would likely only serve one term, and that Bobby's turn would come soon enough.

As the meeting ended, the President and the attorney general stood up and talked a little bit about the polls. When they got over by the door, Bobby looked up with a bit of a smile and said, "Well, you didn't ask me." A wry joke, perhaps. "But I think that I could have done a hell of a job for us."

Johnson replied, "Well, I think you *will* do a hell of a job for us—and for yourself, too."[43]

In the coming weeks, a version of Bobby's parting words, "I could have helped you a lot," was widely reported. To many people, it sounded sad.[44]

"BOB THOUGHT IT was irrevocable," Guthman wrote in a memo-to-file that evening on what the attorney general's mood was like when he got back to the office. A few hours later, McGeorge Bundy called and encouraged Bobby to do as the President suggested and publicly remove himself, either by leaking it or making an announcement. Bundy thought it was a reasonable request— a routine practice in politics, a sign of deference to the President's will. "But it didn't strike him that way," Bundy would remember, saying Bob "got personally angry over it." Kennedy said it would make him look as if he were abandoning all the people who were supporting him—"a blatant disloyalty," as Bundy described Bob's thinking . . . No, he would not remove himself. Lyndon Johnson would have to own his decision.[45]

After the call with Bundy, Bobby figured the news would leak at any moment and called his assistant attorneys general in to break the news. They reacted with silence. "Ah, what the hell," he said, "let's go form our own country." He put on a brave face. "I've had worse things happen."[46]

LESS THAN HALF an hour after Bobby left his office, Johnson wondered if he ought to act before some Kennedy-friendly columnist "writes it up unfairly."[47]

With each passing hour, Johnson's anxiousness grew. By late afternoon, he began checking in with the Democratic power brokers Bobby was close to— the ones who had helped Jack beat LBJ in 1960. He reached Pennsylvania's Dave Lawrence at an airport, telling him to come in to talk the next morning. Mayor Daley couldn't be found for a nervous few hours, and once White House operators tracked him down that evening, Johnson flattered and lied, "You're the only person I've talked to up to now." Johnson asked if "there's any way that you can get any information out" that the President should have the ticket of his choice. "If you can find AP or UP"—an Associated Press or United Press International wire reporter—"or some of 'em that can inquire without hanging it on your name, just say a leader, an outstanding, uh, knowl-edgeable person says that most of the fifty states feel the same way because we've got it from each state, and there's only about three that says some people favor an individual, but they say we'll go with you whoever you want." Johnson also told Daley, "Don't let another human know I talked to you." The first call LBJ made the next morning was to New York City mayor Robert Wagner, asking him to speak out anonymously, too, about how party leaders felt. "They don't want the President to be required to sleep with anybody he doesn't want to sleep with."[48]

Johnson was troubled. He knew that telling Bobby could blow the whole thing up—send the Kennedys into open rebellion against his will—and now he wondered if it was happening. From his hospital room in Boston, Teddy responded to an Associated Press poll of DNC delegates on the vice presidential nomination: "I have only one choice and I'm his brother."[49]

This raised the hair on the back of the President's neck. "I told him yesterday that I wouldn't go with him," Johnson said in a phone call with Secretary of State Dean Rusk that evening. "And there's been stories this morning that Teddy wanted him, and that Ms. [Jacqueline] Kennedy was going to the convention. They put that out this afternoon. And it just means a war."[50]

That day, too, Bundy floated "Joe's idea"—possibly meaning columnist Joseph Alsop, who was also in contact with Bobby that pivotal week. Alsop suggested Johnson pick Robert McNamara, a Republican, with Bobby as his nominator at the convention. Johnson once thought highly of the idea and was widely known to have considered it. But now, the President suspected it would cause an uprising on the convention floor—an uprising that would lead them "to try to cram Bob [Kennedy] down my throat," he told Bundy.[51]

After all, McNamara had been at that New York party with Bobby, and Bundy, too . . . Perhaps this was their plot all along? Perhaps the President was being paranoid?

Perhaps he had good reason to be.

BOBBY HAD GONE along that day as usual, deciding to let Johnson be the one to bring the hammer down. The *Boston Globe*'s Robert Healy stopped by the office for a prescheduled interview the next day, following a group of Democratic leaders from West Virginia whom Bobby had first met during the 1960 primary. It was clear to Healy that they were offering him their support for the vice presidency, and while Bobby didn't let on about what the President had told him the day before, he was circumspect about it.

"It's not fatal if I don't get the nomination," Bobby told Healy, sinking into his chair. "You don't run for the vice presidency. But this thing that was started three and one half years ago with my brother's election to the presidency and the people who came here to serve . . . you have a responsibility not to just disappear."

Healy asked if he would be disappointed if he didn't get the nomination.

Bobby ran his hand across his hair and down over his face. "No . . . all the hurt went in November." Healy pressed him about his chances, and Bobby acknowledged that Goldwater's nomination had diminished them. "Certainly, Senator Goldwater is more acceptable in the South than would be say Scranton, Romney, or Rockefeller," the moderate Republican governors of Pennsylvania, Michigan, and New York. Bobby still didn't know what was next. "I just want to be part of what my brother started . . . I would do whatever I felt was helpful." It was similar to what he had said to Bradlee, and everyone else that year. None of his plans had worked.[52]

After meeting with reporters in a midday press conference, Johnson resigned himself to Bobby's inaction and plotted how to make the announcement. He decided to conceal his true purpose by crossing a whole cadre of Washington officials off the list: all cabinet secretaries and those who met regularly with the cabinet. He telephoned the men in quick succession—including the now-suspect McNamara, who chuckled when he heard what the call was about—to read a statement informing him he was out of the running. To each man, he explained that it was really about Bobby.[53]

Johnson had held an informal news conference earlier that day, so the announcement of a second one in the Fish Room caught the White House press corps by surprise. The cameramen had only fifteen minutes of lead-time to set up. At 6:09 P.M., Johnson entered, put on his glasses, and read a terse statement behind a podium with the seal of the president. He said he did not want high-ranking administration officials distracted by campaign talk. Thus, he would not be recommending them to the convention. "In this regard, because their names have been mentioned in the press, I have personally informed the secretary of state, Mr. Rusk, the secretary of defense, Mr. McNamara, the attorney general, Mr. Kennedy, and the secretary of agriculture, Mr. Freeman, of my decision. I have communicated this to the United States ambassador to the United Nations, Mr. Stevenson, and the head of the Peace Corps, Mr. Shriver." Johnson was in and out of the room within three minutes.[54]

At dinner late that night, Jack Valenti joked, "You just wiped out the whole list right there."

"I just had to eliminate one," the President said.[55]

AN HOUR AFTER the announcement, Bobby issued an official statement through his Justice Department office: "As I have always said, it is the President's responsibility to make known his choice for Vice President. It is in the interest of all of us who were associated with President Kennedy to continue the efforts to advance the programs and ideals to which he devoted his life and which President Johnson is carrying forward."[56]

Bobby's being listed third in Johnson's roundup was such a joke in the capital that the *Washington Star* wrote LBJ could have "accomplished the same result by ruling out any man who lives in McLean, Virginia, or who owns a large dog." Even Bobby made light of it within a week. "At first I thought of saying that the President was premature in eliminating Dean Rusk," he told an audience to laughter. "But then I decided to send a little note to the cabinet members in general, saying, 'I'm sorry I took so many nice fellows over the side with me.'"[57]

For his part, the President relished putting Bobby in his place. He invited three top print journalists over for lunch the day following his announcement and shared a new, slapstick version of his and Bobby's meeting. Johnson said Bobby's "face changed" when he received the news, "and he started to swallow. He looked sick. His Adam's apple bounded up and down like a yo-yo." Johnson was known for his comedic impressions when hotdogging for reporters, and his hubris was plain to the newspapermen that day. "After running through a long list of names" of potential vice presidential nominees, one recalled, Johnson conveyed the sentiment that "he would do better in the November election if he had no running mate."[58]

Bobby was truly defeated. Mary McGrory was with him in the hours after Johnson's announcement, Bill Moyers had heard, and McGrory said that Bobby was philosophical about it. He was disappointed—he had wanted it . . . but he knew how the game was played.[59] Johnson had reversed the Kennedy administration's youthful takeover, and with Humphrey the obvious pick, the future of the Democratic Party looked more like it had in the late 1950s.

Los Angeles Times bureau chief Robert J. Donovan wrote Johnson had "finally closed out the Kennedy Era, the New Frontier, the fabulous period of sisters, brothers, cousins, romping children, Harvard professors, twisting in the East Room and ponies and dogs with names like Macaroni and Charlie." Donovan had once reported from the Solomon Islands, hailing Lieutenant Jack Kennedy's heroics in the Pacific. Now he wrote that Bobby "faces a bleak political future or perhaps no political future at all." He speculated that if a Kennedy ever returned to the Oval Office, it would more likely be Teddy.[60]

The future question had been put to Bobby so many times that year, and the very ability to make a choice seemed to overwhelm him, to leave him doubtful and melancholy. His entire life, the choices had been made for him. He had followed along, taken the jobs and responsibilities that would further the interests of his brother—and therefore, his family. Only he was the new head of the family, and their family business was to lead the nation. The vice presidency seemed like the thing he ought to do. And now, it was out of his grasp.

In a car, driving through the streets of Washington in the days after

Johnson's announcement, Bob Kennedy stared out the window and said to a friend, "I don't think there is much future for me in this city now."[61]

THE WAVE OF sound hit as Robert Kennedy approached the rostrum, dwarfed by two massive portraits of Lyndon Johnson on both sides of him. While smaller pictures of Democratic presidents hung high above the stage, every speaker at the Democratic National Convention in Atlantic City was flanked by giant photographs of the President from Texas, the reigning and undisputed champion of the year's bout. "There's the Democratic ticket," one reporter would write: "Johnson and Johnson."[62]

It was Thursday, August 27, almost the end of convention week. A month had passed since Bobby's elimination, since failing in his quest for a job that would have surely made him miserable, suffocated his political operation, and broken his spirit. What he saw in the convention hall was overwhelming, but it did not overwhelm him—at least, not onstage.

He had spent the week of the convention darting around the beachside resort, sending electric currents through the saltwater air. He flew into Atlantic City straight from New York, right after announcing his candidacy for the U.S. Senate on the lawn of Gracie Mansion, the last realistic option for an independent future in high office. His every appearance in the convention city was like that of a football hero in the homecoming parade—no one else was worth looking at, just him. He was nearly bowled over on the boardwalk trying to cleave his way into the Ritz-Carlton lobby. "Here comes the new senator from New York," a man roared. "He's all right in the [state nominating] convention," a Queens congressman was heard saying, "but the election is going to be close." Bobby and New York district leaders piled into Averell Harriman's suite, where President Kennedy's cigar-chomping press secretary, Pierre Salinger, now a U.S. senator from California, poured himself in for a happy reunion. "I want to see a shirt-sleeved candidate at work," he cracked with a smile, imitating the hard-driving campaign manager they knew in 1960. It was back to the boardwalk, for a two-hundred-foot march to the JFK library exhibit. Bobby and Ethel plunged into the outstretched hands, two of their dogs who miraculously stuck with their owners through the crush following behind them. As if they weren't enough of a spectacle on their own, the green-and-white-kilted bagpipe band of Mayor Daley's Cook County organization led the way—marching backward so as to face them, with half a dozen New Jersey state troopers keeping order along the perimeter.

They reached the exhibit just as President Kennedy's speech in West Berlin played over the loudspeaker. "*Ich bin ein Berliner,*" the voice echoed . . . Bobby's eyes appeared wet.

A woman pulled away from the scene. "I can't stand to watch it."
Bobby parted the crowd and went forward.[63]

THE CAROLINE WAS busy that week, ferrying Kennedys up and down the coast. Jacqueline Kennedy flew in from Newport, Rhode Island, on Thursday, the final day of the convention when the balloting was over. Hubert Humphrey was officially the vice presidential nominee, and it was finally safe to show the tribute to President Kennedy with Bobby's introduction. Jackie didn't wish to stay for that. She had come to thank the delegates for their support of Jack from 1960 to the day he died. Bobby stood by her side for it, as did Ethel and the Kennedy sisters. Bobby wore a dark suit and the women wore black, save for Jackie, regal in white silk brocade. "They'll Shake Hands with 5,000 Friends," read the Washington Post headline. And they did. Hundreds of wistful faces passed by, mouths taut. Smiles. Thank-yous. A Las Vegas delegate—a "gambler" to the moon-faced Jimmy Breslin—with a diamond stickpin in his tie approached and could only offer, "Hello," which Jackie politely returned. "I wanted to say something to her," the gambler said moments later. "But you know, Bobby was right next to her so I just sort of walked off. But I wanted to say something to her."

Jackie stood there for hours, a poised smile frozen on her face, not one tear finding its way down her cheek.

"I couldn't even say anything to her, I just felt like crying," another delegate said.[64]

Bobby never left her side. Notables came by, too. Lady Bird Johnson joined the reception line for an hour. Humphrey passed through. "Congratulations," Bobby said. Only four years after their victory over Johnson and Humphrey, the Kennedys were already being pushed into the past. His brother's likeness hung above the convention stage with Truman's and FDR's, one day to join the portrait of Grover Cleveland, which was lost among the rafters. It might have been an easy thought to entertain until more Kennedy excitement came crashing in. Jackie went out on a balcony to wave, and people on the ground scrambled. A young woman unwittingly burst through a plate-glass door, landing in a glistening mess of shards and some blood. Bobby went down to check on her and apologize for the trouble. After many hours and after the last of an estimated three thousand hands were shaken, Bobby told those gathered, "If events had been different, President Kennedy would have been here personally to thank you for your work for him four years ago." Jackie got back on the Caroline, bound for Newport.[65] Bobby's day was far from done.

He darted from hotel to hotel that afternoon, Ethel and two aides in tow, greeting delegations, shaking hands, and generally being fussed over. It was a feat to see how many he could get to that day. Two hundred West Virginia delegates were camped out at the Burgundy Hotel, and another three hundred from Wisconsin were in the lobby of the Jefferson, whom Bobby addressed from atop a chair. "I remember Hubert Humphrey vaguely in Wisconsin," ruthless Robert Kennedy said to laughs. "But he is on our side now." He told them, and all the other delegations, "I think this is the strongest possible ticket—the best we could get." A parade of Young Democrats discovered his limousine and wouldn't budge until he got on the roof and spoke to them. Ethel, then six months pregnant, climbed up, too. "I learned to campaign this way in Poland," Bobby said. He went up and down Pacific Avenue, meeting with the California, Illinois, South Carolina, North Dakota, and Virginia delegations. Later, he balanced himself on the curving staircase at the Ritz-Carlton, the New York delegates and hundreds of spectators packing the room. "I'm glad to see so many bosses," he joked. Before the West Virginians, the carpetbagging New York candidate said, "I want you to know I am not running for any office in West Virginia." He even let out his black humor, telling Kentucky delegates that he bet they thought the Kennedys would always be around. "Now there are only five or six of us left."[66] It was funny, but so dark.

And then that night, the convention hall.

IT WAS BOUND to come. He could not mourn forever. There were so many things Bobby had said about his brother, and he would say so much more in the future. But the time had come to part with the woeful speeches, for him to look forward and to leave the New Frontier behind. In the minutes before they called his name, he sat on the wooden steps behind the rostrum and nervously scrawled final changes to his speech.[67] He wouldn't look at it again, only taking two cards with quotes written on them: one from Jack, the other from Robert Frost.

Bobby needed to leave the past in the past. Only, the people in that hall had a need, too . . . to release their emotions. They would let them out all at once without prompting or encouragement when the slight blond figure approached the podium.

Over twenty thousand loyal Democrats erupted. Massachusetts governor Endicott Peabody snapped to action, grabbed his state's standard, jumped atop his chair, and shouted, *"Go! Go! Go!"* and the entire Massachusetts delegation hopped up on their chairs, screaming and cheering, too. North Carolina followed suit, while the New York delegation stamped and hollered at the tops of their lungs. The convention hall exploded into a demonstration unlike anything else they would see that week. The place was swaying, with state poles rocking wildly, pennants swirling around as if a tornado were blowing through. There was no stilted organized marching, or beckoning horns or whistles that typically sustained such ovations—just people stomping and clapping and cheering. Teddy White stood among the Illinois delegation, a Chicago delegate barking orders: "Let's not let them stop it—first our row will clap, and then when we get tired, we'll get the row behind us to clap."

The organist could not break in to stop it. A roar and steady hand-clapping. "We want Bobby!" some cried. Each time the demonstration began to wane, Bobby would softly say into the microphone, "Mr. Chairman, Mr. Chairman . . . ," and the applause would surge again—they wouldn't let it stop. It was his voice, *the* voice . . . the voice that sounded so much like one they had known. A woman in her early twenties fell to her knees in an aisle, bowed her head, and held the pose, as if in prayer.[68]

Bobby had no choice in the matter. He soaked it in, his face wrinkled but not wrought. Tears welled in his eyes but he waited until after the speech, during the memorial film, to retreat within the convention hall and sob.[69]

Preparing the speech in the days before, he included a quote by an Irish writer. "When we think of President Kennedy and the future, we can think of what George Bernard Shaw once said: 'Some people see things as they are and say, "Why?" I dream things that never were and say, "Why not?"'"[70]

Bobby cut it from the next draft, though the saying stayed with him, later becoming the optimistic and, in hindsight, haunting finale to his presidential campaign speeches four years later. The words he ended up speaking were ultimately far less important than the thunderous cheering that rang out for over a dozen minutes at the sight of him.

His appearance was not supposed to be the climax of the night. There were other tributes, and President Johnson's formal acceptance of the nomination. But LBJ's speech was stale—"the poorest he made in the campaign," Teddy White later wrote. Everything else that happened on the platform was immediately deemed forgettable. The ovation for Bobby was the moment of transcendence, a *Washington Post* editorial said, when the "banality and blather of political oratory" was thrust aside. The *New Yorker*'s Richard Rovere wrote that Bobby's reception at the convention proved that Johnson's "mastery of the party is not quite complete and probably never will be."[71]

What people would remember about the 1964 Democratic convention were those minutes when Robert Kennedy stood silently before them, waiting to begin.

6

A NEWER WORLD

August 1964–November 1964

IF BOBBY COULDN'T TRAVEL TEN FEET without a crowd swarming him, Steve Smith was just the opposite. President Kennedy's brother-in-law once walked out of the West Wing past a pack of reporters, not a single one recognizing him. Smith was the "Kennedy nobody knew," living anonymously amid New York City's skyscrapers, married to sister Jean, the youngest girl. He had a cool and quiet efficiency that quickly gained others' trust. As a young man, he took his family's business of tugboats and barges along New York's waterways and broke them into the oil business. Joe Kennedy was so impressed with the lucrative turn, he asked his new son-in-law to help expand the Kennedy empire. Soon, Smith was managing the Kennedy family portfolio, valued around $300 million.* When talking business, Smith was either cryptic or uncomfortably blunt in a way that reminded people of Bobby. "He does not play with the 'How's the family?' conversations," a colleague would later say. "He assumes that crap is taken for granted."[1]

It was good that Smith reminded people of Bobby because, as a candidate, Bobby needed a Bobby himself.

"When Steve arrived, he couldn't even spell *vote*," a Massachusetts regular said. They baptized him in Jack's 1958 Senate reelection campaign. He raised millions for the 1960 race and steered Teddy's successful 1962 race, during which Steve lost twelve pounds from an already athletic frame. He often came across as nervous. He chain-smoked and looked at his hands a lot when he talked. Nevertheless, Smith was on track to take the top job in President Kennedy's 1964 reelection operation, keeping a watchful eye over vote-rich Northern states: Pennsylvania, Ohio, Michigan, and New York. He had complete trust, and people actually believed him when he said that he had no personal political ambitions. "Anyone can talk to him and feel he's talking to the

---

* About $2.4 billion in 2017 dollars.

candidate himself," President Kennedy told the *Saturday Evening Post* just a few weeks before Dallas.[2]

Smith had been meeting with leaders throughout New York State all year, prepping RFK's Senate bid, planting ideas in people's heads. And even when Bob pulled out after Teddy's plane crash in June, Smith kept his foot in the door, seeming to understand that the attorney general would have to find something after November.[3]

When Johnson finally excluded Bobby from the vice presidency, Smith put an operation together in short order. One man "working behind the scenes" for Bobby told the *New York Times* about a call he had gotten. "He wanted my home number. He wanted my weekend number. He even wanted the number of the bars where I drink. That's what I call an organization." New York had a state nominating convention, not a primary, and party leaders backing RFK controlled at least 400 of the 573 delegates needed for nomination. So Bobby was the nominee before he even cracked open the state high school civics textbook two aides gave him to brush up on local history.[4]

And that was the problem: "ruthless" Robert Kennedy, swooping into a state he hadn't lived in since he was a child because Massachusetts, where he was a legal resident, belonged to his little brother, and Virginia, where he lived, was its own political dominion. It was classic Kennedy calculation. Bobby was shoving aside lifelong New York Democrats—people who had climbed the party ladder for decades—to claim a power base in one of the largest Democratic bastions in the country. It helped that the bosses liked him. They knew they could work with him, and his name atop the ticket would draw hands to the Democratic lever in voting booths, another way for the grief-stricken rank and file to pay their respects by punching the party ticket. But there were plenty of New York Democrats who couldn't stomach his power play. He hadn't done himself any favors by whipping them so badly for Jack in 1960, telling them quite literally, "I don't care if you survive" this election.[5] Chalk it up to relentless focus; many saw *ruthlessness*. Now Bobby had to convince these people that he wasn't a tyrant; that he could be magnanimous. It was going to be a tough sell.

Arthur Schlesinger went and kissed the ring of Alex Rose, who would get the Liberal Party on board. The state's top Democrat, New York City mayor Robert F. Wagner Jr. was the son and namesake of the Empire State's legendary New Deal senator. Having been in office for nearly eleven years with no Democratic senator or governor to rival him since 1958, Wagner had the most to lose from Bobby's arrival in New York. He had turned on the Democratic bosses in his last reelection campaign, and his continued power depended on keeping his enemies divided. With Bobby, the bosses had the biggest name to unite behind, and Wagner had no alternative. Yet Bobby did not step over Wagner, as his powerful allies would have liked. While he didn't need the mayor's support, toppling him would have been just another "ruthless" mark on his record. As the bosses taunted Wagner, Bobby let him save face by saying he would only run with the mayor's approval, which came within days. Bobby resigned his place as a Massachusetts delegate to the Democratic National Convention and leased a sprawling mansion in Glen Cove, Long Island, from a fashion designer who didn't even know how big it was ("twenty-two or twenty-five or thirty rooms, something like that"). The *New York Times* editorial board begrudgingly likened the operation to a steamroller.[6]

Bobby announced his candidacy from the lawn of Gracie Mansion, the mayor's residence, late in the morning on August 25, only ten weeks before the election. He wore a black tie and black pin-striped suit, "which made him look somewhat older than his thirty-eight years," the *Washington Post*'s correspondent wrote. Ethel, in a lavender maternity dress, stood next to him under the blazing summer sun. Television trucks transmitted the announcement live as he invoked both Presidents Johnson and Kennedy with the first sentence. Bobby's hands trembled as he turned the pages of his speech—betraying an uneasiness that every account of the morning took note of. When he finished, it was Ethel who held the press conference on the porch while Bobby and two of his dogs—a retriever named Battle and a sheepdog named Panda—roamed the grounds. Seven anti-Kennedy picketers marched in a circle across the street with GO HOME BOBBY and NEW YORK FOR NEW YORKERS signs. Some identified themselves as Republicans, some Democrats. Other women and children stood at the mansion's fence calling out, "Mr. Kennedy! Mr. Kennedy!" Bobby walked over and shook their hands. "God love you, God love you," they said. "You're wonderful. We love you." Bob appeared embarrassed. Then the Kennedys were off to the national convention in Atlantic City.

In the car to the airport, Ethel told him about a button she saw a child wearing: I HATE BOBBY KENNEDY BECAUSE . . .

"It will be tough," Bobby said.

Aboard the *Caroline*, he got up from his chair and asked a friend, "Do you think this was the right thing for me to do?"[7]

NEW YORK'S STATE nominating conventions typically attracted a few hundred spectators to watch a thousand or so delegates pick the ticket. Not this time. On September 1, a crowd of four thousand showed to see Bobby's name put into nomination. They crammed the Seventy-first Regiment Armory, an ancient landmark whose usual must was displaced by oppressive steam. It seemed that the aisles and balconies were packed beyond capacity. Balloons popped from the heat. Men and women in paper hats bounced placards with LET'S PUT BOB KENNEDY TO WORK FOR NEW YORK printed on them. The floor looked like "a moving forest of Kennedy banners," wrote one reporter. Ex–Tammany Hall boss Carmine De Sapio, stopped by a *Times*man, said, "I've been attending conventions since I was twenty-one years old"—the days of Al Smith and FDR. "We've had good crowds before. But this is really something." Bobby finally appeared after "five hours of humid turmoil," *Newsday*'s Stan Hinden wrote. The armory was a mess: a giant television and photographers' platform hid the stage from most delegates' view, and the acoustics made it impossible to hear the speeches.[8]

After the convention adjourned at six P.M., Bobby went to a reception at the Sheraton-Atlantic Hotel, where servers and a six-tiered cake announced, "Welcome to New York." Otherwise the ballroom was empty—a glaring oversight: the organizers had forgotten to invite the delegates. Ruinous headlines awaited, so aides scrambled to nearby department stores, where they rounded up whomever they could. Bobby shook hands with more people with Macy's shopping bags than delegate badges.[9]

In New York City politics, a winner's first stop was always the Fulton Fish Market, and Bobby was there before sunrise the next morning. He approached tentatively. The air stank and ice crunched underfoot. The candidate stood out in his gray suit among the rubber aprons of the cutters and packers with fish guts and slime on their chests. Bobby was not a natural, initially pulling back when a worker held up a dripping-wet giant fish for a picture.[10] There was something "off, almost querulous" about his voice, Scotty Reston soon wrote, and that "boyish Bugs Bunny grin." Everyone thought he was tougher than JFK, but he lacked the elegance, the confidence, Jack projected.[11] But no matter his deficiencies, when out in a crowd he became something else: a vessel for memory, a walking touchstone, a symbol of national mourning. The hardy fishermen flocked to him, scrounging for scraps of paper to get his autograph—a squiggly, illegible scrawl. "He's a picture of his brother," one of the men said. "I seen him twice, but I never saw this fellow before. Gee, he sure looks like his brother."

A driver left his haul melting on the dock for the chance to shake his hand. Asked why, he said, "When his brother died, my wife cried for a week . . . I've got to stick around and meet him so I can tell her. She'll be daffy for him."[12]

It was the same on Staten Island, where the borough president, a local pol with an Italian name that Bobby kept butchering, led the procession. The candidate looked taken aback by the commotion. He did not plunge into the crowd, as other candidates might, but was pulled in by it. He did not have pat small-talk lines ready to deploy, but instead spoke only when spoken to. Fortunately, people had lots to say to him. This much was true for Bobby Kennedy: he never had to tell anybody who he was or what he was running for. Love him or hate him, people *knew* him . . . and everyone wanted to touch him. He made short speeches from the roof of a car to stop the crowds from following. Then he would climb down and let them claw at him. In that way, it was like Poland, except he could tell what these people were saying. People were heard wandering away saying, "His brother was a great man."[13]

President Kennedy was on everyone's mind. At an airfield later, a reporter for *Newsday* observed Averell Harriman walk up the *Caroline*'s steps. Flustered by the rush of memories, the former governor blurted to Bobby, "Hello, Jack."[14]

No New Frontier cabinet member had resigned his post in the first nine months of Lyndon Johnson's presidency. On September 2, a day after his nomination, Bobby became the first.

To mark his last day as attorney general, he sent form letters to his closest staffers, looking back on what they had accomplished together. "President Kennedy would have wished to thank you for that—and for your loyalty." He signed the letters, "Bobby."[15]

The candidate and his wife visited President Johnson at 1600 Pennsylvania Avenue to formally submit his resignation. Talking to reporters in the driveway, Bobby said he left "with some regret—perhaps more regret than the enthusiasm when I took over." A reporter gestured to the White House and asked if he dreamed of occupying it himself one day. Bobby smiled. "I think there's someone there. I keep reading that and I never see any statement that he is willing to move out. I think he'll be there for some time."

Bobby attended two going-away ceremonies. One at Cardozo High School, one of the D.C. public schools he frequently dropped in on. Three thousand schoolchildren were there with songs and speeches. A band called the Ambassadors played rock tunes. He looked at a sign that said WE'LL MEET AGAIN and said, "I hope they're all true." Bobby ended his speech to the students with the quotation from Shaw: "Some people see things that are and say, 'Why?' I dream things that never were and say, 'Why not?'"

At the Justice Department, the employees filled a courtyard to present him with gifts: the red leather chair he used as attorney general and a thirty-five-year pin, a joke about how hard he had worked in three and a half years. "When I think of all the things that have happened since that snowy inauguration day in January," Bob told them, "I like to think our role has been the one that is suggested in an old Greek saying: 'To tame the savageness of man, make gentle the life of the world.'"

The ceremony ended at 4:59—a minute before his resignation took effect.[16]

THE CROWDS WERE not fooling him. In an interview aboard the *Caroline*, Bobby gamed the election. "I think President Johnson will carry New York by a million and a half votes"—dwarfing JFK's less than four-hundred-thousand-vote margin in 1960. "I expect to run way behind the Johnson-Humphrey ticket and behind President Kennedy's showing four years ago." Mostly because of the "carpetbagger" rap. He couldn't even participate in the election under New York law. "I could vote in Massachusetts, but as a resident of New York I wouldn't want to do that." So he said that he and Ethel would not vote.

The Democratic tide was stronger than it had been in decades, but his opponent, Kenneth Keating, was his own man. He was the only major Republican officeholder to walk out of the Republican National Convention during Goldwater's acceptance speech. As Bobby told the *New York Times*, "Barry Goldwater is an unpopular figure in the state and Ken Keating isn't. I know that."[17]

Keating was tenacious. Sixty-four years old with stark white hair and a pink face, he looked like the jolly, spry grandfather he was. Underneath was a fighter. He was a Phi Beta Kappa college graduate before he turned twenty, which included time out to serve during World War I. He went on to Harvard Law, private practice in Rochester, and more military service, finishing as a brigadier general after World War II. Keating was undefeated in elective office: six times a congressman from upstate, he then beat Mayor Wagner for the Senate in 1958. He won because he campaigned from dawn till midnight, and a close margin in '58 made him work even harder over his first six years. While Bobby was meek, Keating could spool an old-fashioned political speech. Now against the carpetbagger, he laid out his record, placing an emphasis on his liberalism, showing nothing offensive. Bobby Kennedy was trying to oust him, he said, to deprive the good people of New York his service for no other reason than a "ruthless power play"—to secure a launching pad for his political career. After Bobby announced his bid, Keating told reporters that he was sending him a road map of New York.[18]

"Is this the East River?" Bobby had recently asked his driver in the Midtown Tunnel, *Newsweek*'s Ben Bradlee taking mental notes inside the car. New York's senator ought to know that, Bobby figured. He understood that the carpetbagger issue would be problem, saying to Bradlee, "I'd tell them right out, 'If you want someone who has lived in New York all his life, vote for Ken Keating.'" It was well-known that Bobby needed reminding of local Democratic dignitaries. Privately the campaign provided him with index cards so he wouldn't forget to mention them at rallies in their neighborhoods. Other cards were designed to avoid even more embarrassing mistakes ("*The Bronx is to the north, Queens on your right, Brooklyn below you and New Jersey on your left*").[19]

Now that he was in it, he told the *Times*, he wasn't going to let his residency define the race. "The next eight weeks will determine the winner—not what people think now . . . Goldwater will be an important issue, too, unless Keating completely repudiates him and says he'll vote for Johnson." In an early campaign speech before the state AFL-CIO, Bobby said, "I don't think I'm carrying a bag . . . My opponent is carrying a bag and I think it's kicking. It sounds like someone from Arizona in the bag." Keating refused to endorse Goldwater and demurred about who he would vote for on November 3. Bobby blasted him for this. "I'm for Lyndon Johnson and against Barry Goldwater" was always the biggest applause line in his speeches.[20] Unfortunately for the campaign, too many didn't hear a word.

Bobby's mere presence seemed to create a screaming chaos wherever he went. The earliest example was Jones Beach on Long Island. Plans to walk the sand were scuttled when he couldn't even get there for all of the people grabbing at him. Bobby wore a smile to mask the terror in his eyes as policemen tried to pull him through. Finally, two aides lifted him on their shoulders. Dripping in sweat, he waved his hands to quiet those around him. "There are some little children in here. They're going to get crushed. Won't you please push back a little—please?" The crowd only cheered.[21]

A young woman was overheard saying, "He's a doll; he looks better in person than he does on television."

Said another, "He looks older than he does on television."[22]

The authorities thought the crowd might disperse if people could no longer see him, so they had Bobby get down on his hands and knees while ten park policemen locked arms around him. It didn't help—people kept pushing forward, pushing forward. So Bobby began to crawl toward a bathhouse as a cordon of policemen locked arms at the elbows and inched along with him. When they finally got close enough, RFK popped to his feet and sprinted, dashing to the bathhouse, through a corridor to the pool area, and then over a fence, finding refuge in a locker room. He planned an escape with local authorities while more police barred the door.[23]

It was dangerous. A forty-four-year-old Long Island police officer suffered a heart attack after holding back the surging crowds in the parking lot of a department store in Massapequa. A local Republican official proposed officers receive hazard pay when Bobby came to town.[24]

The crowds often frightened and panicked him in the early days of the campaign. "I think somebody's going to get killed," Bobby said in a crush at Grand Central Terminal, where he was again carried on shoulders so people could see him and move on. A woman was almost trampled at the foot of the escalators, and Bobby hopped up on the partition between the banisters. "Get back! Get back!" he shouted to no effect.[25]

An old classmate, Dean Markham, a former marine whom Bobby dubbed "the meanest lineman at Harvard," joined him for the campaign trail as de facto security. He and Guthman kept the crowds from pulling him out of the car, one gripping him tightly around the belt and waist, the other's arms wrapped around his knees. Sometimes even that wasn't enough, and Bobby would have to make a break for it, hands clawing at his shoes and ankles, jumping from parked-car roof to car roof to escape—leaving a trail of dents behind. Markham came to have a name for the autograph seekers—facepointers. They would thrust at Bobby with a pen or pencil at eye level, and Markham would take one hand to grab their hands and pull them down, all the while hanging on to Bobby's belt to stop other people from pulling him in.[26]

Markham always went prepared for the worst. On blustery motorcade rides in their convertible, the wind blew back Markham's suit jacket to reveal the pistol on his hip that he denied carrying. During a walking tour along Broadway—"more of a shoving tour," the *Times* correspondent wrote—someone dropped a lit firecracker from an apartment house window. Police folded in to cover Bobby, but he just kept shaking hands. He may have been too dazed to notice it.[27]

While the crowds were menacing, opponents and journalists often belittled them as mostly women. "A boulevard of broken heels" was how the *New York Times* described the aftermath of one speech. "The biggest element in the Kennedy crowds are school girls," the *Baltimore Sun* wrote. "Sometimes half or even larger portions of his screamers are teenagers"—teenagers who were under twenty-one and ineligible to vote. The youthfulness of his crowds became so cliché, the *Times* once had to offer a caveat that an audience was "nearly all" adults. Long Island's Democratic boss Jack English played it cool. "We don't count the jumpers and squealers," he said. "We look at adults in the crowd, if they are smiling or applauding. We like what we've been seeing."[28]

Only a week in, they had seen a dozen things that would never happen on a normal campaign. When a campaign rally in the small lower-Adirondacks town of Glens Falls was delayed from eight P.M. to one o'clock in the morning, Bobby was sure the trip was pointless. "This is crazy," Bobby said. "Everybody's gone to bed." But when they landed, the plane door swung open, a brass band struck up a march, and a huge crowd roared the little town to life. Hundreds of people—many in their pajamas—lined the streets.[29]

A woman called out, "God bless you!"

A teenage girl jumped up and down. "I touched him! I touched him!"

A man gripped his hand and said, "Good luck."

A local police captain remarked to journalist Peter Maas of the *Saturday Evening Post*, "This is crazy. I've been on the force for twenty years, and I've never seen anything like it." In the auditorium downtown, thousands were jammed in, and the band struck up "Happy Days Are Here Again."[30]

Bobby was dumbfounded. "Thank you for waiting." He grinned. "Well, here we are, five hours late. That's the smooth, hard-driving, well-oiled Kennedy machine for you." Exhausted, he said he wasn't going to make a speech, and someone yelled for him to say whatever he wanted to. "I'll just say this. I'd like to make my very first commitment of the campaign. I promise that, win or lose, the day after the election I'm coming back to Glens Falls!" He arrived home at four fifteen in the morning, his right hand swollen from shaking hands. It was another day when he didn't get dinner until after midnight.[31]

Physically, it was a miserable start. Day after day, he was scratched, squeezed, pummeled, and thrashed. He began wearing suits off-the-rack since they were shredded within a few days. He sported cloth cuff links instead of the gold ones Jack had given him since they were repeatedly torn from his wrists. He bled mostly from the hands, though a woman gashed his chin. In Plattsburgh, a large man squeezed the back of his neck and pounded his back with exuberance. "*Bobby! Bobby!*" Flowers, confetti, and rice flitted in the air like a disorienting dream. Three times, they bowled him over, Markham and Guthman holding fast to his legs and belt. Riding away from Plattsburgh's dedication of the John F. Kennedy Bridge, Bobby asked in a weak voice, "Do I have to make another speech?"

"One more here, Bob. There are a lot of people waiting in town." Each day ended by cleaning the scratches with ointment to ward off infection.[32]

Mentally, it wasn't much better.

Bobby would later deny feeling any fear amid the crowds. "They were friends gathering round me, all in friendly spirit," he told an interviewer. "Nobody wants to kill me."[33] But the look on his face told a different story. He couldn't hide the terror in his eyes when the crowd rippled one way, then surged violently another way. He couldn't focus. His speeches came out in spurts, awkward pauses between an unsteady voice. He was no longer doing the things in politics that he was good at—strategy, planning. Peter Maas could see his misery, writing, "For Robert Kennedy, campaigning is not fun."

He would wind down only on his way home aboard the *Caroline*, sitting in the chair off by himself, with a bowl of clam chowder or a bourbon on the rocks, staring out the window.

Once, after a whirlwind of upstate events, Bobby and Guthman returned to the Carlyle and ordered up steaks. Bobby was exhausted. He hadn't eaten since breakfast. "I've never seen crowds like you're getting," Guthman said, "they've got to be a good omen."

Bob looked at him pensively. "Don't you know? They're for him—they're for him."[34]

A sense of purpose drove him, even in the dark moments. "I'm not in this for the title or for the hell of it," he gravely confided to a friend. "It's because I think I can do a job."[35]

Bobby pushed himself always. "He's living on nerves," Jack said of him in 1960. Those first weeks wore him down. A reporter counted Bobby shaking 654 hands in twelve minutes outside the Westinghouse Electric Corporation before the seven A.M. shift. After a while, he began stumbling over his words. He looked dazed. The schedulers were summoned to the mansion at Glen Cove. Justice Department aide John Nolan and Justin Feldman, a New York lawyer and Democratic operative, found Bobby next to the swimming pool. He looked so exhausted that Feldman didn't even recognize him. Justin put out his hand. Bobby tentatively reached back with a few fingers, waving his other hand to show how swollen and mangled it was. "This is why I wanted to talk to you . . . Are you guys trying to elect me or kill me?" If they wanted him on the breakneck schedule, he said, "I'll do it. I can physically do it. But I'm going to be so exhausted and I won't be able to think."[36]

The pace had to slow down, and it did. He got a day off the trail every week. The pandemonium kept up. In a way, it was the only thing driving the campaign. Their main message was that Bobby was a Democrat who supported the Democratic platform. "He was shaking hands, he was getting big crowds, he was getting encouragement," Feldman said, "but he was saying nothing on the issues. He was being purely and simply President Kennedy's brother, and he just wasn't coming through."[37]

Nor were the liberals coming around. Bobby was a wiretapper, a McCarthyite, the worst kind of Cold Warrior, an antiliberal, unprincipled political animal. And then some just plain didn't like him. There were plenty of noble excuses to mask their personal disdain. Respectable liberals formed an umbrella group called Democrats for Keating. The journalist-crusader I. F. Stone wrote, "A vote for Kennedy is not just a vote for a U.S. Senator. He acts as if the country owes him the White House." Stone accused Bobby of being insufficiently tough on big business and asserted that "Bobby's only criticism of McCarthy was that he didn't do enough research and relied too much on [Roy] Cohn and [Cohn's assistant David] Schine!"[38]

"It would be very easy to give you a canned speech how I'm all for civil liberties," Bobby told a journalist. "Nothing would be easier than to agree with all the attacks on McCarthy—it makes you very popular. It's easy to sit here and attack McCarthy as an SOB. I'm not going to do it. The facts are I left the committee in '53 because I disagreed with the way it was run. I came back in '54 as counsel for the Democratic minority. I wrote the final report. I'll stand on what I wrote about McCarthy in my book."[39]

The liberals punished him for his past, for not being John Kennedy—or rather, how people *remembered* John Kennedy. The contrast was Bobby's fault. "I want my campaign to be based on the record of the Kennedy administration," he said in an early strategy session. None of his advisers had the guts to tell him "No" or "That won't be enough," one aide later said. Partly because they didn't know what would work, partly because Bob was still in such a fragile state. "You never knew when he was going to just turn off and go and stare out the window," said Milton Gwirtzman, one of Teddy's Senate aides on loan to the campaign.[40]

Being the receptacle of grief for his brother—"a fabulous ghost returned to earth," as a top political reporter described him—was a heavy burden. Murray Kempton called Bobby "the ultimate echo." Everything he was came back to his brother. "He carried himself like an icon through the streets," Gwirtzman said, "so that people could, through him, show how they felt about his brother." Living in New York, he spent more time with his brother's widow, a fellow constant mourner, contributing to his depression and distraction. Jackie shied away from the trail. "I expect that the widow of the late President will be on television before the campaign ends," said the Republican state chairman, certain that a desperate Bobby would stop at nothing. "*Kennedy* is the revered name of a martyred president, but if they keep exploiting it, they'll ruin it."[41]

Once Bobby took John John to see the family's old house in Riverdale in the Bronx. Cynics cried that Bobby was trotting out the world-famous little boy, in red shorts with chocolate smeared on his face, for a ruthless photo op. Aides said he was merely trying to be a father figure to his nephew.[42]

His wife, Ethel, always pulled him out of the pits of grief. She was the sunny counterweight to Jackie's sorrow, living every moment to the fullest. Thirty-six years old, mother of eight children and seven months pregnant with a ninth, Ethel was a shaky public speaker who nevertheless threw herself into rallies to boost her Bobby. She wrote all her speeches herself before running them by Steve Smith. "I deliver the speech by phone to him and he criticizes my diction as well as the content," she told a *Washington Post* reporter. "Sometimes, he says the delivery is fine but that I need a new speechwriter."[43]

Sometimes Jean Kennedy Smith would step in for her very pregnant sister-in-law. "I know you were expecting Ethel, but that's the story of my life . . . They always want Jackie first, then Ethel, then Pat Lawford, but they usually get me."[44]

But often it was Ethel. In downtown Brooklyn, police officers locked arms to keep her safe from all those pushing for an autograph or a touch. She signed whatever people put in front of her—record covers, store receipts, college registration slips—signing with her right while shaking hands with her left. "I suppose it's better to be mobbed than to have nobody show up at all," she said. "If it's helping Bobby, I really like it."[45]

She was his bottomless well of confidence.

LATE IN SEPTEMBER, Bob and Ethel took a car down from the Bronx with Jimmy Breslin in tow. "The Warren Report comes out tomorrow," the writer told Bobby, referring to the findings of the official government investigation into JFK's assassination.

"Yes, I know," Kennedy said.

"Is this going to put the thing right back into your mind all over again?"

"No," he replied. "I don't need the reminder. There are a lot of other things to remind me. I don't need the report."

"Have you read it?" Breslin asked.

"No. I know what is in it. I'm not going to read the report."

"Not at all? I thought it is history and you have a sense of history."

"No." Bobby said, "No," a second time and shook his head, then stared out the window.

They rode in silence for a few blocks while Bobby looked away.

Breslin piped up again. "The papers are going to print an awful lot of it tomorrow."

Bobby snapped. "Bully for them!"[46]

"Few who loved John Kennedy, or this country, will be able to read it without emotion," the New York Times' Anthony Lewis wrote the morning after its release. The paper printed a forty-eight-page insert with the report's findings. Bobby's Senate campaign put out a sterile two-paragraph statement, reiterating what he said spontaneously in Poland that summer—a disturbed young man named Oswald did it and did it by himself. The statement confirmed that Bobby accepted the report's findings and that he would not read it and its story of JFK's assassin and the gory final moments. He did not wish to discuss it further.[47]

As the public devoured the report, Bobby canceled a series of appearances in lower Manhattan, opting to spend the morning with Jackie. Aides said that they strolled unnoticed in Central Park. In the afternoon, he boarded the Caroline at LaGuardia Airport to fly to Ithaca. The Caroline was like a flying living room: sofas, chairs, and tables. One big easy chair was off from the others—the one Jack had sat in. Bobby took off his gray suit jacket and put on a tan pullover sweater he often wore—also rumored to have been Jack's. It hung loose on his smaller shoulders and taut frame. One reporter wrote how going from adoring crowd to adoring crowd aboard the *Caroline* made it feel "like the 1960 campaign all over again," except that Jack was always high-spirited between the stops, "whereas vestiges of the stricken haunted expression still come over Robert Kennedy's face and he stares out the window in long silences." This was one of those flights when Bob said nothing and just stared.[48]

Aides warned him that reporters would ask for his reaction to the conclusion that Lee Harvey Oswald had acted alone.

Bobby looked up with glazed eyes. "Why? What are they going to do that for?"[49]

Kenny O'Donnell told a writer that sometimes he would see Bob talking to himself. Only later did he realize that he was actually talking to Jack. The day was chilly and gray.[50]

Bobby seemed miserable. "He hated himself," Justin Feldman would remember years later, "for being here." It made him awfully tough to deal with.[51]

KEN KEATING WAS suffering in a different way. After a long and successful career in politics, his crowds were being measured against the biggest draw since the Beatles. *Newsday* found his audiences "surprisingly small." *New York Times* veteran reporter Homer Bigart felt embarrassed watching him try to whip up a mere thirty people on a street corner. Startled pedestrians gave him quizzical looks when he reached out for their hands, his aides rushing up behind, whispering, "It's Senator Keating of New York."[52] The old man's only option was an aggressive, multipronged attack campaign.

Conservatives and Republicans already had reason to dislike Bobby, so Keating went after solid Democratic voters: Jews, blacks, Italians. He said RFK had selfishly "deserted" the civil rights struggle "in an hour of great crisis" by resigning to seek office and further his political career. Baseball great Jackie Robinson came to Keating's aid in his syndicated newspaper column, blasting Bobby for urging moderation as churches were bombed, and blaming him for the FBI's "miserable failure" at curbing the brutality toward civil rights workers.[53]

Bobby was labeled anti-Italian for assisting in televised congressional hearings on organized crime featuring Joseph Valachi, a former member of New York's Genovese crime family serving a life sentence for narcotics and murder. Valachi believed he was marked for death and sang for protection, spilling gruesome details. The public was riveted. Italians felt stereotyped as thugs before a national audience. Keating attacked Bobby for his support role—supplying Valachi and the files—to "hearings [that] resulted in nothing . . . He just put on a show to divert attention from other matters"—namely, the LBJ–Bobby Baker gifts scandal.[54]

But the harshest attack suggested Bobby cut a sweetheart deal to allow former Nazis to rake in millions of dollars. The General Aniline and Film Corporation was one of many German assets seized at the outset of World War II, and the Kennedy Justice Department oversaw its transfer to a Swiss company, a common postwar practice that would render millions of dollars to America in claims that Germany still owed. Bobby was aware of the deal's controversy at the time, Guthman later wrote in his memoir. "The Civil Division lawyers on the case were unanimously opposed, primarily on the grounds that former Nazis well might benefit from a settlement." Yet, after numerous meetings, "Bob decided to settle. He believed the terms were equitable; that possible benefit to former Nazis, while hard to swallow, was outweighed by the advantages to the company being free of government control and by the fact that proceeds from the government's share of the settlement would be used to pay claims of American citizens for injuries and property damage suffered at the hands of the enemy . . ."[55] It was a compromise of governing.

Keating called it a sellout. He said Bobby's decision aided a "foreign front" for a "huge Nazi cartel and one of the chief producers of chemicals for Hitler's war machine." Bobby's Justice Department had given a "mere cloak" to transfer $60 million in assets back into dubious hands. Bobby had been prepared for all the other attacks—ruthlessness, be it toward blacks or Italians or liberals. He had faced those questions for years. And while he always knew the General Aniline decision was controversial, the charge took him by surprise.[56]

It was and would remain the boldest attack of the campaign. Even the *New York Times* editorial board—hostile to Bobby from the get-go—said Keating had transgressed the bounds of decency.[57] Keating replied, "I have not said anyone was guilty of any heinous crimes. I have simply criticized my opponent."

"Ruthless" Robert Kennedy was suddenly the aggrieved victim. "I can't believe the campaign has descended to these depths," he said. "I am surprised and shocked—I can't understand for the life of me why he made these statements."

When a reporter in the scrum asked if Keating was being sincere when he said he didn't know how the issue would affect the Jewish vote, Bobby shouted, "No!" He paused to collect himself and added, "He is not, in my judgment, being truthful. I don't think there's a person of the Jewish faith in New York who hasn't had a relative killed by the Nazis. The charge that I made a deal with Nazis can't help but have an adverse effect on how Jewish people feel about me. It will have an adverse effect on every voter—not just Jews. If this kind of charge were true, I wouldn't deserve to be elected to any public office. The charge isn't true. My family, too, has suffered from the Nazis. I lost my brother and my brother-in-law to the Germans. The idea that I would turn over money to the Nazis is ridiculous."[58]

"The charge is not true, of course, but the problem is that you never catch up with these things. People read the first headlines and say that I'm pro-Nazi."[59]

The attacks came just as the air was coming out of his campaign. The crowds were huge, but there was no substance. Three weeks in, and Bobby had made only three formal speeches. The crowds wouldn't listen to staid, thoughtful speeches—he could barely get a full sentence heard in their frenzies. By early October, the lack of substance showed up in the polls: he was fading. Bobby wrestled with the implications. "I think I came into this campaign just as a Kennedy," he told the Boston Globe. "The newspaper stories have all been about the crowds . . . Three girls fainting or a policeman falling off his motorcycle . . . The people have not really been listening to what I've been saying to the issues."

Bobby had worried that if he attacked Keating, he would create a sympathy vote for the old senator.[60] After Keating's Nazi speech, he no longer had to worry.

He set up a strike team to knock Keating on his heels. Bill Haddad, a New York ally from 1960, compiled an opposition-research book titled, "The Myth of Keating's Liberalism." They needed to package it inside of a few inches for the newspapers, so they called in Joe Dolan, a cagey Western operative, to produce ads. Peter Edelman, a pensive, brilliant young lawyer in the Civil Division under John Douglas, helped refine it. Edelman was finishing his tour at the Justice Department and had already accepted a job in private practice, but took a diversion to the campaign. His final nights at Justice included staying after hours and compiling an extensive analysis of Keating's voting record.[61]

Bobby's strategists had sought to conserve their ad dollars for the final weeks of the campaign.[62] They just needed the right commercials to air.

Robert Kennedy was lousy at reading a script straight-to-camera about why he would be the better senator. He came across uncomfortable and stilted; not authentic. But he had to find a way to communicate through the powerful medium of television. It appealed to his aides, New York Times correspondent David Halberstam wrote, "because they do not have to deal with a middle man—the press."[63]

They had some success filming Bobby taking questions outside a suburban supermarket in New Rochelle. "He needed to see people and talk to them face-to-face," advance man Jerry Bruno would write, "and they needed to see him." Once that happened, "the ruthless thing just faded, went out the window."[64] Bobby's aides realized he had a natural outlet—his interactions with young audiences.

He took it for a walk in late September before a thousand students at the University of Rochester. He gave a speech on foreign policy and started taking questions from the students. One asked if he would serve all six years—past the next presidential election. "I intend to serve until my term is up," Bobby said. "But let's just assume I am going to use it as a stepping-stone. Because that is the implication of the question. I don't know where I can *go* . . ." The audience broke into laughter.

"Assume that I was using it as a power base. That's . . . the expression that is used. Using it as a power base, the only thing I can think of is that I want to be president of the United States. Let's just assume then—let's just assume the worst . . . In the first place, truthfully now, I can't go any place in 1968. We've got President Lyndon Johnson, and he's going to be a good president and I think he is not only going to be president in 1964, but he is going to be reelected in 1968 . . . and he'll have my support and my efforts on his behalf . . . Now let's go to 1972. Let's assume I am using it as a power base. I'm going to have to be reelected in six years. That means that if I have done such an outstanding job and I want to be president, I've got to do an outstanding job in the state of New York . . . that means that in eight years I have got to do such an outstanding job that people will be demanding all over the country that I be a presidential candidate . . . I don't see how New York suffers."

An aide ran over and told reporters *not* to take that as a declaration of candidacy for 1972. But they did see something different emerge in Bobby's performance. His coiled demeanor loosened during Q&A. He was most comfortable in the format—conditioned to it after hundreds of hours of combative hearings, sparring with the likes of Jimmy Hoffa and mobsters. Bobby liked the college kids because their questions were tough and direct. "They usually ask the best questions," he told an interviewer, "and when there's opposition in the audience, it's basically more stimulating." Softball questions bored him. His eyes deadened and he gave monosyllabic answers. With the kids, Bob might look annoyed at first, his television man Fred Papert recalled years later. Then Kennedy would remember that they were just kids and he should have some fun.[65] Papert's firm handled accounts for liquors, cigars, and cold medicines. Bottling Bobby's encounters with youth was a breeze.

Papert had his cameras rolling when Bobby and Ethel pushed their way to the front of a packed auditorium on October 5 for a joint session of the Columbia University and Barnard College Young Democrats. A thousand students crowded the aisles inside the hall, another two thousand outside hoping to get in.[66] Bobby took the microphone to applause, and then the room became awkwardly silent, and so did he.

"A, uh, bright group of students," Bobby said sarcastically with a jab of his fist. He grinned. "I've learned—I've learned to say that since I've been a candidate." They laughed. "I thought that maybe you had some questions and we could just proceed . . ."

And proceed they did. *Why New York and not some other place?* He explained that he had lived longer in New York than anywhere else. "If the election is going to be decided on my accent or where I also have other associations with, then I think that people are going to vote for my opponent. I think that the election really should be decided on the basis of whether my opponent or myself can do more for the state of New York and make the greatest amount of difference for this state and the country over the period of the next six years. Again, if it's going to be judged on who's lived here in the state of New York longer, then my opponent has. But maybe you should elect the oldest man in the state of New York." The audience laughed and applauded.

Another asked about his using New York as a "jumping-off place," and Bobby again explained his lack of options until 1972. "Frankly, I don't need the title, because I can be called General, I understand, for the rest of my life. And I don't need the money and I don't need the office space . . . Frank as it is, and maybe it's difficult to understand in the state of New York"—he was speaking from the heart now—"I'd like to just be a good United States senator. I'd like to serve."[67] There came applause.

His aides knew they had the footage they needed. Bobby was playful, earnest, loose. By making him vulnerable, stripping away his standard speech and the laundry list of Democratic cheers and Republican boos, he was able to communicate who he was behind closed doors. What was supposed to be a half-hour forum turned into a two-and-a-half-hour Q&A, and they were getting it all on film, to show the whole state.[68]

Though they would not show the entire exchange, for when he was asked about the Warren Report, the mood changed.

"Now, Mr. Kennedy," a man asked, "in the light of certain speculations of people like Mark Lane about the validity of the Warren Commission report, I wonder, do you still have implicit faith in their findings?"

Bobby's demeanor hardened in an instant. "I've made my statement on that." Jimmy Breslin was struck by the sudden irritation in his voice. Then he bowed his head and ran his hand through his hair, as if he needed to compose himself. A thousand sets of eyes and lights bore down on him. "I don't—I don't think there is anything that I can add to what I have said. I believe . . ." The room hung in anticipation on his pauses. "I answered a question of some Polish students when I visited Poland about the matter, what my judgment was, that Mr.—that this was an individual matter." That was all Bobby would say. The lights for the cameras exposed tears on his eyelashes.[69]

For the most part, student Q&A's were a relief. At New York University, one of his answers landed on an awkwardly solemn note and no one applauded.

So Bobby began to clap gently for himself. The students laughed. The candidate grinned. "A little encouragement makes a big difference. Mr. Khrushchev
always claps for himself. I'm going to introduce that here."

One student asked him the "ruthless question"—why he was running?

"I could have retired and lived off my father," he said. "When I left the
Justice Department, they gave me a flag. I could have run my flag up somewhere
and spent the next sixty years telling people about how I saved the country.
Or I could run for the Senate here. I'm putting a lot on the line. I want to be a
part of the government. There is nothing more sinister to it than that."[70]

Within two days of the Columbia event, the campaign spent tens of thousands of dollars buying half-hour evening blocks on local television—70 to 80
percent of the campaign's expenses ultimately went toward television. Newspaper ads for the spots promised to show Robert Kennedy answering "tough"
questions "from a critical audience of New York college students." These New
Yorkers were young—most under twenty-one. "He is wasting his time," the
Times' Homer Bigart wrote, "the audience is too young to vote. But he likes
young people, and they like him."[71]

"You notice people always call him Bobby instead of Mr. Kennedy," an
aide told Newsday. "They called his brother Jack. This means that people are
identifying with him, thinking of him as a contemporary. It helped Jack and
it will help Bobby."[72]

He still had to stop Keating. Bobby sharpened his rhetoric on the stump,
adding more substantive attacks. Peter Edelman created a visual aid to keep
track of the back-and-forth between the two campaigns, an all-encompassing
sheet of paper Kennedy could absorb it from. Edelman took one of their
campaign handouts with side-by-side comparisons of their positions and
taped on little notes—facts about Keating's record, his attacks, and Kennedy's
counterattacks. They called it the Accordion because of the way it folded out
as they kept adding notes. Edelman would bring in the Accordion before
important appearances or during downtime for Bobby to refresh himself. The
candidate would carry it around the room, tapping his front tooth, as was his
habit. Other times, he would spread it out on the edge of a bed as if it were a
desk, kneel down on the floor, and study it. He would take his glasses on and
off, staring intently. If he asked a question, he would do it without looking up,
trying not to break his concentration on the words before him. Bobby seemed
so focused, Edelman occasionally wondered if he even knew his young aide's
name.[73]

The campaign found its footing. Bobby did enough to rehabilitate his
image from a ruthless political climber to a results-oriented law enforcer, while
hacking away at Keating's liberal credentials with negative ads. Surrogates
worked liberal enclaves to vouch for Bobby's trustworthiness. "I thought

everybody loved and admired Bobby Kennedy until I arrived in New York," Ted Sorensen said, "and found there were some very bitter divisions, even among Democrats." Bobby even swallowed his pride and latched onto Johnson's coattails, ditching the slogan of "Let's Put Bob Kennedy to Work for New York" for "Get with the Johnson-Humphrey-Kennedy Team." The President joined Bobby for a series of campaign stops in the big urban centers, riding through New York City's streets in an open car before tens of thousands, having addressed fifty thousand people in Buffalo and another twenty thousand in Rochester. "This is the largest crowd I've seen in all my travels, from Maine to California," the President boasted in Brooklyn. Meanwhile, Keating remained stuck on the carpetbagger issue and Kennedy's supposed slights to Negroes, Italians, and Jews. A *Daily News* straw poll showed Bobby with a 3–2 lead.[74]

"I'VE BEEN INVOLVED in a lot of campaigns," Bobby told a reporter, "but this one is so different in so many ways. In previous campaigns, our family was so closely bound up together. There was one candidate, but we were all sort of involved, including my father, of course, who felt so strongly about it. Now my brother isn't here, my father can't speak, and my younger brother isn't around. The whole operation is different. Everything is different." Bobby talked about what it was like to be the candidate and not the one running the show. "It's a relief in a way. I like being out of Washington. That's first. And I like seeing so many other people. I like communicating again with that part of American life. I like looking at people, in all the towns and all the cities all over the state. They smile. They don't have an angle. It's very lifting. They're just ordinary American citizens. Washington is so inbred. Washington is a one-industry town. Everyone reads the columnists. Everyone reads the editorial page. Something disturbs them each day. Here, the people that come to an airport to meet you just seem to have sort of a basic confidence that the country is in good hands. They represent the United States so much better than what we have in Washington. They smile. The impression you have is that they look happy, and yet serious at the same time. And they *listen* to you. It's just nice, that's all. It's just the way they look. That's what makes it worthwhile."

"I'm always trying for communication," he said. At a Catholic-sponsored forum in Long Island, where a thousand nuns in habits roamed about, Bobby looked at his prepared text for the schoolteachers—"vaguely about youth," he said—and discarded it. "I was handed a speech written for me at one in the morning, and I was supposed to speak at ten," he complained later. "I found I didn't like the speech. It was very pedantic and routine. It just didn't have any idealism."[75] He began by talking with the sisters about civil rights, and then about where he was two years before that very hour—with his brother, at the start of the Cuban missile crisis. He told them frankly that the President's advisers were split over a strike against the Soviet missile sites—"split almost even—perhaps seven one way, five another."

Bobby said President Kennedy asked how many civilians would be killed in the air strikes on the missile sites. The intelligence advisers came back and said twenty-five thousand.

"These were people who probably weren't Communists," Bobby said, "and weren't involved in bringing the missiles into Cuba." Yet they would have died because the President's advisers believed bombing was "the safer way."

"We would have gone in and knocked out all their bases—there wasn't any question about it—and then started bargaining." The story was frightening—all the more shocking since it was the first time anyone had shared a Cuban casualty figure if the President had chosen to bomb.

But that choice, he told the sisters, would have been a "Pearl Harbor in reverse." He said that the President chose the blockade because "of his education, because of his moral training, and because of his belief in what is right and what is wrong." Political life was hard but worth it, he told the sisters, "because an individual can make a difference." He told them what he had told many others about the life of a politician: "If President Kennedy's life stood for anything, it was the idea that one person can make a difference." Afterward, the nuns surrounded him and Ethel for autographs. Bobby broke away and got to the car. His wife stayed behind, still signing. "Ethel," he called out, "I'm the candidate."[76]

BOBBY'S TROUBLES WEREN'T over. Keating's aides seized on a line in a speech Bobby gave in Syracuse where he said Keating had "ridiculed" the 1963 Nuclear Test Ban Treaty. Everywhere Keating went the next day, he waved a copy of a Senate resolution pressing President Kennedy to secure the treaty. "I was a leader in the fight for the treaty and he says I ridiculed it," Keating said. "That's a falsehood." Bobby was a liar, lying about his record—and had been lying all along. A Keating aide remarked to a young *Newsday* reporter, Robert A. Caro, "We've discovered the flaw now, and we're going to keep hitting it all the way."[77]

The arbiter of political justice, the Fair Campaign Practices Committee, leaked a private letter to the Kennedy campaign calling Bobby out for a "false and distorted"—perhaps "deliberate and cynical"—misrepresentation of Keating's record. Bobby's alleged deceptions were front-page news. "Kennedy Fighting 'Ruthless' Image" was the next day's *New York Times* headline. *Newsday* editorialized that his "show-off" tactics "forfeit for him public respect and stand in sad contrast to those of his late, beloved brother."[78] *Times* reporter David Halberstam wrote that RFK had two opponents: Keating, and his own reputation as "a strong-arm man for his brother's campaigns, an image of a ruthless man interested in power for its own sake." Bobby understood the caricature but chided the press for giving Keating the moral high ground, routinely citing his "principled" opposition to his party's nominee Goldwater.

"That's bravery?" Bobby asked. "How would you like to be associated with someone who's going to lose the state by three million votes?"[79]

In fact, Keating's virtuous reputation intimidated Bobby. "If I were him," Bobby said of Keating just after the election, "I would have run just on my record. I would have remained aloof and talked about my record and said, 'Here is this ruthless young man trying to come into this state and take my job.' If he had done that, I don't know what I would have done. He had been very fatherly towards me in Washington, and I couldn't go after him unless he started in on me first."[80]

Bobby lobbied two members of the Fair Campaign board to resign in protest, while two Kennedy staffers were handed the evidence for their side's claims, sent to the FCPC office, and told to sit on the door until the letter was withdrawn. Within a few hours, another letter was issued citing "additional material" and acknowledging, "The letter should not have been written, and any accusations in it were necessarily unfair to Mr. Kennedy."[81]

For almost the entirety of the campaign, no agreement could be reached on whether the candidates would meet in a face-to-face debate. The decision on both sides rested almost entirely on the polls. When Senator Keating was down in September, he pressed Bobby to debate him, but Bobby, worried about the appearance of beating up on the older man, stayed away. "He looks like your grandfather, and there's no way you can win it." Bobby only accepted the offer after polls showed him sliding, but by then it was Keating with something to lose, and his campaign worried that Kennedy's youth would make Keating seem elderly. Thomas E. Dewey, the Republican presidential nominee in 1944 and '48, who was advising Keating on strategy, warned him that Bobby was better versed in the "sixty-second answers" of the television age.[82] However, the polls swung back in Bobby's direction, and facing a national wave against Barry Goldwater leading the Republican ticket, Keating had no choice but to renew his challenge.

In late October, CBS offered the campaigns a prime-time slot from seven thirty to eight thirty on Tuesday, October 27—one week before election day. Keating bought the first half hour and Kennedy the second for $5,400 each, but they couldn't agree on a format to combine their time slots into an hour-long debate. Rapidly sinking in the polls from the weight of Goldwater, Keating invited Bobby to share his program regardless, saying he would either debate Kennedy or his "empty chair." Bobby was still deciding just an hour before the debate began, sitting on his bed in the Carlyle, shirtsleeves rolled up, his tie loosened and shoes kicked off. His advisers warned that the debate would be dangerous. The Keating campaign had control of the cameras and microphones, and no format had been established to keep things civil—which made it all the more likely Bobby would be painted as the opportunistic interloper badgering a kindly white-haired man.

"I can't let him debate an empty chair," Bobby said to his advisers.[83]

It was decided. Part of his strategy was to rattle Keating by showing up as late as possible. In fact, the plan was to arrive at two minutes to air, 7:28 P.M. . . . It never crossed their minds that the candidate could be barred from entry.[84]

Bobby exited out the back of the Carlyle in order to maximize surprise and reached CBS studios at 7:27 P.M.[85] About fifty reporters and photographers crammed the hallway. "I'm here," Bobby announced. "It's seven thirty, and I'm ready to go in." A CBS executive and two other CBS employees stood in Bobby's way, telling him he could not enter. Kennedy's voice got louder. "Then this is a dishonest show. I'm here. Keating said he wanted to debate. He's going to have that empty chair in there. I want to fill it." The executive told Bobby he had missed the three thirty P.M. deadline for a response. "At least have that empty chair removed," Bobby said.

"That can't be done," the executive said.

Bobby turned toward the newsmen. "I'm wasting my time here."

Inside the studio, Keating said Bobby refused to face him, "man-to-man, toe-to-toe." He pointed to the chair for the camera. "This is how he backs up his charges. This is how he shows his contempt for the voters of New York." Keating was emphatic. "I wanted this debate for the benefit of the people of New York and also for my own sake because I know a face-to-face meeting between my opponent and myself would expose his ruthless attempt to destroy my lifetime character." Republican senator Jacob Javits joined him, complaining that Bobby kept invoking the name of President Kennedy. The camera regularly panned to the empty leather chair behind a desk with a placard reading ROBERT F. KENNEDY.

Meanwhile, photographers snapped pictures of Bobby standing in front of a locked door with a handwritten sign: PLEASE KEEP OUT. NO VISITORS. KEATING. The images of Keating pointing toward the chair and Bobby locked out were juxtaposed on the front pages the next day. It was an utter disaster for Keating.

The hallways of CBS were a pandemonium of shouting newsmen, Kennedy aides, and network security. Guards barred doorways, and Ed Guthman was shoved back when he attempted to enter his own candidate's studio. As Bobby went on the air at eight, reporters gathered outside the front door to Keating's studio. Then a photographer spotted the senator and three aides slipping out a side door and shouted, "There he goes!" The newsmen gave chase. Keating rushed toward an elevator through a narrow corridor with props and furniture shelved along the wall. Attempting to slow the reporters down, Keating's aides knocked down chairs and a table behind them. Artificial palm trees and cue cards started flying. The aides pulled out a sofa to completely block the path. *Newsday*'s Myron Waldman tumbled over it onto his back. Keating made it to the elevator and down to the street. He claimed no knowledge of a chase and said he was merely on his way to another engagement in White Plains.[86]

The day after the debate, Kennedy campaign aides cast off their wariness and began talking openly about "winning big." Keating had lunch with an old reporter friend who said, "He seemed more hurt than angry." The senator collapsed in the polls that weekend.[87]

Bobby spent the final days of the campaign like a winner, whisked from adoring crowd to crowd. "It makes me feel like a Beatle," the *Times* quoted him.[88]

He began election day in Manhattan at early breakfasts for Democratic poll workers with heavy New York accents. "You gonna do awright here," one told him on the East Side.

"That's what we are going to find out today," Bobby said in his Boston voice. He headed back to his campaign headquarters, which had emptied out for the final push.

Alone, Bobby walked across Fifth Avenue at Fifty-seventh Street, his hands plunged in his pockets, his shoulders stooped. He wore his mourning outfit: a black pin-striped suit, black shoes, and a black tie with a gold PT-109 clip. On the headquarters wall, he scanned an editorial pinned to a clipboard. One of the few that endorsed him. His hands were puffed and bruised.

Lonely as he could seem, family was near. He, Ethel, and seven of their eight kids spent the day at the Bronx Zoo. Friendly crowds surrounded them. He held up five-year-old Mary Kerry to feed an elephant named Pinky. News cameras clicked noisily, and the elephant swung her trunk in their direction. "Go get 'em, Pinky," Bobby yelled with a smile. A reporter asked whose side he was on, the elephant's or the reporters'. "I'll tell you after the votes are counted," Bobby said. He and Ethel had a late dinner at Jean and Steve Smith's Fifth Avenue apartment with Joe and Rose, Sarge and Eunice Shriver, and Jackie. Teddy remained in Boston, strapped facedown to a special bed frame, watching the returns on TV through a prism of mirrors on the floor.[89]

The networks called the race before ten o'clock. Keating gave his concession speech shortly after midnight, and Bobby addressed the surging crowd in the ballroom of the Statler Hilton, surrounded by his family and New York's high-ranking Democrats. He thanked his supporters and the Harrimans, Mayor Wagner, Chairman McKeon, local party leaders John Burns and Peter Straus, and "a relative"—Steve Smith—who "went far beyond the effort one brother-in-law gives to another brother-in-law." Bobby said the results were "a mandate to continue the efforts begun by my brother four years ago—the effort to get something started in this country—and a vote of confidence for Lyndon Johnson and Hubert Humphrey." Bobby never explicitly thanked Johnson, though. Then, as he often did during the campaign, he closed by quoting Tennyson: "Come, my friends; 'tis not too late to seek a newer world."

"This is what I dedicate myself to in the next six years for the state of New York."[90]

In Austin, Texas, LBJ watched the speech on his television set, livid. Though Bobby mentioned him, he never *thanked* him.

"If I kept my mouth shut, he'd been beaten," he told Bill Moyers and McGeorge Bundy the next morning. Bobby won his race by ten points, but with less than 54 percent of the vote. LBJ had racked up nearly 69 percent in New York, the state *Newsweek* said he valued "second only to Texas as his personal power base." After all the miles of campaigning he'd done for Bobby, LBJ said to Bundy and Moyers, even Lady Bird "couldn't believe that he wouldn't acknowledge that the President had had anything to do with this landslide victory in the worl—country." Johnson rattled off all the "county judge so-and-so and county surrogate so-and-so and county so-and-so" no-names that Bobby *had* thanked.

"Well, Mr. President," McGeorge Bundy said, laughing, "he didn't realize you were in that room, and all those other sons of bitches *were*."[91]

In fact, Kennedy's victory speech also forgot to mention the Liberal Party, whose early endorsement doomed Keating and bolstered Bobby with skeptical New York reformers.[92] And immediately after, he called the President to thank and congratulate him on his landslide over Goldwater.

"We got a lot to be thankful for, Bobby," Johnson told him. "Let's, uh, let's, uh, let's, uh, let's stay as close together as he'd want us to."

"That'd be fine. That'd be fine, Mr. President. Congratulations—"

"Tell all that staff of yours ain't nobody gonna divide us, and I'll tell mine the same way and we'll—"

"That's right," Bobby said.

"—and we'll move ahead and there's plenty in life for all of us."[93]

The next morning, Bobby sat aboard the *Caroline* in the candidate's swivel chair, on his way to see his brother Teddy, after a promised stop in Glens Falls. He was wearing his horn-rimmed glasses, the morning papers on his lap.

"Now I can go back to being ruthless," he said to the newsmen.

One would write, "Had the phrase been spoken by Adlai Stevenson, it would have been merely funny. But such is the public image of Robert Kennedy that it was also believable."[94]

RFK later told a journalist that he might still have run for the Senate had President Kennedy lived, but as for reality, "I just wanted to keep myself busy and have something to occupy my mind."[95]

One friend said it sounded "corny" but was nonetheless true: Bob was proud of President Kennedy's accomplishments and "he thinks of himself as the guy to whom the torch has been passed. He's not at all modest about that."[96] Doing his best to psychoanalyze, *New York Times* editorialist William V. Shannon would soon write how after the 1960 campaign, John Kennedy stopped using the phrase *the New Frontier* in his speeches, but that Robert Kennedy never did.

Shannon was wrong; JFK hadn't.[97] But his observation was characteristic of how many viewed Bobby: fiercely loyal, sticking to the course his brother had laid out. After all those months of trying to capture the vice presidency, of searching for a way to keep the Kennedy legacy as close to power for as long as he could, Bobby had followed the path as far as it was going to take him.

The New Frontier was behind, and he had no choice but to find his own way forward.

BOOK 2

REVOLUTION

7

THE SIXTIES
BREAKING OPEN

November 1964–March 1965

LYING IN BED AT HIS RANCH early in the evening on election day, November 3, 1964, Lyndon Johnson moaned to his aide Bill Moyers, "Well, I just fell apart. My back's hurting, my head's hurting. I'm aching all over. I've got a headache. I don't know what I'm going to do. I've been in bed *all* day long."

"Well, just take it easy," Moyers told him. "I wish you'd go get some sun somewhere—Key West, or something like that."

The President let out a long yawn. "Well, I'm afraid of Vietnam."[1]

Johnson was monitoring a volatile situation. Minutes after midnight on November 1, Vietcong forces had rained mortars on Bien Hoa airfield. Four Americans died, thirty were wounded, and more than two dozen aircraft were destroyed as the guerrillas—estimated to be eighteen men at most—slipped away in the dark. The embassy would soon report that American B-57 capability "was knocked out in about fifteen minutes," and Ambassador Maxwell Taylor cabled Washington urging air strikes to respond to this "deliberate act of escalation and a change of the ground rules." Taylor called for "the inauguration of a new policy of tit for tat reprisals," in which the U.S. and South Vietnamese governments would "jointly announce that such retaliation will henceforth be the rule, making our statement broad enough to cover major acts of sabotage, terrorism, destruction of industrial facilities, and the interruption of arterial rail and highway communications"—nearly everything Vietcong guerrillas were engaged in. The Joint Chiefs of Staff advised that conditioning policy decisions upon Saigon's agreement was too restrictive, asking that measures finally be taken independently from the South Vietnamese army.[2] Americans were in the country strictly as "military advisers," accompanying Vietnamese soldiers on what were classified as Vietnamese missions, even if it was just one Vietnamese riding in an American aircraft flown by Americans. The required Vietnamese presence was what kept Americans "advisers."

It was all about to change.

American restraint had been unwinding for months. In early August, a U.S. destroyer operating in international waters in the Tonkin Gulf came under attack from North Vietnamese gunboats. A second more questionable high-seas assault led the American military to strike a North Vietnamese oil depot and torpedo bases. Addressing the nation on August 4, President Johnson declared, "We still seek no wider war." Yet within three days, Congress nearly unanimously approved his resolution authorizing "all necessary steps, including the use of armed force" to defend allies in Southeast Asia.[3]

As voters went to the polls two days after Bien Hoa, President Johnson had still not authorized a response. Republicans such as Barry Goldwater, Strom Thurmond, and Richard Nixon accused him of factoring politics into military decisions. White House meetings on what action to take raised concerns about drawing China into the conflict—what would have been a dramatic widening of the war in the dwindling hours of the election.[4] The journalist David Halberstam, who spent the fall covering Bobby in New York after a year in Saigon, later wondered what would have happened if Vietnam had been a bigger issue in the 1964 campaign. He thought Goldwater might have been more vocal for escalation, and LBJ might have moved to the left and entered his first term as "a partial dove." Instead, the President's caution kept the issue at bay until the pressure of winning his mandate was gone. Only his fear never went away.

Robert Kennedy was disconnected from the problems of Vietnam for most of the fall, consumed by his own election. He and Ethel stayed close with Maxwell Taylor, on the ground in the diplomatic role Bobby had volunteered for. It led to an uncomfortable moment on the campaign trail when Ethel asked Halberstam, "Don't you just love Max Taylor?"

"I said rather bitterly that I did not," recalled Halberstam, "that I thought him one of the most overrated men in American life and that I thought he was one of the men most responsible for a growing tragedy. Ethel turned white, hurt and offended, and moved away." Halberstam found Bobby "ambivalent" about the war he had helped start and that his friend Taylor was ratcheting up.[5] Disagreements among those Bobby trusted were becoming more profound.

"There was a group, including myself," National Security Council aide Michael Forrestal later said, "who felt that bombing was dubious as a means of getting a message across to the North and of no use at all insofar as shoring up the Southern government." Max Taylor felt otherwise. Taylor frequently returned to Washington to brief in person, as he did in November of 1964 amid rumors he was quitting over policy differences. Bobby, Ethel, and their son Joe met him at the airport on the trip.

Disillusionment was growing in the Senate Bobby was about to join. Senator Richard Russell, Democrat of Georgia, chairman of the Armed Services Committee and one of the most respected men in Washington, told the *New York Times*, "We either have to get out or take some action to help the Vietnamese. They won't help themselves. We made a big mistake in going in there, but I can't figure any way to get out without scaring the rest of the world." Democratic senator Wayne Morse, a liberal from Oregon, would soon call the State Department's program in South Vietnam "bankrupt," urging a "fair and negotiated settlement." President Johnson insisted, "To ignore aggression" in Vietnam "would only increase the danger of a larger war," echoing his campaign promise.[6]

Another campaign promise was to save the Brooklyn Navy Yard. When President Johnson joined Bobby in Brooklyn late in October to rally votes, he pointed to a banner that read SAVE THE BROOKLYN NAVY YARD and shouted, "That's another reason you should vote for Robert F. Kennedy."[7]

Not three weeks later, the Department of Defense announced the 163-year-old yard's closing as part of half a billion dollars in cuts. Shipbuilding was being shut down. Warfare was changing. The president of the Brooklyn Metal Trades Council lamented to the *New York Times*, "President Eisenhower hit it right on the head when he said, 'Beware the military industrial complex.' Private contractors have everything else in this country but shipbuilding. They can charge anything for missiles, aircraft, rockets, and tanks."[8]

THE DAY AFTER the election, a brash twenty-seven-year-old lawyer named Adam Walinsky volunteered to compile a memo on Kennedy's campaign promises.

Walinsky first got to work with the attorney general in July of 1964, when he was a junior staffer in the Justice Department. Bobby had to testify on the administration's immigration bill, and Walinsky's job was to brief him on all its complicated parts. "Now tell me again, how do I explain this to those guys on the Hill?" Bobby asked.

Walinsky deadpanned, "Several times slowly."

That was Adam Walinsky: like Bobby, endlessly curious yet close to fanatical in his beliefs. The aggressive confidence set in his shoulders and came to a point in the muscles beneath his eyes, a probing gaze and mouth curled in a thinking man's scowl. He was a bold thinker—genetically so, as the grandson of an Eastern European revolutionary who escaped a prison camp to go west. Bobby's discipline and dogged pursuit of organized crime led Walinsky to

the Justice Department after Cornell and Yale Law School. He soon determined that he would follow Kennedy anywhere.[9]

Bobby performed well during his two hours of immigration testimony, but
what happened toward the hearing's end bowled Walinsky over. Congressman
Richard H. Poff, a conservative Republican from Virginia, raised an unre-
lated issue that had been gnawing at him: a group of young American men
had illegally traveled to Cuba and then placed an ad in the *New York Herald
Tribune* saying America was the oppressor in Vietnam and that they would
not serve in the military if drafted. Poff demanded to know whether the Justice
Department was going to prosecute them under sedition laws that counted
discouraging enlistment as a crime.

Bobby said he hadn't seen the ad and would look into it. Then he turned the
question around on Poff, delving into Barry Goldwater's and other Republicans' election-year sniping at President Johnson's war policies. "I suppose
anybody can interpret the general criticism of the war in Vietnam—the criticism by some that it is a 'no-win policy,' that 'people are out there dying for
no reason,' that 'the administration has no policy,' that we are being 'soft
on Communism'—you can also interpret that, I suppose, as undermining the
enlistment of boys in the U.S. Army who are concerned about going to Vietnam
and fighting in a 'no-win war.' I think if you start down that road, there is no
telling who you might indict."[10]

Poff backed down. Bobby had effectively put him in the shoes of the
protesters, and Poff didn't like where he stood. Bobby's ability to engage an
opposing idea and transform it had Adam Walinsky hooked.

Within a few weeks, Bobby left the Justice Department to run in New
York. "That's my state!" Walinsky told anyone who would listen. Determined
as ever, he packed up his wife and baby and fought his way onto the campaign,
staying with his in-laws. He spent September and October crammed into a
small room on the seventh floor of the Chatham Hotel, writing speeches and
policy papers.[11]

After the election, Walinsky spent three days compiling all the policy
papers, responses to questionnaires, and press statements into a booklet, introduced by an eighteen-page strategy memo that became, in effect, the first document of Robert Kennedy's Senate office.

Looking at all the commitments made during the campaign opened Walinsky's eyes to the activist ideas Bobby had moored himself to. "The pressure to
assume this or that position can be fierce," Walinsky wrote to a friend that
winter, "and once taken, a campaign position confers an obligation that is definitely felt by the elected official. At least RFK seems to feel himself so bound.
So the alter ego of a very conservative administration is now committed to
as radical a social-welfare program as is espoused by anyone short of the

Progressive Labor Party." Walinsky's depiction of LBJ and Bobby as polar opposites on social programs was a dramatic way of looking at things. But Bobby also believed that Johnson was much more conservative than people thought, and that exaggerated black-and-white lens of the Kennedy-Johnson relationship that would color Adam's recommendations and Bobby's rhetoric over the next few years.[12]

Walinsky's memo covered twenty policy areas Bobby promised to address in the Senate, along with some political concerns that turned out to be quite prescient. Walinsky toyed with how, if he so chose to, Bobby could challenge Lyndon Johnson's legislative agenda.

Walinsky began by presenting the senator-elect with three paths for the Eighty-Ninth Congress. The first was flat-out support of Johnson's bills as proposed. This would require taking "a pronounced backseat to the committee chairmen and legislative leaders." Public contributions would be limited to some high-profile speeches of support, which would create goodwill with Bobby's senior Senate colleagues and counter the popular narrative of "ruthlessness."

The second path was to introduce legislation of his own in an all-out rebuke of the President's leadership. "I assume that such a challenge would now be premature," Walinsky wrote. Instead, he recommended the third path of offering small amendments to Johnson's bills. It was the easiest way to enact Bobby's promises without antagonizing the President. And it could help him win friends. As a freshman senator, he couldn't possibly pass all the things he wanted to on his own. Walinsky suggested that Bobby be the junior or even silent partner to more senior members and greatly improve their chances. Here, he wrote, "your willingness to work hard without immediate headlines would build your reputation both among your colleagues, and, through the press, in the nation."

From education to jobs programs, taxes to civil liberties, transportation to pollution and immigration—Walinsky surveyed it all. He offered practical ideas and strategies for each area. This was the brunt of his memo: standard, boring deeds, many of which could have been written for any new senator. That it was for Bobby Kennedy at the start of his new life as the junior U.S. senator from New York certainly made it exceptional.

Yet mixed in with the unexciting, Walinsky dared Bobby—over and over again—to establish the opposition camp. "Few voices in Congress are now strong enough to challenge the President's economic policies," he wrote. "I have read that President Kennedy studied economics throughout his time in the White House; you should do the same in the Senate. The choices of which you spoke during the campaign are very real; we are in the position now to set targets for unemployment, [Gross National Product], hours of work, etc., for the next twenty years—and achieve them. All domestic policy, especially on housing, taxes, education, etc., should be considered with these targets in mind."[13]

Even though Walinsky gamed scenarios where LBJ would have his priorities out of order, the memorandum contained nothing on foreign affairs with the exception of one paragraph on Israel. Walinsky completely missed how the war in Vietnam would eclipse 1600 Pennsylvania Avenue's view of the Great Society. He would later explain that there was no practical legislative strategy in foreign affairs. All a freshman senator could do about it was to get up on the floor and talk.[14] Only later would they grasp Bobby's power there.

A Republican senator told columnist Joe Alsop, "That damn Lyndon Johnson hasn't just grabbed the middle of the road. He's a bit to the right of center, as well as a bit to the left of center. And with Johnson hogging the whole road, right, left, and center, where the devil can we go except into the ditch?" Alsop talked to most of the leading Republicans in Washington, and they unanimously agreed that there was one area in which they stood to gain ground: Vietnam. An American defeat would change the political world.

A Republican national committeeman said, "I hate to think that's the most likely way we'll come back, but facts are facts."[15]

TEDDY'S AIDE MILT GWIRTZMAN helped Bobby plan the mechanics of his transition with a two-and-a-half-page memo on how he should staff his Senate office. The legislative assistants were perhaps the most important jobs to fill. They had to work with other senators' aides, "know what is right to say and how you say it," write speeches, and clear legislative hurdles. Gwirtzman suggested Bobby hire two, with one or two "girls"—secretaries—to work under them. Gwirtzman specifically recommended Walinsky for one of the positions, noting that he wrote many of the campaign speeches Bob liked. "He is an accomplished writer, very fast, full of good ideas, and is also a good lawyer," though he qualified the praise with Walinsky's need for "the direction of an older hand" to keep him in line.[16]

Bobby took the suggestion and decided to offer the other position to the "Accordion man," Peter Edelman, from the campaign. Walinsky took the job without knowing his title or even how much he would be paid. Edelman was a little more hesitant; he had already accepted a job at a Wall Street law firm. The campaign was just biding time. But he was astonished that he and Walinsky were offered the jobs they were—as *the* legislative assistants." Edelman couldn't say no.[17]

Justice Department aide Jack Rosenthal figured Bobby didn't even know the pair's names until halfway through the Senate campaign, and they had a long way to go before earning his trust. "It took a long time to get to know him," Walinsky later said, "because he was a very, very complex man who did not reveal himself easily and didn't spend a lot of time trying to explain himself to other people the way so many of us do."

"Hiring them, when they were both under thirty," Rosenthal thought, "was a sign of the kind of politician Kennedy sensed he wanted to become." "The Sixties were breaking open," Schlesinger wrote, "and they, far more than his New Frontier friends, could tell him what it was all about."[18]

BOBBY'S ATTENTION HAD turned local. In December, he toured upstate, territory that Democratic senators from New York City traditionally did not concern themselves with. Bobby wanted to change that. He and his new aides headed to Niagara Falls, Buffalo, Rochester, and Jamestown in the west, on to Syracuse, Binghamton, and the Mohawk Valley, to Plattsburgh, Ogdensburg, and Watertown in the north. The senator-elect had hoped for low-key meetings to avoid the raucous large crowds of the campaign, but hundreds showed. "I'm here to familiarize myself with the problems facing various parts of the state, not on the basis that the federal government has all the answers, but on the basis that it can help, can somehow make a difference," he said. He mostly listened through the two-hour sessions. At every stop, he asked if the locals had organized a community action agency under the Economic Opportunity Act of 1964. He was dismayed that most had never even heard of the new program, telling them, "This is a pile of money that's come along . . . You ought to be taking advantage of it." One of the few places that had heard of it was Clinton County, home to Plattsburgh, where the unemployment rate was 9.3 percent and nearly three in ten dropped out of high school. At Ogdensburg, a reporter wrote that Kennedy "seemed somewhat stunned" to discover the extent of the welfare rolls in St. Lawrence County, the sparsely populated area on the Canadian border. The county had the state's highest poverty rates outside New York City, yet had not applied for assistance. "I'll do what I can to help you," Bobby said, "but you must develop an overall plan." At night, he and Walinsky or Edelman would either stay for a soup and Scotch before hopping on the *Caroline* back to the city or spend the night at a tiny country motel.[19]

That winter, an aide would say, "It's funny, but the problems of places like Glens Falls and Rochester seem to be a tonic to him." RFK had spent so much time on national and international affairs, localizing his attention was an important, almost calming experience.[20]

It struck him most when he returned to Washington for new-member orientation, where Bobby heard briefings from his former colleagues in the cabinet. "Rusk made a good speech about foreign policy," he told the writer Murray Kempton, "but everyone else talked about how the main thing was to save money. I'm afraid you lose perspective in Washington."

"We have to concentrate on our own failures," Bobby told Kempton about his fellow politicians. He said he was shocked to find that the Mohawk Valley was just as impoverished as Appalachia. "It worries me a little," Bobby said, "when I read these stories about how much the President is thinking about [Franklin] Roosevelt and how he lost his popularity in 1936 because he did too much. But you can lose popularity by doing something or you can lose it by doing nothing. You lose it anyway. It's there to be spent."[21]

Bobby knew he wanted to spend his popularity and influence somehow, but wasn't yet clear what he would spend it on.

AFTER TAKING LEAVE for Bobby's campaign, Joe Dolan returned to his job as assistant deputy attorney general in the Justice Department, where he expected to remain for some time. Then Bob asked him to run his new Senate office. Dolan was a wise pick for administrative assistant. A Long Island native educated in New York before moving out West, he had been in the thick of the civil rights battles, on the ground for court-ordered integrations at Montgomery, Oxford, and Birmingham. As John Seigenthaler would later say, "*Loyal* was Joe's middle name." In early 1960, Dolan was a state assemblyman and the top John Kennedy man in Colorado when Ted Sorensen called to say that a *Time* magazine reporter looking at Kennedy's strength around the country was headed to Denver, and Dolan shouldn't tell him anything. Dolan took the reporter out to lunch and played dumb. When the reporter circled back after his trip, he told JFK his operation looked good—except in Colorado, where there was "some dumb son of a bitch who didn't know anything about what was going on."[22]

Bobby had to select the committees he would serve on, and Dolan quickly took charge. Democratic majority leader Mike Mansfield sent Bobby a letter saying that just about every one of the sixteen standing committees would have a vacancy. The Mansfield-chaired Steering Committee decided who went where, and Dolan sent Bobby a list of its members, saying that lobbying them "is not regarded as unseemly."

"Which committees you stay off are more important than which you get on," Dolan wrote in a memo. Judiciary was too obvious a choice for a former attorney general; Dolan told Bobby that he needed to add "new dimensions" to his image. Government Operations, whose investigations Bobby had led as a staff attorney in the 1950s, had an open seat. Dolan thought taking it a bad idea that would only reinforce the ruthless stereotype. "Not good for you with a Democratic President," he wrote in his memo. "People would expect you to carry on as 'the investigator.'"[23]

Bobby took the seat on Government Operations, in part because he got along so well with its chairman, Arkansas's John McClellan. He also joined the committee on the District of Columbia and the Labor & Public Welfare Committee, whose oversight of education policy, welfare, and work would put him at the epicenter of Johnson's War on Poverty.[24]

Labor and Government Operations were also the committees where President Kennedy began his Senate career in 1953.[25] On the day of Bobby's swearing in, a committee aide made the mistake of asking if he wanted the same assignments that "*Jack* had."

Bobby said nothing—he didn't have to. The icy stare in his eyes said it all. The aide knew he had crossed the line and mentioned how he would have said "*Senator* Kennedy" if only there hadn't been so many of them.

"You could have said *President* Kennedy," Bobby said before walking away.[26]

SEVEN MINUTES TO noon on January 3, 1965, Bob and Ted Kennedy entered the Senate chamber side by side, each with one hand tucked in his suit-coat pocket. Ted was frail after months in the hospital, fifteen pounds lighter. A fully pregnant Ethel brought seven of their eight children to the gallery, where the rest of the Kennedy women—Jean, Pat, Eunice, and Joan—watched as Republican senators Jacob Javits and Leverett Saltonstall escorted their junior colleagues to the rostrum. The roll was suspended from alphabetical state order, allowing two brothers to be sworn in simultaneously for the first and only time in American history. "Mr. Kennedy of Massachusetts and Mr. Kennedy of New York" raised their hands as Senate president pro tem Carl Hayden of Arizona administered the oath of office. The applause was sustained as Ted, stiff from his broken back but betraying no pain in his face, fulfilled a vow to walk to his back-row desk. Ted sat where JFK had last, a tribute he would continue through five decades. Bobby's seat was in the *back* back row. Johnson's landslide gave Democrats a majority with sixty-eight seats, one of the largest in the Senate's history. To sit all the Democratic members on one side, an extra row with two seats had to be added. That's where Bobby was, ranked ninety-ninth out of a hundred senators in seniority. "Well, at least I got inside the building," he joked. "If there was one more Democrat elected, I would be out in the cloakroom."[27]

After an open house in Teddy's office, the party moved across the Chain Bridge to Hickory Hill. On the car ride over, a reporter asked how Bobby felt to be carrying on the "family tradition" in the Senate. Bobby was silent for a full minute, then said that his feelings had been "somewhat mixed."[28]

"I was remembering and regretting the situation that gave rise to my being there. That affected everything." It was certainly going to be a change of pace. "We were making decisions every day," he said of the White House. "It will be a totally new life," he added quietly. "I expect my manners to be good. I have no complaints."

Bobby's manners had to be good. One of his new colleagues told columnist Mary McGrory that the junior senator had a long way to go. "Bobby was always the one who said, 'No.' Jack was the one who said, 'I'm sorry.' Of course, if a president is going to be popular, he can't do the refusing. But Bobby did it without trying to soften it much."

Teddy was the opposite, McGrory wrote—"one of the darlings of the Senate" for his patience and humility. He had sat long hours presiding over the Senate for the three-month civil rights debate, never begging off from his duty. Teddy's youth, combined with the disclosure of his expulsion from Harvard for cheating and stories about his diving into the pool at Hickory Hill fully clothed gave the impression that he was less than serious. His 1964 plane crash changed that. He used those months confined to bed as an opportunity to reeducate himself on the important issues of the day. He received private tutorials on state and local government, economics, and science. Arthur Schlesinger, who was "dismayed" when the family wanted to make Teddy a senator, thought the injury turned out to be "one of the luckiest things that ever happened to him." Teddy was already being talked about as a potential running mate for Hubert Humphrey if and when that time came.[29]

The *Wall Street Journal*'s reporter found Bob stiffer than Ted, "more introspective, more intense, less inclined to casual conversation." Bobby himself said, "Teddy is a better natural politician than any of us."[30]

Teddy was taller, dashing with his "toothpaste smile" as one reporter called it.[31]

"It's painful when Bobby comes in the dining room," one Democratic senator confided in 1965. "We try not to look. Nobody likes him yet. Somehow you don't mind Teddy. He's so outgoing." Once it was Teddy, the freshman at Milton Academy, tagging along with Bobby and his Harvard football teammates on their weekend trips to Cape Cod. Now, Teddy was the one guiding his older brother on protocol so he wouldn't look foolish, signaling to him which way to vote. They were in constant contact, walking from their offices to the Senate floor together, talking politics.[32]

Teddy was by Bobby's side on the day of Lyndon Johnson's inauguration. The morning's bleak weather was in keeping with Robert Kennedy's mood. Before the ceremony at the Capitol, the remaining Kennedy brothers trekked up the hill at Arlington National Cemetery to pray at the President's snow-covered grave. Then they paid their respects to the new President, watching him take the oath. As they had four years earlier, the Kennedys sat bareheaded in the cold, except their seats weren't as good this time—about fifty feet from the inaugural platform with those of the other senators. Neither stayed for the balls or festivities, and Bobby stopped once more at his brother's grave on his way home. Thomas Collins of *Newsday*'s Washington bureau was present for the second visit. Fifty people looked on while a uniformed sergeant opened the white picket gate for Bobby. He knelt, crossed himself, and bowed his head. He dug his left hand into the snow, picked up a handful, and crushed it to melt some drops of water over a bouquet on the mound. He flung the snow back to the ground, crossed himself, stood up, and walked away. A photo of him kneeling before the eternal flame appeared on page A2 of the next morning's *Washington Post*. A rumor emerged that he only stopped a second time because no camera was around the first. An unnamed senior Republican senator told journalists Nick Thimmesch and William Johnson, "This is a pretty sophisticated and hard-boiled crowd. They notice stuff like that."[33]

Anyone close to Bobby knew otherwise. A year after Dallas, he still went to the grave often. Reporters had spotted him there twice in recent weeks: once when he returned to Washington after the election, and again on the November 22 anniversary, when he knelt hatless and coatless against the bitter chill. He laid a white carnation and then prayed. John Seigenthaler was staying at Hickory Hill that night. Bob abruptly asked if Seigenthaler would take him to confession. As they drove in the dark, Bobby told him to stop at Arlington. They pulled up in front of the locked gates, but before Seigenthaler could ask how they could get in, Bob was out the door and over the fence . . . Seigenthaler was alarmed until he saw Bobby send the night guard back to his station with nothing more than a knowing wave. That's when he realized, *This isn't the first time he's done this.*[34]

The next day, November 23, Walinsky was with RFK at the airport, on their way to Los Angeles. Ethel was there to see them off and give Bobby a striped tie. Walinsky overheard them talking about how it was Bobby's first one since Dallas that wasn't black.[35]

BOBBY'S MOTIVES AND abilities had been questioned before. He would prove himself the way he always had—through the work.

On January 12, 1965, the Veterans Administration announced an economy drive that would close 4 old soldiers' homes and 11 of its 168 hospitals across the country. Three of the facilities were in small upstate New York towns: Bath, Castle Point, and Tupper Lake. These were places where the loss of federal money and jobs would have a profound effect. Shut down the Brooklyn Navy Yard, and the workers were still in New York City. Shut down these hospitals, and the local economies collapsed. Bobby's seat on Labor gave him a platform to fight from as the Veterans Administration's director, William Driver, was called before the Subcommittee on Veterans' Affairs to account.

Bobby entered his first hearing through the public entrance instead of the committee room, his coat over his arm, looking for a place to put it and the way up to the rostrum with the other senators. He made the unusual choice of standing up behind the committee table, "seeming like even more of a prosecutor than before," the *Times* wrote.[36]

"Mr. Driver."

"Yes, Senator."

Over the next few days, Bobby would dismantle the VA's rationale for the closings, focusing on the millions the federal government had spent modernizing the facilities up until that very month, and prying out specifics—many of which the VA officials did not know. When Driver admitted that veterans in the Northeast would be relocated to a West Virginia hospital for domiciliary care, Bobby scolded, "I suppose if we applied the same criteria to the post office, we would close up every post office in every small town in the United States." He asked if the VA would change its decisions if their information proved to be factually incorrect. Driver said he would consider it. Bobby then dragged Driver through contradiction after contradiction, much of it backed by the testimony of VA employees sitting by Driver's side.[37]

Bobby's performance received rave reviews—"the same surprise technique which he used to confound labor racketeers," the *Chicago Tribune* wrote. The *Washington Post* said the "finely honed Kennedy scalpel" and "machine gun style cross-examination" was back in use.[38]

The administration was startled by the blowback to its cost-saving measures. President Johnson was forced to personally defend the decision at a news conference, while the Senate closed ranks, tagging a rider on an appropriations bill preventing any spending on the closing of the hospitals. Soon, Johnson turned the matter over to an advisory committee, and in May, word leaked that the administration had relented and would halve the number of facilities slated for closure. Bath and Castle Point were saved, while a deal was worked out to put Tupper Lake under the state's control.[39]

Yet Bobby's desire to craft education policy was what had truly drawn him to the Labor committee. There, Walinsky was shouldering the workload for hearings on one of the biggest domestic items of the year: President Johnson's $1.3 billion Elementary and Secondary Education Bill, groundbreaking in its amount and the scope of aid to school districts. Over and over again in the committee hearings, Bobby objected to allocating the money without a way of measuring progress: "We are going forward with a billion dollars the first year and perhaps two or three times that the second year, the third year, the fourth year, and the fifth year, without anything really written into the bill which is going to test or determine whether a particular program should be put into effect," he said. "Large sums of money are going to be lost, but much more importantly, another generation of young Americans is going to be lost." Walinsky drafted an amendment to adopt the New York Board of Regents' model for testing and, working through the administration, submitted it as a White House amendment in the House, where the bill was being marked up. Its addition didn't bear the title of "The Kennedy Amendment" and barely had Bobby's fingerprints on it. Later, columnist Joseph Alsop would write that the subtle move showed how Bobby valued accomplishment over publicity.[40]

However, his biggest accomplishment in his first month as a senator was all too public.

The Johnson administration was pressing an aid bill for Appalachia, distributing $1.1 billion to impoverished rural counties in eleven states. New York's Southern Tier, some 350 miles of rugged hills stretching from west of the Catskills to Lake Erie, was originally in the bill's range, but Governor Rockefeller asked that they be left out. He was concerned the impoverished "Appalachian" label would somehow harm the international brand of New York's economy. Bobby disagreed, only the bill seemed to be passing New York by. His office learned late on the last Friday in January that it was headed for a floor vote. Senate and administration leaders had discouraged any more amendments, promising future projects for New England, the Ozarks, and the Northern Great Lakes Region. Only Walinsky recalled that Bobby had specifically used the Appalachian aid program in his campaign, and so the aide spent the weekend drafting an amendment allowing the inclusion of thirteen New York counties. A floor speech was set for Monday morning.

Bobby questioned whether or not he should address the chamber. He knew the tradition: freshman senators were supposed to remain silent on the floor and learn the Senate's rules, with rostrum duty. John Kennedy had sat by for over four months before addressing his colleagues. Teddy waited almost a year and a half. Bobby made his first speech on the Senate floor on February 1, a mere four weeks into his career.[41]

"The Senator from Massachusetts is recognized," New Mexico Democrat Joseph M. Montoya, the presiding officer, announced, mistaking Bobby for Ted. After some laughter, Bobby asked, "Mr. President, will the record show that it is the senator from New York?"

"The record will so show."

Bobby's short speech touched on his relationship with Appalachia, going back to his time campaigning in West Virginia during the 1960 presidential primary. He noted that the economic situation of the Southern Tier was no different from that of the areas across the invisible border where the

Appalachia aid program stopped, even though these places "are in this respect more like West Virginia . . . than the counties of Pennsylvania which they enjoin." The senator cited statistics to show young people had no choice but to leave for better economic prospects, saying, "A region's future, like a nation's future, is in its youth; if these counties continue to lose their young people, they will have no future."[42]

Bobby's senior Republican colleague Jacob Javits quibbled with the wording of the amendment, and Bobby accepted the change to please him. This was typical Javits: ever present on the Senate floor, papers spilling off his desk while others' remained pristine, waiting to begin condescending debates with his colleagues. Bobby once responded to a Javits interjection with "I thank the Senator . . . I think."[43]

The amendment passed on a voice vote, and a grin spread across Bobby's face. Senator Albert Gore of Tennessee pumped his hand in congratulations. Full passage of the bill followed, and though West Virginia's senator Jennings Randolph had steered the billion-dollar legislation through Congress, Bobby's photo was on the front page of the *Chicago Tribune*.[44]

Still, Bobby had an even bigger speech in mind: publicly pressuring the Johnson administration on Vietnam.

In December 1964, President Johnson had approved more aggressive, large-scale actions against North Vietnam but was waiting to enforce them so Maxwell Taylor could work on the political situation in the South. Bobby seemed pleased with Taylor's work. He idolized the general, a hero of World War II whom Bobby had worked closely with to uncover what went wrong in the Bay of Pigs fiasco during his brother's administration. His regard for Taylor was such that when Ethel gave birth to a baby boy that winter, their ninth child and first since JFK's assassination, they named him Matthew Maxwell Taylor.[45] Every now and again, Johnson would ask the general, "How is that Kennedy boy named after you?"

"I wasn't sure he was joking," Taylor would later say.

Bobby feared Taylor was becoming Johnson's scapegoat for why Vietnam was sinking deeper into chaos. In a handwritten letter to Taylor that January, RFK acknowledged, "The news from Viet Nam does not seem to be improving . . . I detect at least an effort on behalf of at least some important segments of the administration to place the blame on you. I notice it in the newspapers and I detect it in other ways . . . And I don't think there is anyone back here who defends you or who speaks up on your behalf."[46]

Bobby's speech may have been his way to support his friend and restore faith in the effort. The South Vietnamese army was near its breaking point; its government was unstable; and the U.S. footprint was light enough to withdraw quickly. In January, United Nations secretary-general U Thant restarted his drive for talks between the Americans and the North Vietnamese. He chose the hermit kingdom of Burma as the venue for its inaccessibility to Western journalists. The work continued into February, as Bobby considered his next move. The United States was in no position to negotiate, and if what Bobby had heard was true, it could mean disaster for U.S. allies.[47]

Roger Hilsman, a friend of Bobby's and a former State Department official specializing in Southeast Asia, prepared some thoughts, and Guthman wrote a draft that opposed "unthinkable" withdrawal from Vietnam in favor of more political tactics. "The counter-insurgency steps taken by President Kennedy," the draft said, "which President Johnson has carried forward, have had their effect, but have been undercut somewhat by the political instability of the South Vietnamese government." One of the truths of U.S. involvement in Vietnam, Bobby was to say, was that the conflict "is not now and never has been a 'war' in the true sense of the word. It has been a guerilla action—a war of terrorists, assassins and saboteurs—not of armies pitted against one another." Bombing targets in North Vietnam, as Johnson had approved, would "not bring peace to South Viet Nam. In the last analysis, the way to defeat terrorists is to increase our capability to fight their kind of war." Bobby was to call for the use of programs the Kennedy administration created "to spur our anti-guerilla efforts" against "totalitarian aggression," invoking what President Kennedy said in 1961: "This nation was born of revolution and raised in freedom. And we do not intend to leave an open road to despotism."

Bobby was hesitant to make these critical observations and suggestions less than a month into his Senate career. Ed Guthman would recall how RFK was convinced "it would add substance to the stereotype of the ruthless power-seeker and, worse, be interpreted as a personal attack on President Johnson, rekindling the public fight between them, rather than an honest disagreement on strategy."[48]

Then, everything changed. On February 7, the Vietcong launched a well-coordinated attack on the American airfield at Pleiku, planting dynamite charges to destroy aircraft and spraying small-arms fire and sixty rounds of mortar shells into the barracks and nearby targets. Eight Americans died immediately and 126 were wounded. Pleiku was on a high plain with only some brush nearby—a much more difficult target than November's assault on the jungle-shrouded Bien Hoa. This and the efficiency of the strike suggested the attackers had been inside the compound before.[49] It was a stunning failure for the American operation.

McGeorge Bundy had been in Vietnam at the time and wrote while en route from Saigon to Washington that "without new U.S. action defeat appears inevitable—probably not in a matter of weeks or perhaps even months, but within the next year or so." Bundy introduced a paper proposing "a policy of sustained reprisal" against the North, without the need to connect each "reprisal" with a particular action. "The object would not be to 'win' an air war against Hanoi, but rather to influence the course of the struggle in the South."[50]

Johnson read the memo in his bedroom the night Bundy got back and said to him, "Didn't we decide all that earlier?" Bundy was shocked. It seemed the President had made up his mind about what to do back in December.[51]

In a meeting of the National Security Council following the attack, the President lamented delaying more military action to help Taylor work on the political situation. Johnson "was concerned that in December we placed the establishment of a stable government as a first priority," a State Department memorandum said, "and things had gone down hill since then, not up."[52]

The response was swift and firm. Johnson authorized strikes against four targets after Pleiku, but three were fogged in and he decided not to go back for them. "We all felt," Johnson later wrote referring to his top advisers, "that a second-day strike by U.S. planes might give Hanoi and Moscow the impression that we had begun a sustained air offensive."[53] Things quickly began to spiral out of control.

In Moscow on February 9, two thousand Russians staged a violent protest against America's retaliatory bombing raids outside the U.S. embassy, hurling stones through more than two hundred windows and against the facade. The following morning, the Vietcong detonated a powerful bomb at a hotel housing American soldiers in Qui Nhon. Twenty-three U.S. servicemen died, the largest loss of American life in a single attack since the involvement began.[54]

Later that month, Johnson spoke about the situation in Vietnam with former President Eisenhower, who advised him to shift from retaliatory strikes to a "campaign of pressure." They both agreed, Johnson later wrote in his memoirs, that Diem's 1963 assassination was a political setback and that "a leader of courage and ability" had yet to emerge. It was also at this time that the President continued to elevate Thomas Mann within the State Department.[55] Bobby and the New Frontier liberals felt Mann was a step back to the colonialist approach. Johnson believed he was the "nut-cutter" the world needed. For fourteen months, Johnson had continued the Kennedy policy objectives, keeping the promise he made before a joint session of Congress in those shocking hours of November 1963. Now, with his own mandate secured, the President was beginning *his* administration, following *his* instincts, and he tended toward the traditional power ideas that Eisenhower had favored.

To Bobby, this regression was a mistake. Others believed there was no good option—least of all in Vietnam. David Halberstam would later write of this "arrogance" among Kennedy partisans, who believed "they were tougher, brighter and more contemporary than the Eisenhower people." They believed that the conventional way of willing victory through bombs and overwhelming force was outdated, and Robert Kennedy, Halberstam observed, "was one of the worst offenders. He became the New Frontier's leading student on guerrilla warfare and Green Beretism, the latter being something of a Washington fad."[56]

Now the government had moved away from that position, back toward Eisenhower's conventional-force pressure campaign. The war was escalating. On March 2, more than a hundred American aircraft launched an attack on military targets in the North, the first strike in a massive bombing campaign, Operation Rolling Thunder. From February to April, sorties in Vietnam would increase from 122 per week to 604 per week.[57]

Bobby put away his Vietnam speech and entered, Guthman wrote, a period of "vexing second thoughts and self-doubts." Visiting college students in Ithaca, Bobby said he believed in "taking whatever steps are necessary" for the United States to keep its commitment. "I'm not in favor of staying a minute more than is necessary. If our word means anything, we must remain as long as it is evident that the people favor it."[58]

On March 8, Maxwell Taylor wrote to State Department headquarters, "It appears to me evident that to date [North Vietnamese] leaders believe air strikes at present levels on their territory are meaningless and that we are more susceptible to international pressure for negotiations than are they." That day, thirty-five hundred U.S. marines landed to protect the air base at Da Nang, near the border with the North. They were the first American combat troops on the ground.[59]

"It was the black year," Taylor later said.[60]

8

RUTHLESS

March 1965–May 1965

BOBBY'S REPUTATION FOR RUTHLESSNESS followed him to the Senate, the centerpiece of a *Look* magazine interview on newsstands in February 1965. Oriana Fallaci, a blunt Italian journalist, met him in his suite at the Carlyle, surrounded by framed photographs of President Kennedy arranged like votive candles. The room felt more like a chapel than a hotel suite, she would write. When she pointed it out to Bobby, he said he understood why people wanted to know if he was always thinking of his brother. "But I am not obsessed. I do not always think of him, not a lot, anyway." Photos of other family members were around, too, he said.

She asked Bobby about a cigarette case Jack had given him in 1960 with the inscription AFTER I'M THROUGH, HOW ABOUT YOU? "Have you always thought of taking his place? Were you thinking of having yourself elected, in one way or another, in his stead?"

"No," Bobby answered, saying that this was a misinterpretation. Jack's inscription wasn't about Bobby running for office, but rather, what purpose he would serve in life once he had finished working for his older brother. "That sentence did not mean literally 'Take my place,'" Bobby said. "Its meaning was more in the nature of 'What will you do when I have finished . . . *you as a human being?*'"[1]

Bobby said to Fallaci that he wasn't the ruthless, calculating politician that haunted the imaginations of conservatives and liberals alike. He said running for office had never even occurred to him before Dallas. "I began to think about it a lot, continuously in fact, after he died: as a means to continue what he had begun, what he and I had begun together."

He told Fallaci, "I am so well aware of being disliked by many that it no longer surprises or disturbs me. I no longer care. On the contrary, I do understand the reason: I have been too closely involved in too many struggles, in too many battles. But there are also people who do like me: They elected me, did they not? The poorer people like me. Negroes and Puerto Ricans, for instance. The deprived, if you like. They are for me, I know . . . So let the others say whatever they like. Oh, I know what they are saying about me."

Ruthless. Bobby said it wasn't up to him to judge his most infamous trait: "I am not going to psychoanalyze myself."[2] Others, particularly old enemies, would do that for him.

Appealing a guilty verdict for jury-tampering, Teamsters president Jimmy Hoffa minced no words about the man who had led the federal investigation of his union. Hoffa told a news conference that the "flood of subpoenas" had ceased since Robert Kennedy had stepped down at the Justice Department, suggesting his impending jail sentence was the result of Bobby's "conspiracy" against him. "He took an interest in me first to further his own ambitions," Hoffa said, "and secondly because he is a spoiled brat, one who thinks he can dictate policy to everybody. He was not a good attorney general and he'll probably make a worse senator. I hate to think what he would be like as president. We'd probably have a fascist government."[3]

In New York politics, Bobby provided a power center for the ruthless. His involvement brought a new respectability to aligning with the patronage-driven county political machines. Democrats who signed up weren't just with the bosses; they were with Kennedy now, too. As the state legislature flipped to the Democrats in the Johnson landslide, the bosses set their sights on who would be the new Speaker of the Assembly and president of the Senate in Albany. The incumbent Democratic leaders were both supporters of Mayor Wagner, which mattered little to the bosses before, but now that they were in the majority, those leaders controlled $5 million in patronage jobs. Wagner and the bosses couldn't agree on compromise candidates, and a weeks-long standoff ensued—the scheduled start of the new legislature passing without leaders being elected. Wagner was outspoken in supporting the incumbents, while Bobby claimed he was neutral, though he and Steve Smith were privately aiding the boss candidates, who had more support within the Democratic caucus. "What I see here," Wagner privately told President Johnson, "is a little power play on the part of those Kennedy people that'd like to take over this operation here and the governorship in '66 and the delegates in '68 . . . I've talked to him [Bobby], and he gives me one story, and then he'll give somebody else another story the next minute." Wagner eventually brokered a deal with Governor Rockefeller to get the Republican caucus to elect his candidates, and Bobby called the decision "unfortunate," telling a reporter he considered it "a victory for Mayor Wagner." Bobby was so agitated that he penned a righteous letter to the winning legislative leaders warning against the ills of patronage and invoking President Kennedy's "talent search" in staffing his administration. Rockefeller remarked that Bobby's "holier-than-thou attitude" had only arisen after "boss-control leadership didn't pan out."[4]

That same winter, a former low-level Justice Department staffer published an article in *Esquire* magazine with a withering aside about Bobby removing heavyweight boxing champion Floyd Patterson's autographed picture from his office wall after he lost a title bout.[5]

Then Bobby's character came under assault from the very institution he had just joined.

The accusation came on March 2 from a minor Judiciary panel holding hearings on government invasions of privacy. Testifying before the subcommittee was Roy Cohn, perhaps Robert Kennedy's first and fiercest enemy in national politics. A decade earlier, Cohn and Kennedy had been the Republican and Democratic counsels of the Senate Investigations subcommittee, where Cohn was Joe McCarthy's right arm in his Communist witch hunts. A year apart in age and about the same height and weight, the two nearly came to blows in the hearing room at least once in 1954, when Bobby told Cohn not to threaten him. "You hate me," Cohn said to Bobby. "If I hate or dislike anyone," Bobby said, "it's justified." Reporters ran over when they heard voices rising.[6] Bobby would always blame Cohn, not McCarthy, for the Wisconsin senator's excesses. The animosity was mutual and never subsided.

By March 1965, Bobby was a senator and Cohn was an attorney in Manhattan enduring his own legal difficulties—tried for perjury and obstruction of justice in 1964. In the run-up to his trial, by which he was acquitted, *Life* magazine ran an unfavorable article about Cohn. His lawyer suspected that then–Attorney General Bobby Kennedy had planted the story to influence the jury and subpoenaed *Life*'s correspondence with the Justice Department. They received something that had nothing to do with Cohn: evidence that Bobby had planted a Jimmy Hoffa exposé at the same time the Justice Department had the union leader under indictment. Specifically, a 1961 memo from *Life*'s Washington correspondent to an editor in New York detailed a backroom meeting where Kennedy introduced the reporter to Sam Baron, a high-ranking Teamsters official turned government witness. The memo explained how the informant feared for his safety and wanted to tell the inside story of Hoffa's corruption in the pages of *Life* in case he turned up missing or dead.

At the subcommittee hearing, Cohn's lawyer unveiled the memo and accused Bobby of a federally funded "cloak-and-dagger operation" to smear someone the government was prosecuting before his day in court.[7] The subcommittee chairman, Democratic senator Edward Long of Missouri, denied any prior knowledge of the accusation and said he would have invited Senator Kennedy before the committee to defend himself had he known.

The next morning, Bobby appeared by his own request to testify under oath about the allegations. Yes, he had set up a meeting, but he insisted an article was only to be published in the event the informant was killed or wound up in the hospital. Baron's beating at Hoffa's hands came one year after Bobby introduced the informant and the magazine, and the Teamster exposé appeared a few months after that, with photos of the scars on Baron's nose, cheek, and forehead. The reporters in the hearing room found Senator Long startled by Bobby's forcefulness when answering his questions. Then the subcommittee's chief counsel, Bernard Fensterwald, set Kennedy off.[8] "This was an arrangement whereby I understand it," Fensterwald said, "you were putting what would normally be described as a 'fink' in touch with *Time-Life* to write a magazine article?"

"Normally described as what?" Bobby asked.

"*Fink*. F-I-N-K."

"I never heard that."

"A *stool pigeon*," Fensterwald replied. "Does that word strike a chord?"

Bobby was not amused. "I thought it was a citizen who was reporting information and evidence in connection with illegal activities."

"That is correct," Fensterwald began. "That would be a very good definition."

"That is your definition of *fink*?" Bobby said.

"Wait."

"Let me say, I am shocked to hear that. There have been a lot of loyal people, if I may say, Mr. Counsel, who have provided information to the U.S. government in connection with Communist activities, underworld activities, and narcotics activities at great risk to their own lives, and I think that has been very, very helpful to the United States."

"And it is also your position, sir," Fensterwald replied, "that it is proper for the attorney general to take such people, even when a case is under investigation and indictment and attempt to see that their testimony is printed in the public press rather than taken into court?"

"That is not the way it was done, Mr. Counsel."

"Well, I would—"

"I never did anything like that. That was the implication of the testimony yesterday," Bobby said. "As I understood it, there was no evidence or information ever given to any magazine by the Department of Justice. I would have no control over what this individual would do other than the fact that I urged no article be published unless something happened. I would have no control beyond that. No article was ever published until some eighteen months later when Mr. Hoffa beat up Mr. Baron."

Bobby was on a roll. He lectured the committee and its chairman on how to conduct a public hearing, accusing them of spreading "an implication across this country that I had acted improperly . . . Now, if this committee is going to look into improper activities or activities that are unfair, then I think that the practices of the committee might be studied as well."[9]

Ruthless Bobby had reared his head. "Gone was the modest diffidence which [Kennedy] has practiced during his first two months in the Senate," the *Chicago Tribune*'s correspondent wrote. The irony of Bobby—the hard-nosed investigator of Senate inquiries past—decrying an aggressive panel was not lost on the national press. An editorial from the *Toledo Blade* read, "Isn't it rather late for Bobby Kennedy, of all people, to be complaining about implications and insinuations, which were his chief stock in trade when he was often employing the investigating powers of Congress for political advantage?" The more cynical observers thought Bobby played it brilliantly, one remarking that he came across on TV like "an outraged choir boy, and nobody votes against that."[10]

Asked how he thought Bobby was doing so far, Republican senator Hugh Scott of Pennsylvania said, "Quite loudly." The sparring with Senator Long, Scott said, "was enough to keep him out of the Senate club." Years later, Long was exposed for being on Jimmy Hoffa's payroll in 1963 and 1964, while Fensterwald, too, later became a Hoffa legal fixer.[11] But these details would remain secret for some time, and Bobby's disrespectful tone was the story of the day.

The high-profile spat obscured Bobby's other efforts to win allies. Washington columnist Roscoe Drummond praised his forging relationships with the older Southern senators while cultivating newer ones, like with his back-row seatmate, Joseph Tydings of Maryland. Bobby took his dog Brumus by to visit old fiscal hawk Harry Byrd's dog in the Virginian's office. Pets were the topic of discussion, not politics, and Bobby needed the practice talking colleague to colleague. He was still adjusting to addressing them by their first names instead of "Senator," unwittingly mangling some, calling out to Oregon's Maurine Neuberger, on the Senate subway, "Good morning, Marion!" Given his ability to outshine senior members, his staff deliberately subdued his press operation, avoiding news conferences, though reporters still gathered at his office to gossip, just as they had when he was attorney general.[12]

The demand for contact from citizens in New York and around the country was overwhelming. Eleven weeks in, Bobby was getting more than a thousand letters a day, and his office's responses were woefully behind: less than six hundred a day by mid-March. Peter Edelman had already begun stuffing his backlog in a desk drawer so people couldn't tell how far behind he was. The phone lines were constantly jammed, the *New York Times* writing that it took four or five tries to break through the busy signal. Once SENATOR KENNEDY; NEW YORK; WALK IN was stenciled on the door of suite 1205 opposite the elevator, the "girls," as they were universally referred to, would keep the door open all the way in the hope that hiding the glass would reduce the number of autograph seekers. When Joe Dolan's secretary from the Justice Department left in March of 1965, he hired a young woman working in Senator George Smathers's office. Her name was Mary Jo Kopechne.[13]

The layout kept the office in a constant state of upheaval. Senators from large states like New York were entitled to seven rooms according to Senate rules. Only no seven-room suites were available to the ninety-ninth in seniority, so Bobby received a four-room main office and three others: a windowless one across the hall from the main office, one on another floor, and another in the building across the street. "I used to complain there wasn't enough space when we were in the Justice Department," Bobby's secretary, Angie Novello, told a reporter. "I must have been crazy!" Dolan suggested they "go slow on hiring" since whatever was left over from the staffing subsidy could be used for other office needs at the end of every month. Judging by the amount of mail they were receiving, Joe recommended putting the money into their constituent-response operation: more robotypes, flexotypes, letter openers and sealers. "For God's sake," Peter overheard Bobby telling Dolan and Guthman, "don't tell Ethel that we're free to buy furniture. Tell her it's all government-issue."[14]

Bobby's blue-carpeted office was the only comfortable space to assemble, though meetings were rarely more than a few people and never official. Staff meetings were seen as a waste of time; there were too many things to do. Kennedy's windows faced out to Constitution Avenue and First Street, with the Capitol dome a few hundred feet in the distance. Watercolors by his children decorated the walls, while above the couch hung a large oil painting of the late Lieutenant Joseph Kennedy Jr., smiling in his pilot's gear. On another wall were photographs of family and achievements: his maternal grandfather, Honey Fitz, sharing a laugh and a handshake with President Taft in 1912; the elder Joseph Kennedy in an inscribed picture with President Hoover, and another of Teddy next to President Truman. President Kennedy was atop them all. Elsewhere hung a framed yellow legal pad that Bobby described as "the last doodle"—notes from JFK's final cabinet meeting, in which he scribbled and circled the word *poverty* seven times.[15]

Washington Post columnist Marquis Childs once stopped in that spring and could feel the energy in the air. The constant chirp of ringing phones, hundreds of little yellow while-you-were-out messages spilling off desks, the girls huddled over stacks of paper trying to keep it all together. Bobby's office was like Jack Kennedy's, circa 1957–58, Childs thought. These people were working with the White House in mind.[16]

* * *

In February of 1965, the *New York Times'* Tom Wicker wrote that "civil rights, that most divisive of issues, does not loom so large in this Congress as in the last several," even though it was public knowledge that Johnson had met with Dr. King and said more action to make it easier for Negroes to vote was necessary.[17] The path was unclear. Then in March, events unfolded in Selma, Alabama.

In 1965, more than half of Selma's population was black. Its voting rolls, however, remained 99 percent white, far from an Alabama anomaly. Voting rights activists chose the city as the point of origin for a fifty-four-mile march to the state capital in Montgomery. State-sanctioned resistance was instantaneous. On Sunday, March 7, the march halted at the foot of the Edmund Pettus Bridge where gas-masked state troopers set upon them in a melee of nightsticks, shrieks, blood, tear gas, horses, and sirens. The mayhem—captured on film—interrupted regularly scheduled television programming across the country that night. "Bloody Sunday" had gone national. A tense week followed. More marches were promised, as was more segregationist resistance. On Tuesday, racists ambushed a group of white Unitarian ministers in town for the protests. "Now you know what it's like to be a real nigger," one of the racists shouted after a club to the head knocked the Reverend James Reeb to the ground. He succumbed to the wound hours later—hours through which Lyndon Johnson received more than fifty calls on the minister's condition. Legislation guaranteeing voting rights was necessary. A nationally televised address to a joint session of Congress was arranged for the soonest possible date: Monday, March 15.[18]

Johnson turned to his speechwriter Dick Goodwin, the Harvard-educated intellectual and holdover from the Kennedy days. Goodwin wrote the address in a few frantic hours with no time for it to be edited or posted to the teleprompters. The President read from typed pages on the dais as he said, "At times history and fate meet at a single time in a single place to shape a turning point in man's unending search for freedom. So it was at Lexington and Concord. So it was at Appomattox. So it was last week in Selma, Alabama." He spoke of the race problems in America and reached back to distinctly American language: *"All men are created equal—Government by consent of the governed—Give me liberty or give me death."* Some paragraphs later, the President added another, more recent phrase to the pantheon: "And we . . . *shall* . . . overcome." At Johnson's own suggestion, the speech included mention of his time teaching dirt-poor Mexican-American kids in a little town halfway between San Antonio and Laredo, and how he could feel "the pain of prejudice" in their eyes. He said that he did not want his presidency to be about empires, grandeur, or dominion, but about educating children, feeding the hungry, helping the poor, and extending the right to vote. "I want to be the president who helped end hatred among his fellow men . . . who helped to end war among the brothers of this earth."[19]

It was an amazing declaration. "He's got some guts," Bobby said to a friend afterward. Arthur Schlesinger observed in his journal that Johnson's "ability to transmute boldness into banality may be, in the short run, a source of strength." Bobby had a reputation for caution when it came to civil rights, which sometimes made him seem uncaring. He seemed to pay only lip service to the issue, such as his 1961 statement that America could elect a black president within a few decades. James Baldwin shook his head sadly. "You should have seen the laughter and scorn with which that was greeted in Harlem," the writer said in 1965.[20]

Yet Bobby's care was genuine—enough for him to ignore his advisers and take a seat on the Senate's District of Columbia committee. The Constitution gave Congress control over local government in the nation's capital, and the D.C. committee provided oversight. "Too many cooks . . ." Joe Dolan wrote of its morass of federal and local jurisdiction. But Washington was the only big city in the country with a Negro majority. Its problems mirrored many of those in New York. And the position allowed him to do more for Washington's black community. Bobby would often appear to be the only senator truly engaged on the issues in its hearings, dressing down a city commissioner for offering half-baked solutions. He asked why Washington was kept under the thumb of Congress, wondering aloud at an early committee hearing whether "home rule" was being held back for fear of a city run by Negroes. At a town meeting for D.C. residents on public education, Bobby told them that because their city was majority black, "there are many people who don't want progress made here."[21]

His care about the issue was hard for the average person to see, however, for as soon as Congress began its meetings and negotiations to draft a voting rights bill, Bobby took off on vacation. The Canadian government had named a mountain in the Yukon for his brother, and he intended to be the first one to climb it.

Even Bobby may have recognized how badly it looked to step away during such unrest. Just before he left, he agreed to an interview with the *Christian Science Monitor*'s Godfrey Sperling in Kennedy's Carlyle Hotel suite. As Sperling settled in, Bobby was dressing for the day, buttoning up his shirt and carrying his shoes, with shaving cream still behind his ear. Breakfast was carted in and Bobby defended his civil rights record between bites. He said he had fought for voting rights legislation "back in 1962 . . . but I couldn't stimulate interest." Soon, he would claim before a group in D.C., "If the clergy, for example, had exhibited the same interest in 1962 that they have this year, we'd have been able to pass that legislation and Selma wouldn't have happened."[22]

To Sperling, Bobby added, "[Alabama governor George] Wallace is right about the problem being as bad in the North as it is in the South." Bobby said that while the Civil Rights Act had outlawed racial discrimination in public places, the bigger problem of poverty had to be contended with. "This answer might frighten people," he said. "And I don't mean it that way. But I think we may well have other Selmas and Birminghams here in the North before we will be willing to take the corrective action that is necessary."[23]

Sperling asked Bobby about a recent, sensational crime that was grabbing headlines in New York City: a "black nationalist" teenager brutally stabbed a white teenager to death while passengers of their subway car looked on. Bobby replied, "I don't like to say this, but I'm afraid it is going to get worse before it gets better . . . The great problem is the lack of family life among the Negroes. So often there is this pattern: There is illegitimacy. Or if there is a father, he isn't the one who brings the paycheck home. He isn't the one who comes home in the evening and helps provide discipline. Often he lies around the house. The mother may not be there much of the time . . . Little wonder that our studies in Harlem schools show students losing ten points in their IQ between the third and sixth grade. Often there is no place for them to study at home, nothing to encourage them to move ahead in school."[24]

This was clearly an issue in D.C.'s crime problem, with the majority of troublemakers coming from broken homes. Poverty was another factor, since the District's "man-in-the-house" rule prevented families from getting welfare as long as the father lived at home, a rule that persisted at the insistence of West Virginia senator Robert Byrd. "If we are not going to provide adequate welfare services, an adequate education, recreation for young people, and employment opportunities, we aren't in any position to ask why there is rising crime in the city," Bobby said about Washington.[25]

THE CLIMB UP Mount Kennedy was rushed. Bobby originally planned to conquer what was then the tallest unclimbed peak in North America during the Yukon's summer climbing season, but a National Geographic Society member told him in early March that other teams were about to set out. If he wanted to make the summit first, he had better do it within the next two weeks.[26]

On his way out West, Bobby told reporters, "I've been practicing. I've been running up and down the stairs in my house, [yelling] 'Pull me up!'" Then he became serious. Standing in the New York airport bearing Jack's name, he said he had one intention. "I'm going because it's named for my brother . . . It's just this one. This is the mountain I am going to climb." Security was tight due to a phone call the FBI had received from a "weeping and hysterical woman" insisting two men with guns would threaten his life. On the plane to Juneau, Alaska, Bobby told reporters that his kids were excited, but not Ethel. "She's frightened."[27]

The newspapers made the 13,900-foot mountain sound incredibly dangerous. The Associated Press described "a sharp, granite spire sheathed with ice and snow and raked by gale-force winds at this time of year. Temperatures drop as low as 40 below zero." The *New York Times* likened the final four hundred feet to "climbing up the side of a triangle." The team included mountaineer Jim Whittaker, who had become the first American to summit Everest two years earlier. Asked if it was unusual to take a man who had "literally never climbed before" on such an expedition, Whittaker said, "Yes, it is, but Senator Kennedy is an unusual man."[28]

The papers offered daily updates on the ascent, even though few details were to be had. The radio transmitter at the base camp was out, so they were literally cut off from the world at the start. Reports included Bobby's position on the mountain—observed by flyovers from the *New York Times*—and preclimb information such as the weight of their packs or how they were snacking on fruit juice and nourishment bars with honey. The weather on the mountain was warming, the *Times* reporter on assignment in Whitehorse relayed, which added the danger of sliding snow. An avalanche had just occurred below the senator's position, with two smaller snow slides on the mountain as well.[29]

Later, Bobby and his teammates would reveal that the weather had been a concern at camp before they set out. The other climbers suggested waiting a day, but Bobby insisted they go. "I want to get there," he said.[30]

"We thought that we would have had to climb at the senator's pace," said twenty-six-year-old Barry Prather, the third member of Bobby's team and another athletic professional. "But we didn't. We climbed at a regular mountain climber's pace." A second three-person team with a photographer climbed behind, along with Sherpa guides, who earned seventy-five cents a day for their dangerous work. Bobby asked Whittaker why a man risked his life for such meager pay. For his son's education, Whittaker said.[31]

The trek was easy until the final ascent, when Bobby began to feel the mountain's toll. "The air was thinner and I had a continuous headache," he would write. "Soon, the very act of placing one foot in front of another required intense effort." He began counting out each hundred steps, or reciting a poem to distract himself.[32]

Then, about nine hundred feet from the summit, Whittaker heard a cry and felt a jerk on the long rope between him and Bobby. "I turned around and saw the senator up to his chest in the crevasse," Whittaker later told reporters. Bobby had plunged through ice, a hazard of the constantly shifting glaciers.

The fifty-foot rope attached to Whittaker had slowed Bobby just enough to pull his arms out to hold himself up. Whittaker drove an anchor into the snow and fastened the rope. Bobby braced himself and kicked his spikes up and into the ice and lifted himself out. It was a shock, but to be expected; the much heavier Prather fell through three times on the climb. Climbers either had to go around the crevasses or jump over them.

Bobby would write of his partners, "They had almost all been on difficult expeditions, with men who had been killed," yet they never "dwelt on the dangers of mountain climbing." Each man wore a PT-109 tie clip.[33]

They rested before the final five hundred feet. Bobby looked up. The mountain seemed to rise almost straight into the sky. He thought going any farther was impossible. "I turned around and started back," he said later. But before he could, Whittaker drove his ice ax into the snow and began pulling himself straight up. After thirty feet of strength and will driving him, he looked down at Bobby and commanded, "Now you climb."[34]

After a few minutes of only a rope and some tools between him and thousand-foot drops, Bobby was overcome by the thought "What am I doing here? *What am I doing here?*" Filled with dread and doubt, he looked at his surroundings. The Pacific Ocean spread out to the southwest. Giant mountains filled the horizon. His only choices were to fall, turn back, or continue. So he did. The incline decreased for the last hundred feet, and Bobby removed his hat while the other climbers hung back to let him go ahead and take the summit alone.[35]

He reached the top, dropped to his knees, and drove a flag into the ground, black with the Kennedy family crest in white. The clear weather left him with a view for miles and miles. Bobby would write that at that moment he felt "pain." Not the physical pain after a grueling climb, but rather "a feeling of pain that the events of sixteen months and two days before had made it necessary." He would also remember feeling relief and exhilaration and gratitude in recounting his journey. But the pain was the emotion he recalled first.[36]

A little more than a day later, Bobby reached a hotel room in Seattle, stripped to his waist, and phoned Ethel before turning to reporters to share stories from the climb. The publicity was tremendous. "Bobby Kennedy conquers mountain" appeared on the front pages of the *New York Times*, *Boston Globe*, the *Los Angeles Times*, and the *Chicago Tribune*, among many others, often accompanied by a wire photo shot from the plane making passes overhead. The climb was featured on ABC's *Wide World of Sports* less than three weeks later, in a segment narrated by Bobby himself. It coincided with the publication of his account in *Life* magazine, featuring color photos by the cameraman in the trailing team. Bobby donated the payment for the article to the education of the Sherpa guides' children, garnering another round of positive stories.[37]

Later, Fred Dutton would write a memo suggesting Bobby make "one major, exciting personal adventure or activity" every six months. "So much of your support in the country is non-political, non-ideological. You need to allow dramatic insights into your own life and interests occasionally, especially for the younger people for whom you are almost a personal model." Dutton wrote that Bobby's "verve and vitality" would stand "in contrast to the dull middle aged tone that President Johnson and Hubert have hanging like a pall over the country." He proposed spending a week on a kibbutz—a rural Jewish settlement in Israel—or an archaeological expedition in Peru or a "non-shooting" safari in Africa with the boys. Bobby passed Dutton's memo on to Joe Dolan with a note: "As usual . . . he has some good points."[38]

Bobby knew how to deflect criticism of his attention seeking. *Times* editorialist William Shannon observed that Bobby was "sophisticated enough to know that others may poke fun at his own heroics, so he beats them to the punch and does it first."[39] The *Life* article had its share of self-deprecating jokes and displays of humility, but it didn't mean he was beyond barbs.

Bobby had stepped away at a grave time. During his return from the mountain, another protestor was killed near Selma. Viola Liuzzo, a white housewife and mother of five from Michigan, was gunned down while shuttling demonstrators from Selma to Montgomery.[40] As Bobby was getting back into his freshman duties that April, he presided over the chamber while Maine's veteran Republican senator Margaret Chase Smith held the floor. Her speech mentioned a famous Mainer getting a mountain named after him. "I would like to go to Alaska to climb that mountain," Smith said. "But official Senate business does not permit time out to be absent. We have important matters, like the civil rights bill before us."

An observer saw Bobby wince slightly.[41]

WHILE BOBBY WAS on the front pages, his staff had been hard at work on the voting rights bill. Peter joined a bipartisan staffers' drafting group in a basement room of the Old Senate Office Building, where they worked over the weekend debating the bill's sections. Most of it centered on the triggering mechanism: defining official voting rights violations that would spring the federal government into action. From time to time, the phone would ring with Attorney General Katzenbach or one of the Justice Department lawyers writing the administration bill on the line. The person would ask what the staffers' draft had to say on a topic, and Edelman later recalled the "embarrassed silence" on the other end before the person thanked them and hung up. The staffers could tell that the administration's bill was getting stronger and stronger through hearing what the Senate liberals had in store.

Only there were limits to what the administration and the Senate leaders could add for fear of sinking the bill. The most prominent piece belonged to Ted Kennedy, with his amendment to ban the poll tax—monetary charges for voting—at the state and local levels. Katzenbach claimed it threatened the entire bill with a constitutional challenge. Mansfield and Dirksen added a compromise measure to prompt a fast court test on the constitutionality of state poll taxes, but Ted stood fast on principle and insisted on registering a floor vote. "I never thought Teddy would have the guts to buck Lyndon," a senior senator anonymously told the *Boston Globe*. "We felt he was too soft to try anything like this." He went down fighting on a 45–49 vote, winning praise from his colleagues on both sides of the issue. However, some questioned whether Bobby's support for his brother's measure was part of a larger political ploy. The *New York Times* soon wrote that "gallery observers" thought Bobby voted with Teddy against leadership to get to the left of Vice President Humphrey, "the man with whom he might contest the Democratic Presidential nomination in 1972." In truth, Bobby had actually served as an intermediary between Teddy and the White House on the amendment. Katzenbach assured RFK that the administration had the votes to defeat it, and that if it was good for Teddy, they might as well submit it.[42]

Bobby successfully tacked his own amendment to the bill, outlawing a literacy-test requirement that largely affected Puerto Rican New Yorkers. Despite his cosponsoring it with Senator Javits, a Republican, it, too, was considered for its political impact: enfranchising three hundred thousand Puerto Ricans to potentially defeat the telegenic liberal Republican John Lindsay in the 1965 New York City mayoral race.[43]

Within months, the voting rights bill became the Voting Rights Act, enshrined alongside other landmark laws. Johnson's landslide had changed the political terrain. "A crazy time," Adam Walinsky later described it. "I mean, we were going to reshape American society, all of us! There was a new bill every day."[44]

Newspapers told of how Johnson broke the congressional stalemate under JFK's presidency with his "special attention" to members, evidenced by the autographed color eight-by-ten photos going up in offices all over Capitol Hill. Kennedy had courted Congress, the *Wall Street Journal* wrote, "but Mr. Johnson goes at it harder, day and night, weekday and weekend." Kennedy friend Charles Bartlett wrote, "The President's energy and talents are causing his program to move through Congress with startling ease." Another, Arthur Krock of the *Times*, praised LBJ's "driving pace" and personal courting of members—"the warm handclasp, the whispered 'secret.'"[45]

Bobby was one of those on Capitol Hill who supported the President's domestic programs in the Eighty-Ninth Congress. But privately he and other

Kennedy hands deeply resented how the press fawned over Johnson's abilities while denigrating JFK's. Arthur Schlesinger would write that it was simply "arithmetic"—larger margins in Congress—that made LBJ superior. Schlesinger even imagined how if roles had been reversed, with Johnson assassinated and Kennedy defeating Goldwater in a landslide, "then Kennedy would have had those extra votes in the House of Representatives, and the pundits of the press would have contrasted his cool management of Congress with the frenetic and bumbling efforts of his predecessor."[46] But not all of Johnson's decisions were being heralded as genius.

"WHY MUST WE take this painful road?" President Johnson asked in his April 7, 1965, address on Vietnam. The speech, before a live and applauding audience at Baltimore's Johns Hopkins University, was broadcast nationally to tell Americans why he had escalated hostilities so dramatically—a fivefold increase in bombing and landing the first of thousands of combat troops. Johnson had campaigned and won on "no wider war," and he said these actions would keep that promise, since the other option—"to abandon this small and brave nation to its enemies"—would only lead the United States to return in greater numbers.

"The central lesson of our time is that the appetite of aggression is never satisfied. To withdraw from one battlefield means only to prepare for the next."

After two months of expanded bombing and troop deployments, Johnson said, "We do this to increase the confidence of the brave people of South Vietnam . . . and we do this to convince the leaders of North Vietnam—and all who seek to share their conquest—of a very simple fact: we will not be defeated." The auditorium broke into twenty-two seconds of applause, broadcast coast to coast.

Yet the audience also applauded when Johnson extended his hand for negotiations. He said the United States stood ready for "unconditional discussions" to reach "a peaceful settlement" based on an independent South Vietnam. He looked beyond the days of war, speaking of an aid program to Southeast Asia that even North Vietnam might participate in. "This generation of the world must choose," Johnson said. "Destroy or build? . . . Kill or aid? . . . Hate or understand?"[47]

Bobby didn't watch the speech, but he was often hearing from his constituents on Vietnam. A one-week sample in early March 1965 showed 319 letters for a negotiated settlement, 119 for withdrawal, and 40 for fighting. The staff was still formulating a response.[48]

Two weeks passed from Johnson's speech with no sign of improvement, just more bloodshed. At a meeting of the National Security Council on April 21,

Secretary of Defense McNamara estimated that the North would not move toward a political settlement for at least another six months, if not a year. CIA director John McCone agreed, telling the President that the Communists saw the war turning in their favor. McNamara suggested the bombing shift its focus: from pressuring the North into a negotiated settlement toward a heavier campaign against infiltration of the South. In other words, wider war.[49]

The next day was a busy one for Bobby. He spent part of it presiding over the Senate as debate began on the voting rights bill. In the afternoon, he attended a ceremony naming the flower garden on the east side of the White House for Jacqueline Kennedy. And then in the evening, he met privately with President Johnson in the small room off the Oval Office for an hour and thirty-six minutes. In a newspaper account of the meeting, Bobby was said to have again expressed his reservation over the direction in Vietnam, finding too much emphasis on military solutions and too little on the political and diplomatic aspects. He stressed that the White House needed to make it plain to Saigon: the U.S. was not staying and would not fight their war for them. According to Johnson, Bobby had two propositions for him that evening: fire Dean Rusk as secretary of state and replace him with the youthful White House aide Bill Moyers, which made Johnson wonder "if there was something wrong with his thinking processes"; and halting the bombing of North Vietnam. A bombing pause could be a sign of goodwill, Bobby argued.[50]

"I told him that we had been considering a pause for some time and were giving the matter careful study," Johnson recalled in his 1971 memoir. "[Bobby] suggested that we try it for a few days, even one or two. A brief pause would do no harm, he said, and maybe something useful would come out of it. I repeated that we had been discussing such a move and he could rest assured it was receiving very serious consideration."

Privately, Johnson feared a bombing pause would make the United States look desperate for a settlement. "I was also worried that a pause might afford Hanoi a military advantage," Johnson wrote in line with the advice he was receiving at the time, "making it easier to send more troops and supplies into the South." Bombing, Johnson felt, would show "our determination."[51]

It was a poor time to test the President's will. Within days, Johnson ordered an invasion in the Caribbean and asked for hundreds of millions more to fund the fighting in Vietnam.

AMONG JOHNSON'S EARLIEST affronts to JFK's legacy in Bobby's eyes came in his December 1963 restoration of Thomas C. Mann to assistant secretary for Latin American affairs, upending the Kennedy White House's approach to the region. President Kennedy had sought to prevent more Communist revolts like Fidel Castro's and increase partnership with southern neighbors through the Organization of American States. Its centerpiece was the Alliance for Progress, with benchmarks for economic growth, so "every American republic will be the master of its own revolution."[52]

Mann's approach was completely different. "I think in the Latin American mind, one who talks about 'revolution' is understood to be saying that he favors violence in the streets and disorders," the career diplomat would privately say. "I thought we should favor orderly evolution and be careful of what we said and orient our program so that that would be made clear." Mann's was an old worldview—a "Tex-Mex" lens of the hemisphere that Johnson shared. He "not only didn't have charisma," a White House speechwriter later said, "he didn't believe in it." Averell Harriman had threatened to resign when Mann was brought back to the State Department in late 1963, and by 1965, Mann had replaced Harriman as undersecretary for economic development, the third most powerful job at Foggy Bottom.[53]

President Johnson leaned on Mann's counsel on April 24, when leftist rebels in the Dominican Republic mounted an attack to overthrow the ruling triumvirate and restore power to Juan Bosch, the country's first democratically elected president. Bosch had been deposed within a few months of taking office and was living in exile in Puerto Rico. When the rebels in Santo Domingo gained the upper hand, he told the world he was ready to return.[54]

Lyndon Johnson knew Bosch—LBJ had attended his inauguration in February 1963 on behalf of the Kennedy administration. Johnson shared the popular assessment of him as a persuasive speaker with limited knowledge who was incapable of governing. In a recorded telephone conversation with Mann, the President fretted over what the new situation would portend. "We are going to have to really set up that government down there, run it, and stabilize it some way or another. This Bosch is no good. I was down there."[55]

As the fighting intensified and the rebels armed civilians with submachine guns, the United States announced plans to evacuate American nationals who wished to leave. Reports said hundreds were dying in the fighting. Supporters of the fallen government got behind a military junta to preserve the old order.[56] Johnson had to choose which government he wished to "stabilize": the established authoritarians, or the popular revolt whose outcome was unknown.

His advisers stacked the deck. Tom Mann cared little for what the people wanted. He told the President that Bosch failed to understand "the Communist danger" among the rebels who would return him to power. "We do not think he is a Communist but what we are afraid of is that if he gets back in, he will have so many of them around him; and they are so much smarter than he is, that before you know it, they'd begin to take over."[57]

Hours later, the military junta telephoned the American embassy requesting the U.S. military's presence "to help restore peace." U.S. ambassador Tap Bennett relayed the junta's message claiming that the rebels were Communists, engaged in "mass assassinations, sackings of private property," and seeking to "convert this country into another Cuba." The President's national security team in Washington asked that the request be rephrased to emphasize the threat to American lives and "not refer to the communist angle."[58]

President Johnson gave the order, and helicopters carrying 405 U.S. marines landed in Santo Domingo. After a meeting with congressional leaders where the CIA director explained that Communists were leading the revolt, Johnson announced his decision to the American people in a brief televised address and then proceeded to a party for his daughter's senior prom.[59] Johnson had acted without consulting the Organization of American States.

"I am not willing to let this island go to Castro," the President told a White House Cabinet Room meeting. The Organization of American States, he said, "is a phantom—they are taking a siesta while this is on fire." Yet world opinion worried him, and he ordered the officials to manage the damage to America's image: "I want [the United States] to feverishly try to cloak this with legitimacy."[60]

Johnson followed up by sending another thousand Marines and twenty-five hundred paratroopers, with the Joint Chiefs chairman instructing their commanding officer: "Your announced mission is to save U.S. lives. Your unannounced mission is to prevent the Dominican Republic from going Communist." Amid heavy fighting and the first American casualties, more troops deployed—over six thousand within four days.[61]

Johnson went before the nation once again, this time with a longer, more determined answer to why he had acted unilaterally. He spoke of the ambassador's cable about the threat to American lives—the subject Washington had suggested emphasizing. Johnson said the message meant, "If you do not send forces immediately, men and women—Americans and those of other lands— will die in the streets . . . I knew there was no time to talk, to consult, or to delay."

Johnson concluded by invoking the infamous words of deposed Soviet premier Nikita Khrushchev, whom JFK squared off against in the Cuban missile crisis.

"We do not want . . ."—Johnson paused—"to *bury* anyone, as I have said so many times before.

"But we do not intend to be buried."[62]

Inside of a month, more than twenty-one thousand U.S. troops had landed in country.[63]

*   *   *

THE U.S. INTERVENTION helped radicalize the opposition in the Dominican Republic. Within days, the *New York Times*' correspondent found, "There are many observers, including foreign diplomats here, who believe that while the U.S. exaggerated the Communist influence at the outset of the revolution, it may have pushed a great many people into the arms of the Communists because it gave the rebels no alternatives." The Communists could sit back and watch "the rebellion become increasingly nationalistic and anti-American."[64]

This was the price of unilateralism. A price LBJ seemed perfectly willing to pay.

"We don't propose to sit here in our rocking chair with our hands folded and let the Communists set up any government in the western hemisphere," he said in defense of his deployment in the Dominican Republic. Republican House minority leader Gerald Ford said the reference to a rocking chair was a dig at JFK, who famously used one to soothe his back, for his unwillingness to escalate at the Bay of Pigs and deploy American troops to overthrow Castro. Bobby stayed silent, and Kennedy partisans privately fumed. Dick Goodwin believed Johnson's sidestepping allies in the region "would be seen as a return to the worst days of gunboat diplomacy." Arthur Schlesinger penned a gloomy memo about the risks of intervention.[65]

Johnson continued to display his prowess, attending a union event at the AFL-CIO headquarters that he originally turned down once they sent a telegram supporting his decisions in Vietnam and the Dominican Republic.

"We are not the interveners in the Dominican Republic," he said, but rather the defenders of freedom. "They actually thought pressure on an American president would get so great that he'd pull out of Vietnam . . . *They don't know the President of the United States.* He's not pulling out." Johnson then recalled a passage he memorized for a recitation contest as a child: "I have seen the glories of art and architecture, and mountain and river. I have seen the sunset on the Jungfrau, and the full moon rise over Mont Blanc. But the fairest vision on which these eyes ever looked was the flag of my country in a foreign land."

Bobby's speechwriter Adam Walinsky heard this rhetoric and was particularly chilled by the line about the "flag in a foreign land." How much worse it would have been if he had known: Johnson lost that grade school contest.[66]

"THE IMPRESSION IN Washington," the *Los Angeles Times*' bureau chief wrote of President Johnson on May 2, "is that he is encouraged to take forthright action abroad because he is riding so high politically at home."[67]

Early on the afternoon of May 4, LBJ sent a special message to Congress asking for an expedited $700 million to fund the growing war in Vietnam—bringing the year's spending to $1.7 billion. Johnson said it was the only way to start negotiations.

"They think they are winning and they have won and why should they sit down and give us something and settle with us?" Johnson told a news conference. "I have searched high and wide—and I am a reasonable good cowboy—and I can't even rope anybody and bring them in who is willing to talk and settle this by negotiation."[68]

But the funding vote was an unnecessary request. "He did not have to go to Congress at this time for the $700 million," read the lead story in the *Washington Post*. "As he explained in a talk in the East Room of the White House, he already had the authority to use monies appropriated earlier for the Defense Department for 1965.

"The Chief Executive wanted to give Congress another chance to demonstrate to the world . . . that it is with him all the way in Southeast Asia."[69]

This was the final straw for Bobby's silence. He understood the decision in Vietnam ultimately rested with the President. He had even once advocated an intervention in the Dominican Republic.[70] But Johnson was shirking responsibility—seeking to make Congress equally as complicit for any missteps. Bobby later told a reporter that had the President not forced Congress to quickly take the plunge into drastic escalation on short notice, he would have said nothing. Bobby would vote yes, but he would have his say first. He revisited the ideas in the Vietnam speech he abandoned in February, working off a new draft by Arthur Schlesinger.[71]

Bobby's junior staffers offered their thoughts, too. Walinsky was dismayed by Johnson's "no prettier sight than an American flag in a foreign land" attitude, finding the words "terribly, terribly revealing and very scary to me."[72] He put together a memo "in our not-very-informed judgment" on behalf of himself, Peter Edelman, and another aide, Wendell Pigman. Walinsky wrote that the vote was "close to a declaration of war, a declaration that covers North Vietnam and China by implication . . . A silent vote in favor is a flat endorsement of every major aspect of [Johnson's] policy—commitment of ground troops, continued bombings, and whatever else may be used to increase pressure in future."

From Walinsky's point of view, America's relations with the world had "shifted radically in the last year" under Johnson, to "a foreign policy based on force, a reliance on military pressure almost to the complete exclusion of political solutions, and a simplistic equation of revolution with communist conspiracy." And now, "with almost no serious debate," the President was asking Congress "to confirm that shift, and to surrender any right of stopping the present course.

"Though all of us feel somewhat silly trying to tell you what to do in this area, we do feel that the debate is necessary. And it will be a more constructive and meaningful one if you take part . . ."[73]

Walinsky was insecure about offering the senator foreign-policy advice. A short time earlier, the two legislative assistants tried to arrange for a State Department briefing on the situation in Vietnam. When Bobby found out, he told them that if there were going to be any briefings on Vietnam, "I'll do them."

"Not 'I'll *get* them,'" Walinsky later recalled, "but 'I'll *do* them.'"[74]

Neither Walinsky nor Edelman had a hand in the final draft of Bobby's speech. Schlesinger and Burke Marshall, who remained one of Bobby's all-purpose advisers, were in the office with him before the speech early that afternoon.[75]

Bobby appeared in the chamber to packed galleries but an almost empty floor.[76] Two Democrats, Mississippi conservative John Stennis and Oregon liberal Wayne Morse, yielded him thirteen minutes for his statement.

In a display of deference to his senior colleague, Bobby quoted Stennis from the day before. Bobby said that while he was voting for the resolution, "It is not a blank check."

He spoke against both withdrawal and escalation, saying to leave would be "a repudiation of commitments undertaken and confirmed by three administrations"—his brother's included. "We cannot hope to win a victory over Hanoi by such remote and antiseptic means as sending bombers off aircraft carriers.

"The course of enlarging the war would mean the commitment to Vietnam of hundreds of thousands of American troops. It would tie our forces down in a terrain far more difficult than that of Korea, with lines of communication and supply far longer and more vulnerable." Worse, he said, it would bring China and the Soviet Union closer together to aid another Communist regime and foment political instability at home. "It would lead to heavy pressure on our own government by thoughtless people for the use of nuclear weapons, and it might easily lead to nuclear warfare and the third world war.

"There remains a third course—and this, I take it, is the policy of the administration, the policy we are endorsing today. This is the course of honorable negotiation . . . President Johnson has expressed our American desire for honorable negotiations. So far there has been no satisfactory response. It seems that North Vietnam thinks it will win anyway and therefore sees no point in negotiation," Bobby said, acknowledging Johnson's core rationale. "This is the reason and the necessity, as I understand it, for the military action of our government." But seeking a settlement was still necessary.

"I believe that we have erred for some time in regarding Vietnam as purely a military problem when in its essential aspects it is also a political and diplomatic problem. I would wish, for example, that the request for appropriations today had made provision for programs to better the lives of the people of South Vietnam"—what President Johnson had spoken of in his Johns Hopkins speech.

Turning to the Dominican Republic and the President's bypassing the Organization of American States, Bobby said, "Of course, unilateral action is easier than collective action; but we are much stronger when we act in concert with the rest of the hemisphere than when we act alone; and consultation is the price we must pay for the extra strength our alliances give us.

"I note some tendency to criticize the OAS. The OAS has its imperfections, of course . . . but one way to make it stronger is to use it."

Bobby also stood up for the non-Communist democrats in Santo Domingo fighting for their vote. "Our determination to stop Communist revolution in the hemisphere must not be construed as opposition to popular uprisings against injustice and oppression.

"Mr. President," he said addressing the well, "our objective must surely be not to drive the genuine democrats in the Dominican revolution into association with the Communists by blanket characterizations and condemnation of their revolution . . ."[77]

"HIS REMARKS WERE so measured," Mary McGrory wrote, "that as many auditors thought he had spoken for the administration as against."[78]

The *Washington Post*'s correspondent wrote that Bobby's speech "seemed to sum up the dominant mood of the Senate," in reference to the "blank check" some feared they were signing over to Johnson.[79]

Sign it over they did. Eighty-eight senators gave Johnson their symbolic votes, with another 408 representatives in the House. Only three Senate Democrats—Wayne Morse of Oregon, Ernest Gruening of Alaska, and Gaylord Nelson of Wisconsin—stood in opposition. Gruening said LBJ was dragging Congress around "like a dog on a leash," while Morse predicted the President would soon send "thousands of more troops in Vietnam."[80] However, what Bobby said to the *New York Times* the day after his speech would receive far more attention.

"I don't think we addressed ourselves to the implications of what we did in the Dominican Republic," he told veteran Washington correspondent John D. Morris. "I think there should have been consultation prior to any action we would take," and that if speed was vital, the Organization of American States could have passed a resolution supporting the marines' deployment in the time it took them to reach Santo Domingo.

Morris, who covered the Kennedy administration, asked Bobby if the Organization of American States had been consulted before supporting the band of troops landing at the Bay of Pigs to overthrow Castro in Cuba.

"No," Bobby replied. "I don't think we handled the Bay of Pigs very well."[81]

"Kennedy Critical of Johnson Move" was the front-page headline in the *Times*, and it didn't stop there. Newspapers across the country picked up on the interview as fresh news of rivalry. The worst of all was another paper in New York.

Ted Knap, a reporter at the *New York World-Telegram and Sun*, called Edelman and asked, "Is the senator saying that President Kennedy would have done it differently?"

Edelman hadn't worked on the speech and honestly couldn't tell. "Gee, I don't know, Ted. If you read that in there, then I suppose it's in there," he said.[82]

The next day—under the headline "What Would JFK Have Done?"—Knap prominently cited a "reliable source" confirming, "It is the privately expressed opinion of the Senator that his brother, President John F. Kennedy, would have acted differently."[83]

"The senator was just livid," Edelman later said. He owned up to being Knap's source, but insisted he had been misquoted. He tried to explain: "I don't think it's fair because *this* is what I said—"

But in that moment, Bobby rolled his eyes heavenward. "How do we know what he would have done? *He isn't with us anymore.*"[84]

Unnamed "informants" familiar with Bobby's thinking sought to repair the damage through young *Boston Globe* reporter Andy Glass, who wrote that while Kennedy recognized the newsworthiness of his comments, "The senator is distressed, however, that the name of his brother . . . has been injected into the issue. He has never speculated, either privately or publicly, over what course of action President Kennedy might have taken in the revolt-torn Dominican Republic."

Glass revealed details about Bobby's private meeting with Johnson on Vietnam in April, how the senator stressed political reforms over military pressure, and that the United States could not fight their war for the Vietnamese. RFK had only gone public with his thoughts because he was voting *with* the President. "If I voted for it without saying anything," Glass quoted Bobby, "it would have appeared that I approved of it—which I didn't."

According to the article, leaders from the Latin American left had reached out to Bobby to express their concern about the President's labeling the Dominican revolt Communist and his acting unilaterally. So Bobby included in his speech: "Our determination to stop Communist revolutions in the hemisphere must not be construed as opposition to popular uprisings against

injustice and oppression just because the targets of such popular uprisings"—
including dictators—"say they are Communist-inspired or Communist-led
or even because known Communists take part in them." Bobby added, "It is
not a question of intervening or not intervening, but rather of doing it legally
or doing it illegally."[85]

Try as Bobby might, JFK's ghost remained in the debate. The editor of the
Atlanta Constitution wrote how President Kennedy reacted to 1961's failed
Bay of Pigs landing by hitting his hand against the lectern and saying unilateral action was "contrary to our traditions and to our international obligations. But let the record show that our restraint is not inexhaustible . . . Should
that time ever come, we do not intend to be lectured on intervention by those
whose character was stamped for all time on the bloody streets of Budapest"—
a reference to Soviets crushing an uprising of Hungarian students in 1956.

President Johnson, the editor concluded, "must have been startled to find
the lecture coming from President Kennedy's brother."[86]

Another columnist, James Wechsler, read the Bay of Pigs experience
differently. He wrote that the Kennedys seriously vetted so-called "authorita-
tive" intelligence reports since "their hands had been burned by such 'hot'
documents" in Cuba.[87] It appeared Johnson had never learned such a lesson.

The effect of Bobby's criticism on LBJ seems to have been minimal. And
having just received overwhelming support, the President was ready to take
Bobby's suggestion—at least for the moment.

On May 12, he suspended the raids above North Vietnam. Through Canadian intermediaries, Washington told Hanoi that bombings were suspended
for an indefinite period. The pause lasted six days and succeeded only in
proving Johnson right. The North had no interest in negotiations.[88] And
though several people contributed to the decision, Johnson later referred to
this cessation of hostilities as "Bobby Kennedy's pause," explaining, "I was
anxious to have his cooperation, his support."[89]

Time would tell.

9

THE REVOLUTION NOW IN PROGRESS

June 1965–July 1965

ROBERT KENNEDY SPOKE IN ECHOES.

The sound of his voice echoed his brother's.

His opinions echoed his judgments.

His slightest disapproval of any presidential action echoed how his brother might have responded.

And the echo rang in Lyndon Johnson's ears.

John F. Kennedy was the phantom executive, looming over the administration. His foreign-policy deliberations near the end of his life offered no clear direction—no right or wrong answer. As President, Kennedy had lashed out at the Soviets at the Bay of Pigs on one hand, but trusted them in nuclear negotiations. He began the march into Vietnam, increasing the commitment from 948 military advisers to 16,000. Yet in his final two months, he began preparing their withdrawal, with a thousand to leave at the end of 1963 and the entire force to return home by December 1965. Within days of the assassination, Johnson amended the plan.[1]

Lyndon Johnson had battled for an administration of his own—free of the Kennedy factor in decision making and comparison. Despite his landslide victories in Congress and at the ballot box, foreign policy always came back to echoes of Jack Kennedy. Every action Johnson took was haunted by the thought begun, its sound bouncing from wall to wall, then disappearing in the air before it was complete.

But to many, Bobby *was* the echo—the finisher of the thought. And so everything Bobby said or did was vested with great importance. As Bobby wrote in December 1963, "What happens to the country, to the world, depends on what we do with what others have left us."[2] In echoing his brother, Bobby found the path to his own voice . . . to words that would define him for generations and be carved in stone at his gravesite.

On May 29, 1965, what would have been President Kennedy's forty-eighth birthday, Bobby went to Fort Bragg, North Carolina, to dedicate a facility for the Green Berets in JFK's name. In November 1963, some of the commandos had come up from Fort Bragg to form the honor guard at the funeral, and after the ceremony, one placed his lid beside the eternal flame. The impromptu tribute became a permanent memorial.[3] Bobby adopted it as well. "A green beret lies always on my desk," he told them.

Special Forces members from Fort Bragg had bled in Vietnam. Others had died. Bobby marked their courage in a speech. "You fight what President Kennedy called, 'another type of war—new in its intensity, ancient in its origin—war by guerrillas, subversives, insurgents, assassins, war by ambush instead of by combat; by infiltration instead of aggression, seeking victory by eroding and exhausting the enemy instead of engaging him.'"

It was, Bobby said, "the struggle of the coming decades. It is not like other wars."

"We cannot win with mere military force," he told these decorated veterans of combat, "for guns cannot fill empty stomachs, napalm cannot cure the sick, and bombs cannot teach a child to read." Bobby said that their objective was to "build on hope—the hope that we, the wealthy and comfortable and educated part of the world, will meet our obligations to those less fortunate than we are; the hope that we will stand, not for the status quo, but for progress; and the hope that we work, in these far-off places, not just to preserve our advantages—but to ensure that these advantages are spread to all men everywhere.

"If we do this," he continued, "if in Vietnam and elsewhere, we fulfill the hopes that your work must build on—if we, remembering our own revolutionary heritage, seize the chance to lead the world revolution now in progress, rather than trying to block its path—we need not fear for the future."[4]

"*The revolution now in progress.*" The idea was an echo of President Kennedy's inaugural, the words Bobby quoted in his December 1963 memorial foreword to *Profiles in Courage*: "We dare not forget today that we are the heirs of that first revolution."

"The Revolution Now in Progress" became the title of his address to college commencement ceremonies in Buffalo and Plattsburgh, New York. It was his statement on youth and the future, taking all of human history and comparing its plodding steps to the whirring pace of the 1960s.

"In hundreds of thousands of years—until a century ago—men increased the speed of their travel only by the difference between walking and riding a horse," he said at Buffalo State. Referring to the astronauts aboard NASA's Gemini IV, he spoke of astounding change. "As we sit at this ceremony, two brave men circle the earth."

But every change was not so easy to appreciate—especially not for "the dispossessed people" living in the most impoverished places on the planet. "For uncounted centuries, they have lived with hardship, with hunger and disease and fear. For the last four centuries, they have lived under the political, economic, and military domination of the West." But the relatively short burst of technological and democratic advancement had revealed the West's stunning prosperity to them.

"We have shown them that a better life is possible," Bobby said. "We have not done enough to make it a reality."

"A revolution is now in progress. It is a revolution for individual dignity . . . to bring hope to their children . . . for economic freedom . . . for social reform and political freedom, for internal justice and international independence." And it was a revolution with an unsettling twist.

"This revolution is directed against *us*—against the one third of the world that diets while others starve; against a nation that buys eight million new cars a year while most of the world goes without shoes . . ." The revolution was against the world that spent $100 billion on weapons that would destroy mankind if used while the rest of the globe could not get a fraction of that to keep its infrastructure in line with its growing population. But the revolution was also the United States' legacy.

"We ought to understand the legitimacy of these ideals," Bobby told them, "for they are only what our own forefathers sought. We ought to recognize their power—for they have sustained us throughout our history.

"The status quo, after all, seems comfortable," Bobby said to the graduates. "The established order seems safe. And the opponents of change too often call themselves our stoutest supporters—and hasten to brand *their* enemies as *our* enemies.

"We must, nevertheless, remember our revolutionary heritage. We must dare to remember what President Kennedy said we could not dare to forget—that we are the heirs of a revolution that lit the imagination of all those who seek a better life for themselves and their children . . ."

As the frontiers of human possibility expanded, faraway borders drew nearer. And therein lay the challenge, no less grand than those of the explorers who drew them. "You, college graduates, have an unparalleled opportunity—not to find a world, but to make one."[5]

Bobby also delivered an extended version of this speech at Queens College, nearly a year to the day after one of its students, Andrew Goodman, left for Mississippi to register Negro voters amid sweltering Southern resistance. Goodman's twenty-year-old body, beaten and shot, was later found in an earthen dam alongside those of two other civil rights workers.[6]

Bobby told Goodman's classmates that their sit-ins, their teach-ins, their civil liberties protests, and their marches on Washington were restoring the "essence of the American Revolution."

"So when Andy Goodman went from this college to Mississippi," Bobby said, "he was building freedom for all of us."

For Bobby demanded that the graduates take their educations with them when they went to protest. He insisted they know what was factual, what was fair, and what was civil. Protest, he said, was not their "toy."

"It is not helpful—it is not honest—to protest the war in Vietnam as if it were a simple and easy question, as if any moral man could reach only one conclusion. Vietnam admits no simple solution."[7]

THE VIETNAM QUAGMIRE was deepening with every hour.

The Johnson administration anticipated a major Vietcong offensive during the monsoon season—a swift shove to move America toward withdrawal. Johnson believed that if the United States showed resolve, the Vietnamese might come to the negotiating table.

Senators feared another doomed experiment, pitching more troops into the country only to be told even more were needed. They began to resent what was celebrated as LBJ's greatest strength—his cajoling. "The Senators do not complain that Mr. Johnson does not call them in," the *New York Times* wrote on June 6, 1965. "He is forever summoning them to the White House. But, they say, he does not consult, or even discuss, with them; he delivers lectures."

Johnson's successor as Senate majority leader, Mike Mansfield, publicly warned that rejecting criticism on Vietnam "in the name of national unity" could lead to "delusive weakness." One senator told the *Times* that LBJ suffered from "overbriefing and underconsultation."[8]

But there was no stopping it. "GIs Get Viet Nam Combat Role" was the banner headline on the *Washington Evening Star* on June 8. The paper's Saigon correspondent reported that "military strategists here appear to have resigned themselves to throwing tens of thousands of American soldiers into jungle combat with the Communist guerrillas this summer if the South Vietnamese army continues to suffer heavy losses." Bobby did not comment about the rapidly expanding American force level—approximately 53,500 by mid-June 1965.[9] He was too much in the press already that month.

New books about the Kennedy administration landed with loud thuds in Washington. The first was an earnest book by JFK's postmaster general, J. Edward Day, claiming that Bobby was "the chief political manager of the Kennedy administration"—"very much in charge" of doling out patronage. Day said that on political appointees, a White House staffer had ordered him, "All recommendations are to clear through the attorney general." The book said Bobby "passed on applicants for the top appointive positions" and would often telephone about lucrative property leases—the dirty dealings of politics that built his ruthless reputation.[10]

Only it paled in comparison with Theodore White's *The Making of the President: 1964*. Despite the title, its first excerpt centered on the 1960 campaign and Bobby's backstairs mission at the Democratic convention to drive Lyndon Johnson from his brother's ticket. This was White's second bite of the apple. *The Making of the President: 1960*, his chronicle of the Kennedy-Nixon race, offered a more staid version of Bobby's opposition to Johnson: a passing mention of a meeting Bobby and Kenneth O'Donnell had with some Johnson advisers about the objections some labor leaders had to LBJ as the running mate.[11] But an eyewitness, *Washington Post* editor Philip Graham, disagreed with White's original account and gave White what he had written down in July 1960. "If ever," Graham told him, "you want to write about it again, this is the way it was." Graham committed suicide in August 1963, never knowing if Johnson's story would ever be interesting again.

With Johnson now in charge, Graham's account was key to the making of President Lyndon Johnson. In late June 1965, the memo appeared alongside White's excerpt in *Life* magazine.

Graham wrote that Jack had offered Lyndon the vice presidency but was getting opposition from a strong liberal faction. Bobby had gone to the Johnson suite to pressure him to withdraw. There were tense moments between Bobby and the Speaker of the House, Sam Rayburn of Texas. The old bald bull spat curses in young Kennedy's direction and told him he couldn't speak for his brother on a matter this big. Bobby left the suite and returned again, still adamant that Johnson could not join the ticket.

Finally, Jack called and said it was settled—Lyndon was on the ticket. Graham told him, "Jack, Bobby is down here and is telling the Speaker and Lyndon that there is opposition and that Lyndon should withdraw."

"Oh," Jack said calmly, "that's all right; Bobby's been out of touch and doesn't know what's been happening." Graham put Johnson on the line, and after speaking with JFK, Lyndon handed the phone back to Graham.

"You'd better speak to Bobby," Graham said, and Bobby entered the room, "looking dead tired."

"Bobby," Graham said, "your brother wants to speak to you," thinking to himself it was "the silliest line in the whole play."

Graham left the room slowly enough to hear Bobby say, "Well, it's too late now," and slam down the receiver.[12]

A week later, White rolled out another excerpt, this one on Bobby's and Johnson's clashing accounts about their 1964 Oval Office meeting on the vice presidency. "In New White Book—Bobby Claims LBJ Didn't Tell Truth," ran the headline in the *Boston Globe*. "Bare Bobby Kennedy Spat with Johnson: Told Texan He Spoke Untruth," the *Chicago Tribune* said. Both men declined comment.[13]

AT THE SAME time, Bobby's political power was on the rise. Mayor Wagner had decided not to seek reelection in New York City, and Bobby was the clear inheritor of the state Democratic Party. He soon after installed the chairman of his choice: Binghamton mayor John Burns, who, columnist Drew Pearson wrote, "would be under the domination of Bobby's backstage henchman, Paul Corbin." And Bobby continued to curry liberal favor by working successfully with Jacob Javits, defending him when the *New Republic* suggested he barely helped with the Puerto Rican voting rights amendment. Bobby wrote a letter showing deference and respect to his senior colleague, whom he credited with the amendment's passage. He even supported other senior senators he locked horns with. Connecticut Democrat Tom Dodd made his displeasure with Bobby's critiques of LBJ's foreign policy known, yet Bobby assisted Dodd by testifying in support of his bill to eliminate mail-order rifles like the one used to kill President Kennedy. As Bobby entered the hearing room, Senator Dodd asked him to pose for photographers in front of a display board with the different types of rifles available by mail. Bobby shook his head no and kept walking, though he delivered powerful remarks denouncing the National Rifle Association's "massive publicity campaign" for having "distorted the facts" and placing "their own minimal inconvenience above the lives of many thousands of Americans who die each year as the victims of unrestricted traffic in firearms."[14]

Some, such as columnists Evans and Novak, saw bigger designs in the stars. They wrote that Hubert Humphrey scuffed his liberal credentials walking the administration line on the Dominican Republic and the poll tax amendment, benefitting Bobby.[15] Soon followed reports of a liberal "Kennedy bloc" forming in Congress. Senators Birch Bayh of Indiana and Joseph Tydings of Maryland, and Congressmen John Tunney of California and Teno Roncalio of Wyoming were "gunning to embarrass the Administration at every turn," the *Wall Street Journal*'s political correspondent wrote. Worried about a challenge, the White House was "straining to woo away such early John F. Kennedy supporters as Mayor Richard Daley of Chicago and Senator Abraham Ribicoff of Connecticut." The *Journal* admitted much of it was "highly exaggerated and premature" since Bobby and Teddy still needed the administration to pass legislation. "Even the more pugnacious Robert Kennedy seems to be leaning over backward to minimize public differences with the President and Vice President. Realizing that any criticisms he utters get far more attention than those by other Senators, and deeply conscious of the burdens of the Presidency, he has been showing marked restraint in his public comments."

The restraint was unique in a body of attention seekers. An anonymous Senate colleague told the paper, "Bobby has to start living his own life sometime, without always worrying how the press will interpret each remark."

The *Journal* wrote that his staff members seemed more aggrieved than their boss. "Robert Kennedy aides have shown signs of a Johnson persecution complex, convinced the President is always out to 'do in' the Senator. On occasion they have been known to alert reporters to an anti-Administration amendment coming up in committee or on the floor."[16]

Bobby was sensitive to the tension. He discouraged members of his staff from speaking poorly of the President, Adam Walinsky later said. "If you get used to talking about somebody as a bad guy or a booby at the dinner table," Walinsky recalled, "you're going to do it when you sit down and talk with reporters over lunch."[17]

There was only so much Bobby could do.

Perle Mesta was a Washington hostess who backed Johnson for the nomination in 1960, then switched to Richard Nixon in the general election. She was never once invited to the Kennedy White House, a brutal snub for someone of her social reputation. Mesta had scheduled an administration party for Mike Mansfield on June 25, the same night Teddy had a party for Bobby and Ethel's fifteenth wedding anniversary. Washington society had to choose.

Convertibles snarled traffic for blocks around the Edward Kennedys' Georgetown home. The party had ten senators, four ambassadors, two cabinet members, President Kennedy's mother, and some three hundred others, compared to Mesta's reserved, thirty-person dinner party.

Mansfield and his wife attended each, saying, "Things went swimmingly at both parties, and I hope that the mountain they tried to make out of this molehill will be allowed to sink into the sea." Wyoming senator Gale McGee stood outside Teddy's with a guest-counting reporter and yelled to Bobby on the porch, "Who's ahead, Perle or—" and clasped his hand over his mischievous mouth.[18]

Humphrey told the Associated Press that he wasn't concerned about the Kennedys rising up against the administration, noting his long-standing friendship with Ted. "I've never had the same friendship with Bobby that I've had with Ted, but this means nothing more than the fact that it's not been my privilege. I think he's demonstrating great qualities as a senator."[19]

Robert Healy of the *Boston Globe* wrote that Bob and Ted were not running against the White House, but leading instead. "They have picked up the support of a number of liberals in the Senate who have been leaderless since the day when Vice President Hubert H. Humphrey joined the administration team." Healy wrote that Bobby's chase of the vice presidency had made him all too aware of the power of being on Johnson's ticket in '68 for him to offer anything more than helpful criticisms.[20]

Criticism was the only thing Bobby had to offer on foreign policy. At one time, he had a direct line, assured that the Oval Office was listening. But as he had lamented to Murray Kempton in the winter of 1964, "What is different now and what makes me sad is that I see a problem . . . and I can't do anything about it . . . you can't just pick up the phone."[21] Other senators also groused to the *New York Times* that Johnson wasn't listening to them on Vietnam and world affairs, but nearly all of them had more seniority and influence over the legislative process than Bobby. And despite reports, Kennedy did not have a meaningful coalition in Washington, or operational control of his state Democratic Party.

What Bobby had was the ability to speak and be heard, which he had not used to its full potential. Adam Walinsky would later say that his memo on campaign promises contained nothing on foreign policy because all Bobby could do as a senator was get up on the floor and "blah blah."[22]

Only once he began doing it, his Senate office realized how much they could shape the world.

STILL FEEDING BOBBY ideas and advice, Fred Dutton sent a memo in May of 1965 suggesting he speak out for nuclear nonproliferation. The second anniversary was approaching of President Kennedy's landmark address at American University calling for diplomacy in the age of extinction-level weapons, where he had said, "Our most basic common link is that we all inhabit this small planet. We all breathe the same air. We all cherish our children's future. And we are all mortal."[23]

Dutton asked Bob to help the future by calling to the past. "I strongly urge you seize this moment and provide a striking, hopeful contrast to the military clanking and diplomatic grating of most of our present national efforts." Dutton urged him to go to American University as his brother had, where students would provide a "fresher, livelier backdrop," and "sustain what I believe should be an emphatically recurring theme of yours—talking to younger people about the future . . ." Dutton recommended that "the timing should be the day before the anniversary of President Kennedy's speech so that you will be in the papers that day and just ahead of others [who] will likely at least passingly note it, as President Johnson and Hubert."[24]

Bobby took the advice on the subject, but instead chose to make it his first "official" Senate floor speech later that June. Dutton was assigned to write it,

The nation stood still as millions watched Bobby and his family mourn, November 25, 1963.
UPI VIA GETTY IMAGES

Bobby photographed smiling for the first time since his brother's death as he watched his daughter, Kerry, play at the Justice Department Christmas party, December 20, 1963.
ASSOCIATED PRESS

Hundreds of students waited for Bobby in the rain at Japan's Waseda University where he had been booed and heckled two years prior, January 18, 1964. BETTMANN VIA GETTY IMAGES

President Johnson's chilly reception for Attorney General Kennedy after sending him to settle an international dispute amid vice presidential speculation, January 28, 1964. ASSOCIATED PRESS

In March 1965, Bobby became the first person to summit a 13,900-foot Yukon mountain named for his brother.
WILLIAM ALBERT ALLARD VIA GETTY IMAGES

DEMOCRATS
WRITE IN

ROBERT F.
KENNEDY
FOR
VICE PRESIDENT
BE SURE TO PUT AN X AFTER THE NAME
W. LaChance, Manchester, N. H., Fis. Agt.

CANDIDATE OF THE

DEMOCRATIC PARTY

FOR

VICE PRESIDENT

OF THE UNITED STATES

I HEREBY DECLARE MY PREFERENCE FOR CANDIDATE FOR THE OFFICE OF VICE PRESIDENT OF THE UNITED STATES TO BE AS FOLLOWS:

⟶ *Robert F. Kennedy*   **X**

Palm card from the 1964 New Hampshire Democrats' vice presidential write-in campaign.
WILLIAM DUNFEY PAPERS, JFK LIBRARY

Students stormed the ballroom in Scranton, Pennsylvania, at Bobby's first major speech after JFK's assassination, urging him to run for vice president, March 17, 1964.
THE LIFE PICTURE COLLECTION VIA GETTY IMAGES

Kennedy with his daughters Courtney and Kerry, sons Michael and David, and the children of President Kennedy in his lap at home in McLean, Virginia, June 1964. GEORGE SILK VIA GETTY IMAGES

Bobby wandered aimlessly alone along the foggy hospital grounds in Springfield, Massachusetts, hours after Ted Kennedy was nearly killed in a plane crash, June 20, 1964. BETTMANN VIA GETTY IMAGES

In Communist Poland, RFK left a trail of dents in car hoods after impromptu speeches to the hundreds of well-wishers who stopped his motorcade wherever he went. STANLEY TRETICK, PHOTOGRAPHER, LOOK MAGAZINE PHOTOGRAPH COLLECTION, LIBRARY OF CONGRESS, PRINTS & PHOTOGRAPHS DIVISION, [REPRODUCTION NUMBER E.G., LC-L9-60-8812, FRAME 8].

President Johnson handed RFK pens in a terse exchange at the Civil Rights Act signing after the fallout of Bobby's interview with Ben Bradlee about the vice presidency. FRANCIS MILLER VIA GETTY IMAGES

Bobby's eyes brimmed with tears as he waited for the ovation to end at the Democratic National Convention in Atlantic City, August 27, 1964.

At campaign stops across New York in the fall of 1964, Bobby began as a wooden speaker (top, in Coney Island) and was often pulled in by the surging crowds in New York City street rallies (bottom). BETTMANN VIA GETTY IMAGES

Tumbling atop a car in New Rochelle (top) and stumping amid a hostile crowd in his Republican opponent's hometown of Rochester (bottom). RFK's breakneck schedule around New York State often left him with torn clothes and swollen, bleeding hands.

5 CENTS
FINAL EDITION
● 1964 NEWSDAY, INC.

Newsday

LONG ISLAND
Wed., Oct. 28, 1964   Vol. 25, No. 47

THE GREAT DEBATE: RFK, KEN DON'T MEET

Shut Door, Empty Seat, Chase...

Story on Page 3

RUNNING DEBATE. The New York Senate race looked more like a 50-yard dash in CBS' Manhattan studio last night as the candidates did some fast maneuvering during time set aside for a debate that never came off. Democrat Robert Kennedy is barred, above, from a studio. At right, corridor where Republican Kenneth Keating made a hasty exit is blocked by a seat cushion (center) and smashed potted plants (foreground) dumped to slow down reporters. (Story, other photos on Page 3.)

UPI Telephoto

Newsday Photo by Morseman

Senator Kenneth Keating invited Bobby to debate but locked his opponent out of the studio and berated an empty chair. After the broadcast, Keating's aides flung props and a couch in the path of reporters chasing the senator through the hallway. COURTESY OF NEWSDAY

Bobby visited his brother Teddy, strapped to a Boston hospital bed for his broken back, on November 4, 1964, the day after they won six-year Senate terms from New York and Massachusetts. BETTMANN VIA GETTY IMAGES

RFK visited President Kennedy's grave at least twice on the day of President Johnson's 1965 inauguration. ASSOCIATED PRESS

Bobby, with Senate leadership and new members of the Eighty-Ninth Congress, entered ranked ninety-ninth out of one hundred senators in seniority. BETTMANN VIA GETTY IMAGES

Bobby's withering questioning of witnesses during Senate hearings drew headlines and sometimes produced results. Pictured here on the Veterans Affairs subcommittee in 1965. BETTMANN VIA GETTY IMAGES

JFK's stone likeness loomed over President Johnson and Defense Secretary Robert McNamara at a July 1965 meeting on Vietnam in the White House Cabinet Room. LBJ LIBRARY PHOTO BY YOICHI OKAMOTO

RFK voted as a New Yorker for the first time in the New York City mayoral primary, September 14, 1965, nearly a year after winning office. A Republican official challenged Bobby and Ethel's residency when they voted in the general election, requiring them to file affidavits.
ASSOCIATED PRESS

Before delivering the Day of Affirmation address on June 6, 1966, RFK visited Ian Robertson, a student leader persecuted by the South African government, and gave him a copy of *Profiles in Courage* signed by Jackie Kennedy. ASSOCIATED PRESS

Robert Kennedy looked to the sky with a smile in Capetown, South Africa, June 1966. ASSOCIATED PRESS

and the address was set for a Wednesday. Walinsky and Edelman got his version on the Friday before. The draft didn't work—Dutton knew the subject but was no speechwriter. "It's a disaster," Walinsky told the senator at the office cocktail party, suggesting a rewrite. It was typical of Adam and Peter, Ed Guthman would later write: "short on foreign policy experience but long on chutzpah."[25] Walinsky was assigned to come up with a new speech from scratch, and that's when it hit him: he had no idea what he was doing.

"I didn't know a damn thing about it. Absolutely nothing. A total blank."

He spent the weekend in the backyard of Averell Harriman's Georgetown home and Roswell Gilpatric's farmhouse on the Eastern Shore of Maryland for bull sessions with President Kennedy's top minds on disarmament, before heading back to Hickory Hill for edits. Walinsky brought his wife and two-year-old son with him to show Bobby and Gilpatric a draft at Washington's National Airport. Ethel, a carload of Kennedy kids, and their ridiculously large Newfoundland dog, Brumus, came, too, amusing Gilpatric, the former deputy defense secretary, as they "nearly succeeded in dismantling" the waiting area. Gilpatric had led Johnson's Task Force on Nuclear Proliferation, which months earlier turned in a report on the spread of nuclear arms to smaller countries. Their findings were labeled top secret and sealed even to members of the Senate.[26]

It was an especially hot day, and the subject matter was thicker than the air. Walinsky's son was fretting and crying until Bobby picked him up, sat him on his lap, and calmed him instantly. Gilpatric was impressed by Bobby's attention to detail despite the distractions, later recalling, "Bob's powers of concentration were unparalleled . . . Obviously he had thought out the whole complex subject of nonproliferation and knew precisely where he came out and what he wanted to get across."[27]

Once the final draft was completed, Walinsky sat down with McGeorge Bundy at the White House to clear the speech with the administration. There didn't appear to be any problems.[28] Only later did the extent of Gilpatric's input become controversial.

Bobby's official debut on the floor was well attended for a Senate speech. Vice President Humphrey was presiding over the chamber, and more than a dozen senators went to their desks to watch.[29] "I rise today to urge action on the most vital issue now facing this nation and the world," Bobby said. Vietnam and the Dominican Republic were being fought in the streets, while the true threat was assembling in laboratories and silos. He said that with a few years and a few million dollars, nuclear capability would fall into the hands of "small, remote countries"—even "private organizations"—and then there would be no shortage of ways to "stumble into catastrophe." Disaster could come in the form of "an unstable demagogue, or the head of one of the innumerable two-month governments that plague so many countries, or by an irresponsible military commander, or even by an individual pilot." In the hours after a bombing, the circle of suspicion would be too wide. Retaliation, inevitable.

Bobby said that President Kennedy had taken "the first step" with 1963's Nuclear Test Ban Treaty, and that President Johnson was as "deeply committed" to his journey toward peace. "But we have not yet taken the second step."

Thereafter, every word of Bobby's six-point proposal—fleshed out through the expertise of Johnson's Task Force on Nuclear Proliferation chairman— must have seared the President. For though Bobby said he was committed, he implied Johnson was not fulfilling the first promise he made as President: *to continue.*

Bobby's speech proposed a new treaty with the Soviet Union to stop the spread of nuclear weapons to more countries by creating "nuclear-free zones of the world," and expanding the test ban to underground detonations. He called for halting the arms race between the United States and Russia, given stockpiles "more than adequate to destroy all human life on this earth," and a mutual commitment to direct world militaries toward "nonnuclear forces," so that countries "need not choose between defeat and mutual annihilation." Bobby also said the efforts should include the "profoundly suspicious and hostile" Communist China, which the United States had broken ties with after its revolution in 1949. "China will have nuclear weapons," he said, without noting its two recent detonations. "And without her participation it will be infinitely more difficult, perhaps impossible in the long run, to prevent nuclear proliferation." Questioned by reporters after the speech, Bobby said he still opposed admitting China to the United Nations, but that negotiations were possible.[30]

Bobby yielded the floor to Majority Leader Mansfield, who praised the speech and JFK's work on the issue. Fifteen other senators rose to congratulate Bobby and reflect on the speech's content, including Republicans Aiken of Vermont and Cooper of Kentucky, along with Democrats Moss of Utah, Church of Idaho, Pell of Rhode Island, Gruening of Alaska, Hart of Michigan, Tydings of Maryland, and Harris of Oklahoma. Senator Javits chimed in with unusually positive comments, saying Bobby had "stuck his neck out" and done a good job.

Senator Clinton Anderson, Democrat of New Mexico and chair of the Joint Committee on Atomic Energy, wondered if Senator Kennedy might do something about getting the Gilpatric Report released to members. Gale McGee of Wyoming started a colloquy about who had the most to gain from nuclear regulation, and Bobby talked about some of the obstacles. "People will say, 'There is nothing that we can do about this because we are involved in a war in Vietnam.'"

Senator George McGovern agreed that the Vietnam conflict could not be allowed to divert necessary attention and heralded the address "as the most significant speech that has been made on the floor of the Senate this session."

John Pastore of Rhode Island, the Senate's most vocal advocate for nuclear arms control, endorsed Bobby's urgency, describing the detonation effects of a twenty-megaton bomb, and said, "God bless you for making this speech today. It was time someone whose name is recognized over this country and around this world talked about this."[31]

After, reporters asked Bobby if he thought his brother's nonproliferation policy was being neglected.

"No," he said. "But I think we need a fresh initiative." Pressed on Senator Anderson's question about why Gilpatric's task-force report hadn't been released, Bobby replied, "You better ask the executive department."[32]

Walking over to the congressional gymnasium later that afternoon, Bobby felt good about the speech. He told Walinsky there would need to be a second one on nonproliferation. There was more to say about the Chinese bomb.[33]

THE NEXT MORNING Walinsky woke to a ringing phone.

It was the senator. "You seen the paper?" Bobby said. "What is this?"

"I don't understand," Walinsky replied. The *Washington Post* had put the speech in a small item on page A7 and called it an imitation of Johnson administration policy.

"Is that true?" Bobby asked. "Is this just a rehash of administration proposals? I didn't think that's what it was."

"I don't think so either, Senator," Walinsky reassured him. "I don't think that's what we were doing, and I don't think that's what it was about."

"Well, what are we going to do about this?" Bobby sounded uncharacteristically upset.

Walinsky asked what the *New York Times* was saying. Bobby didn't know—it hadn't arrived yet. The papers came earlier at Walinsky's place on Capitol Hill than they did out in McLean. "Wait a minute," Walinsky said, "They just delivered it downstairs. Let me go down and see." He put down the receiver and went to the door. The speech was covered on the front page with a two-column headline, "Kennedy Proposes Treaty to Check Nuclear Spread." Inside, there was another column about "the emergence of the brothers Kennedy as powerfully independent figures within the Democratic Party," along with a showcase of the full text—extraordinary attention for a maiden speech.

Bobby was satisfied. "All right. Well, that's okay," he said. "So that's just the

Washington Post. They're just screwing around with Johnson. The hell with them." He hung up.[34]

Bobby probably hadn't even gotten through the *Post*'s story when he called Walinsky, for its write-up of the speech was in fact laudatory, and the message received. His words "left the impression that the Administration was moving too slowly on the issue," the *Post*'s report said. The *Times*' Tom Wicker wrote that the speech "left strong implication that Mr. Johnson was not doing as much as he might in this field—or as much as President Kennedy had planned to do," but also that it "probably would have caused little stir if it had been delivered by any number of other Democratic Senators—even considering its remarks on Communist China."[35]

The White House was forced to explain its foot-dragging. Its comment, in the words of the *Times*, was "short and chilly." Press secretary George Reedy said, "Of course we are glad Senator Kennedy is also interested in this field," and noted that it was President Johnson—and by implication, *not* President Kennedy—who had appointed the special task force. Reedy said the State and Defense departments, as well as the Atomic Energy Commission, were reviewing the findings, which were still highly classified.[36]

The President was livid. Bobby had just used the expertise and information from the task force Johnson commissioned before he could use it himself. He was most stung by *Times* columnist Scotty Reston, who wrote that LBJ was a neglectful "soaker," who required bathing in information before solving a problem. "He has been devoting most of his energies to the Vietnam and Dominican affairs—and to the critics of his policies in these two places," Reston wrote. "Thus, the nuclear problem has not had the attention it deserves, and therefore Senator Kennedy raised the question."[37]

Johnson had, however, been planning a major address on curbing nuclear weapons for the anniversary of the United Nations. A draft was completed in May. He had even put his Kennedy speechwriter, Dick Goodwin, on it. Johnson's address was scheduled for Friday, June 25. Bobby had delivered his on Wednesday the twenty-third.

On Thursday, July 24, Johnson called Goodwin into his office. "I want you to take out anything about the atom in that speech. I don't want one word in there that looks like I'm copying Bobby Kennedy."

Goodwin tried to save his draft. "But Mr. President," he said, "the Kennedy speech is very different from yours, and it's only his opinion. These are formal proposals from the President of the United States. The entire world will be listening."

Johnson picked up a copy of the *Times*. "Here's Reston's column on Kennedy's speech. You make sure we don't say anything that he says Bobby said. I'm not going to do it." The speech was gutted. It would be a year and a half before President Johnson made another move toward halting the nuclear arms race, and he would never achieve one. The task force he commissioned would not receive even a passing mention in his memoirs.[38] Bobby's speech had effectively erased it.

Stories soon emerged of how Johnson "angrily rewrote his recent UN speech," and of Bobby's ruthless attack on the White House with the potential use of classified information. Washington columnist Drew Pearson claimed Bobby refused the President's entreaty through Averell Harriman not to deliver his speech before his United Nations address. Pearson wrote that Bobby had allegedly told another emissary he would defer only if the President personally asked.[39]

"That's pure horseshit," Walinsky would later say, remembering that even Harriman said Johnson wasn't moving fast enough during their pre-speech meetings. And the stories didn't even take into account that Walinsky had gone to the White House and sat in the basement office of McGeorge Bundy to clear it.[40]

Joseph Alsop tweaked the President's nose for his "habit of constantly ordering ferocious 'security' investigations"—the latest "now in progress because of alleged leaks to Senator Robert Kennedy of the quite ordinary information" in his speech. Richard Wilson wrote in the *Los Angeles Times*, "If he is irritated because government officials feed both the press and to Senator Robert F. Kennedy the same ideas for speeches they are feeding to him then this is another example of Mr. Johnson's self-centered mania." The *Christian Science Monitor* wrote of the President's "extraordinary sensitivity to criticism and an almost obsessive determination to keep matters in his own hands," even when he was still incredibly popular—70 percent approval in the polls. "He has a quirk of personality which forces him to magnify minor affronts, thus overshadowing major achievements," Robert E. Thompson wrote in the *Boston Globe*, adding that his "peevish attitude . . . added prestige to Kennedy's words."[41]

The *New York Times* editorial board, which often saw ruthlessness behind Bobby's acts, praised his recent foreign-policy speeches. "It is possible to read narrow political concerns into Senator Kennedy's remarks, but this interpretation can be overdone. His observations flow naturally out of his experience in the Cabinet and as a close adviser to his brother . . . The nation and the Administration can benefit from this kind of informed criticism."[42]

Bobby joined Ethel out west for a family rafting trip down the Yampa and Green rivers in Colorado and Utah, where the children carried "dinosaur-hunting licenses" through the area where the animals once roamed. The trip's progress made daily news, with photos of Bobby shooting treacherous rapids solo in a fifteen-foot kayak. The papers noted that it was his first time. He was a natural in rough waters.[43]

THIS AS AMERICAN military planes hit North Vietnamese targets only eighty miles from the Chinese border, and Vietcong agents set off bombs just five hundred yards from the U.S. embassy in Saigon, immediately killing twenty-nine. Radio Hanoi announced the execution of a captive American army sergeant in retaliation for the South's public execution of V.C. prisoners. The State Department condemned the "wanton act of murder" and said it was considering freeing the other nineteen captured servicemen by force. "Losses on both sides have been heavy," Secretary Dean Rusk said in a speech, noting the thousands of Vietnamese and one hundred Americans killed in three months. "We must expect these losses to continue—and our own losses may increase."[44]

The United States was breaking into all-out war. Seventy-five thousand troops were in country, having quadrupled in just one year. "Military experts anticipate heavy battles," the *New York Times* reported, "perhaps even 'set pieces' of conventional warfare that the Communists so far have avoided."[45]

Bobby always believed the war would be unconventional—the new kind of conflict he spoke of at Fort Bragg. He had raised concerns before, but did not feel the urgency until that summer to make his mark. With even his antagonists at the *Times* editorial board having recently called his words on foreign policy helpful, there was no better time.

On the day of the Senate nuclear speech, Joe Dolan sent Bobby a memo that the State Department wanted him to address the International Police Academy graduation on July 9. The program sought to professionalize security forces in the developing world and had 147 students from twenty-two countries, many from Latin America and 4 from Vietnam, training in operations against guerrilla tactics and Communist infiltration—"counterinsurgency," Dolan told Bobby.[46]

It was a last-minute assignment, and Bobby wanted a draft based off his speech at Caltech the year before. It had discussed the United States' troubling support for "tyrannical and unpopular regimes that had no following and no future . . . colonial rulers, cruel dictators, or ruling cliques void of social purpose." It said that "guerrilla warfare and terrorism arise from the conditions of a desperate people" that "cannot be put down by force alone." The speech continued, "Over the years, an understanding of what America really stands for is going to count far more than missiles, aircraft carriers and supersonic bombers."[47]

Walinsky's draft took that sentiment and turned it into a biting critique of America's unblinking support for South Vietnam.

"Victory in a revolutionary war is won not by escalation, but by de-escalation," the draft said. And: "If all a government can promise its people, in response to insurgent activity, is ten years of napalm and heavy artillery, it will not be a government for long."[48] Bobby was forecasting the fall of Saigon.

Bobby signed off on these bold, blunt words. They may well have been his. In the run-up to the speech, he and Walinsky discussed America's efforts in the developing world to work its will on smaller countries. The senator believed that no amount of aid or military pressure could overcome what the people wanted. They would get the government they desired, one way or another. What the United States had to do was resist the temptation to answer terrorist violence with more violence, to reward people-oriented governments, and steer the bad ones in the right direction.[49]

"In conventional war," the speech said, "the aim is to kill the enemy. But the essence of successful counterinsurgency is not to kill, but to bring the insurgent back into national life."[50]

An advanced copy of the text was released to the press late in the afternoon the day before Bobby was to give it. News of his latest foreign-policy jeremiad quickly reached the White House. A reporter messengered a copy to Sherwin Markman, a young lawyer and assistant to top Johnson aide Marvin Watson. Markman gave it to Watson, who took it to the President. Johnson said they should try to get Bobby "to back off."

"Do you really want me to take that chance?" Markman asked Watson. "What if Kennedy tells the press that the White House tried to pressure him? Won't we be putting ourselves into his hands if he decides to say that? Or, if he does change his speech, how is he going to explain himself without involving us?"

"See to it that we don't get blamed for anything" was Watson's parting advice.

So Markman headed over to suite 1205 in New Senate Office Building early that evening and introduced himself. Bobby was still in, and Walinsky and Edelman joined them in the senator's office. Markman argued to change the speech with the strongest appeal he could think of: pleading to Bobby's loyalty.

The International Police Academy was operated by the Agency for International Development, and its director, David Bell, would be introducing Bobby. "David was an old friend of President Kennedy," Markman said to the senator. "Your brother brought him into the office he now holds and his agency is deeply involved in Vietnam."

"So what?" replied Walinsky, wary of a Johnson man invoking JFK.

"I don't think the senator wants to embarrass David Bell."

Bobby listened. He and Bell had served on President Kennedy's counterinsurgency group on these very issues. They had worked closely together, week in and week out.[51]

"Perhaps you have a point," Bobby said. After all, the advance copy had already put his thoughts out there. "Adam here writes a pretty firebranding speech. Maybe it does go a little too far." They began a line-by-line reading. Markman made objections and Walinsky and Edelman argued against deletions. Bobby listened until he had to go to Hickory Hill for dinner guests, leaving them to debate. When he returned around midnight, they had reached a compromise, deleting the most offensive portions about de-escalation and napalm, and adding language that approved military measures in difficult situations like Vietnam. It was neither an endorsement nor condemnation of the administration policy.

Markman was still worried how Bobby would explain the changes to the press. "What are you going to tell them?"

"That the advance text they received was merely a draft. It was delivered to them too early and by mistake. I had not cleared it. It is not what I intended to say and it is not what I said. The only words that count are the ones I say. Won't that do it?"

"Almost," Markman said, asking what Bobby would say if reporters brought up pressure from the White House.

"Then I will lie," Bobby said, laughing.[52]

The next morning, he delivered the speech in an old streetcar barn at Thirty-sixth and M streets in northwest Washington.[53]

"In the 1960s, it should not be necessary to repeat," he said, "that the great struggle of the coming decades is one for the hearts and minds of men. But too often, of late, we have heard instead the language of gadgets—of force ratios and oil blots, techniques and technology—of bombs or grenades which explode with special violence, of guns which shoot around corners, of new uses for helicopters and special vehicles." But popular support was not won through "superior force."

"Guns and bombs cannot build—cannot fill empty stomachs or educate children, cannot build homes or heal the sick. But these are the ends for which men establish and obey governments; they will give their allegiance only to governments which meet these needs."[54]

"It is sometimes said the political methods are ineffective against terrorists," he said toward the end, citing the thousands of local officials the Vietcong had murdered. "Without question, terror is an effective and important weapon for the enemy. But even the use of terror is sometimes limited by political considerations—and can be sharply limited by political action . . . No matter what assistance they receive from outside . . . insurgents stand or fall in their political success. Without popular support, they become conventional invaders—and can be dealt with by conventional means.

"I think the history of the last twenty years demonstrates beyond doubt that our approach to revolutionary war must be political—political first, political last, political always."[55]

In the added section on Vietnam, Bobby said, "We must realize that Vietnam has become more and more an open military conflict . . . in which military action on our part is essential just to allow the government to act politically.

"What I say today is in the hope that the lessons of the last twenty years will be applied in other places—so that we are able to win these wars before they reach the stage of all-out military conflict now apparent in South Vietnam." He concluded, "We can all do better."[56]

As Bobby stepped off the stage, reporters surrounded him. "Why did you change your speech?" was the first question.

"I didn't change a thing. I said what I intended to say." Bobby told them that the release of the text had produced phone calls, though he would not say from whom, and he decided on rewrites to avoid "confusion."[57]

The "official explanation," the *Times* wrote, was that Bobby heard reporters were taking the advance text as evidence that he was breaking from Johnson's foreign policy. The *Baltimore Sun* would label the speech changes "radical." The *Boston Globe* wrote that they "seemed to alter the focus from an attack on the President's politics to what could be interpreted as an endorsement of them." Joseph Alsop would write that Bobby's changes to his speech "were no doubt primarily motivated by his sense that his brother would never have been willing to accept a catastrophic defeat in Southeast Asia."[58]

The reporters continued to press Bobby on what the United States should do next in Vietnam. He told them he would not presently halt the bombing. He had no alternatives to the President's policy or, at least, was unwilling to voice them. "We are in a very difficult situation," he said, "and I expect it will get worse before it gets better."[59]

At the White House, smoke trailed from the thin cigar between Bill Moyers's fingers as he calmly told reporters that what Senator Kennedy said in his speech was not much different "from what we have said."[60]

"We expect that it will get worse before it gets better," Johnson said a few hours later, using the same words Bobby did, at his press conference to announce Henry Cabot Lodge was returning to South Vietnam as ambassador. Bobby's friend and counterinsurgency adherent Maxwell Taylor had finished a year of service and promised his wife a calmer retirement than Saigon. But the change also coincided with a rapid expansion in the war effort. Johnson added, "Our manpower needs there are increasing and will continue to do so."[61]

Bobby's statement on the transition praised Taylor but did not mention Lodge. The choice was the President's, he said, and he would vote to confirm the nomination. Asked if Lodge was the "most effective" choice, Bobby demurred. "That has to be decided."[62]

Sherwin Markman had attended Bobby's speech and sidled his way into the press conference to make sure all went as planned. He returned to the White House optimistic about the future. When they had first learned about the contents of the speech, Marvin Watson had predicted to President Johnson in a memo that Vietnam "will be another Kennedy vs. Johnson issue." But as Watson and Markman enthusiastically reported Bobby's cooperation to the President, he remained unimpressed.

"It's only temporary," Johnson said. "Bobby intends to cause me as much trouble as he can. Count on that."[63]

DAYS LATER, *LIFE* magazine began its serialization of Arthur Schlesinger's forthcoming book, *A Thousand Days*—excerpting the portion in which Bobby tried to remove Johnson as the vice presidential nominee.

The Kennedy court historian began with JFK privately mocking LBJ as "the riverboat gambler" while at the 1960 Democratic convention, and saying that he only discussed the vice presidency with him "because he thought it imperative to restore relations with the Senate leader."[64]

"I didn't offer the vice presidency to him," Kennedy said in Schlesinger's account. "I just held it out like this and he grabbed at it." Schlesinger wrote that Kennedy told aides, "You just won't believe it. He wants it!" Though party liberals expressed grave misgivings about Johnson as vice president and said there might be resistance on the convention floor, JFK confirmed LBJ as his choice, reading him the prepared text of the announcement over the phone. But before the announcement was made, Bobby went to the Johnson suite to see if—given the objections—LBJ might step aside. The Texan wouldn't budge.

That Bobby had resisted Johnson's selection was long accepted as fact. But a damning detail from the Kennedys' inner circle made it all the worse. Schlesinger wrote that when the selection was announced, Bobby put his head against a wall and said to the last man in the room, Johnson adviser James Rowe, "My God, this wouldn't have happened except that we were all too tired last night." In Bobby's eyes, Lyndon Johnson's vice presidency was illegitimate—a product of sleep deprivation.[65]

Bobby declined to comment to the *Times* about the aspects of the story, except to say he did not remember saying those words, and if he had, it didn't mean he was referring to the selection of Johnson. Though it did not appear in the *Life* excerpt, Schlesinger's book would include the caveat that when Bobby said "this" wouldn't have happened, he was "referring not to the candidate but to the confusion."[66]

"There was no disagreement between President Kennedy and myself on this matter," Bobby told the press in a blanket statement. "If you accept the relationship between myself and my brother, you know that I would not have tried to undo a decision that had been made." The only thing further he would say was that he had recorded his recollection of his meetings with Johnson on the vice presidency, and according to the *New York Times*, it "would not be released for publication anytime soon."[67] Unknown to readers, Bobby recorded those recollections with Arthur Schlesinger. The version in *A Thousand Days* was more or less Bobby's, with the exception of the sensational quote. According to him, JFK did not expect Johnson to accept their offer. "We both promised each other that we'd never tell what happened," Bobby told Schlesinger, but he admitted that after going back and forth for hours, "we decided by about two o'clock that we'd try to get him out of there and not have him." So when Bobby released his cryptic statement of "no disagreement" between JFK and himself, he was really confirming that he was acting on his brother's behalf. Neither of them wanted Johnson to be vice president.

The White House was publicly cool to the matter. "The President hasn't seen *Life* magazine, so obviously I can't comment on it," a press assistant said.[68]

Privately, between the books and the speeches, the President and his aides felt Bobby was wielding the past like a knife. White House counsel Harry McPherson sent a memo to the President that month about the wall coming up between the Kennedy and the Johnson sides, and how they would be poorer in the public's perception for it. "There was a mystique about the Kennedy staff," McPherson wrote, "that it was a free-swinging, free-spirited collection of brilliant and independent intellects; each man became a personality, and oh what a good time they had running the government. On the other hand, we are rather bright, nice young men who lost our independence of mind the day we signed on. It wasn't true about the Kennedy staff, and it's not true about us, but it is a myth that dies hard."[69]

McPherson encouraged tolerance toward Bobby Kennedy, whatever they believed he might be conspiring toward. "You have the office, the policies, the personal magnetism, the power to lead and inspire, and above all the power to put good ideas into effect," McPherson wrote. Johnson would hear none of it, and just glared at Bobby and his allies for trying to turn him into an accident of history.[70]

"I don't see anything to be gained by that," the President soon said to reporters about arguing with historians like Schlesinger and White. "I don't know just how much these men may know about what actually happened, but they are entitled to their opinions . . . Of course, I know why I did what I did," he said. "The President asked me on his own motion to go on the ticket with him, and I gave him my reasons for hesitating. He told me he would speak to Speaker Rayburn and others, and he did."[71]

McPherson was wise to advise Johnson against a battle of perceptions, for the White House would never win. They were making hard choices—governing—while Bobby was showing glimpses of what might have been. In the yet-unpublished words of William Manchester—whose book on the transition of power would also spark controversy—the President was contending with a man who "looked like, sounded like, and thought like the slain leader . . . It was as though Edwin Stanton had been Abraham Lincoln's twin."[72]

Bobby made token offers of support to LBJ at this time. Speaking at a Democratic fund-raiser in Wisconsin that summer, he said President Kennedy "knew" Lyndon Johnson was committed to the Kennedy domestic agenda, and "that he shared their dreams, that he was the best man to carry on this fight."[73]

But the comparisons and the mythmaking showed no signs of letting up—something even loyal JFK aides recognized. The *Washington Post*'s Ward Just counted nine Kennedy aides with books in the works. "They are building Jack Kennedy into a legend ten feet tall," said Larry O'Brien, who was lining up a book himself. "No one will recognize either the pedestal or the man when they get through."[74]

Columnist James Wechsler, who was close with Arthur Schlesinger, wrote that life would be easier for Bobby if these books weren't coming out. And yet, "he is profoundly concerned about his brother's place in history and hardly disposed to resist this kind of thoughtful immortalization. Beyond that one suspects he believes there are large lessons to be derived from even the cruelly brief tenure." Specifically, Wechsler wrote that Bobby wanted to apply Jack's lessons to Vietnam.[75]

Many of Bobby's foreign-policy speeches echoed Jack's thinking, his quotes. Utilizing the rhetoric of President Kennedy came naturally to him. Walinsky and Edelman kept books of JFK's speeches and statements handy when preparing Bobby's. It was the natural thing to do: his life and beliefs had been so intertwined with his brother's. Marguerite Higgins's column said, "intentionally or not, the tone" of Bobby's foreign-policy speeches "suggested that if the Kennedys had still been in power, they would have done things better." Roscoe Drummond wrote, "He has given no speeches helping the President. He has given a whole series of speeches critical of the President," with barbs that were "limited and slanting, not head-on."[76]

Nor was Johnson eager to publicly engage Bobby on these matters. In an interview with *Newsweek*, LBJ downplayed his differences with the senator, saying his critics were sending the wrong message. "The Communists think we've lost. They think they can run us out. I've tried thirteen peace offensives to get them to talk, but no." He invoked commitments from Presidents Eisenhower and Kennedy, saying, "We cannot just get out," and had one word for American success in Vietnam. "Power. Power on land, power in the air, power wherever it's necessary." So on a summer day in July, he told the nation he was increasing the American troop commitment by fifty thousand—a total of 125,000 in the combat zone—and doubling the monthly draft call to meet the demand. High-level sources told the *New York Times* that continuing the war without a troop increase would have resulted in a "dangerous deterioration of the military situation." Victory seemed plausible. Alongside the 500,000-man South Vietnamese military, the Americans would take on a North Vietnamese fighting force estimated at 165,000.[77]

This was what truly mattered: the power to make war that Johnson possessed, and which Bobby could only offer opinions on. But to some, Bobby's words held meaning beyond what could be measured in the daily back-and-forth of politics. Halfway around the world, a group of young people locked in a revolution against a racist regime heard Robert Kennedy's call for progress, reform, and freedom for all. On July 12, the National Union of South African Students moved to invite Bobby to speak before their annual affirmation of human rights in the spring of 1966. One of their leaders would say the request grew out of his representation of "the younger generation of political leaders and the new ideas of youth."[78] In short, they invited him not to honor his brother or to unveil a monument; but to speak for himself.

10

SLOW BOIL

August 1965–November 1965

THE NIGHT PRESIDENT JOHNSON vaulted U.S. troop levels in Vietnam over 125,000, an hourly poll taken by a marketing company and shared with journalists measured the response of the American public. The first hour registered 54 percent support of the administration's Vietnam policy. Twenty-four percent disagreed and 22 percent replied, "Don't know." But by the final hour, support dipped seven points to 47 percent. "Don't know" had suddenly doubled to 43 percent.[1]

Johnson was especially sensitive to polls and their findings. In an interview soon after with *Newsweek*, he produced two thick booklets of polling and proudly chided the press on how wrong they had been to criticize his decisions abroad. "The polls on Vietnam run about eighty to twenty in favor of what we're doing," he declared. In his mind, the public wasn't the problem; it was the other end of Pennsylvania Avenue. "Congress isn't eating out of my hand," the President said.[2]

Johnson's announcement included a request to Congress for an additional $1.7 billion for the war, but members were still bitter about being cornered into May's funding vote. "Some say privately they will never allow the President to get by with this trick again: he must fully demonstrate the need for any more war funds," the *Wall Street Journal* reported.[3]

The skeptical were tight-lipped on the issue. Supporters were brazen. "Several influential Democrats in Congress" noted to the *New York Times* "that the principal support for an increasing military commitment came from Republicans who were ardent followers of Barry Goldwater." South Carolina's Strom Thurmond said the United States had to go as far as possible to win the war, including "the tactical A-weapon" if necessary. "After all," he said, "they are coming into South Vietnam and cutting off ears of mayors and other officials. It may take something drastic to bring them to their senses and stop this war." However, Johnson could not fully enjoy his conservative support. Gerald Ford, leader of the House Republicans, endorsed the Vietnam policy while urging the President to cut back his domestic programs "to marshal the nation's strength for the military effort." Johnson responded to such criticism by saying he would not allow "this problem in Vietnam to lock the door of opportunity . . ."[4]

The Senate had outright Democratic critics of the policy, such as Wayne Morse of Oregon and Ernest Gruening of Alaska. But most of the skeptical spoke only in off-the-record interviews. These senators believed the bombing had failed, that Saigon was incapable of gaining popular support, and that more American troops meant taking over the fighting. If the United States was lucky, the war would end in partition like Korea, with an American occupying force needed to prop up the government. These silent senators were also said to question the "domino theory" that Vietnam's fall would lead to a wave of Communist takeovers—doubting Thurmond's prediction of Red China reaching "all the way to the shores of Hawaii." Yet they had no alternative to the President's course of action and understood the need for a united front while American men were fighting and dying. Many also feared being labeled weak on Communism. Still, a bipartisan handful led by the strident Senator Morse openly called for further Vietnam action to go before the United Nations Security Council.[5]

On August 9, the President held a briefing for senators to offer what he described as a balanced view of his Vietnam policy. It began with Maxwell Taylor delivering a report on the military, diplomatic, and political situations. Secretaries Rusk and McNamara, Under Secretary Harriman, and newly appointed UN ambassador Arthur Goldberg were all on hand for discussion. Johnson later appeared unexpectedly at Bill Moyers's press briefing. Asked if members of Congress were "disagreeing privately" with his policy, the President said, "I find that members of my party, and the other party, and people throughout the country frequently disagree with me on a good many things. I don't think it's private though."[6]

However, Bobby was not one of them. He attended the briefing and had nothing critical to say about the troop increase. Teddy took the lead on Vietnam, championing the budding refugee crisis amid the Vietcong's butchering of pro-Saigon villagers.[7]

Teddy spoke for both of them on Vietnam after Bobby's controversial foreign-policy speeches. Sitting in a high-backed chair in the Senate reception room, the youngest Kennedy brother told Robert Healy of the *Boston Globe*, "We support the President as much as any senator here."[8]

THE WAR WAS the slow boil of the summer, but Bobby's attention reached beyond Southeast Asia. After all, 83 more Americans had died in car wrecks over the Fourth of July weekend—553—than in five years of fighting in Vietnam. The rate of U.S. traffic deaths had climbed for a third straight year after a two-decade decline.

Bobby sat on the Senate subcommittee that asked the highly profitable auto industry why it invested so little in protecting its passengers. Executives claimed caution didn't sell. They said their new safety features led to a sales drop in 1956. Automaker AMC removed seat belts after customer complaints.[9] But Bobby believed the car industry would not cut into their profits to understand the problem, let alone spend what it took to reduce it.

Questioning three executives from General Motors, Bobby brought up a study from Cornell University about faulty doors and locks on GM vehicles that spilled passengers onto the pavement, turning fender benders into deadly collisions. The executives said they were unfamiliar with the Cornell report and needed more data to understand why their doors were more likely to fall off.

"What shocks me," Bobby said, "is that Cornell makes the information available, and here are three top officials of General Motors and they aren't even aware of it. It doesn't indicate a very high priority for traffic safety."[10]

He dug into their financial statistics, beginning with safety. "Tell me: How much money does General Motors spend on those matters?"

Board chairman Frederic Donner said they were *about* to spend a million dollars on a university-backed safety study.

"What have you spent so far?" Bobby asked.

Donner said, "We don't know, Senator, how to add all these things up."

The admission was stunning. Auto industry executives prided themselves on their data-driven decision making.

Bobby pounced. "You *don't*?"

Donner scrambled. "Because they are scattered all over," the chairman said. "I mean, research may do something in this activity—"

"General Motors doesn't know how to add them up?" Bobby said.

"—through AMA—what?"

Bobby repeated himself. "General Motors doesn't know how to add these matters up?"

"It isn't adding," Donner said. "It is dividing."

Bobby quickly reminded Donner that he was the one who used the word *add*. The rough estimate was $1.25 million. Bobby asked whether GM had any idea how many children had fallen out of their cars.

"Nobody knows that," said GM's president.

"I don't quite know how you would find that out," said GM's chairman.

"Nobody knows that answer," said GM's vice president for engineering.

Bobby moved on to the bottom line. "What was the profit of General Motors last year?" he asked.

GM president James Roche began, "I don't think that has anything to do—"

Bobby cut him off. "I would like to have that answer, if I may. I think I am entitled to know that figure. I think it has been published. You spent one and a quarter million, as I understand it, on this aspect of safety. I would like to know what the profit is."

Donner interjected, "The one aspect we are talking about is safety."

"What was the profit of General Motors last year?" Bobby repeated.

Chairman Donner snapped, "I will have to ask one of my associates."

"Seventeen hundred million dollars," President Roche offered.

Bobby: "What?"

Donner: "About one and a half billion dollars, I think."

Bobby: "One billion dollars?"

Donner: "Yes."

Bobby: "Or one point seven *billion* dollars. You made one point seven billion dollars last year?"

Donner said, "That is correct."

"And you spent one *million* dollars on this?"[11]

The *Washington Post* article in the next day's paper said Bobby dealt with the high-paid executives "as if he were examining a couple of youthful applicants for a driver's license who hadn't done their roadwork." The *Wall Street Journal*'s reporter wrote that the GM men's pleas of ignorance "were unconvincing, especially in view of Detroit's penchant for cranking out figures when they're more self-serving—the allegedly astronomical cost of switching to the metric system of measurement, for example, or the claimed investment in bringing out each new car model."[12]

The questioning got results. When Ford's chief executive came before the committee next, he was prepared with a lengthy statement addressing all of the senators' concerns. And within days of their Capitol Hill grillings, both Chrysler and GM released multimillion-dollar figures on their safety spending. Bobby's high-profile rebukes were prominent in the stories.[13]

As a senator, Bobby rushed headlong into challenging powerful interests, even when it was futile—such as in his battle with the tobacco industry. An alarming surgeon general's report publicly released in early 1964 found an inextricable link between smoking and a slew of fatal illnesses. Federal action seemed a given, so the boardrooms of the notoriously competitive "Big Six" tobacco companies banded together to stop it. Through a year and a half of negotiations, whenever regulation began to get any real teeth, their lawyers defanged it.[14] One of those lawyers was Robert Wald, a friend of Peter Edel-man's, who met with him for dinner one night and said how upset he was over his work. Wald wondered if Senator Kennedy could do something. Soon after, Bobby passed by Edelman's desk and his aide mentioned the cigarette lobby's runaround. Edelman casually suggested that they make a statement.

"That's fine," Bobby replied without hesitation.

"Well, you know," an astonished Edelman said, "don't you want to think about it a little, because you're taking on this big, all these big companies—"

"No, that's fine," Bobby said, as if he were ordering lunch. "I'm glad you mentioned that. We should do it."[15]

They were up against a well-funded lobby marshaled by Abe Fortas, close friend and adviser to President Johnson. Fortas assembled a coalition beyond the crop's Southern base to include farmers and manufacturers of all stripes, plus every broadcaster and publisher in the country—the recipients of $250 million a year in tobacco advertising. The Federal Trade Commission, regu-lator of deceptive practices, wanted health warnings in every cigarette bill-board, magazine ad, and broadcast commercial. Fortas's lobby had decided to give way and put labels—CAUTION: CIGARETTE SMOKING MAY BE HAZARDOUS TO YOUR HEALTH—on every pack. But not on the ads. The Senate Commerce Committee slapped a moratorium on the FTC's regulatory power to insert warnings in cigarette ads for at least three years. Senator Ross Bass of Tennessee said it would allow for "further research" before forcing a company to "contra-dict its [pro-smoking] views as shown in the advertising."

The fight went to the floor, with Bobby cosponsoring an amendment. In his speech, he spoke of studies showing that half of high school students were regular smokers by the time of graduation. "The alarming fact is that if present smoking habits continue, one million of the children who are today in school in our country will develop lung cancer," Kennedy said. "In Congress and around the nation, we have spent a great deal of time talking and debating about American boys dying in South Vietnam . . . yet our death toll in Vietnam so far is about four hundred." RFK found no scientific or medical reason justifying a lengthy moratorium.

Senator Bass, a fellow Democrat, challenged his colleague, the former attorney general. "The senator has much experience in the field which concerns the protection of the laws of the country," Bass said. "Does the senator know of any other item in the nation, in any area . . . in which, if the manufacturer advertises his commodity, he is required to make the affirmative statement 'We want you to buy our product, but if you use it, it might kill you?'"

Bobby began listing examples of medicines with FTC-mandated warning labels.

Bass interrupted sarcastically, "I appreciate the doctor giving me all of those statistics . . . If the senator from New York says we should ban the use of all tobacco products, that is his privilege."[16]

Bobby's amendment failed handily, and the final bill overwhelmingly passed against his and four other lonely nays—not even Teddy joined him this time.[17] Tobacco and money had won the day, and Abe Fortas would get a seat on the Supreme Court before the summer was out.

Bobby hated losing and hated it even more when people in politics wore "noble" losses like a badge of honor. He said that reform liberals preferred defeat because they were "in love with death . . . For an awful lot of them in this kind of group," he said privately, "action or success makes them suspicious, and they almost lose interest."[18]

Bobby had failed, but he was failing with a purpose. It was good politics for him to be a liberal warrior, as Stewart Alsop wrote in the *Saturday Evening Post*. "With Hubert Humphrey boxed in, Robert Kennedy is filling the resulting vacancy as leader of the liberal Democrats." That summer, he would vote to repeal the federal right-to-work law that hampered union membership, vocally oppose immunity for bankers in an antitrust suit, and fight a controversial measure to give Washington, D.C., police more leverage to extract confessions from suspects. While it was indeed good for him politically, these were battles Bobby cared about. In the case of cigarettes, he was so sincere that the writer Truman Capote would later find him outside their Manhattan apartment tower haranguing two youngsters he caught smoking "like some sort of avenging angel who had fallen out of heaven upon them."[19]

Yet his reputation left his sincerity forever in doubt. Stewart Alsop wrote, "Kennedy's critics in his own party have often expressed doubt that he is a 'real liberal' at all." Bobby agreed, saying he disliked the word *liberal* since nobody really knew what it meant. And he still refused to condemn Joseph McCarthy to Alsop because, Bobby said, "the man is dead, and I'm not going to do it."

"McCarthy was hated more by liberals than any other politician in modern times," Alsop wrote, "and yet the man who refuses to say bad things about him is becoming sort of a liberal lodestar."

"I hope I've learned something in the last ten years," Bobby told him.[20]

THE CHILDREN OF the city concerned Bobby. He had walked the broken concrete lots of New York City, littered with shards of glass and metal, and stained by exploded trash bags tossed from apartment windows high above. A federal program paid youths to convert these disasters into tiny parks. Alongside Senator Javits, Bobby was constantly announcing federal funds to fight poverty, introducing new projects and initiatives.[21]

A thousand people filled a block and hung out of brownstones in the Puerto Rican section of Harlem on August 12 to see him and Ethel take part in an induction ceremony for Volunteers in Service to America—a kind of domestic Peace Corps. The forty-three new VISTA workers would spend the next year on projects to help alleviate poverty in the community. Under floodlights, Bobby gave a short speech: "Your job is to help relieve poverty; to make the people dissatisfied with landlords and politicians—dissatisfied even with this United States senator." He was surprised to hear that there was no official swearing in, so he decided to make up an oath, telling the workers to raise their right hands and repeat after him, "I solemnly swear . . . that I will be faithful and true to the VISTA concept . . . and help my own and take care of my baby brothers and sisters . . . and vote for Robert Kennedy in 1970." After, he and Ethel wandered off into the crowd as hundreds of children moved in to touch him. They joked how they would love to get a game of stickball going. "You be Willie Mays," Bobby said to one child, "and you be [Orlando] Cepeda . . . And who will I be?" he wondered. "Well, I'll just be myself."[22]

He knew the smiling faces in the streets would return to homes stricken by poverty. "I have been in tenements in Harlem," Bobby had said in Chicago that April, "where the smell of rats was so strong that it was difficult to stay there for five minutes, and where children slept with lights turned on their feet to discourage attacks." He talked about crumbling homes, failing schools, and an infant-mortality rate in Bedford-Stuyvesant that was twice the rate in more affluent parts of the city. "Thousands marched for James Reeb"—the Boston minister clubbed to death in Alabama—"but who marches for our own dead children?"[23] No one would, until something got their attention.

That began in August, nearly as far as could be from Selma, in a poor Negro section of Los Angeles. The Watts neighborhood was demographically separated from much of the city: 93 percent black, four times as overcrowded, a fifth of its homes crumbling, lower incomes and higher crime. Then one night the drawn-out drunk-driving arrest of a black youth created a spectacle, turning into rumors and then a riot. The police pulled out and sealed the neighborhood off from the city, letting it burn. More than thirteen thousand National Guardsmen mobilized to regain control as the crisis spread over six days. Then followed an eruption in Chicago after an undermanned fire truck killed a black woman. In Springfield, Massachusetts, the arrest of civil rights demonstrators led to arsonists marauding through the streets.[24]

At least one California politician blamed Bobby for Watts in the immediate aftermath. Joe Shell, the former Republican leader in the state legislature, told the *New York Times*, "When Bobby Kennedy was attorney general, he said as long as people are mistreated, they are going to riot. This is no attitude for an attorney general to take. The moment we accept violation of law, we are giving open sesame to this kind of action."[25] More criticism was to come, especially once Bobby began sharing his thoughts. General Dwight Eisenhower said in a Capitol Hill news conference, "I believe the United States as a whole has been becoming atmosphered, you might say, in a policy of lawlessness. If we like a law, we obey it; if we don't, we are told, 'You can disobey it.'"

Bobby took on the former president in interviews. "There is no point in telling Negroes to obey the law," he told David Broder. "To many Negroes, the law is the enemy. In Harlem, in Bedford-Stuyvesant, it has almost always been used against him." The challenge was greater because it concerned pocketbooks, not ballots—housing, not drinking fountains. Securing rights in the South, he said, "was an easy job compared to what we face in the North."

"The only answer is massive relief with the real help going to the young," Bobby said, though Los Angeles already received millions in antipoverty funds—some of it locked up in political disputes. The *Herald Tribune*'s Andy Glass wrote that Bobby "acknowledged there would be ample stealing and graft in the programs. But, he added, people will just have to live with it and understand it." The next day's *Boston Globe* juxtaposed thirty-nine-year-old Bobby's and seventy-four-year-old Eisenhower's quotes in large type. They epitomized the coming generational and ideological divides of white major-party leadership in what some called the Negro Revolution.[26]

But Bobby also spoke of a geographic divide. The United States is "strangely insensitive to the problems of the Northern Negro," he said to a largely white civic group in a New York suburb later that week.

"In the last four years, the Negro has made great progress; and the Civil Rights Act of 1964 and the Voting Rights Act of 1965 are rightfully regarded as achievements of which we can all be proud. But as we are learning now, it is one thing to assure a man the legal right to eat in a restaurant; it is another thing to assure that he can earn the money to eat there . . ."

The Southern model was not applicable for Negroes in the North. "Civil rights leaders cannot, with sit-ins, change the fact that adults are illiterate. Marches do not create jobs for their children." And so, Northern slums were "places of blighted hopes and disappointment"—ignited by injustice to violence.

And while Bobby said many rioters were "simply hoodlums" and "only a small minority" of Negroes, he reminded his white audience of "the harsh fact" that "just saying 'Obey the law' is not going to work."

"The law to us is a friend, which preserves our property and our personal safety. But for the Negro, law means something different . . . The law does not fully protect their lives—their dignity—or encourage their hope and trust for the future."

Bobby noted how a *Time* magazine report said that one leader of the Los Angeles riots was a biochemistry graduate. "We should not be surprised," he said. "After all, we are very proud of the fact that we had a revolution and overthrew a government because we were taxed without representation. I think there is no doubt that if Washington or Jefferson or Adams were Negroes in a Northern city today, they would be in the forefront of the effort to change the conditions under which Negroes live in our society."[27]

The reaction to Bobby's diagnosis was profoundly negative. The *Christian Science Monitor* editorial board called his statements "deeply disturbing" and warned that it gave rioters "the impression that influential national figures look with sympathy upon their breaking of the law." The *Times*' Tom Wicker observed with irony that Bobby, whose name was "a cussword" in the South over civil rights, was now declaring Northern racial problems to be "more urgent." *Time* magazine included the statement with other "irresponsible postmortems," including that of a "husky [Negro] youth" who said, "Last time we weren't out to kill whites. Next time is going to be different."[28]

But in an interview in his office on September 3, Bobby stood by his radical words, calling Watts a "clear warning of what will happen in other cities, all across the nation, if we don't act quickly." He had vague ideas of what needed to be done, including that the solution needed to come from within the Negro community. He said that many blacks "who succeeded in climbing the ladder of education and well-being fail to extend a helping hand to their fellows on the rungs below. I think we white people must demand a lot of ourselves in the years ahead. We should demand as much from the many Negroes who already share the advantages of our affluent society." Meeting at Hickory Hill, he instructed his Senate staff to begin researching a program—a plan to attack conditions in the slums and redirect the energy of the Negro Revolution.[29]

Two years earlier, Bobby might have done things differently—tempered his rhetoric and found a compromise. It might have even achieved something. But he was a legislator now, and the swiftness of executive office was gone, as he told Jack Bell of the Associated Press:

"As attorney general I was involved in matters in which action could be taken quite quickly, and also, of course, I had a particular relationship with the President of the United States," he said. "In the Senate . . . my decisions have less of an immediate effect, and of course, legislation is not passed as rapidly as action can be taken in the executive branch."

"Would you say that you get somewhat less satisfaction out of it?" Bell asked.

"No. A senator is free to range over a broad area. They are matters of considerable significance. So although my role is quite different from what it was when I was attorney general, the job is still of great interest and offers great satisfaction."

Bell measured Bobby's interest in returning to the executive branch. "Have you any present intention of running for any other office in 1968?"

"No, no."

"How about 1972?"

"No," Bobby said. "No. I have none."

"You'd like to stay in the Senate?"

"Yes. I run again in 1970 for the Senate."

"You intend to do that?"

"I intend to do that," he said.[30]

Bobby talked about the reports of his single-handed attempt to remove Johnson from the ticket at the 1960 Democratic National Convention, insisting he did everything "at President Kennedy's request." Whatever "erroneous conclusions" others made resulted from their applying "preconceived notions" to "a particular sentence or phrase of a sentence without knowing what the rest of the conversation was." Even one of the controversy-stirring authors, Ted Sorensen, would soon tell CBS's Mike Wallace in an interview that the stories of Lyndon Johnson's selection didn't conflict, and Bobby had merely played his role "of delivering bad news to the Johnson camp."[31]

Bobby also defended LBJ when Bell asked, "Are we following the right course in Vietnam?"

"I support the effort that's being made in Vietnam by President Johnson. I believe this to be most important. If the effort in Vietnam becomes merely a military effort, we shall win some of the battles, but we will lose the overall struggle. The people of Vietnam need to feel that their future should rest with Saigon and not Hanoi. We need to give them security—that is going to require police and military action—but at the same time, social, political, economic, educational, agriculture progress has to be made for the peasants of that tragic land. And we need to do much in this field."[32]

After the foreign-policy sniping of early summer, some saw reconciliation. The Kennedy office's constituent newsletter featured a smiling picture of the senator and President Johnson at the White House, which Evans and Novak wrote "symbolizes a cooling of the country's hottest political feud." The books from JFK's aides kept coming, with longtime personal secretary Evelyn Lincoln releasing hers, which included an account of the selection of Lyndon Johnson. UPI wrote that Lincoln's book upset Bobby as much as Schlesinger's had, and that President Kennedy's widow shared this feeling. The report said Jackie had read parts of Schlesinger's and Sorensen's books, and "insiders said she was displeased with some of the reminiscences." The first lady had made

White House residential staffers sign papers that they would not write about their relationship with the Kennedys, and Evelyn Lincoln had allegedly received a copy of such an agreement, but never signed. Jackie was intensely private, secluding herself and her children as best she could on the fifteenth-floor apartment at 1040 Fifth Avenue, accessible only by private elevator. She was hounded by the press, and it sometimes fell to her brother-in-law to manage her image. When newspapers published photos of a woman in light-colored slacks and a black sweater aboard Frank Sinatra's yacht in Hyannis Port, Bobby personally telephoned to clarify that it was not Jackie.[33]

Bobby was still the protector of his family. Late that summer, his eldest, Kathleen, was show jumping in front of five hundred people when her horse, Attorney General, somersaulted over a barrier and landed on her. She was still unconscious when they removed her from the field. Bobby and Ethel were aboard a boat with their other children, sailing on Long Island Sound, and the Coast Guard dispatched a cutter to inform them of Kathleen's accident. There had been seventy-mile-an-hour winds the night before, and fifteen-foot-high waves made it impossible for the boats to heave. Coast Guard coxswain Sam Harris yelled through a bullhorn that Kathleen had been injured. "Don't be concerned," Harris announced. But Bobby was determined. He stripped off his shirt and shoes, fastened a small orange floater around his neck, and jumped overboard into the waves. With all his might, he swam the fifty yards to the cutter in a few tense minutes, his head at times disappearing amid the swells.[34]

Some saw recklessness in the dangerous swim, likening it to his mountain climbing and white-water-rapids shooting.[35] But fear had driven him into the water. Bobby knew little more than his daughter had a serious head injury. While Kathleen would be okay, with a mild concussion and some internal bleeding, the outcome could have been much worse. The Kennedys had faced such things before.

President Kennedy had been nearly two years into his term before the family finally revealed his nearest sister, Rosemary, was mentally retarded. A single sentence in 1960's *The Remarkable Kennedys* explained the "quiet" and "only unmarried" sister's absence from her photogenic family's exploits: "teaching in a school for retarded children in Wisconsin." In truth, Joseph Kennedy's attempt to improve Rosemary's mind through a lobotomy had left her mute and memoryless at age twenty-three—what her mother called "the first of the tragedies that were to befall us." She disappeared from her mother's round-robin letters within a month of the 1941 surgery, and as Jack's political career took off in 1947, the family moved her a thousand miles away to Jefferson, Wisconsin, on the advice of Boston archbishop Richard Cushing, who feared the "publicity" of her living in New England. Her mother, sisters, and brothers waited until after her father's stroke before visiting or publicly acknowledging her condition. Rose would speak out about feeling "frustrated and heartbroken" for the lack of "concrete information" to help Rosemary when she was a child.[36] The Kennedys atoned by becoming the highest-profile champions for the mentally retarded.

In the summer of 1965, Bobby's Senate office began receiving desperate letters from mothers of children at the Willowbrook State School. Located on Staten Island, Willowbrook housed over six thousand patients from infants to the elderly, making it one of the country's largest state-run institutions for the mentally retarded. The letters claimed the patients—often called "inmates"— were filthy, idle, and abandoned. Some died from the neglect, like eight-year-old John Taylor when he was taken for a shower. Faulty plumbing had corroded the cold-water pipes, and an inexperienced ward attendant did not notice that the water she was spraying on the boy was boiling. Taylor screamed in agony, but the ward attendant did not heed him—patients at Willowbrook often screamed for no reason. The boy was taken back to an isolation room, where he butted his head against the wall until a doctor came to stitch him up. Stripping the child for a penicillin shot, the doctor discovered the blackened burns covering his body. It was too late to save him. Taylor died the next morning. Willowbrook merely dismissed the young ward attendant responsible and put up a sign reminding others to check the water temperature before administering showers. Many others died for the lack or inattention of staff. A patient died after another pushed his wheelchair under a burning-hot shower. A severely retarded child was beaten to death by an older, more capable boy, put in with the slower ones as punishment. One inmate punched another in the neck, breaking his larynx and suffocating him.[37]

The letters arriving at Kennedy's office told similar stories of misery. Their children were supposed to be in the care of the state and Governor Rockefeller, except Rockefeller wasn't helping them. No one was. Some letters had clippings from a *New York Daily News* series on the school's conditions, validating their claims. The parents reached out to Bobby because the state wouldn't act . . . because he was their senator . . . because he, more than anyone else in power, might understand.

The letters landed on Adam Walinsky's desk, and he sent for a complete set of the *Daily News* stories from the Library of Congress. He put them with the letters in a packet for the senator, and just days after Kathleen fell from her horse, Bobby took the *Daily News* reporter with him for a surprise inspection of the Willowbrook State School.[38]

As they entered Ward C in Building 9, the smell of urine fell like a damp cloud, accompanied by the sounds of seventy-five severely retarded men, grunting and gibbering, shuffling feet and rustling clothes. The quarters were decades old and overcrowded. Rows of metal beds lined a narrow aisle, spaced ten inches apart. Bobby thought it looked like *three* inches. Patients had to walk across one another's beds to get in and out of their own. The dayroom walls were drab; urine and spit puddled on the floor. Everywhere was "dimness and gloom and idleness and stench." Their clothing looked like rags. Fights were common. There were too few attendants for too many men. And it was the same throughout Willowbrook.[39]

Two hundred children under the age of five lived in Building 12. Some had been abandoned at birth by parents who wouldn't even look at them. Bobby would later talk about seeing "young children slipping into blankness and lifelong dependence."[40] He walked through the children's dayrooms and saw no toys or books or games—no space for personal possessions—"for any shred of individuality." Bobby said he thought of his own children, and how they prized their toys and books—the only things they knew were truly and fully *theirs*. These children would never get to experience that feeling.

As they toured the grounds, Willowbrook's director told Bobby that his staff were doing all they could—and he was right. However, the State of New York was not providing the funding to hire the people they needed. The director had less than half the number of teachers he requested—only an eighth of the therapists he wanted. The rest were overworked—a staff defeated by the stink of it. When a reporter later asked the director whether Bobby's criticisms were more or less true, he said they were, though he wished he had offered a kind word for the men and women doing the best they could.[41]

Bobby phoned Walinsky in Washington and told him he had to visit and collect more information. "I've got to say something about this." Walinsky had never heard the senator so outraged. Walinsky arranged to go to Willowbrook, and to take the *Caroline* up to another institution in Rome, New York, with Kennedy family friend and physician Dr. George W. Thorn. It was better at Rome, but not by much. The problem wasn't Willowbrook; it was statewide, with a badly neglected mental health system. Thorn helped Walinsky devise a list of recommendations, with a list of federal programs that could make up for the state's financial shortcomings.[42]

Bobby took the findings and his outrage to the New York Joint Legislative Committee on Mental Retardation's hearing in the Bronx, where he testified a little more than a week after Kathleen's fall from her horse. His words were righteous and inflammatory—written for people to notice, to make them remember, to make things change.

He spoke of children "living in filth and dirt, their clothing in rags, in rooms less comfortable and cheerful than the cages in which we put animals in a zoo—without adequate supervision or a bit of affection—condemned to a life without hope." He told of the misery he saw, the men walking over one another's beds, the smells and the sounds. He spoke of the children with no toys or play or teachers in their lives. "We hear a great deal, these days, about civil rights, and civil liberties, and equality of opportunity, and justice. But there are no civil rights for young retarded adults—when they are denied the protection of the State Education Law." The law commanded that every child between the age of five and twenty-one receive the fullest education he could absorb. This was nowhere near the case in Willowbrook, where one misbehaving seven-year-old boy was placed with low-functioning adults for *five years*. Now at twelve years old, his exile from childhood had destroyed him. All that could have been salvaged from this boy's mind was gone. His life was over.

"There are no civil liberties for those put in the cells of Willowbrook—living amidst brutality and human excrement and intestinal disease... Nobody who has ever raised a child would want him to live for a moment as thousands of the mentally retarded now live in New York," Bobby said. "I have an older sister in an institution. She's fortunate not to be in this type of institution."[43]

He gave his report and recommendations and said that it was just a matter of action. "Nothing that I have said today is new," he noted, inviting the committee members to read a pamphlet on mental deficiency. "You can open it to almost any page and measure another way in which we fail to meet these standards... We cannot tolerate a new snake pit in New York." Bobby quoted Sophocles asking, "What joy is there in day that follows day, some swift, some slow, with death the only goal?"

"We can do better," he said. "We must do better."[44]

The testimony had its intended effect. The committee chairman sent two state senators straight from the hearing to Willowbrook for an inspection. Governor Rockefeller's spokesman said they were aware of the "difficulties" within the system. The committee had already commissioned a report, which Rockefeller had bottled up. Bobby wanted its release, not a political fight. "Our shortcomings are due to no one man, and no one single administration," he said in his testimony.[45]

Only Rockefeller, a year from reelection, didn't trust him. The report leaked anyhow, and within days of Bobby's testimony, the governor's office released a master plan on overhauling the state's mental health institutions with a network of small community centers. Within another month, Rockefeller authorized the immediate hiring of dozens of therapists and teachers to fully staff Willowbrook. Bobby's words would appear again and again as the story went on, and patients' families felt heard, blasting the Rockefeller administration. "For years you've called us paranoid every time we complain," one mother shouted at a hearing of the State Department of Mental Hygiene.

"When Senator Kennedy told the public how bad things are at Willowbrook and Rome, you said he was exaggerating, too. Then public opinion forced you to take a few short steps in the right direction."[46]

Words were the only lever of power Bobby had, and Rockefeller had many. Bobby's office wrote the governor multiple times offering to partner on securing federal funds, but the letters went unanswered. In December, Rockefeller would tell reporters Bobby's testimony on Willowbrook was wrong. "In sum, he was misrepresenting the situation," he said. "A responsible official should know the facts, and he has the responsibility to tell the public all the facts." The governor paused for emphasis. "Of course, he is new here."[47] Bobby let the dig slide and continued to write, pointing out all the places the state wasn't taking advantage of federal funds. Rockefeller replied with a telegram calling Bobby ruthless.

"I trust that the continuing relations of state officials with their Federal counterparts and the obtaining of assistance for the mentally retarded will not depend on your acting as the political broker," Rockefeller's letter said. Bobby countered with a press conference at the Carlyle, but there was no way for him to win in a contest of ruthlessness. With the 1966 governor's race around the corner, Bobby backed down. "We had to go away from it," Walinsky would say years later. "We got out of it during the whole election campaign of 1966 because the senator just didn't want it to be a political thing." When Bobby returned to the topic after the election, Rockefeller was still in control, and the governor's office "wanted to do it their own way," Walinsky said.[48] In a short time, the children of Willowbrook would be forgotten and abandoned once again. Robert Kennedy's retreat was one of the few times he removed himself from an issue he cared about over such a small personality clash. It was the worst of politics.

POLITICS WAS JUST as difficult in the Senate with the profile of a Kennedy.

Francis X. Morrissey was a loyal man. From South Boston, he had an up-by-the-bootstraps story and was dispatched by Ambassador Kennedy to guide Jack through his first congressional race in 1946. Morrissey continued to squire JFK and then Teddy through the political world, while looking after any other needs. He was always at the airport or train station, no matter the time or weather, with a car and reservation in hand.[49] "A kind of personal factotum," as Dick Goodwin described him.[50] By the time Jack reached the White House, he was a Boston municipal court judge. The Ambassador thought he deserved a spot on the federal district bench.

But opposition to his ascension was overwhelming. Critics said he lacked trial experience and the proper education. He was a laughingstock to the faculty of Harvard Law School. The Boston Bar Association unanimously voted against a recommendation in 1962, writing to then–Attorney General Kennedy that he "is entirely lacking in the qualifications of education and training necessary to carry out the duties of the office of a federal judge." The district was too important to let someone of his caliber preside over it. President Kennedy took the nomination under consideration but never moved on it.[51] Morrissey's chance had passed him by.

Then with Jack gone from power and the Ambassador's stroke leaving him wheelchairbound and incapable of communicating, many friends stopped visiting lonely Joseph Kennedy. But not Frank Morrissey. "He came to see him almost every week," one aide to Teddy would recall. "He didn't do it to ask him to propose his nomination. He came to see the Ambassador as a long-time friend." The only favor Joe Kennedy ever asked of Teddy—or of Jack, Ted had heard—was that Morrissey be nominated. And so Ted nudged the White House, without any anticipation of the President's sending it on.[52]

Then on September 23, Johnson did. "I don't believe it," Teddy said to his staffer Milt Gwirtzman. "Johnson's just nominated Frank Morrissey for district judge."

"He wasn't tossing any bouquet" with Morrissey, Walinsky later said. Gwirtzman thought Johnson was genuinely doing a favor for Teddy. The suggestion of Johnson's sabotaging the nomination before making it was dismissed as a "cocktail theory" in the *New York Times*. In reality, the President only decided to make the appointment after he knew Morrissey was unconfirmable. The nominee was more than inept—he was duplicitous, as his Senate confirmation hearings would soon reveal.[53]

Gwirtzman warned Morrissey not to trust Republican minority leader Everett Dirksen to give him a fair hearing, but Morrissey didn't listen. "Frank felt that if he could show the senators that he was a nice obliging fellow," Gwirtzman said, "they would confirm him. He regarded it sort of like being interviewed for admission to a Boston club." Morrissey had taken three tries to pass the bar exam, and Dirksen genially mentioned how he had "flunked" the bar exam on the first pass. Then his sandy, mellifluous voice transformed into a growl. Morrissey and his family watched from red leather chairs as Dirksen turned to his character witness, Senator Edward M. Kennedy of Massachusetts. "Tell me, Senator, do you regard the federal court as an in-training court?"

"No, I do not."

"Does the Boston Municipal Court try jury cases?"

"No."

"Was Judge Morrissey endorsed by the Boston Bar?"

"No." The questioning went on like that.[54]

Morrissey had to come clean when the Bar Association revealed his secret.

Morrissey had had trouble getting his start as an ambitious young man from a poor family in Depression-era Boston. An older friend advised him that Georgia allowed anyone with a degree from a state law school immediate entry to the bar. The friend told him about a fancy-titled crash course that would give him a diploma—and thereby, a law license—within weeks. And so, Morrissey paid for the "quickie" degree and entry to the bar, bypassing years of learning and expenses. He would later spend nights attending Suffolk University Law School in Boston and graduate at the top of his ninety-six-member class, but his youthful mistake followed him. In his application, Morrissey listed his Georgia law license without mentioning his so-called degree from the Southern University Law School.[55]

The Bar Association officials revealed this information at his hearing, and when Morrissey's turn to testify came, the room became quiet as he spoke of his shame. He said he spent six months in Atlanta, trying to find cases, only no one would hire him, so he returned to Boston. The ballet of political loyalties got more insidious when the *Boston Globe* revealed Morrissey's sworn testimony about trying to make an honest go of it in Georgia conflicted with his simultaneous candidacy for the Massachusetts state legislature. The *Globe* won a Pulitzer Prize for its coverage, and the lead reporter later revealed that he was tipped off by Kenny O'Donnell, Bobby's teammate and one of Jack's closest aides, who disliked Morrissey.[56]

Other Kennedy allies began to peel off, so Bobby entered the picture to help. He had paid his dues that summer, leading former Mississippi governor James P. Coleman along the path to the Fifth Circuit Court of Appeals. The appointment gave Coleman—whom the *New Republic* labeled a "stout segregationist"—jurisdiction over several Southern states and many civil rights cases. Baseball great Jackie Robinson wrote in his column that "Senator Bob" had backed Coleman "to repair some of those Dixie fences he has broken down" and restore his national chances in the South. Coleman's friends stressed that his support for the Kennedy-Johnson ticket had probably ended his political career, and Bobby was acting out of loyalty. Edelman later said that on nominees like Coleman, the senator would look at him and shake his head as if to say, "Sorry about that." Bobby, the only Kennedy male who never required Morrissey's services, had actually been influential in blocking his nomination in 1961, though in 1964 Bobby thanked Johnson for considering the Morrissey nomination—in writing. Now, he had no choice but to back the family friend. "I'm supporting him," he said at a campaign stop on behalf of New Jersey's Democratic governor. "He's a good judge. The mere fact that he was associated with the Kennedy family should not make him unavailable."[57]

This was the Kennedys' view—that they received no senatorial "courtesy." The *Globe* reported that Teddy "complained privately that if Morrissey had not been sponsored by him he would probably be confirmed without a whisper." Then again, most senators were not considered presidents-in-waiting, and both Kennedys were. Bobby, now head of the family, believed he was the only one who could reason with Everett Dirksen, who saw the Morrissey nomination as a shaft of light after spending the session buried under Johnson's agenda. In opposing the appointment, the minority leader finally had a fight he could win. Bob went to see him in his office, where the Republican claimed at least forty votes likely to oppose. Dirksen was still holding even more embarrassing information about Morrissey and Teddy's consorting with a deported Mafia hit man on a 1961 trip to Italy.

Bobby erupted at the minority leader and said bitterly, "You hate the Kennedys."[58]

"I'm not interested in you or Teddy," Dirksen responded, "but I'm out to get Morrissey. You think I'm out to cut your neck—to ax you." He extended his arm toward a likeness of President Kennedy. "You see that bust on the mantel?" Dirksen said in his smooth voice. "That was one of the best friends I ever had."[59]

Bobby and Teddy furiously worked the phones during the final hours of the Morrissey lobbying, with one senator receiving calls from both brothers as well as two Kennedy staffers. But the votes weren't there. Even if Morrissey could be confirmed, Dirksen and others would continue to drag his name through the mud, with the prospect of impeachment if more damning details emerged. The brothers decided they had gone as far as they could. Teddy would recommit the nomination, sending it back to committee to expire within thirty days—the least humiliating option.[60]

Milt Gwirtzman was the first staffer they told. "It's a fine strategy," he said, "but how about your commitment to Frank Morrissey?"

Bobby fixed on him and said directly, "I think we've more than fulfilled our commitment to Frank Morrissey." Bobby believed that if Morrissey were truly loyal, he would have withdrawn voluntarily after all of the trouble he caused.[61]

Teddy informed the President, but few others knew what he had planned. The younger brother entered the Senate Thursday morning, his desk stacked with folders, law books, and documents—signals of a long night ahead to the observers in the gallery. Some guessed the debate could delay the vote into Friday. Only when Teddy began his sentence "*If* we took up the nomination this morning . . ." did it dawn on the reporters that something else was happening. His voice cracked while praising his family's friend and admonishing the American Bar Association for attacking Morrissey's character and training "perhaps because he attended a local law school at night rather than a national law school by day." Teddy's voice trembled as he recalled the poverty Morrissey sought to escape pursuing his dream of a legal career: "one of twelve children, his father a dockworker, the family living in a home without gas, electricity, or heat in the bedrooms; their shoes held together with wooden pegs their father made . . ." He then asked for unanimous consent to recommit the nomination. The first one to cross the aisle and pump Ted's hand was Ev Dirksen.[62]

It had all been a test of loyalty. Of the fourteen senators who had not responded to the quorum call the morning of the Morrissey vote, all were Democrats and many of them were Kennedy allies—members of the liberal bloc they were supposedly leading. One frequently mentioned ally, Joseph Tydings of Maryland, was present and waiting on the floor. Tydings, who owed his political career to a U.S. attorney appointment from President Kennedy, was holding a high-handed speech to reject the Morrissey nomination as a matter of conscience, borrowing the spirit of JFK's private words to Schlesinger, just published in *A Thousand Days*: "Sometimes party loyalty asks too much." Edelman, there to staff Bobby, watched Tydings's face fall as Ted revealed the motion to recommit. Bobby and Teddy felt betrayed.[63]

On its surface, the Morrissey nomination was about one man's lack of qualifications for a lifetime appointment. Within, it showed how fragile loyalty could be in Washington, D.C. Morrissey's defeat was also a harbinger for what would be done in the name of John F. Kennedy. Jacqueline once said Bobby would have her "put on my widow's weeds . . . and ask [LBJ] for tremendous things like renaming Cape Canaveral after Jack."[64] No longer. The period of mourning that had got the Kennedys whatever they wanted was over. Loyalty only lasted so long.

BOBBY HAD A bad reputation for senatorial courtesy. Where others would interrupt a speech by asking "the distinguished senator" or "my friend," Bobby would simply nod his head or wave his hand.[65] Teddy kept a cooler head, capable of engaging with disagreeable senators without antagonizing them. He was the floor manager of the administration's immigration bill, the picture of Senate decorum in a debate with Southern Democrat Spessard Holland. Florida's senior senator was dismayed that newly organized African nations were receiving what he considered "equal status" with "our mother nations of Western Europe" under the proposed revisions to the immigration quota system.

"I believe that one of the most laudable aspects of the entire bill is the elimination of the racist factor," Teddy said of easing restrictions on immigration from non-European nations. But Holland kept on until Bobby rose to ask if the senator believed Americans with roots in Africa had the same right to be here as those with European ancestors.

Holland said yes, but he did not know many African Americans "who have the slightest ideas as to what tribe or nation or area or geographic region their people came from."

Bobby asked, "Perhaps he could suggest to the Senate why it is that those who came from Africa are unable to say where they came from."

"They did not come as immigrants, let us put it that way," Holland said in a strained acknowledgment of the slave trade. "I have no fault to find with them. I am only stating what is the fact, that those good people have no nationality now, no race to look to, and no home country to look to except the United States, whereas the distinguished senator from New York has a mother country to which he can look, as I think every senator present has."

Whether Holland truly cared or not, he believed there was no solution to the problem. Bobby felt otherwise. "I am very pleased of the fact our family came from Ireland. I think some of the people the senator has described to us, whose mother countries are the Scandinavian countries or perhaps Ireland or England or some other countries, were responsible for bringing the people from Africa to the United States in the first place, as slaves. So when the senator says, after we have performed that kind of unforgivable act, that we should penalize them because they do not know where they came from, nor where in Africa their grandfather was born, as I am fortunate enough to know, I am surprised to hear the senator from Florida suggest such a philosophy, and that is why I rise in the back row of the U.S. Senate to speak."[66]

Holland was an outlier. Immigration reform passed the Senate 76–18, and Johnson signed it into law on October 3 near Ellis Island, with the Statue of Liberty towering above. Bobby and Teddy were there standing around the President smiling. Bobby's Justice Department had helped sculpt the bill, but diminished from his powers, his contributions as a senator amounted to rising in the back row to speak. Yet many saw value in this. People even began to see new dimensions to the win-at-all-costs younger brother. In another revelation from Sorensen's book, Bobby was named "the best performer" among the cabinet during the Cuban missile crisis, one of the dual shocks to the national psyche of the early 1960s. Sorensen wrote of Bobby's standing against a preemptive strike against Cuba without warning, calling it "a Pearl Harbor in reverse [that] would blacken the name of the United States in the pages of history."[67]

Fred Dutton had advised Bobby not to spread his portfolio too thin—to bear down on one or two topics and establish his credentials. As early as July,

Dutton was pressing for a second major address on nuclear weapons. Bobby had told Walinsky immediately after the June 23 speech that there was going to have to be another on Red China and the bomb—"a policy maker's speech," with direct suggestions for containing the nuclear threat.[68] And so, Bobby's second major Senate address suggested inviting the Chinese to disarmament talks in Geneva.

"If they accept," he said on the Senate floor that October 13, "the negotiations will be more meaningful—for they will then include all nuclear powers. If the Chinese refuse, we will have lost nothing," reminding them that the United States was already in talks with China's ambassador in Poland. "We will have opened another door to peace, and the Chinese will show to the world that they are not interested. I think no one, looking at United States foreign policy since 1961, will interpret our civility as a sign of weakness." He added, "We can never know the results until we make the attempt."[69]

Kennedy used floor debate to drive his point home. He sent out advance copies of his speech to draw other senators into a colloquy with him. Six senators were there to comment on Bobby's remarks, while Ethel watched from the gallery. Senator Ralph Yarborough of Texas came down to praise the men for continuing "the best tradition of the Senate" in developing "ideas on the floor." Neither the White House nor the Chinese engaged the proposal, and the State Department declared China had shown no "serious interest" in nonproliferation.[70] Nuclear politics took a back seat to the issue driving world affairs: the conflict in Vietnam.

Fifty-eight Americans died there one week in early October 1965, bringing the U.S. military's killed-in-action list to 806. Another twenty-five had died by the time that week's casualty number could be reported. On the day Bobby spoke out against nuclear proliferation, students burned their draft cards in defiance of a new, largely symbolic law. That weekend, ten thousand people marched in Berkeley, California, while smaller demonstrations came together in New York, Michigan, Chicago, and Columbus, Ohio. A student marching in Berkeley said, "We won't end the war. Bobby Kennedy, or someone like that, will have to end it. But we've got to do something."[71] Bobby was not there yet, but he was willing to defend those who were.

In New Jersey, free speech around Vietnam was the biggest issue in the reelection campaign of its Democratic governor, Richard Hughes, who was being pressured to fire a Rutgers University professor who had welcomed a Vietcong victory at an antiwar teach-in. Bumper stickers demanded RID RUTGERS OF REDS, while the Republican candidate for governor used a recording of the professor, Eugene Genovese, in his radio commercials—and was rising in the polls as a result. Governor Hughes resisted calls for him to dismiss

Genovese from the state university for his views on the war, and Bobby praised him for it. "I would not be here today if Governor Hughes put any pressure upon the [Rutgers] board of governors to fire Mr. Genovese," he said. "This would destroy the whole idea of academic freedom." Bobby warned three thousand college students in East Orange that when "a single political figure can decide who will teach in our universities, it would sound the death knell of higher education."[72]

Former vice president Richard Nixon, on his years-long comeback quest, became the top Republican surrogate against Genovese. "Does an individual employed by the state have the right to use his position to give aid and comfort to the enemies of the United States in wartime?" Nixon asked. He said that Bobby "misinterpreted and confused" the issue, and that he was rejecting the traditions of Democratic presidents like Wilson and Roosevelt.[73]

Some saw Bobby's defense of free speech and calls for diplomacy with Communist adversaries as a naked political play—"romancing ADA-type liberals who always distrusted him," columnists Evans and Novak wrote. His strength, they said, is "rooted in city machines." Indeed, Bobby was more comfortable with ward bosses. Campaigning in New Haven that October with Mayor Richard Lee in the smoky lodge of the Knights of St. Patrick Club, Bobby said, "I know, looking at your faces, what President Kennedy must have seen when he visited Wexford." He went on. "I asked Dick Lee about the Knights of St. Patrick on the way in. I asked, 'What good works do they do?' He said, 'They just drink a lot!'" The men raised their glasses and laughed.[74]

William Shannon wrote that Bobby felt most at home with Democratic regulars "even when he recognizes they are narrow-minded or not wholly trustworthy"—at least he could count on them to vote the right way.[75]

WITH THE RETIREMENT of Mayor Wagner, keeping New York City in the Democrats' hands was Bobby's chief political aim of the fall.

Looking at the numbers alone, a Republican winning in New York City seemed impossible in 1965. There were 687,397 Republicans on the voting rolls—less than a third of the 2.35 million Democrats. There were more Democrats in Brooklyn than there were Republicans in the entire city.[76]

But Republican congressman John Vliet Lindsay had just run a citywide campaign, plastering his 1964 slogan—"The District's Pride, the Nation's Hope"—far outside his tony slice of Manhattan. LBJ carried Lindsay's district with 70 percent of the vote; Lindsay walked away with 71 percent. Six feet four inches tall, dashing and youthful, a *Times* columnist wrote that Lindsay's Republican colleagues thought him "a little too good looking, a little too Ivy

Leaguish and a little too curt and abrasive." The forty-two-year-old Lindsay sought to tap into the Kennedy style for his campaign. He even tried to hire Bobby's 1964 admen.[77]

Bobby looked for a suitable candidate for mayor. Steve Smith and Bobby's New York–based Senate aide Tom Johnston drew up a list of whom they could get to run, but as they began vetting them, they found out one wasn't registered in the city, another wanted Bobby to clear the field, and a third was actually a Republican. Meanwhile, all the candidates already vying for the job wanted Bobby on board. One even tried to get Steve Smith to join his slate at the urging of Mayor Wagner. "I don't think it's my role to become involved in a primary election such as this," Bobby wound up saying in late July. Privately, he had already resigned himself to Lindsay's impending victory. "It appears . . . that John Lindsay will win the election," he wrote to a friend in London on July 19. "People want a change and they feel Lindsay will give it to them."[78]

While the Democrats angled, Lindsay took bites out of their base. Candidates could run on the ballot lines of multiple parties, and Lindsay locked up the Liberal Party's nomination and organized a third line for independents who didn't feel comfortable voting for him under the Republican or Liberal designations. In Congress, Lindsay voted with his party just 6 percent of the time, marginalizing the right wing and drawing firebrand publisher William F. Buckley Jr. into the race for mayor on the Conservative Party's line. Buckley's opposition to civil rights and social programs benefiting Negroes attracted working-class Irish Catholic voters—another blow to the Democratic coalition. Though a resident of Connecticut, Buckley insisted, "I have no problems that Bobby Kennedy didn't have" in finding an address to run from as a carpetbagger.[79]

Bobby and Ethel had recently moved their New York residence from Long Island to a corner apartment in a new thirty-eight-story building at United Nations Plaza, but their polling place was still linked to their New York driver's licenses, listing their address as the Carlyle Hotel. They arrived late on primary night, September 14, to cast their ballots. A reporter outside the school polling place asked Bobby if he finally felt like a New Yorker. "I thought when I was elected I became a New Yorker," he said.[80]

The primary's big winner was a quintessential New Yorker—one who never missed an election, Abe Beame, all of five feet two inches tall, the classic machine politician. New York City's chief financial officer, he ran for mayor because it was the next rung on the ladder. He bore no sweeping vision; his campaign announcement consisted of four hundred words, read in under five minutes. While he had few beliefs, Beame did believe in the machine. His support from bosses Charles Buckley, Adam Clayton Powell, and Stanley Steingut made his candidacy tick. He didn't give a hoot about Lindsay's getting the pivotal

Liberal nomination—"a foregone conclusion," he called it. His campaign manager told the *Times* they were unconcerned by Lindsay's appeal, saying, "You can't run this city on grammar."[81]

Beame's surprise primary win was a mixed blessing for Bobby. On one hand, the defeat of Wagner's choice made Kennedy the state's undisputed Democratic power broker. On the other, Beame was a terrible candidate who drove Bobby nuts.

Nevertheless, Bobby committed a significant amount of time to the mayor's race. Joe Dolan sent him a list of fifteen speeches to groups they had agreed to "per your oral okay" in the latter part of September and October. Bobby scribbled at the bottom, "Joe, I have never heard of half of these!!!" But with Lindsay and Buckley eating into the Jewish, Negro, and Irish votes, Bobby looked at the election as a matter of will. He believed Beame had to make a strong push in black and Puerto Rican neighborhoods, and an aggressive appeal to party loyalty. He could lose almost half of the city's Democrats and still win. Anyone would agree with the *New York Times* observation that Bobby campaigned harder for Beame than any other Democrat. Evans and Novak praised the senator's "valiant" effort for a man they called a "bookkeeper" and "non-personality." Bobby was on the docks in an icy wind, making his pitch to pier workers rounded up with hot coffee. He rolled through the city's boroughs in the back of a truck with the candidate—sometimes alone when Beame was late—urging Democrats to stay loyal.[82]

Bobby gave freely of Steve Smith's talents and assigned Peter Edelman to Beame's campaign all month, as the Kennedys' eyes and ears inside the operation. Edelman was on hand for a recording session with Beame and Bobby. It started fairly well. Beame talked about his hard upbringing, and Edelman thought he sounded good. Bobby wanted more out of him and began coaching. "Look at me, Abe. Get mad at me. Bring your fists down . . . All right, Abe Beame, tell us why you think you deserve to be mayor of New York."

"That's great . . ." said Beame. "And then what do I say?"

So Bobby gave Abe Beame an idea or two why Abe Beame might want to be mayor. After they wrapped, they walked out of the studio together and Beame said, "Senator, thank you very much for coming and doing this with me. I really know better now why I want to be mayor."

Bobby went for a bite to eat with his aides and asked them who they would vote for. Tom Johnston said Lindsay. Edelman recalled saying, "I guess I would vote for Beame, but only because I'd been working on the damn thing."[83]

Everything about Beame's campaign seemed wrong. Rolling through the streets of Manhattan with Beame, a campaign worker kept calling through a portable sound system, "Here he is, the man of the hour, Senator Robert Kennedy, and Abe Beame!"

"Just say, 'Robert Kennedy and Abe Beame,'" Bobby finally told him.[84]

Beame was glad for Bobby's help, if sometimes deflated by it. His pride was bruised when Bobby would introduce him, step away from the microphone, and the crowd's attention would dissipate. "A lot of people would be going to *him*, asking for his autograph," Beame later said, adding that Bobby was embarrassed for both of them. "I think he really would have preferred it not happen because he knew that it would sort of have some kind of an effect on the candidate." Though Beame wouldn't have wished for the attention RFK got. Standing between Bobby and the crowd was like "taking your life in your hands," Beame said. "We'd go there and they'd just pull him down, drag him down and push everybody in his way."[85]

Count Basie and his band warmed up a predominantly Negro crowd at a nighttime rally in Brooklyn's Bedford-Stuyvesant section. Bobby finished his remarks, and the crowd rushed forward to touch him. A mother at the front struggled to shield her baby from the crush. Kennedy reached down and scooped the baby out of her arms and onstage with him. He cradled the child through Beame's speech and then, as Basie struck up the band, took the baby for a spin as if they were on a dance floor. He kissed the baby on the head as he handed him back to his mother.[86]

William White wrote in his column that the "emotion-prone" and "image-worshippers" had shifted their allegiance from Bobby to Lindsay. On a walking tour on Fourteenth Street, an elderly woman rushed up to Bobby, grabbed his hand, and said, "It's good to meet you, Mr. Lindsay." Between one of the rolling rallies in Manhattan the weekend before the election, a man in a leather jacket came up to Bobby's car, held out his hand, and said, "I'm still for you, but I can't go along with Beame. To me, he's the antithesis of everything I thought you stood for."[87]

RFK's campaigning on Abe Beame's behalf served only to remind reformers of his ties to Charles Buckley and the machine. Murray Kempton wrote that "the contest seemed very like those occasions when John F. Kennedy used gracefully to go to the sidelines and simply watch, making it clear by his abstention that he could not be expected to go down for a hopeless Democrat against an appealing Republican." As leader, Bobby would do no such thing, even though Kempton had heard he was talking about Beame's hopelessness. "I think what's happening to Abe Beame must be rubbing off on me," Bobby was alleged to say. "I'm not sure I can afford to make these trips with him any longer. I've never seen crowds so cold. It'll take me six months to get anyone to speak to me again." Yet the loyal Bobby marched right on alongside the Beame team.[88]

The *Daily News* and *Herald Tribune* polls showed the race neck and neck in the final weekend. On the last day of campaigning, Bobby and Beame had eight rallies in the Bronx and another six in Brooklyn.[89]

Bobby and Ethel waited more than an hour to vote at Public School #5 on East Eighty-first Street and Madison Avenue. When their turn came, Republican city councilman Theodore R. Kupferman contested their eligibility for the cameras: "I challenge your right to vote because I don't believe you're a resident of this district." Bobby and Ethel had to sign affidavits that they maintained a residence at the Carlyle Hotel a few blocks away.[90]

"It's nice publicity for him," Bobby said of the final indignity before defeat.[91]

John Lindsay won with about 45 percent of the vote, only three points ahead of Beame—sapped by Lindsay's inroads with blacks and Jews, and William F. Buckley's support among Irish Catholics—while the down-ballot Democratic candidates won. Loyalty carried them through.[92]

Across the river in New Jersey, Governor Richard Hughes was reelected despite an onslaught of attacks over the pro-Vietcong professor. New Jersey Democrats credited Bobby for leading the charge in defense of free speech. Landing in Los Angeles for meetings and appearances three days after the election, Bobby kept up the discussion of civil liberties at the University of Southern California. A capacity crowd of seventeen hundred packed the school's main auditorium, while even more jostled to gain entry. As Bobby began his remarks, some of the locked-out students began banging on the doors. Bobby paused and said, "I'd let them in," into the microphone, and the university president relented. Making noise had gotten them somewhere—but it wouldn't solve everything, Bobby assured them.[93]

He began by talking about the incredible change between his experiences with student activists and his brother's. "In 1960, people spoke of youth as the Silent Generation—the uncommitted. No one would say that now." And yet "sometimes," he said, "it is made more difficult by those acting not so much as youths but as children."[94]

"I defend the right to dissent, the right to criticize . . . But we must be careful not to let disagreement with national policy jeopardize the success of the efforts in which student participation has been so important."[95]

"The fact is that disagreement need not and should not bring disengagement," Bobby said, citing a declining interest in the Peace Corps because of the war in Vietnam. "It would be most ironic if dissent from other phases of our country's policy were to damage the programs which the dissenters feel we should be doing more of."[96]

Yet within a few hours, Bobby's message was overshadowed by stray comments in a news conference at the Ambassador Hotel.[97] "Have there been any instances in which the anti-Vietnam-day demonstrations and protesters have gone too far?" one reporter asked.

"Yes, I think they have," Bobby said. "For example, where they won't let those with opposite views speak. Or where violence is used." Asked about draft-card burning, whose punishment was increased after a unanimous voice vote in the Senate, he said, "If a person feels that strongly and wants to make that kind of sacrifice, he can go and burn his draft card and take the consequences. But I don't agree with it personally."[98]

"Will it have a snowball effect?"

"I don't think it will," Bobby said. "No."[99]

Then a reporter asked about a new, sensational form of protest just coming to light. As a backlash to the antiwar demonstrations, more than 150 Stanford University students in favor of the war organized a blood drive to benefit American and South Vietnamese soldiers. In response, a few dozen antiwar Stanford students controversially pledged their blood to those fighting for the North.[100]

A reporter asked Bobby, "What about giving blood to the North Vietnamese? . . . Is that too far?"

"If we've given all the blood that is needed to the South Vietnamese, I'm in favor of them having blood."

"Even to the North Vietnamese?"

"Yes," RFK said. Someone started in on another question before Bobby cut back in, "—I'd rather concentrate on the South Vietnamese and those who need it at the moment," but it was too late. Bobby's humanitarian impulse put him knee-deep in a campus controversy. Without realizing it, he had effectively endorsed a fringe suggestion to ship Americans' blood to the Vietcong.[101]

Veteran *Los Angeles Times* reporter Carl Greenberg, whom Richard Nixon singled out for fairness at the end of his disastrous 1962 gubernatorial campaign, returned to the issue. "Senator, so that it may be abundantly clear," Greenberg asked, "are you now saying that even though we are in combat with North Vietnamese, who are killing our troops, that if the North Vietnamese need blood, it's okay to give it to them?"

"Yes, I would do it through—if the Red Cross is making a drive for blood and feels that can be helpful, as our own—" Bobby stopped and started his sentence over. "Any North Vietnamese that are captured, for instance, by our troops in Vietnam are treated, they're helped by blood, they get help by assistance. If more of that kind of blood is needed through an organization such as the Red Cross, then I would—"

"Then you are speaking of prisoners of war, and not the shipment of American students' blood into Vietnam—North Vietnam?"

"No, I'm talking about through an organization such as the Red Cross."

"Which is not making such a drive, to our knowledge."

"The blanket question as to whether we would furnish blood to anybody from North Vietnam, I would furnish it under the circumstances I have described. I think that that's in the oldest traditions of our country."[102]

Bobby had made a giant mistake, one he would only realize after. Later that afternoon, he clarified that he opposed sending blood to the North Vietnamese because "it might violate our laws." The comments opened up a floodgate of criticism. "Bobby Bleeds for the Enemy," the *Chicago Tribune* declared. "Sending blood is a very special thing," columnist Marguerite Higgins wrote, "a sign of sympathy." Joe Dolan eventually added a rare public statement that "Senator Kennedy has always opposed any direct action by groups in this country to send blood or other supplies to the North Vietnamese."[103]

Barry Goldwater was by far the harshest critic, telling Republican activists in New Mexico that the Democratic Party was "in the hands of the extreme, radical left," supporting war opponents "to the edge of treason." His voice rising with anger, Goldwater boomed, "Why the silence today, when a United States senator says—as he did last night—that there was nothing wrong with sending American blood to our Communist enemies? It is appalling to me that the press of this nation hasn't jumped down his throat even though he retracts and retracts and retracts and retracts."[104]

Goldwater remained bullish on the fighting in Vietnam. "I see a chance the war could end by Christmas," he said of the growing troop levels on October 14. Bobby was hearing the opposite. *Times* correspondent R. W. Apple Jr. updated him in a letter from Saigon. "You had suggested before I left that I suggest, and not simply criticize," Apple wrote. "We seem to believe that General Motors can overwhelm guerillas . . . But the acceptance of guerilla warfare *as* guerilla warfare must be extended to the whole U.S. military effort here . . . Bombers aren't the solution; I truly believe that they make as many new V.C. as they destroy." The American death toll crept higher. The Pentagon said 902 had died in combat. Nearly five thousand had been wounded.[105]

Edelman was along for the California trip and spent much of the day trying to stem the blood comments' damage, calling reporters, saying, "Please, he didn't mean it. What he said was . . ." He and Bobby stopped into the offices of the *Los Angeles Sentinel*, a Negro newspaper in Watts, where a KENNEDY FOR PRESIDENT sign greeted them. Bobby got a kick out of it, which surprised Peter amid all the uproar. They walked around and talked to people. On one street corner, Bobby spoke with a middle-aged man, who looked perfectly healthy, about what he thought was wrong with his neighborhood.

"Flustration."

"Excuse me?" said Bobby.

"Flustration."

"What do you mean?"

"Well, man," he said, "when you're over fifty and you is black, you can't get a job nohow."

Later, Bobby and Edelman walked into the Ambassador Hotel, where he was speaking at a Democratic Party fund-raiser, and an aide to the district's congressman approached them in the lobby. "Senator," the aide said, "you went into Watts this afternoon and didn't tell us." On the streets, Bobby had heard again and again from people complaining that their congressman was missing in action. Some claimed that he hadn't even been by since the riots three months earlier. With a small group standing around, Bobby didn't flinch. "When was the last time your boss was there?"[106]

Like the youths he focused so much of his attention on, Bobby was quick to stand up for ideals, even if the truth was reckless. His words reflected an attraction to change that couldn't come fast enough. And it resonated—in Watts, and around the world.

FAR AWAY, IN SOUTH AFRICA, a young student leader named Ian Robertson had heard Bobby's appeal to youth. Robertson was head of the National Union of South African Students, the largest multiracial organization in South Africa, which resisted the apartheid regime that grew more and more belligerent with each passing year. In July, shortly after Bobby first spoke about the "revolution now in progress," Robertson invited him to address their group at Cape Town University in the spring of 1966 for their annual Day of Affirmation. It was the day in which the members rededicated themselves to the ideals of freedom—a holiday the organization had created in 1959, when the government barred nonwhite students from the universities. Authorities alleged NUSAS members were part of a violent rebellion against the government. South Africa's minister of justice—the equivalent of the U.S. attorney general—called NUSAS "a damnable and detestable organization," and its leaders "the offspring of snakes." He offered to remit sentences of political prisoners whose parents signed statements that said their children were misled into joining.[107] But mostly, they were thousands of young people trying to create change.

The students had already invited Dr. Martin Luther King Jr. to speak, but his admittance to the country seemed unlikely after state media, the South African Broadcasting Corporation, suggested he was a Communist. He was unlikely to get a visa. "I very much look forward to SABC's attempt to prove that Senator Kennedy is also a Communist," Ian Robertson said. The ruling Nationalists in the South African parliament said Robertson and his allies were "playing with fire."[108] They soon put Robertson under house arrest and marked him a legally "banned" person, who could not thereafter appear or be mentioned in public.

In late October 1965, Bobby wrote back that he was "very happy to accept" the students' invitation. The decision marked a dramatic turn for those trying to control South Africa's future. The government was faced with a dilemma: blocking a world leader from their country, or seeing him denounce their policies in its streets. The South African regime was fiercely anti-Communist, but stopping the entry of someone with Bobby's stature would be an admission that the regime had broken completely from open society. Bobby drove this point home, speaking in New York: "I have visited more than fifty countries on every continent in my lifetime, and I look forward to meeting the people of South Africa."

Some thought the government might ban NUSAS to prevent Kennedy from visiting, or that the government would not formally refuse his visa but indicate they could not show the required "hospitality" to protect him.[109]

"It is unlikely that he will ever go," Murray Kempton wrote of the South Africa trip. "What is extraordinary is the fact of the invitation . . . Senator Kennedy has a name then at which lonely men grasp in their loneliness."[110]

REVOLUCIÓN

November 1965–December 1965

IN A MEMO TO BOBBY written in the summer of 1965, Fred Dutton had urged him to go abroad in the fall and spend some time at a foreign university as "a platform for your projecting moral and intellectual leadership." The Soviet Union, Britain, Israel, Sweden—any place, Dutton advised, except Latin America. Anti-American demonstrations in the wake of the Dominican invasion had been vicious, "and that would obviously be undesirable for a number of reasons right now." But that was exactly where Bobby wanted to go—carrying on with John F. Kennedy's promise to the region of "an alliance for progress"—"*alianza para progreso.*"[1]

The decision to tour Latin America was to put himself in the middle of danger. It meant hostile questions amid unstable governments in a place where his brother's extended hand had become Johnson's fist.

In October, Under Secretary of State Thomas Mann continued to defend America's military actions in the Dominican Republic while insisting that "non-intervention is the keystone of the inter-American system." Mann said that April's invasion was self-defense against Communists taking "a base for further aggressions . . . The facts we already have would fill a volume. Each passing day brings additional facts to light. The danger will soon become apparent even to the most skeptical."[2]

Bobby was considered the chief skeptic, and the administration was unhappy with the very premise of his privately funded trip, which became clear early on in his November 3 State Department briefing. The meeting was in a conference room with a long table. Bobby sat down in the middle on one side, with Adam Walinsky pulling up a chair from the wall to sit slightly behind him. Then the State Department people filed in, all sitting on the other side of the table. More entered and the room filled up, but still, no one would sit on the Kennedy side of the table.[3]

Presiding over the briefing was Jack Hood Vaughn, assistant secretary of state for inter-American affairs, U.S. coordinator of the Alliance for Progress, and a disciple of Mann's foreign policy. Vaughn had been in Santiago, Chile, when Bobby's trip was announced—there on a fence-mending tour to garner good publicity for President Johnson. Yet on the front page of the major newspaper *El Mercurio* was an extensive story on the pending visit from the brother of the Alianza's "founder," pushing the current administration's top official to an inside page.[4]

Vaughn brought his embarrassment to the meeting with him. "I mean, he didn't raise his voice or get mad, but it was clear that he was very angry," one attendee later said. From the outset, he was aggressive toward Bobby. The senator asked how he should address the invasion of the Dominican Republic. Vaughn brushed it aside. "In the first place, nobody will ask you about it because they don't care about that issue. No one asks about that anymore."

"Well," Bobby said, "you haven't been talking to the same Latins I have, because that's all they ever ask me." He offered to bet $5 that it would be one of the first three questions asked.[5]

Vaughn replied indignantly, "If they *do* ask you, you can always tell them what *your brother* said about Cuba."

Walinsky saw the glare come over the senator's eyes. Walinsky knew the look well: a "dead flat cold" stare that could "wither tree branches a hundred miles away."

"What in particular were you suggesting?" Bobby said.

"Well, the statement he made after Cuba that we'll never tolerate Communism in this hemisphere."

Bobby stared at him and quietly said, "I just hope you're not using anything that President Kennedy ever said to justify what you did in the Dominican Republic."[6]

It went from bad to worse as Vaughn continued to reference "your brother" as they went through the list of countries Bobby would be visiting, with the corresponding representatives from State briefing on American policy and other flash points.[7]

The discussion reached Peru, where its government and the International Petroleum Company, an American oil interest, were in an eighteen-month battle over oil profits. The newly elected Peruvian leadership thought the foreign company had made enough money off their national resources to start paying more royalties. International Petroleum thought the Peruvians had forgotten their place. Thomas Mann had the company's back and announced the United States would be slowing down its aid to Peru. This angered Bobby. Peru was doing exactly what the Alianza intended: peacefully electing a non-Communist, pro-democracy candidate and exhibiting self-determination on its citizens' behalf. "Unequivocal support to democracy" had been one of the pillars of JFK's policy.[8]

"Why," Bobby asked in the briefing, "should the government get into a contest between the Peruvian government and a private American oil company?" Vaughn insisted it was vital to U.S. interests and needled Bobby on how mistaken it was of "your brother" to suspend relations during its military coup.[9]

They moved on to Brazil, where the military had taken control and the situation was dire. In March of 1964, a bloodless coup overthrew leftist president João Goulart. President Humberto Castelo Branco, former army chief of staff, took over with an anti-Communism line that pleased the United States, while dissolving the existing political parties and subjecting free speech to strict punishment.[10] Bobby asked what he should tell these people about democracy. A Brazil desk officer started into a formulaic diplomatic statement that neither endorsed nor condemned.

Bobby cut him off. "I don't talk like that."

Silence.

Vaughn said, "Well, why don't you just say nothing?"

"Are you kidding?" Bobby said.

In that tense moment, Frank Mankiewicz, Latin America director for the Peace Corps, interjected.

Mankiewicz already knew what Bobby was up to in South America—John Nolan had consulted him about the itinerary. Mankiewicz had grown up in Hollywood, the son of *Citizen Kane*'s screenwriter and the nephew of the world-famous director Joseph Mankiewicz. Approaching middle age and with combat tours in Europe and advanced legal and journalism degrees under his belt, he quit his entertainment law practice and joined the Peace Corps. By the fall of 1965, Mankiewicz was the director in Latin America, overseeing four thousand volunteers in eighteen countries. This eye-opening experience radicalized his view of foreign affairs. "The Peace Corps volunteers were always on the side of social change," Mankiewicz said years later, "but whenever people in Latin America tried to emulate the American Revolution, the U.S. government tried to emulate George the Third."[11]

Witnessing events in the Dominican Republic had changed Mankiewicz's thoughts about American foreign policy everywhere. He was in Santo Domingo when thousands of marines landed with the mission of keeping the peace and restoring order. The rebels were on one side, the military government on the other, and the marines were in the middle. The Peace Corps volunteers' sympathies were with the rebels, which is why senior White House aide Bill Moyers made sure the Latin America director was there to keep his volunteers out of trouble. Mankiewicz felt for the rebels as the kids did, but recognized that these decisions were made a lot higher up the chain of command. If the mission was to keep the two sides from getting at each other, then so be it. That's why what he saw next was so unforgettable. He was with *New York Times* foreign correspondent Tad Szulc at Santo Domingo's Hotel Ambassador, from which they could actually see the marines parting their lines to allow the Dominican army to roll through and crush the rebels. Mankiewicz was on the phone talking to his wife, who was watching the news on television back in Washington. They were saying that the marines were there to keep the two sides apart. He couldn't believe what he was hearing. They were helping the military rulers, and everyone in the Dominican Republic knew it. It occurred to Mankiewicz at that moment, "If they're lying about *that*, then maybe they're also lying about Vietnam."[12]

Frank's suggestion in the meeting was for Bobby to split the difference. "Well, you know, at least you're identified with one of our political parties and you are a United States senator," Frank said, "and I would think the minimum that they might expect—and I don't see why it would be *wrong*—would be to say, 'In our country we like strong political parties and strong legislative parliamentary institutions, and we wish you'd have them.'" Bobby liked the sound of that.

Vaughn would hear none of it.[13]

"Well, Mr. Vaughn," Bobby said, summing up the briefing, "as I see it, then what the Alliance for Progress is come down to is that you can abolish political parties and close down the Congress and take away the basic freedoms of the people and deny your political opponents any rights at all and banish them from the country, and you'll get a lot of our money. But if you mess around with an American oil company, we'll cut you off without a penny. Is that it?"

"That's about the size of it," Vaughn replied.

The meeting ended, and Mankiewicz approached Bobby. Kennedy asked him, "Are these people real? Do they really believe that stuff, or do they just talk that way?" Mankiewicz said they really believed it. "It sounds like we're working for United Fruit again," Bobby would soon tell a reporter, a reference to how the Eisenhower administration bent American foreign policy to help big business against the government of Guatemala.[14]

In Latin America, the Kennedy name meant "change," and someone like Bobby could wield enormous influence. Columnists Rowland Evans and Robert Novak reported that a Venezuelan government official contacted the State Department to encourage Bobby to visit Central University in Caracas— "a hotbed of over-aged Communist 'students' and a staging ground for Red terrorist bands." They wrote, "Venezuelan authorities usually don't want a touring United States Senator within shouting distance of the University. But Kennedy, they feel, could cope with the leftist students as he did in Japan and might actually get through to those not committed to communism." Newspapers predicted embarrassment for the administration, with reports of students "preparing pro-Kennedy and anti-Johnson placards." The fear at the State Department was "that the romantically-inclined Latin mind will view Kennedy as a sort of government-in-exile who will give them what Tom Mann won't—thereby undercutting U.S. policy."[15]

A few days after Bobby's contentious briefing with Vaughn, National Security Adviser McGeorge Bundy reached out to RFK to smooth things over. Bundy told Bobby he understood why he was upset, and that he was right: Alianza aid was being used to do the corporations' dirty work. But nevertheless, that aid was in Tom Mann's hands now, and if he mouthed off down there, the situation would only get worse.[16]

Bobby would heed Bundy's advice on his rhetoric, but would torture the administration in another way: by taking Dick Goodwin along.[17]

Goodwin had shaped the Alianza under JFK, along with President Johnson's best lines—including his address to Congress after Selma. "Don't you know a liberal Jew has his hand on the pulse of America?" Johnson scolded Jack Valenti for not originally assigning Goodwin the speech. Goodwin had been trying to split from the White House all summer, negotiating with the President over when he could leave. Johnson finally relented—with the promise that Goodwin would come back to write the 1966 State of the Union. Less than two months later, he was joining the Kennedy party as a "friend," not a staffer. He later heard that the President scoured wire reports of Bobby's trip looking for the sentences that "could only have been written by Goodwin."[18]

THE KENNEDY PLANE landed in Lima, Peru, to a dishearteningly small crowd. Only two hundred had turned out as the embassy kept Kennedy's schedule confidential for "security precautions." His aides suspected the ambassador of sabotage to please Johnson.[19]

It was the last time they had the complaint. The country buzzed in search of "¡Roberto!"—which they chanted along with "¡Presidente! ¡Presidente!" Standing in an open car shaking hands through the streets of Lima, Bobby joked, "Be sure to vote for Abe Beame." Communist students carrying signs reading OUT YANKEES could barely fight their way within three blocks of him.[20]

Bobby had spent the year talking to American college students about the revolution now in progress—acknowledging the speed of change, the racing pulse of their generation, rooted in the United States' greatest traditions. Latin America's students—many of whom had lived through actual revolutions—shared this sense of upheaval, only not through American eyes. Bobby needed to weave their revolutions into his words—*their* Washingtons and Jeffersons and Lincolns—to connect with them, to appeal to what they loved about their people, their past, and tap into their hope for the future.[21]

And so, as he had in Plattsburgh and Buffalo and Queens, Bobby depicted the Peruvian students as the heirs to revolution. He said that just as Jefferson was thirty-three, Hamilton thirty, and Madison thirty-six when they challenged an empire, Peru's San Martin and O'Higgins were thirty-six. Bolívar a mere twenty-eight.

"You can do as they can," Bobby told them. "You cannot do less."

He spoke of the "justice of the Incas—who punished nobles more severely than peasants for identical crimes," because the privileged person's responsibility to society was the greatest. He closed by invoking Manco Cápac's proud establishment of the Inca civilization eight hundred years earlier—a controversial point that his speechwriter, Walinsky, a twenty-eight-year-old rebel himself, was well aware of. For hundreds of years, the conquistadores had subjugated the Indian people of Peru, discarding their native history for one that exalted the Spanish. By 1965, things had started to change. The Indian and mestizo—mixed-race Spanish and Indian—were now attending the universities and stepping up in society, but race and class relations were still fragile. For Robert Kennedy to come in and recognize an Incan hero was an emotional and proud moment for those students whose families felt the boot of colonization on their necks. Walinsky knew it had struck a chord when the Q&A portion began. He saw the face of the first student to ask a question after the speech. His features were Indian, plain as day, and Bobby had spoken directly to his revolutionary history. And just as Bobby had predicted, the student asked about the United States' invasion of the Dominican Republic. "You lose the bet," he cabled Vaughn in Washington.[22]

In speeches across the continent, Bobby reprised his words from June's commencement speeches in New York, telling students in Lima, Santiago, and Buenos Aires, "The responsibility of our times is nothing less than revolution." It "will be peaceful if we are wise enough; humane if we care enough; successful if we are fortunate enough. But a revolution will come whether we will it or not. We can affect its character, we cannot alter its inevitability."[23]

"Kennedy Preaches Revolution!" was the headline in one Rio newspaper. The word littered his speeches (more than a dozen times in his Chile appearance alone). Your hemisphere, Bobby said, "was the birthplace of freedom's revolution." Lexington and Concord weren't named, weren't even settled, when Santa Fe had its first uprising against colonial powers in 1580. He quoted the astonished words of a defeated British general after Argentina delivered Latin America's first great victory against Europe in 1807, and spoke of continual revolution in the United States.

"We have had other revolutions since our independence, for mine is a revolutionary country: in the 1820s, to open political life to all regardless of birth or property; in the 1860s, to abolish the great plantations and the slavery which supported them; in the early twentieth century, to break and control the power of the great corporations. But it was the revolution of the New Deal that showed the power of affirmative free government—the government which joins the ideal of social justice to the ideals of liberty."[24]

THE KENNEDY ENTOURAGE was a circus. Many were left behind for Bobby's trip to the high-altitude city of Cuzco in Peru, and the traveling party still amounted to more than two dozen reporters and aides, bumping American tourists from a flight and costing them their hotel rooms. At the capital of the Inca empire, two thousand cheering Indians and a brass band waited for Bobby behind a barbed-wire fence by the dirt runway. Police with Czech-made machine guns stood between him and the people, but Bobby blew past them and toward the crowd. For a moment, the people appeared startled, as if expecting him to keep his distance, and then they pushed forward to embrace him. The barbed-wire fence came tumbling down into Bobby and others, tearing his pants at the knee and gashing his cheek. He kept on to deliver a short speech, dabbing at his cheek with a bloody handkerchief. He refused a tetanus shot and walked around in ripped pants for the rest of the day. People followed him, shouting, *"¡Viva Kennedy!,"* while waving Peruvian and American flags. Hundreds of children ran after the open-paneled truck carrying him.[25]

A fleet of Land Rovers took them to visit an American-run farm program, and along the way Bobby spotted Indian peasants working a cornfield by the road. "Stop the car," he said, jumping out and leaping over a ditch to shake hands with them. The workers earned about twelve soles—about forty-five cents—each day and had never heard of Bobby Kennedy, but they thought he might do something for them. One explained that he was paying high prices for powdered milk donated through the U.S. Food for Peace program. Bobby turned to the Peace Corps aide accompanying him and demanded, "You look into this."[26]

He relied on Frank Mankiewicz's Peace Corps volunteers for honest information about AID (Agency for International Development) projects. The embassies had tried to steer him toward safe ventures, but Bobby carved out time in most days to veer off the official path and visit shantytowns on the fringes—*barriadas*—such as Pampa de Comas in Lima, Peru. A hundred thousand called it home. Few had shoes. Bobby looked in on the small brick shacks with slat roofs, some with crude-looking Soviet hammer and sickles painted on them. The neighborhood lacked electric power, and clean water had to be trucked in because the dispute with the oil company had choked off American aid. A U.S. official told Bobby that the impasse made securing the funding for a water tank impossible. "It's outrageous," he told Goodwin. "Those people are living like animals, and the children—the children don't have a chance. What happened to all our AID money? Where is it going?" America's ambassador in Peru, J. Wesley Jones, "might as well have been the ambassador from Standard Oil," Walinsky said. The streets were dusty, the stench of sewage powerful as Bobby looked in on the brick-and-straw shacks, shaking hands. With the press, he kept his peace. "I have learned that the Alliance for Progress has taken hold," he said in his first formal news conference of the trip. "It has been slower than we had hoped, less certain than we had expected, but it is working."[27]

There were those in Peru who really suffered, and then there were those who liked to think that they suffered. Bobby met a few of the latter when he attended an exclusive cocktail party at the apartment of one of Dick Goodwin's artsy Peruvian friends. The guests were intellectuals, poets, artists, and other members of Lima's upper crust. "It was exactly like a meeting on the West Side of Manhattan," Walinsky would recall. The discussion was about the Dominican Republic, the Rockefeller-owned oil companies, the things the United States had done wrong and "very little, if anything, to do with any notion of social justice inside Peru."[28]

Bobby had heard enough. "Look, why do you always look to the United States?" he asked.

"Well, the United States won't let us do anything about the International Petroleum Company."

"Well, if it's so important to you, why don't you just go ahead and nationalize the damn oil company? It's your country. You can't be both cursing the United States and then looking to it for permission to do what you want to do; what you have to do is act on your own and take the consequences."

"Well, imagine the State Department," someone said. "Why, David Rockefeller has just been down here and he told us there wouldn't be any aid if anyone acted against the International Petroleum."

"Oh, come on," Bobby said. "David Rockefeller isn't the government. We Kennedys *eat* Rockefellers for breakfast. So if you want to assert your nationhood, why don't you just do it? What's going to happen to you after all? The United States government isn't going to send destroyers or anything like that."

A few days later, Bobby's quote about the Rockefellers appeared in the press—someone had hidden a tape recorder at the party. It raced around the continent, and when Bobby landed in Buenos Aires, a reporter who had garbled the translation asked, "Tell me, Senator, is it true that you have breakfast with Rockefeller every morning?"

"Not *every* morning."[29]

* * *

BOBBY DID NOT do as the State Department suggested and deny tensions altogether. He publicly admitted through an embassy-supplied interpreter that the slowdown of the Alianza over an oil contract was troubling. But he also said that President Johnson was fighting the aluminum companies' attempts at price gouging, just as President Kennedy had fought the steel companies. Standing atop a car, chopping the air with his arm, Bobby declared, "President Johnson is interested in *you*; he wants to help *you*."[30]

"It might have been easy for him in these circumstances to criticize the Johnson Administration," *New York Times* correspondent Martin Arnold wrote in his column. After all, the crowds were cheering Kennedy—not the United States. Arnold thought it must have been confusing for the Latin Americans. They were accustomed to leaders flouting laws of democratic succession. "It was very hard to explain to South Americans why he wasn't President of the United States," Arnold later said, describing the thinking as, "*Here is this man's brother. Why didn't he just march on Washington and* take *the presidency?*" One member of the traveling party said, "They don't want him for president. They want him for *dictator*."

Instead, Bobby swallowed his hard feelings for the President and even pushed his humble narrative, that "Lyndon Johnson had come from the soil and that he would understand their type of problems."[31] Bobby defended America in his continuous question-and-answer sessions at universities. Hearing student after student deriding American dominance took its toll on him. "Sometimes I wish somebody would say something nice about the United States," he said in a soft voice.

Ethel asked reporter Andy Glass how it went.

"Bob made quite an impression," he said.

"Oh, aren't you *nice* to call him Bob."

Glass said he didn't find it "dignified for a man who's nearly forty to be called Bobby. I wish everybody would call him Bob."

Ethel told Glass he would always be *Bobby* to her.

Then, just like a child, Bobby raced Walinsky and friend Bill vanden Heuvel the hundred yards up the hill back to their hotel.[32]

THE MEMORIES OF JFK were strong in Chile, where a thousand waited and women wept as Bobby stepped from his plane at Santiago's Los Cerrillos Airport. The ambassador, Ralph Dungan, was a familiar face from the Kennedy White House, and the party went to dedicate a school named for the President they had known and served.

With white-uniformed students lined up before him, local official after local official described Bobby as "a future President of the United States" as he nervously drummed his fingers on a copper plate.

Bill vanden Heuvel turned to Andy Glass and said, "You're not going to write that 'President' thing, are you?"[33]

Bobby said that he had come to see Chilean president Eduardo Frei's "revolution in liberty" up close. Frei's Christian Democratic Party was helping to guide the continent toward democracy, yet the Johnson administration had a tepid relationship with him. Kennedy spent two hours with him and Dick Goodwin, walking the grounds of Frei's summer residence overlooking the sea, discussing the Dominican Republic and land reform. When Bobby returned to Santiago, his car stopped traffic for blocks as he shook hands and praised President Frei. "Of all the heads of government I've met around the world and all their administrations . . . I am as much impressed with this group here as any I've seen," Bobby said. "If this administration does not succeed, there is a good chance the country will go Communist, because the people will have lost faith in a democratic government." That was exactly what some of Chile's radical university students were hoping for.

During Bobby's first campus visit in Santiago, about two dozen students shouted, "Kennedy go home!"—until other students rushed them and they fled. When order was restored, the first thing Bobby said was "I'm sorry they left. I'd have liked to learn from them."[34]

In Concepción, Chile's third-largest city, authorities warned Bobby not to be fooled by the adoring crowds—the Communists were well organized there, and the Marxist student group would not abide the senator speaking at the university. Bobby hoped to head off a conflict. He called the Marxist leaders to ask them to meet him at his hotel that afternoon. A dozen showed. They didn't look like revolutionaries. They were students, some in ties. For two hours, the two groups sat across a wooden table from each other, discussing what was respectable for both sides. Finally Bobby said, "Why do I give a damn? Why do I sit here and listen to you? There are a lot more pleasant things to do in Concepción. But I'm here because I'm interested in the revolution in Chile. Certainly, Chile has differences with the United States, I know that. Yet Chile gets more assistance, per capita, than any other Latin nation. Do you ever think about that? No. Because it doesn't fit your position."

The Communists sat there uncomfortably.

Bobby slapped the table. "I'm not coming to fool you," he said. "I've had a candid conversation with you. I doubt we could have had this meeting in Havana, Peking, or Moscow. I'm delighted we could in Chile. That's why I'm against Communism . . . Would you like me to come up to the university?"

"No, not me," their leader said in English. "We do not condemn you personally, but as a representative of a government whose hands are stained with blood. It if it was up to me, I would not let you speak."

Bobby became more agitated. He jabbed his finger toward the students. "Fifty or sixty persons can stop a speech. I know that. I don't mind getting hit by an egg. I've been hit by worse in my career." He paused and looked down for a moment. "In my judgment, if I can say so, the great indictment of your position is that you won't let me speak. You describe me with blood on my hands. I haven't had a marine stick a bayonet in *you* yet." He doubled back. "Let me make a deal with you. You speak for fifteen minutes and I'll speak for fifteen minutes . . . Aren't you confident? You don't sound it." Their leader said no and the students filed out quickly before Bobby could shake their hands.[35]

Occasionally, Seigenthaler had joked with Bobby, standing off to the side of a speech and yelling, *"Kennedeee, go home!"*[36] Now he and vanden Heuvel were warning him. Tradition kept police and military from entering university grounds. The Communists were unpredictable, they said. He could be hurt if he went. Bobby took a bath.

Two students from Frei's Christian Democratic Party arrived at Bobby's door next, saying that they needed him. "If you don't come, it will be a great victory for the Communists. I don't know how long it would be before we could show our faces." Then the rector of the university arrived, advising against the visit as he could not guarantee the senator's safety. Then the top American Catholic priest in the city arrived. "It would be great if you could go," he said.

"I've *got* to go," Bobby replied. Ethel walked into the crowded room and said she was going, too, and there wasn't a second's hesitation from Bobby.

Crowds pounded on the windows of their motorcade as it left the hotel. *"¡Viva Kennedy!"* But the mood changed the farther they went, until at last they neared campus and their police escorts peeled off one by one. They entered the university completely and frighteningly alone.

Bobby entered the gymnasium flanked by Seigenthaler, Goodwin, vanden Heuvel, and some reporters. Two thousand packed the stands. A hundred Communists claimed one section, overpowering every other voice, and as Bobby passed, they unleashed eggs, coins, small stones, and garbage in his direction. Bobby crowed to Seigenthaler, "If these kids are going to be young revolutionaries, they're going to have to improve their aim." They managed to hit everyone *except* Bobby, including some of the people in front. A fight broke out in the middle of the gym, delaying the program by ten minutes. The jeering was relentless. The Communists shouted, *"¡Kennedy, paredón!"*—"Kennedy, to the wall!" Martin Arnold feared more violence. Cries continued— *"¡Guatemala!" "¡Paraguay!" "¡Brazil! ¡Brazil!"*—echoing off the walls. "Go home, go home, you Yankee son of a whore." Then they sang the national anthems of Chile and Cuba. Bobby stood for both. *"¡Santo Dom-in-gooo! ¡Santo Dom-in-gooo!"*

The anti-Communist students had their own chants about Soviet aggression—*"¡Hungary! ¡Hungary!"*—but were no match.

Finally Bobby began. He jumped atop a table with his translator leaping up behind him. "I believe in freedom," he said toward the Communists. "I believe in free institutions. And I *will* speak tonight." Only those standing within a few yards of him could hear for all the shouting. "I do not come tonight to say the United States is without fault. All human beings make mistakes. But we support your revolution with our hearts because you are making the same effort we are making in the United States." The Communists began the Chilean national anthem again. Bobby kept right on. "We support your effort to build a new society. But we believe, most of all, in the right of free expression. We don't believe in spitting on people. We don't believe in throwing eggs." He called the Bay of Pigs "a dark day" for the Kennedy administration, "but don't judge the United States by this," he said. "This is not the true spirit of the United States—the true spirit of the United States is found in the work of four hundred or five hundred young people who come down here and volunteer to live in the rural areas and the slums to help Chile better itself." Every time he began to speak, the protesters drowned out his voice.[37]

In a corner, some set an American flag on fire. Ethel, stone-faced, spied a man from the U.S. embassy giggling nervously. "Don't you laugh when the American flag is being burned," she said.

Bobby jabbed his hand toward the Communists. "If they are so right, let one of them come down here and debate me. Let one of them be a spokesman and let the people in this room decide."

"Assassin!" they screamed, amid a string of curses.

"Will you come down and join me in debate? Come on down! Come on down! I challenge you to a debate! I am willing! Will you test your ideas before the students of this university? Do you want me to come up there?" Bobby immediately leaped down and made a path toward them, his entourage following.[38]

A photo in the *Washington Post* showed students shoving and tumbling before Bobby in a frantic, packed gymnasium. Walinsky would look back on the moment thinking someone could have swung a knife or drawn a pistol, yet Bobby remained cool and calm. Danger was just a part of his life. Walinsky remembered thinking that the senator was astounding at dealing with it—"physically, about as courageous a person as I've ever seen."[39]

Bobby climbed on a chair just below the Communists' section and extended his right arm to shake hands. A student in front spat directly into the senator's eye, the liquid streaming down his face. Next to him was one of the young

Communists in the meeting earlier, looking dismayed. Still, Bobby kept his hand out while another student swung his legs under the railing to kick at him.

Bobby jumped down. "Let's go. We've done what we came to do," he said, dabbing at his eye with a white handkerchief.[40]

Despite their venom—or perhaps because of it—Bobby sought out the most virulently anti-American students. In fact, he demanded the danger. He rejected police protection and was distressed to learn that participants were screened before a youth rally in Argentina. It was his way of proving his commitment, Martin Arnold thought—to show that the idealism John Kennedy stood for did not die with him.[41] It made him a part of something bigger, and if he couldn't get close, they couldn't learn from each other.

Before he was booed and assaulted at the *universidad*, crowds in the streets had gathered around his vehicle to touch him, and Bobby stood on the roof and sang "The Battle Hymn of the Republic" as they listened solemnly.[42] These moments mattered. He was a national phenomenon in Chile, dominating the headlines, and radio stations suspended their programs to provide coverage.

Even in the face of insults, he wanted to know more. Asking the Chilean officials why the Communists were so strong in Concepción, they told him of the working conditions in the undersea coal mines nearby. The place was miserable, dirty, and dangerous, with a heavily Communist union. To the officials' dismay, Bobby asked to go at once. That night, Bobby's group had a party, with many staying up until two in the morning. At four thirty, vanden Heuvel began rousing others: "Come on," he said, "the senator wants to go to the coal mines."

The Chilean police worked through the night to secure the route, fighting narrow roads, the cover of darkness, and a thick fog—perfect ambush conditions. Chilean soldiers were stationed at what looked like every hundred yards. When Bobby arrived and asked to make the long journey with the workers into the mine beneath the Pacific Ocean, the site manager protested. "Those men are Communists, they'll kill you," he pleaded. Bobby was unafraid. "Senator Kennedy, you can't go down there, you'll tear your suit."

"Haven't you heard that I can afford another suit?" he said before sneaking into a closing elevator and descending fifteen hundred feet. The tunnel train at the bottom was ordered to leave immediately, with the hope of stranding the senator. Bobby saw what was happening and sprinted down the narrow, damp track, running the train down and diving into the open car on his hands and knees. Once Bobby caught it, the train halted and let some others join. And so, within a few hours of the clash at Concepción, Bobby and his party were on their way to the bottom of a coal mine.

He looked around at the low-hanging, high-voltage wires just inches from their heads. The conditions got worse the farther down they went. Four had died this year, and four the year before. Bobby went the three miles to the end of the rail line, then walked two miles to the working area. "Senator Kennedy from the United States," he said to workers passing in the dark. It took half an hour for Bobby to make the trip. He shook hands with everyone he could find. "If you worked here as a miner," Bobby said to a supervisor, "would you be a Communist?"

"I'm afraid I would," the man said. "We breed them here."

When Bobby returned to the surface, the onetime aide to Red hunter Joseph McCarthy told the American journalists, "If I worked in this mine, I'd be a Communist, too."[43]

BOBBY KEPT RETURNING to the slums. His entourage jokingly called his trip the "all-expense-paid slum tour of South America."[44]

After his fourth visit to Lima's shacks, a Peruvian official was overheard saying, "Why does he want to see all this? I've lived here all my life and I've never been in one of these places."[45]

Bobby stepped over sewage and into homes, asking questions, smiling and handing out PT-109 tie clips. He trampled car hoods and roofs, pulling Ethel up beside him and raising her hand. "I give you the mother of nine children!" In Chile, Ethel toured the shanty home of a mother and her eight small children in one of Santiago's slums. There was one room, six small beds and a few blankets. Ethel complimented the mother on her home, looked over the children's homework, and hugged them. The mother fought back tears.[46]

In Buenos Aires, thousands of Argentineans, many of them teenagers, turned out to greet him outside the ambassador's residence, chanting "Bo-bee! Bo-bee!" and waving signs. One addressed Bobby as if he were an old friend, with a simple WELCOME, BOB.[47]

Others saw danger. An embassy security officer in Argentina said Bobby was crazy to go near the crowd. "These are volatile people. Their mood could change at any moment. They could *kill* him." Military police in blue helmets wildly swung clubs at anyone within reach. Photojournalist Steve Schapiro was stepping backward snapping photos when Walinsky saw one of the officers' eyes zero in on Schapiro's head and raise his club. The speechwriter caught the officer's arm before he could complete his swing. Even Ethel had to punch a cop in the stomach. Walinsky would remember seeing the blank-faced soldiers carrying submachine guns and thinking, "The relationship between the government and its people is expressed most precisely in the kinds of sidearms that the police carry." Yet Bobby climbed out of the ambassador's car and waved his way past the police into the crowd.[48] "I bring you cordial greetings from President Lyndon Johnson," he said.[49]

In São Paulo, Brazil, he was asked if the United States would have a better world image "if they had kept President Kennedy's policies." Bobby said, "I would not make a comparison between President Kennedy and President Johnson . . . My judgment is that President Johnson is continuing the same efforts that were begun by President Kennedy."[50]

"Go back to when President Kennedy was alive," he told students in Brazil. "He wasn't always so highly thought of as he is today."[51]

"We have made mistakes," Bobby told them, "but you have probably made mistakes, too . . . Not all of your troubles are the fault of the United States, and nothing the United States can do will solve all your problems . . . We have had arguments, but so do friends argue and husbands and wives fight. That does not mean we are not friends nor does it mean the husbands and wives will be divorced."

An embassy official in Rio said, "His humble way of admitting our own mistakes has done a lot to blur anti-American feelings."[52]

His youth, his manner, and his Catholicism made him instantly popular. In the Chilean farming community of Linares, the people tossed so many flowers that the group's cars looked like floats in a parade. The *Wall Street Journal* wrote that Bobby "has been a surprisingly staunch defender of President Johnson's foreign policy—despite what must have been heavy temptation to increase his popularity by disavowing it." Bobby would redirect their affection, leading a crowd of Chilean schoolchildren in a *"¡Viva Johnson!"* chant.[53]

Asked if he would become a presidential candidate, Bobby said he was backing President Johnson and would be running for reelection in 1970. "That's a long ways off," he said of 1972. Only in private did he invoke the future, telling Americans stationed at the embassy in Lima to stop using Alianza aid to bludgeon the Peruvian government. "I'm not in the administration *now*," Dick Goodwin remembered him warning.[54]

Bobby awoke on the morning of November 20 and turned forty years old—a reminder of just how young he was, and how much promise he held. A new biography came out that month, titled *Robert Kennedy at 40*, documenting the short life that had once reached the height of American power and seemed destined to return to it. "Even in 1984," the book's authors wrote of a White House bid, "Bobby will be just fifty-eight—not at all too old to run."[55]

"It is foolish to talk about anybody in the presidency now except Lyndon Johnson and maybe Hubert Humphrey," Scotty Reston would write that fall. "The future is mercifully shut out" for Bobby, "who should get himself a new nickname after 40." Reston wrote that Bobby "is not wildly popular in the Senate. He is still not a good extemporaneous speaker, and he has not yet mastered the art of looking at himself and the other public figures in his world with either detachment or humor. But who has at forty?"[56]

Ethel threw a birthday party at the home of friends in São Paulo with funny songs and gag gifts. Bill vanden Heuvel saw the memories of President Kennedy deep in the senator's eyes—two years earlier was the last time Bobby had seen him alive. His mind was clearly in another place when someone pulled the ends of party favors, eliciting sounds of gunfire: *pop-pop-pop!* Kennedy plunged his face into his hands and cried, "Oh, no . . . Please don't." And then the moment was over . . . [57]

Walinsky, who had only gotten to know him well that year, would later say that Bobby "was a very secret man in many ways. There were things he carried around in his head that were unimaginable, things that he just had to live with, all by himself. Knowledge about other people, and other things." It was a lonely burden to carry.[58]

NOVEMBER 22 WAS harder to bear. Bobby passed the anniversary of his brother's death in Salvador, Brazil. He and Ethel began the day with morning mass at a magnificent two-hundred-year-old church. There, with a few dozen impoverished locals, his face was twisted in pain and he bowed his head. Bobby and his wife stayed and prayed at the altar for a long time after Communion, and then went to the slums, where his five-man Brazilian security team retreated to their cars, cursing the stench under their breath. He stopped at a community center renamed for his brother. Children sang "God Bless America," and Bobby wept openly. Some of the kids had no shoes. He gathered them around and said quietly, "President Kennedy was most fond of children. Can I ask you to do a favor for him? Stay in school, study hard, study as long as you can, and then work for your city and Brazil."[59]

The children liked the sandy-haired visitor who talked a lot about learning. When asked if he knew who Bobby was, one child answered confidently, "Yes. He's the minister of education."[60]

On the flight to Natal, Brazil, Bobby sat by himself with his head buried in his arms. He had tears in his eyes when he placed a wreath at a memorial bust of JFK at the Praça da Imprensa. Firecrackers in the crowd made him wince, and in the twilight he climbed atop a truck and spoke to hundreds at an impromptu memorial service lit only by flashlights. "Every . . . child . . . an . . . education!" he said, pausing between each word. "Every family adequate housing! Every man a job! As long as there is a Kennedy in public life in the United States, there will be a friend of northeast Brazil."[61]

Love mingled with fear. Three university students under the age of twenty-one were arrested on the anniversary of President Kennedy's murder, in an alleged plot to throw acid in Bobby's face during a speech. Police described the woman and two men as agents of "a continental Communist conspiracy directed from abroad" to inspire violent anti-American demonstrations. The authorities scaled back the accusations the next day, saying the students only planned to hurl plastic bags of ink—*not* acid. Bobby asked that they be released to attend the rally, but the police refused. Bobby sent an emissary to the jail to see if the students cared to submit questions for him to answer, and they sent two. One of the students wrote him a note saying that because of his respect for President Kennedy, he did not "have the cowardice to make an attack against your life."

In Recife, Brazil, Bobby spoke jacketless, sleeves rolled up before a thousand students, talking for two hours, and answering questions—including the written ones sent by the jailed students, though he never called attention to that detail.[62]

"Freedom of speech and freedom of protest are essential in Brazil as in any country of the world," he said in a country that had just seen its rights curtailed.[63]

Some students criticized the United States for its invasion of the Dominican Republic, its history of segregation, and its continued discrimination against Negroes. "Looking at this audience," Bobby said, "I don't see many dark-skinned faces." A stunned silence . . . followed by cheering.[64]

"Though I come from the richest state in the most fortunate of nations, there are still far too many families living in poverty and ignorance and filth," he told four thousand students and faculty members at Catholic University in Rio. "New York, like Rio de Janeiro, has its own favelas." He told them of the extreme poverty he had seen just miles from their campus and that young people bore a special responsibility to their countries. "How many of you have ever been in a favela?" he asked. A few raised their hands. "How many of you have ever worked in a favela?" Even fewer hands went up. "If all we do is complain about the universities, criticize the government, carry signs, make speeches to one another, and then leave to take a job with United Fruit or a Brazilian company and then not pay any attention to those who need our help, then we have not met our responsibility. It is not enough just to talk about it. Unless we do something, there's not going to be any Brazil—or any world."[65]

"We are in the middle of a revolution here. It can be violent or not. It depends on what we make it," he said often.[66] "I come to Brazil to see what leadership you will give to the great war or revolution of our time—the war against the age-old enemies of man: tyranny and disease, hunger and ignorance. And there is a danger, growing out of this very university experience. That you will not do so. The very education which has helped expand your awareness of the problem of other men is the same education which prepares you for a place in society far removed from those problems. As the skilled and professional people of your nation and the world, you will be moved out of the contact with the large number of people in the world whose principal worries are hunger and hope. You will be equipped to live, work, think, and travel in the very latest day of the twentieth century. You will read and hear about poverty and tyranny; you will be aware, concerned, and sympathetic. But will you also work to lend your talents to the service of your society—and of all societies on this shrinking planet?" He concluded, "If we fail to meet our responsibilities now, the judgments of the moment may excuse us. But there is no escaping the judgment of posterity."[67]

At University Hall, they cheered.

"The imbalances and injustices, the people out of time, out of money, out of hope—these are yours and yours alone to change."[68]

"These things you can do. *These things you can do.* These things you *must* do."[69]

The *Washington Post* called his reception in Brazil "some of the most enthusiastic" of the entire tour.[70]

He provoked and provoked and provoked. When sugarcane cutters told him of working six days for three days' wages, he made a beeline for the landowner, in a white linen suit, snapping pictures on an expensive Japanese camera. "Let me just say this to you," Bobby said. "I think you are breeding your own destruction. You are tearing down your society if you don't pay people a decent wage."[71]

Many of Bobby's appointments with government officials in Brazil had been scrapped in late October, when the military coup dissolved political opposition and everything else that could be deemed "antirevolutionary." Instead, Bobby spent an hour at the Presidential Palace in private conversation with President Humberto Castelo Branco. Back in the streets of Rio, Bobby saw another crowd abused by soldiers' elbows and rifle butts and decided to jump on a car and yell, "Down with the government! On to the palace!" He talked about revolution and called for the restoration of democracy.

"Of course," his aide Tom Johnston remembered, "a lot of these things . . . were not reported back in the States, or if they were, were not reported in any context. But they obviously really were upsetting for the embassy."[72]

One stunned Brazilian minister pulled Dick Goodwin aside that night and asked, "Can't you do something about this young revolutionary?" Goodwin had no recourse for the minister, but Bobby's office paid a cumulative $300 for all the car hoods he damaged.[73]

* * *

AFTER THANKSGIVING WITH Peace Corps volunteers, Bobby, Ethel, five aides, and nine reporters chartered a special flight to Manaus, a port city deep in the Amazon jungle, on a mission into Brazil's "green hell" to visit Catholic missionaries. They took an old white paddle wheeler down the Amazon, dragging their mattresses out from the stuffy staterooms and onto the decks to sleep beneath hammocks.[74]

The Amazon trip was meant for relaxation, "but the pace Senator Kennedy set here and elsewhere in the Amazon has been grueling," one reporter along for the journey wrote. Firecrackers announced the Kennedys' arrival, and hundreds of children would follow them wherever they went, talking and asking questions. He was the first politician of any nation they had ever met. Someone hooked a wagon to a tractor for Kennedy to survey the local sights, and he rode along like the pied piper of the jungle, with dozens of children riding or running alongside. At one point the vehicle swerved and Bobby was thrown into some bushes, but he simply picked himself up, borrowed a bicycle, and, with two kids hitching a ride, pedaled the two miles left on their tour.[75]

Looking for even more adventure, Bobby headed for missionaries living with a remote Indian tribe, translating the Bible into the local tongue. A few of the men chartered a single-engine seaplane from 1939, heavy with cargo and bodies. "I must be crazy to get on this thing," Bobby said before kissing Ethel good-bye. They flew for what seemed like hours and landed near a collection of thatched-roof huts. The missionary couple translated their conversations with the local tribe, who had never heard of Presidents Kennedy or Johnson. Bobby asked the twenty-four-year-old chief for his impression of the United States. "I guess," he said, "that it's bigger than this place." Bobby was interested in their culture, quizzing the missionaries on the tribe's family structures.

After a daring midnight fishing adventure amid "a blinding rainstorm which dropped the temperature from nearly 100 to about 55 degrees," as one reporter wrote, they made for home. Their canoe's motor failed, and they needed eight hours to get to a place where the water was deep enough for their plane to take off. Bobby eagerly hopped out into the water to help when they got stuck on rocks. He seemed genuinely free, splashing around and doing an impression of Walter Cronkite as he said, "It was impossible to pinpoint the exact time and place where he decided to run for president. But the idea seemed to take hold as he was swimming in the Amazonian river of Nhamundá, keeping a sharp eye peeled for man-eating piranhas." He paused and added, "Piranhas have never been known to bite a U.S. senator."

Bobby confessed that he would like to cross the North Atlantic in a sailboat alone.

"That would take six weeks," one person told him. "You're a United States senator. You could never get away with it."

"I guess you're right," Bobby said. There wasn't enough time.[76]

BOBBY ARRIVED IN Caracas, Venezuela, to anti-American riots. A public bus was burned and leftist students exchanged gunfire with police, though no one was reported hurt. Threats were made to kidnap Ethel and gun down the motorcade. Bobby debated Communist students on television. "I don't accept your description of the 'facts,'" he said. "Why isn't the President of the United States a Rockefeller if big business really runs our country? What you're saying is simply ridiculous . . . Now follow up," he demanded. "Come back at me."[77]

The senator delivered a culminating speech to the national labor federation, saying, "Latin America can speak to the nations of Asia and Africa from the platform of common problems and understanding which we in the United States do not completely share." He urged Latin Americans to take a bigger role in "the peaceful settlement of disputes" in the region and to make it a nuclear-free zone. He suggested a more Western-like approach to continental relations and with the world, so that they could take part "in the councils of the West" before—not after—a decision was made. He also walked through the slums with Venezuelan president Raúl Leoni, followed by easily a thousand of their inhabitants. Leoni had just succeeded Rómulo Betancourt in the country's second consecutive presidential election—a democratic milestone made possible, Bobby believed, by stabilizing Alianza aid.[78]

The Kennedy group stayed at the residence of Ambassador Maurice Bernbaum, whose wife could be heard through the walls asking, "Where did all these people come from? Who are they? Why are they sleeping here?" Followed by the ambassador quietly urging, "Calm down. We have to do this." When *New York Times* reporter Martin Arnold wandered the compound shortly before the diplomatic reception, he found Bobby neck-deep and alone in the swimming pool.

"Come on in," he called to Arnold.

"I haven't got a bathing suit," the reporter said.

Bobby shrugged. "I'm in here without a suit."

So Arnold stripped down to nothing and jumped in. They swam for a while as guests began filling the residence and garden. That's when Bobby got out of the pool—wearing swim trunks.[79]

BOBBY'S TRAVELING PARTY returned to Kennedy International Airport in New York on the first of December, after nearly three weeks of rambling around Latin America. The senator was set to make his first Sunday-morning talk show appearance four days later on *Meet the Press*, where Vietnam would be the focus.

Secretary of State Dean Rusk had just spoken about rejecting peace feelers from the North Vietnamese before further escalation. "Our attitude was and is that we are not interested in saving face but in saving South Vietnam," Rusk said. In Saigon, Secretary of Defense McNamara said that the "decision by the Vietcong to stand and fight" against heavy bombings "can lead to only one conclusion—that it will be a long war."[80]

In the studio, Bobby was reminded of his "blank check" statement before the spending vote in May. "In view of the recent escalation of the war," reporter Bonnie Angelo asked, "do you think the President should go back to Congress for further discussion of the whole Vietnam situation?"

"I think if there are going to be troops beyond the numbers that President Johnson mentioned in his speech in August, if we are going to carry the bombing beyond the area that it is presently being aimed at, then I think it should be discussed with the appropriate committees in Congress and with Congress itself."

Angelo followed up, "Do you think a formal declaration of war would clarify our position?"

"I do not at this moment," Bobby said.

The question of a bombing pause came later. Bobby said he would support one under circumstances that brought parties to the negotiating table—or even "if it would make once more clear to the world that we are interested in peaceful negotiations of the problems of South Vietnam." Still, he equivocated by saying he hadn't had the proper intelligence briefings to judge whether "the moment is the appropriate time."

Chief moderator Lawrence Spivak returned at Bobby, "Senator, as you know, there have been a number of press reports . . . May I ask you the direct question: Do you support fully his present policy on Vietnam?"[81]

Bobby was silent. His eyes darted away to the left. He blinked. Three seconds of dead air had passed.

"I basi—I basically support the policy," he finally said.[82]

The *New York Times* would write the next day, "Mr. Kennedy stared at Mr. Spivak for what began to seem a long time before he replied."[83]

"I have some reservations about whether we are doing enough in the economic and political field, and I also have felt for some period of time that a major effort had to be undertaken in the diplomatic field. I think more has been done on that in the last six or eight months than had been done prior to that time, but I think that within Vietnam military bombings, military action, and military troops, military forces of the United States, cannot by themselves win the war. I think we emphasize continuously the military aspects without the political and the economic areas or efforts that have to take place in Vietnam."

Bobby and Spivak exchanged words. "You don't think at the present time we are doing enough?"

"Let me just say that I think we can do more, and I have made it clear that I think that more has to take place . . . I would like to see visits by representatives of the civilian side, once again to emphasize and promote a program within Vietnam that has some meaning for the people, because I think a military program by itself, or alone, is going to be self-destructive."[84]

At the end of 1965, Joseph Kraft wrote a column about Bobby's reluctance to speak out on Vietnam for fear of creating discord with the President. "He had talked about the difficulty of saying anything because it would be put down to political ambition rather than to a statement of the case. And it did take something—because he was constantly aware of that—to trigger it." Kraft felt Bob opened up to him about it because Kraft was against the war but thinking strategically—unlike some of the Kennedy staffers. Bobby, Kraft said, "knew I was very sensitive to danger . . . in favor of his lying low."[85]

A Gallup Poll taken in November had just found people growing more inclined toward Bobby: 60 percent of the public could name something they liked about him, while only 38 percent could name an unlikable characteristic. For the most part, people admired his intelligence, aggressiveness, sincerity, and energy; 8 percent said, "Because he's a Kennedy," while 10 percent said, "I just like him." People least liked him for capitalizing on the Kennedy name and being "pushy."[86]

"In the American lexicon," Martin F. Nolan wrote for the *Boston Globe*, "Bobby Kennedy is ruthless, just as Jack Benny is stingy, Dean Martin playboy and the New York Yankees invincible."[87]

Some 40 percent said they would like to see Bob become president one day, while 46 percent did not. When asked if RFK himself would like to become president, 74 percent agreed.[88]

A reporter who tagged along aboard the *Caroline* for a flight to Albany in mid-December asked Bobby how long he would feel compelled to work hard. "I suppose as long as I stay in politics and government," he said. Bobby asked the reporter for a notebook and pencil and wrote down a quote from Aeschylus that ended, "But when the height is won—then there is ease."[89]

1 2

POWER AND
RESPONSIBILITY

December 1965–February 1966

A LITTLE LESS THAN a year after he died, a bust of John F. Kennedy's head was installed in the White House Cabinet Room to honor his calm amid the missile crisis of October 1962. From then on, JFK's stone likeness would appear like a silent sentry in the background of photographs of Johnson and his advisers discussing how to handle Kennedy's malignant legacy: the escalating war in Vietnam.[1] Kennedy floated like a specter over the large oval table. Some may have viewed him as a monument to past commitments. Others, a spur to think anew.

In November 1965, previously unreported complaints about the lack of American diplomacy with North Vietnam came from beyond the grave. Adlai Stevenson, ambassador to the United Nations, had been engaged in a frustrating search for peace when he died of a heart attack on a London street four months earlier. The headline announcing his death appeared alongside ones he had been unable to stop: U.S. jets striking targets forty miles from the Chinese border and rumors of a larger military draft.[2] CBS reporter Eric Sevareid wrote in *Look* magazine that Stevenson had told him just before he died that senior Johnson administration officials resisted a secret peace conference arranged by the U.N. secretary-general—a heavy allegation since the White House claimed escalation was its last resort. Sevareid wrote that in the early fall of 1964, an anonymous "someone in Washington" asked to put off peace talks until after the election. Then, once Johnson had won, Secretary of Defense Robert McNamara opposed it. Months passed. The U.N. secretary-general offered to let the United States write the terms of the cease-fire, but according to Stevenson, Sevareid wrote, Secretary of State Dean Rusk did not respond.

The article sent a shudder through the administration. In Rio at the time of its publication, Rusk cabled back that there was always "a touch of Hamlet" to Stevenson, and that Sevareid's story was "probably" motivated by "a very substantial fee," the only explanation for why a television newsman published his scoop in a magazine. "Under these circumstances, such an article is not likely to avoid the temptation of dramatic effect," Rusk wrote.[3]

As that controversy was unfolding, a new one was in the offing. Italian foreign minister Amintore Fanfani was at the United Nations in New York on November 19 when associates delivered a detailed peace feeler from North Vietnam's Ho Chi Minh. Fanfani gave the North's terms to America's new U.N. ambassador, Arthur Goldberg, on November 20. "Fanfani said that one of the sources reported to him orally that Ho Chi Minh said that he is so eager to get this settled that he would be willing even to go to Washington," a State Department official wrote in a memo. Analysis to the President from National Security Adviser McGeorge Bundy found that "although worded in the most palatable form possible," the proposal demanded the establishment of a coalition government in which the National Liberation Front—the political arm of the Vietcong—"would play a leading and probably dominant role." Giving the NLF power was a deal breaker for the United States. Still, the administration deliberated and dallied for two weeks before making a counteroffer—by which time newly ordered air strikes appeared to sink the talks. Another embarrassing story spilled into the press.[4]

Bobby was apprised of the back-and-forth between the State Department and Fanfani and was disappointed at how the situation turned out, comparing the indecision and delay with the fast de-escalating action of the 1962 Cuban missile crisis.[5]

"How could the State Department wait for two weeks?" Bobby said at a holiday party in comments recorded by Stephen Schlesinger. "If we had acted that way in the Cuban crisis, we might have had war." He said that he would have agreed to Hanoi's four points the way they agreed to Russia's during the missile crisis: by taking "our own interpretation" of them. "This would make us look good whether the offer was real or not." Bobby said he had told LBJ he should have taken these steps with Hanoi a year ago—presumably after the 1964 election. "I don't think we've shown an open approach." Still, Bobby said, "I really think Johnson wants negotiations . . . Fifty percent of the government is for them. Fifty percent is against them. We're in a stalemate."[6]

As time went by, Bobby became more and more disillusioned by failings like these. He would occasionally pop into columnist Joseph Kraft's office to talk about Vietnam, and Kraft remembered how upset Bobby was over the "intellectual dishonesty" in missed opportunities for negotiations—"people who said they were doing one thing and really doing another."

"I guess there was a naive side to him," Kraft later said. "I can remember not being very bothered by it because I assumed that [Johnson] would mess it up since I assumed that he was trying to win the war and not negotiate a settlement." Bobby felt deceived.[7]

At the holiday party with Schlesinger, Bobby said that he didn't blame Johnson or McNamara; he blamed Rusk. "I'd like to speak out more on Vietnam. I have talked again and again on my desire for negotiations. But if I broke with the administration, it might be disastrous for the country."[8]

McGeorge Bundy would later say that Fanfani's peace feeler was like dozens of others they received in those years: "the more you poked, the less he had." But at the time, reports of missed opportunities for peace were taking a toll. Bundy observed to the President in a November 1965 memo how "the Sevareid episode, rightly or wrongly, has strengthened the impression among critics at home that we have not gone the full distance in seeking negotiations. There is now increased value in proving our good faith by a new pause."[9]

Vietnam was quickly taking over the capital. "Washington has, in fact, become a single-issue city," Tom Wicker wrote. The cost for Vietnam soared above the estimates the administration had made just months earlier. White House sources had said it would cost $2 billion yearly, yet the $5 billion predicted by congressional Republicans Gerald Ford and Melvin Laird now looked to be more accurate. The White House knew as much. Bundy wrote the President, "McNamara's budget shows that the alarming figure he mentioned at the Ranch may turn out to be an understatement." With Congress unlikely to pass a tax increase in an election year, spending cuts loomed. Republicans argued the nation had to choose between "guns and butter." And they had already paid for the guns . . .[10]

"This nation is now making a major effort and great sacrifice in Vietnam," Bobby said in a mid-December speech in downtown Brooklyn. "The question here in New York City is what sacrifices all of us are prepared to make, what changes in our way of doing things we are prepared to accept to make this a city and a nation which deserve the sacrifices being made in our name half a world away.

"What are we prepared to do," he asked, "when children I have seen in Harlem must keep lights turned on their feet so that the rats will not bite them as they sleep? . . . What are we prepared to do for the fifty percent of the young men in Manhattan who are not even physically or mentally qualified to enter the army?"

To forsake the war at home for the war abroad "would be a terrible mistake," Bobby said, for it would "invite a society so irretrievably split that no war will be worth fighting, and no war will be possible to fight."[11]

Bobby had borrowed his words from the McCone Commission, which had studied the causes of the Watts riots and insisted that without a "revolutionary attitude toward the problems of our city," the breaches between race and class "could in time split our society irretrievably." Bobby took that message and applied it toward America's priorities in Vietnam. The *Wall Street Journal* believed he was setting the bar "for a full-dress Vietnam debate next year." He was joined by the likes of Martin Luther King Jr., who said that if "a roll-back on the domestic front is necessary, we will have no alternative but to use our lobbying and protest activity to get Congress to reverse it."[12]

In December, Hanoi proposed a twelve-hour Christmas Eve truce. The administration was wary, suspecting it would only lead to another major attack like the assault on Pleiku, which came two hours after the annual Tet holiday truce ended. Secretary McNamara had been pushing the President toward an indefinite bombing pause since November, and Bobby did, too, telling reporters in New York that the White House should accept the cease-fire and extend it "on an open-ended basis."[13]

Teddy expressed his skepticism, as well. "I'm sure we could obliterate North Vietnam this afternoon," he told college students asking about bombing Hanoi. "But is that what we want to do?"[14]

For these comments, former President Harry Truman took the Kennedy brothers to task. "They are outsiders, just as I am," Truman said to huffing reporters on his brisk December-morning constitutional through New York City, "and they have no more business sticking their noses in than I have. I would recommend to the people to whom they are talking not to pay any attention." Truman added that Hubert Humphrey would be the Democratic nominee in 1972. "And that's not a prediction—*that's a fact* . . . Johnson is a good Democrat and he knows how to run the country," he said, dismissing "silly" draft-card burners.[15]

What Truman's decades of experience missed was the shift within the country. Nineteen sixty-five had begun with sixteen thousand Americans in Vietnam. Roughly two hundred thousand were there by year's end. The public speculation was that as many as four hundred thousand could be there by 1967. As the troop levels gradually built, so did the burden on the White House. In the same memo fretting over the Sevareid story and the soaring costs, Bundy wrote, "[General] Westmoreland's recommendations for 1966 deployments have increased, and the fighting in the Plei Me area shows that we may have to look forward to a pretty grim year. This again strengthens the argument for one further demonstration that our determination to seek peace is equal to our determination on the battlefield."[16]

And so, with just days remaining in 1965, the Johnson administration took a hard look at the Vietcong's proposal of a twelve-hour Christmas truce. Soviet ambassador Anatoly Dobrynin suggested a twelve- to twenty-one-day pause to McNamara and Bundy, promising that negotiations were "impossible" for North Vietnam if bombs kept falling.[17]

America countered by offering a day and six hours, which administration sources unofficially said would likely extend past that pause if the cease-fire was honored. Bobby urged that the Christmas truce be lengthened so the conflict could move "from the battlefield to the conference table." Speaking by phone from a skiing trip in Sun Valley, Idaho, he said, "It is my view that Americans and South Vietnamese troops should not be the first to attack if the Vietcong substantially honor the additional hours of the truce established by our side."[18]

The respite from battle let South Vietnamese families return to the streets of Saigon, while relaxed American soldiers danced the Watusi with girls from Bob Hope's entertainment troupe. On December 28, a U.S. government spokesman acknowledged that the bombing pause would continue indefinitely, the military concerns superseded by political ones. Washington wanted to test Hanoi's willingness for peace. Members of the administration canceled their New Year's plans and fanned out across the globe, looking to start peace talks.[19] Though skirmishes would soon resume, the air war stopped. From the outside, the prospect for peace looked real.

BOBBY PUT HIS focus toward New York City, taking a few days to visit Christmas parties for children in housing-project basements in low-income areas in the Bronx and the Bedford-Stuyvesant section of Brooklyn, paid for by a small trust he and others endowed. Ethel, Jackie, and six of his nine children joined him at the end of a long day of singing carols. "I have a special treat for you," the former first lady said with a big smile. "I will give the microphone to Senator Kennedy, and he will sing for you. He has a beautiful voice." Bobby sang a few off-key bars of "Silent Night" as the children giggled.[20]

He had been weighing policy prescriptions for the ghettos ever since Watts. Once the McCone Commission released its findings on the Watts riot's causes, Bobby called for similar, community-led initiatives to probe the conditions of slums in every American city. Most were already tinderboxes. They had to be vigilant about sparks. And here, too, he saw friction from Vietnam. In his mid-December speech, Bobby reminded his audience that some of the worst race riots in history had occurred during World War II "because Negro soldiers were asked to give so much, and their families at home were allowed so little."[21]

Back in the summer, Bobby had asked his aides to start thinking about a comprehensive approach to the cities. It was primarily a reaction to the violence, but was also to set new goals. A promise had been made in the civil rights movement and propelled into the mainstream by the New Frontier, and that promise was still woefully unfulfilled even with the achievement of the Civil Rights and Voting Rights acts.

Bobby's staff spent the next months speaking with experts and visiting communities such as Bedford-Stuyvesant. By winter, they were struggling to pack all their ideas into one speech, so they decided to break it into three parts: speeding the end of de facto segregation in Northern cities, improving the slums for those who stayed, and how the rest of America—primarily the white middle class—would benefit. It amounted to what Peter Edelman later called "a total impact project for the ghetto." It was radical, comprehensive, and possibly exceeded the senator's ambition.[22]

Edelman was responsible for the first speech on breaking up urban ghettos, by far the most sensitive subject. Government-forced integration was harder to argue for in the North, based on the premise that segregation there was somehow different from Jim Crow: it was by choice, not code. Yet Bobby's speech on January 20 argued that was just a step farther along the path from America's original sin. The Negro had traveled from enslavement, to open discrimination, to neglect.

"For three hundred years," Bobby said, "the Negro has been a nation of people governed by a repression that has been softened to the point where it is now only massive indifference." He blamed Northern white flight to the suburbs as Southern Negroes poured into the cities for "a situation of segregation unparalleled in our country's history." Bobby proposed federally sponsored actions to allow Negro families some mobility: aid for relocation housing out of the ghetto; aid to educate kids in better schools; and aid to hire community-information officers to help newcomers from falling prey to slumlords.[23]

The ideas were explosive. The speech, however, was a dud. "An utter, total bomb," Edelman said. The audience was four hundred philanthropists at a luncheon at the Americana Hotel in midtown Manhattan. They had come for a Kennedy and chicken à la king; not a statistic-laden jeremiad on how their city was worse than Jim Crow.[24]

The second speech two days later, on improving the ghetto in the short term, was at a more receptive venue uptown: a group of black leaders at a Harlem YMCA on 175th Street. Bobby knew the crowd was his from the moment he walked in. Mayor John Lindsay was holding a question-and-answer session, but his nationally rising star was no match for that of Bobby, who turned the room's focus and embarrassed the great Republican hope. Lindsay stayed twenty minutes into Bobby's speech before exiting, with Bobby slyly acknowledging, "Bye, John," from the microphone.[25]

This second speech recognized that the topic of the first was a "task of years, perhaps of decades," and that the present generation of Negroes could not be allowed to languish. The solution, he said, would begin in Harlem and Bedford-Stuyvesant.

"Clearly, the most important problem in Harlem is education of every kind," he said. "Fathers must learn job skills, and mothers how to buy food economically. Students must learn to read, and little children how to speak. And teachers must learn how to teach and employers how to hire."

Bobby said "too little" was expected of ghetto children in the classroom, and that the "extreme position" of describing "welfare as the worst thing that could have happened to the Negro" had "factual support." He insisted that his proposal was "not a massive extension of welfare services," because there were "not enough social workers, psychiatrists, or indigenous workers in the country to minister to all the broken families and hopeless children on a case-by-case basis." Welfare could not "confer respect" to "men without work, for in the United States you *are* what you *do*."

Besides improving ghetto residents' self-image, Bobby said that society at large had a responsibility, too: to stop treating slum denizens "as liabilities" and begin thinking of them "as a valuable resource, as people whose work can make a significant contribution to themselves, their families, and the nation."

His solution was jobs: created immediately, offered exclusively to residents, on projects that improved their lives. Older workers would be sent back to school, high schoolers would be allotted academic credit for work-study programs, and those who exhibited leadership traits would be introduced to advanced classes set up by state and city universities. Businesses would be lured with tax breaks, having big corporations treat the ghetto as they would a foreign country by setting up satellites and gradually letting the locals run them. Labor unions would be prodded to desegregate their ranks and train Negro and other minority apprentices. And residents would be empowered by establishing groups of tenants and volunteers to address problems with slum landlords and superintendents, and to repair their crumbling housing.

Bobby believed an economic overhaul through the existence of jobs and the pride of employment could reinvent the slums. "For this is man's work," he said, "work which is dignified, which is hard and exacting, which is at the same time rewarding to the man who does it and the community around him."[26]

Tough talk and all, the speech was well received. If the McCone Commission was a diagnosis, this was medicine. However, these programs were expensive, in cost and commitment. The price could only be borne through consensus like the kind that carried the New Deal through to fruition. And consensus was fracturing. Middle-class suburban whites, many of whom supported civil rights in the South, were bitten by ghetto violence. The passage of civil rights legislation alleviated some of the national shame from nonviolent protesters clubbed on their television sets. The destruction in Watts left them puzzled, worried, and bitter. Many felt less and less responsible for the plight of the ghetto, and less and less inclined to do something about it.

Walinsky pushed the senator to transcend race and fix his focus on class.[27] The young legislative assistant had long believed that the middle class—the postwar American majority "with almost no characteristic common to all"—defined itself "largely by the fact that the poor exist." He had published this thesis in a cover story for the *New Republic* magazine shortly before joining the 1964 Senate campaign.

"Doctors are middle-class," Walinsky wrote, "but so are bookkeepers; factory workers vacation with lawyers, drive bigger cars than teachers and live next door to store-owners, and send their children to school with the children of bank tellers." Some in the middle class were wealthier than others, but none of them were at the very bottom, and that was what their status and societal self-worth depended on. For this reason, Walinsky concluded, "the middle class majority *does not want* to improve significantly the lot of the poor, or . . . actively desires to keep the poor in their place."

In order to build consensus for a new fight against the grittiest poverty, Walinsky believed the broad American middle had to gain from it. "A serious program must offer the middle class a new lifestyle in return for the raise in status it would give to the poor; it must deal not only (or even primarily) with pockets of economic poverty but the poverty of satisfaction, purpose and dignity that afflicts us all." Walinsky was certain that if they could alleviate the poverty of satisfaction, they could make a revolution in the ghetto without the middle class batting an eye.[28]

That was the goal when Robert Kennedy rose to speak that Saturday night, January 22, in a Statler Hilton ballroom packed with white middle-class members of the United Auto Workers. To combat resentment before it metastasized.

"We are now engaged in a great experiment," Bobby said, to benefit "the poor and the distressed" of urban ghettos and Appalachia. "But we have not exercised that same imagination . . . on behalf of Americans who are not poor, not cut off from the twentieth century, not handicapped by racial discrimination or age or youth.

"The question will be, why should we? What help do these more fortunate Americans need in a time of a record gross national product, of increasing prosperity throughout our society?" It was because the gross national product did not measure all inequalities—least of all, "the inequality of time." It was far easier to afford and attend college in 1965 than it was in 1955. "The graduating high school senior of ten years ago . . . is still only twenty-seven or twenty-eight, a young man in the prime of his life, with over thirty years of productive life and work ahead. If that young man, for financial reasons, went to work instead of college at the age of eighteen, there is little chance that he will ever get a college education." Ultimately, choices made between the ages of fifteen and twenty tended to limit workers' potential for a lifetime.

"Our society changes rapidly," he said, "but we have not provided enough opportunity for people to change with it." It was the change-oriented message Bobby had directed at the world's idealistic youth. He had now recast it for the middle-aged middle class.

If the government could offer college scholarships to teenagers who agreed to serve in the navy, it could make similar deals with older students serving their country in Harlem or Appalachia. It could help them with loans and financial arrangements to make their sacrifices viable. He listed more ideas to offer the middle-aged middle class the opportunities and benefits they had seen politicians handing out to every group but their own. They were ideas, and only the start. "The foregoing is no exhaustive list," he recognized. "By its very incompleteness, it demonstrates that we are only at the beginning of a beginning in thinking about opening opportunities for all. More thinking must begin now. For the pace of change—in our economy, in our politics, in our whole society—can only accelerate . . . Let us now then prepare the minds of all our people . . ."[29]

Of *all* our people.

Bobby's inclusive policy message was overshadowed that night by politics. His speech didn't begin until nine thirty so he could attend to political business in Boston earlier—a rollicking black-tie testimonial dinner for Kenny O'Donnell's campaign for Massachusetts governor. "I'm pleased to come to a place where they understand my accent," Bobby said. That's what got the headlines that night. After all, his city speeches were announcing ideas; not actions.[30]

Finding the place for his antipoverty plans was the next challenge. Harlem was politically fractious with competing power brokers who all demanded a taste of the action. Brooklyn's Bedford-Stuyvesant was so troubled that even those who were exploiting the community were disorganized. Bobby had visited the neighborhood multiple times, including a trip with Senator Javits in the fall for "A Slumless Bedford-Stuyvesant" conference at a junior high.[31] He returned there just days after the speeches on the city.

"What, another tour?" one exasperated Bed-Stuy leader said when hearing that Bobby wanted to come through. "Are we to be punished by being forced again to look at what we look at all the time? We've been studied to death. The writers of sociology books have milked us of all the information." Another Brooklyn ghetto leader said she had been on enough tours. "You know what?

I'm tired, Mr. Kennedy, I'm tired . . . We got to have something concrete *now*, not tomorrow. *Yesterday.*"

After much speaking, it was time for him to listen. Bobby sat through a reception, hearing resident after resident chide and scold him for a million lies of a thousand politicians. They told him off again and again and again. "We're here to hear from our senator what he plans to do," said one, causing Bobby to pitch forward and let out a startled—*audible*—scoff. "We're not even in the pipeline!" state senator William C. Thompson said. "How do we get a priority?" The people living there were through being polite. They had had enough photo ops and didn't care how many eyes were on Kennedy. Civil Court judge Thomas R. Jones met the senator to take a walk. "I'm weary of study, Senator. Very weary. The Negro people are angry, Senator, and judge that I am, I'm angry, too." The *Times*' photographer, Meyer Liebowitz, captured Bobby talking to a little boy in the doorway of a home at twelve thirty in the afternoon. Bobby asked him why he wasn't in school. The five-year-old told him, "I went," then slammed the door in his face. The skepticism toward what a politician could achieve came from every corner.[32]

AS BOBBY EMBRACED a progressive agenda, the progressive agenda embraced him. A few days after the speeches on the urban crisis in late January 1966, he was the guest speaker at the annual dinner of Americans for Democratic Action—the warhorse organization of intellectual liberal politics. An invitation to ruthless Bobby Kennedy was once unthinkable, since even President Kennedy at one time had a strained relationship with the ADA. "I'm not comfortable with those people," he said. Bobby was even worse. In late 1965, Fred Dutton wrote him a letter with a sidebar listing all the old "liberal wing" doubts: "too much latent hostility . . . a cop . . . soft on McCarthyism." Bobby scrawled in the margin, "What about eavesdropping + listening devices?"[33]

But despite liberalism's flourishing under a Democratic president and massive majorities in Congress, the ADA faced a surprising vacuum in leadership at the start of 1966. This was the ADA's first year without Adlai Stevenson and just a few since the passing of Herbert Lehman and Eleanor Roosevelt. Hubert Humphrey, its former rising star, had dimmed in the vice presidency, pressed into the defense of Vietnam. And so, Joseph McCarthy's committee counsel was now the ADA's keynote speaker.

Bobby was enjoying a broad public appeal that he could have only dreamed of three years earlier. When a Gallup Poll asked, "What man that you have heard or read about, living today in any part of the world, do you admire the most?," Bobby was third, behind Presidents Johnson and Eisenhower, while Vice President Humphrey had come in eighth. And though 55 percent thought Bobby would one day win the Democratic presidential nomination, only 26 percent thought the same of Humphrey.[34]

As the year turned over, columnist after columnist diagnosed Humphrey with a Bobby problem. "There is nothing this Capital likes so much as a contest framed in terms of personalities," Marquis Childs wrote of the Humphrey-Bobby battle. Some of the vice president's men even feared that Johnson might replace him on the ticket in 1968 to build up a stronger rival to Bobby for the '72 nomination. "Humphrey's looks are ordinary," Mary McGrory wrote. "He has a rather flat face, prominent eyes, a narrow mouth. His manner is that of a man from North Dakota who has realized the American dream in his life and likes people and politics. His problem has always been that he has been taken for granted . . . What he needs is to demonstrate toughness. But the vice presidency is that last place in the world to display that particular characteristic."[35]

With Bobby moving in on his crowd, Humphrey played it cool.

The vice president was giving a speech to party regulars in Brooklyn the same night as Bobby's Americans for Democratic Action speech and offered him a ride aboard Air Force Two from Washington to New York.[36]

Because of the city speeches tying up Walinsky and Edelman, Arthur Schlesinger, an esteemed figure in the party's ADA wing, wrote Bobby's first draft.

Walinsky was appalled. "It's useless; you can't give any of this," he told the senator.

"Yeah," Bobby replied. "It's too bad, isn't it?"

"You know, it's all this old Hubert Humphrey crap."

RFK grinned. "Well, you know . . . he does awfully well with those people."[37]

Walinsky and others in the Kennedy office didn't want to recast Bobby in the Humphrey mold, rejecting the New Deal nostalgia that so many liberals were locked into. As such, Bobby's final remarks that night urged them to live and deal with the twin prosperity and poverty created in the wake of Franklin Roosevelt's reforms.

"Truly, he made a revolution," Bobby said of FDR. "But what is required of us is that we do more than recite those accomplishments and talk of dreams fulfilled. For to be true to his legacy and to speak of his name we must be prepared to work a revolution at once as profound and as compassionate as the struggle he began just thirty years ago." They could no more look to Roosevelt for answers than Roosevelt could look to Grover Cleveland.[38]

At a speech for newspaper editors a short time after, Bobby cited a spate of federal programs and said, "The inheritance of the New Deal is fulfilled. There is not a problem for which there is not a program. There is not a problem for which money is not being spent. There is not a problem or a program on which dozens or hundreds or thousands of bureaucrats are not earnestly at work. But does this represent a solution to our problems?" he asked. "Manifestly it does *not*."[39]

And so, Bobby's staff began the process to go beyond the New Deal, beyond swollen government and toward a solution for the last third of the twentieth century. Over the next several months, they developed a hybrid program in Bedford-Stuyvesant—a community development corporation mixing public and private interests.[40]

MEANWHILE, WASHINGTON WATCHED the White House for signs of falling bombs. A column in the *Los Angeles Times* described the peace offensive as typical of Johnson to "over-dramatize" in trying to convince the world he was doing all that he could. "He has Ambassador Goldberg rushing to see the Pope and Prime Minister Wilson. Ambassador Harriman and a jet-load of experts bouncing from Warsaw to Budapest to Belgrade en route to India. Ambassador Soapy Williams running through Africa. Undersecretary Mann makes a hurry up visit to Mexico. Ambassadors, worldwide, are alerted. Brother, are we for peace!"[41] The war was about to get worse, the politics more fraught, and Johnson wanted to prove to his critics and opponents that he wanted peace most of all.

Inside the White House, the President fretted over the military consequences of diplomacy. At a meeting early in the bombing pause, McNamara reassured Johnson that any bridges the North repaired could easily be knocked out. "Bombing them has not reduced infiltration." Ambassador Lodge in Saigon sent a steady stream of bad news about North Vietnamese soldiers crossing into the South and dim prospects for peace. "I believe the Communists are determined to drag this thing out until the '68 elections," the ambassador cabled.[42]

Bundy tried to reassure the President, saying, according to Jack Valenti's notes of their January 3 meeting, "For the first time we have made headway with the *New York Times*."

Dean Rusk replied that he told Scotty Reston, "No matter how long we stopped bombing it will never be long enough for the *Times*."

"I think this will disarm our critics in the Congress," Under Secretary of State George Ball offered.

The President said he saw no reason to resume the bombing. "Our big problem will be they'll let us stew in our own juice. Then we'll stew in theirs."[43]

Days passed. Then weeks. The President's concern was growing. McNamara and Bundy counseled patience. Joint Chiefs chairman General Earle

Wheeler and others saw Hanoi gaining military advantages.[44] And while Johnson monitored Hanoi's reactions, he watched the Senate's just as closely.

"What do you hear from the Kennedy boys on this?" the President asked McNamara on the morning of January 17, twenty-four days into the pause.

McNamara didn't know about Teddy, but Bobby "was very pleased to see the pause started. I think he feels that we've got to continue to increase our forces there, but that we ought to carry on efforts toward negotiations or some form of nonmilitary settlement. As do I."

"Will Bobby oppose resuming bombing in light of the *New York Times*?" Johnson asked. "I assume they will. They're gonna oppose anything we do, aren't they?"

"Well, I don't know if they'll oppose it," McNamara said. "I think they'll say we didn't wait long enough or we didn't handle it right during the intervening period. They may oppose it as well. I talked to Scotty Reston, Friday or Saturday. My impression was that he personally would oppose it."

Later in the conversation, Johnson said, "I want to be patient and understanding and reasonable. On the other hand, I think you know my natural inclinations."[45]

On the evening of January 25, Johnson met in the Cabinet Room with bipartisan leaders in Congress, including the chairmen and ranking members of the committees on Appropriations, Armed Services, and Foreign Affairs. Jack Valenti took notes. Johnson's mentor Armed Services chairman Richard Russell said, "This is the most frustrating experience of my life. I didn't want to get in there, but we are there. I don't think the American people take this war seriously. I don't credit the polls on Vietnam. Those people have been ground under so long, all they want is peace . . . I think we have gone too far in this lull—although I recognize the reason. This pause has cost you militarily. We are going to lose a lot of boys as a result—casualties of our care for peace."

Senator J. W. Fulbright, chairman of the Foreign Relations Committee, rejected the argument, saying the United States was trying to "reimpose colonial power" and "take the place of the French." He advised against resumption and urged Johnson to "find a way out. After large casualties," he said, "we will come to a negotiation."[46]

The "full-dress Vietnam debate" was at hand. The Associated Press surveyed eighty-nine members of the U.S. Senate and found fifty willing to take a position: twenty-five senators against resuming air strikes, twenty-five in favor.[47]

Reports of division over the bombing pause multiplied.[48] Familiar with the pressures of the Oval Office—and likely the internal deliberations via administration sources—Bobby sent Johnson a four-page handwritten note in late January:

"Reading the newspapers and their columnists and listening to my colleagues in Congress (including myself) on what to do and what not to do in Viet Nam must become somewhat discouraging at times." The note came with a book, Bruce Catton's *Never Call Retreat*, about Lincoln's solitary burden during the Civil War. "I thought it might give you some comfort to look again at another President, Abraham Lincoln, and some of the identical problems and situations that he faced that you are now meeting." Bobby concluded by saying "how impressed I have been with the most recent efforts to find a peaceful solution to Viet Nam. Our position within the United States and around the world has improved immeasurably as we face the difficult decisions of this year."

What effect the letter might have had is unknown. Jack Valenti ghosted Johnson's tender reply on January 27, thirty-four days into the pause: "You know better than most the gloom that crowds in on a President, for you lived close to your brother."[49]

"I don't want war with Russia or China," Johnson said in a meeting with aides that same day. "I feel less comfortable tonight than I felt last night. I don't want to back out—and look like I'm reacting to the Fulbrights."

Later in the meeting, he turned to McNamara. "What did Bobby say?"

"He says the burden of proof is on us."

Johnson: "What will he say when we resume?"

McNamara: "I don't know."[50]

THE BOMBS BEGAN falling again on January 31, the same day that five thousand marines undertook the largest amphibious landing since the Korean War. Johnson announced the resumption and asked the United Nations Security Council to convene a meeting where his representative would "present a full report on the situation in Vietnam, and a resolution which can open the way to the conference table."[51]

The Senate discussed the move for three hours that day. Ted Kennedy released a short statement sympathizing with the President's decision. Bobby's came later: longer, tepid, and warning of "disaster."[52]

"We should not delude ourselves that [bombing] offers a painless method of winning the war." Bobby described the persistent economic inequality in Vietnam—rooted in its concentrated land ownership. "To such conditions, military action in the South or in the North is no answer. Military action is needed to allow social reform to take place. But if American soldiers are to fight and die to buy time for the Government of South Vietnam, that time must be used." Education, land reform, and public health needed investment. "But we have not yet made the effort necessary . . . And the best talent and brains in our Government are focused far more on military action than they are on programs which might help the people of South Vietnam—and in the long run, help our effort as well. This imbalance must change."[53]

Bobby said, "If we regard bombing as the answer to Vietnam, we are headed straight for disaster. The danger is that the decision to resume may become the first in a series of steps on a road from which there is no turning back—a road which leads to catastrophe for all mankind."[54]

On another of Bobby's trips to Republican-dominated towns upstate, more and more people were curious about Vietnam. "First it's a war offensive and then it's a peace offensive," one man asked him. "What does it mean?"[55]

Congress deemed to find out. On February 3, Chairman Fulbright decided to reassert the Senate's role in American war-making. He convened the Senate Foreign Relations Committee for immediate public hearings on the war's conduct, beginning at eight thirty the next morning. The Tonkin Gulf Resolution had approved "all necessary measures" for preventing aggression in Southeast Asia, but hardly any senators had had a large-scale land war in mind at the time of the August 1964 vote. The President had now requested millions more in funding. Fulbright said an inquiry was necessary before further approval.[56]

Bobby had been unable to get a seat on Foreign Relations but followed the hearings closely. The committee wanted top administration officials to testify on the record and in public. Secretary McNamara replied that the hearings could harm national security and suggested closed sessions. Senator Wayne Morse of Oregon said, "Let's have it out with the secretary of defense because the American people are going to have it out with this administration at the ballot box." Morse, who cast one of two original votes against the Tonkin resolution, had introduced legislation to rescind the authority, which he said was unconstitutional and being misused for "an undeclared and illegal war."[57]

Johnson took the premise of the hearings as an affront, especially for the request that Humphrey appear. "No vice president has ever testified before a committee," the President would later tell a group of congressional leaders. Fulbright insisted to reporters, "The committee will work out something civilized. There's no war on with the White House." But when the first six-hour hearing began on February 4, the New York Times wrote the committee turned out "in almost unexampled force," with seventeen of its nineteen members on the dais. Sixteen of those present were critical in their questions for foreign aid administrator David Bell.[58]

Within hours of the hearings' announcement, Johnson had come up with a distraction. He took top cabinet and military officials and flew to Honolulu for an abruptly called conference with South Vietnamese leaders. Johnson wanted Prime Minister Nguyen Cao Ky's government, still struggling for legitimacy after eight months in power, to explain how they planned to win the war and what the United States could do to help. The conference was really meant to display confidence in Ky, not discuss strategy.[59]

Most of all, it stole attention from Fulbright.

BOBBY'S OFFICE HAD been swept up in the city's single issue—in some cases literally, when part of a delegation of fifteen hundred women peace marchers clogged the hallway by his door in the New Senate Office Building, making it impossible to get to the elevators.[60] The chaos added to his leverage.

McNamara and others were urging Bobby to visit Vietnam, though he knew how unlikely it was he would get an accurate picture of the situation. Teddy had gone in the fall, and correspondent Neil Sheehan wrote that refugee villagers had been living under rickety lean-tos until officials learned of the senator's impending visit, and suddenly "tidy huts" appeared "in neat rows along dirt streets freshly scraped by bulldozers."[61]

Fred Dutton responded with a letter advising Bobby against a trip, warning him not to become "a six-day specialist" on the war. "Putting yourself in the middle or with the Johnson Administration on the Viet Nam war will disrupt the effect of so much that you have done in your basic personal course for the last two years . . . Why louse all that up on a trip which can likely have little tangible benefit to the country or yourself and appears to me to be an unconscious effort by McNamara, Taylor and Harriman to have you help pull their and President Johnson's badly charred chestnuts out of a fire that they are letting get out of control?"

But Dutton also advised Bobby that he could not "duck" discussing Vietnam completely. "To talk about subjects like reforming [New York] divorce laws and nuclear non-proliferation but not Viet Nam would look like you are afraid of the really tough, immediate problems and are equal only to nibbling around the fringes."

Dutton told Bobby that he had reached a special place in politics. "It can even be said you are really now at the center of the Democratic Party and increasingly, if reluctantly, the rallying point of the preponderant liberal majority of that party . . . You have conducted yourself faultlessly in attracting that broad new support without alienating past strength."[62]

Bobby expanded his discussions with the generation fighting the war. He was scheduled to deliver an address before about 250 college-newspaper editors at Columbia University, but instead of speaking, he decided to hold a Q&A from the floor. Question after question had to do with Vietnam, so he polled the audience. Asking for a show of hands, a slight majority favored the current policy. Bobby asked the editors if they thought their views matched those of the students at their schools. Most said they did.[63]

He continued on another upstate tour to Clinton, Little Falls, and Gloversville. Of about nine hundred college and high school students, about 25 percent told him they not only supported the policy, they favored increased bombing of Hanoi and Haiphong.[64]

The public's remove from the conflict troubled him. Speaking to three hundred high school students in Rochester that month, Bobby said the current military draft policy was unfair. He said the price of a deferment was tuition to college, and the kids who couldn't afford it or wanted to be printers or plumbers were no more expendable than their shielded peers. He said the laws needed a change, and he was considering proposals.[65]

He was also considering making his private thoughts on the war known, once and for all.

AT SEVEN O'CLOCK on a midwinter's morning a week into the Fulbright hearings, the phone at Dick Goodwin's Middletown, Connecticut, home started to ring. Goodwin, who had recently sent Bobby a letter about not developing too hard of an image as an ideological antibusiness liberal, had been up until three A.M. and wasn't about to pick up.

But the caller was persistent.

It was Bobby and he made no apology for the hour. "Have you been following the hearings?"

Goodwin said that he had, and Bobby asked whether his voice might add anything constructive. Goodwin said he'd call him back.[66]

Watching the televised Fulbright hearings was frustrating. One observer wrote that after a while, the scene became surreal: "The senators did not look like senators; they looked like actors playing senators, and the generals were not generals but only actors playing generals." Among the critical witnesses were Lieutenant General James M. Gavin, former chief of plans at the Pentagon, and the preeminent Cold War thinker, Ambassador George Kennan, who suggested the conflict was a quagmire that the United States should not want to sink deeper into. Kennan warned the panel against a "precipitous and disorderly withdrawal," suggesting that the Vietcong "be locked into unpromising positions" for the best diplomacy to run its course. He also believed that the Vietcong should be granted a role in the South Vietnamese government.[67]

In a memo, longtime Johnson aide George Reedy warned the President to temper his reaction, for the men were coming from "a moderate standpoint," and his opponents "are anxiously hoping the Administration will blast Gavin and Kennan and thus drive them into the 'dove' camp, which now lacks really respectable leadership."[68]

Even without respectable leadership among the opponents of escalation, talk of a political toll on the White House and the Democrats increased. There were even rumblings on Capitol Hill that President Johnson would not seek reelection in 1968. The Associated Press ran with the story on February 13, 1966, suggesting that "an enlarged U.S. military commitment in the unpopular war is likely to drag on into the presidential election year without any definitive signs that it can be ended successfully." The assessment was almost identical to Lodge's telegram from Saigon a few weeks earlier.[69]

There was also the issue of the political sentiment in South Vietnam. Prime Minister Nguyen Cao Ky had recently proposed a democratic regime that would hold national elections in 1967.[70] But members of the U.S. Senate Foreign Relations Committee were skeptical about every promise surrounding Vietnam. Secretary of State Dean Rusk had been batting away their questions for several hours during his testimony on February 18 when Chairman Fulbright said he struggled to explain the rigidness against negotiation from both sides, "unless we just assume the world has gone mad."

Secretary Rusk, calm and chain-smoking, decided he had a few questions of his own for the combative Fulbright. "Mr. Chairman," Rusk said, "I wonder if I might ask you to amplify your statement in one respect. What do you want Hanoi to do in these circumstances?"

Fulbright responded that he would like to get the interested parties around a negotiating table. "I get the impression," he said, "that we are in an unlimited war, and the only kind of settlement is unconditional surrender." Fulbright added that the United States "can probably impose our will," but that the enemy needed assurances—for example, "that if an election is held in Vietnam, we will abide by it regardless of the outcome. I do not think that has ever been said in any convincing way by this administration."

Rusk initially balked. "The only convincing way in which you could say that to the other side, apparently, is to let them have, to start with, the government that would conduct the elections"—a reunified Vietnam, South and North. The Communists "with some seventeen million people up there," Rusk said, had "seventeen million votes in their pockets. They want some elections in the South so that the combined numbers would clearly mean that they then would take over South Vietnam through that process." But, he clarified a few minutes later, if the South held a free election, the United States would support and accept it. "What we are saying," Rusk declared, "if that is the issue, let us have the elections. Let the South Vietnamese decide."[71]

The conversation shifted away, but to Bobby, this was the key exchange of the hearings. Until the United States could firmly answer what it would do with election results, the South Vietnamese could not gain the peace to actually hold elections, because the National Liberation Front had no assurances for laying down their arms. Rusk had seemed to offer it there, giving Bobby the opening he had been waiting for to emphasize it.

Dick Goodwin had spent the week since Bobby's call trying to phrase the assurance in the most palatable language possible. He settled on inviting the NLF "to a share of the power and responsibility." This was politically treacherous. At best, it was a tacit admission that some in South Vietnam favored the party backed by Ho Chi Minh over the American-supported government. At worst, it looked like abandoning our ally at the ballot box by agreeing to an election that the Communists would rig. Goodwin read the draft to RFK over the phone that afternoon and sent it to Washington with a note. "Please protect me absolutely on this. Even from your notoriously discreet associates. Say your wrote it yourself." Goodwin had joked at a recent speech in Washington, "I have to come down here once a week and report my phone calls." But it was more than President Johnson being touchy about his former staffers. Some would see the speech as questioning the cause that thousands of U.S. servicemen were fighting and dying for. The American people had been told that their blood and treasure were protecting the South Vietnamese from tyranny. To suggest putting their freedom—and those boys' sacrifices—up for a vote that could end in a Vietcong victory was breathtaking. "I think this really reaches to the edge of political danger," Goodwin's note said, "and I have put in as many protections as possible."[72]

It appears Bobby didn't see the danger or, if he did, was unconcerned by it. He was simply enunciating the position that Dean Rusk had subtly confirmed at the hearings. There was still great trepidation about even the whiff of concessions. Days earlier, the senator's close friend General Maxwell Taylor asked the Foreign Relations Committee, "How do you compromise the freedom of fifteen million South Vietnamese people?"[73] For all Bobby's ruthlessness and calculation, real and imagined, he showed tremendous courage on issues of right and wrong—along with hazardous abandon.

Others on his staff grasped the consequences. When Wes Barthelmes learned that Bobby had called a Saturday news conference on Vietnam, the first thing the press secretary did was call his wife to let her know that he wouldn't be home for a day and a half. Bobby asked Barthelmes, "Do you think there's any news in it?"

"They'll be writing about it till the end of the world," he said.[74]

More than thirty reporters attended on February 19, with klieg lights, television cameras, and a dozen microphones—"all the trappings of a Presidential news session," wrote the *Los Angeles Times*.

Bobby said that both Washington and Hanoi needed to bend. "If negotiation is our aim, as we have so clearly said it is, we must seek a middle ground. A negotiated settlement means that each side must concede matters that are important in order to preserve positions that are essential." Without that, escalation would only continue. He said that "any negotiated settlement must accept the fact that there are discontented elements in South Vietnam, Communist and non-Communist, who desire to change the existing political and economic system of the country." Bobby said the United States had only three options: "kill or repress them; turn the country over to them; or admit them to a share of the power and responsibility." The United States needed to accept the uncertainty that a free election would bring, he said. It was setting priorities, just as in October 1962, when the United States' ultimate goal was the removal of missiles from Cuba; not the humiliation of the Soviets. "If our objective had been much greater than it was," he said, "there would have been war." It was near verbatim to what he had privately said to Schlesinger's son two months earlier, before the bombing pause and hearings. It took the course of events, the public outcry, and the sluggish slide into wider war to draw him out—to let him feel comfortable to speak.

"We are not going to get a complete surrender from them," Bobby said to reporters after his prepared remarks. "And they certainly are not going to get one from us." He called a military victory "at best uncertain, and at worst unattainable," and suggested that the United States might be addicted to "clichés" about freedom instead of getting "down to specifics." He also suggested America was too beholden to South Vietnamese leadership, right or wrong. "I don't think our policies in the United States should be controlled by the government in Saigon."[75]

"There are hazards in debating American policy in the face of a stern and dangerous enemy," he said. "But that hazard is the essence of democracy."

One reporter asked Bobby, "What happens next with this speech?"

He replied with a smile, "I'll show it to my wife and see what she thinks." And he did. If he believed there would be a significant backlash, he did nothing to prepare for it, as he immediately went off to Vermont for a skiing vacation. His family was already there, with Teddy remarkably back on the slopes some fourteen months after leaving the hospital for his broken back. There, Bobby quickly found himself snowed under by what *Time* magazine dubbed "a blizzard of criticism."[76]

* * *

THOUGH INVOKING THE lessons he had learned alongside his brother's advisers, Bobby had stepped out of line with the men who had counseled JFK and continued to advise President Johnson. He may have thought that those he worked with in close quarters during crises would be roused by his bold leadership, just as JFK's restraint and compromise had near single-handedly steered them away from war with Russia. These were the few men on the planet who knew that President Kennedy had cut a secret deal to remove the Soviet missiles in Cuba, sacrificing America's Jupiter missiles in Turkey.[77] The arrangement was so politically toxic that it remained hidden for decades, written out of RFK's posthumously published account, *Thirteen Days*, and Schlesinger's Homeric biographies of both Kennedy brothers.

The *New York Times* called Bobby's speech "a dramatic policy break," and a proposal "more concrete" than anything put forward by Fulbright. "By such a move, it was believed here today, he may well put himself in the position of leadership of those who actively oppose or have the deepest reservations about the administration's policy."[78]

Bobby knew that his voice carried further than other congressional critics of the current policy—his bustling news conference could only have confirmed that. He knew the dynamics of the administration better than any other senator and truly believed he was amplifying something Dean Rusk said in his testimony. Bobby had even called Bill Moyers the day before and read him the major points. His office sent a hard copy of the speech to the West Wing the morning of its delivery.[79]

It allowed Moyers to issue the White House's firm response within minutes of when Bobby finished speaking. No talks until "Hanoi changes its mind about aggression and the subjugation of South Vietnam by force."[80]

Vice President Hubert Humphrey, one of the few members of the administration who had not been in the meetings with JFK, was caught completely off guard. In New Zealand on a tour to rally Pacific allies, Humphrey ripped Bobby's proposition of shared power—seeing it as completely countermanding the resolve his trip was trying to spread. "I do not believe in writing a prescription for the ills of South Vietnam that includes a dose of arsenic," he said. "This is more or less like putting a fox in a chicken coop," Humphrey told reporters on his way to Manila. "There are usually not many chickens left after the fox has been around. Or let me give you an even better analogy. It would be like putting an arsonist in the fire department."[81]

Reporters asked South Vietnamese prime minister Ky what he made of the remarks. "The so-called National Liberation Front does not liberate anybody. They killed eleven thousand of our troops last year and twenty-two thousand of our innocent people in the countryside. They murdered them. They are a thousand percent Communist and they are illegal in free Vietnam, so let's not talk about the National Liberation Front anymore." Hungary's ex–prime minister volunteered his analysis as the former leader in a coalition government overrun by Communists, telling the Associated Press that while not impossible, keeping democrats in power depended on the strength of outside support.[82]

Opinions in the American press were derisive, if not hostile. The *Chicago Tribune* titled its editorial "Ho Chi Kennedy," writing, "Sen. Kennedy out of his ignorance and political ambition, has compromised his loyalty to the United States when it is at war by subscribing to communist myths and adopting them as his own, in opposition to a national policy, which is supported by an overwhelming majority of American citizens. He is not the junior senator from New York. He is the senior senator from communist North Viet Nam—Ho Chi Minh's Trojan horse in the United States Senate." In a more measured response, Eugene Patterson of the *Atlanta Constitution* wrote, "Sen. Kennedy felt we had to show more of our cards to persuade our adversaries that a settlement is possible. But the card he turned over was not his to show," encouraging Ho Chi Minh with concessions in advance. The *Washington Post* editorial board posited that "such a surrender would not buy peace in Southeast Asia" and only reward aggression.[83]

Others reduced the statement to politics. "Senator Robert F. Kennedy is becoming the new hero of the Democratic left," David Broder wrote for the *Times*. "Some self-described liberals who formerly regarded him as a ruthless, cold-blooded and even unprincipled political operator now look to him increasingly as the symbol and exponent of their dissatisfactions with the Johnson Administration." Mary McGrory wrote that Bobby "sounded very much like the Humphrey of the old days." Minnesota's Senator Eugene McCarthy, hungry to be quoted, told the *Washington Post* that he had made a similar suggestion weeks earlier, but received no attention.[84]

This was the risk of Bobby's statement. Those who took a firm stance against escalation were labeled doves and treated like caged birds from there on out. Any further skepticism was diminished or even discounted as coming from someone set in his or her view. McCarthy, Morse, and Fulbright all struggled with this. But Bobby had the potential to break out of this box. He had been a direct participant in deepening the Vietnam commitment. He had a reputation for being an overzealous Cold Warrior fixated on Castro. And he had become the walking conscience of the Kennedy legacy—the echo of his brother's voice.

That was why the words of National Security Adviser McGeorge Bundy stung the most. Bundy came to the White House with the New Frontier and had recently announced his impending departure. "He understood the

President's thinking as well as anyone," Bobby had recently said of how the national security adviser marshaled the facts for JFK.[85] But now Bundy's facts served a different President, and when Bundy was scheduled on *Meet the Press* the day after Bobby endorsed working with the NLF toward elections, he came prepared.

"I am not impressed by the opportunities open to popular fronts throughout the world," Bundy quoted JFK from 1963. "I do not believe that any democrat can successfully ride that tiger." The point, Bundy said, was that there could be no free and fair elections with Communists involved. They rig them.[86] But don't take his word for it; take President Kennedy's.

Bobby was shocked and hurt by Bundy's criticism. He even drafted a note to him that said, "Perhaps a call would not have taken any more time than for someone to look up the quote of President Kennedy to use against my position," though Bobby filed it in his papers, never to be sent.[87] Instead he returned to New York to downplay his differences with the administration in an early-morning network interview with *NBC*'s *Today* show.

"The Senator came like an uneasy ghost at the obscene hour and to the bizarre place," wrote Murray Kempton, who shadowed him at the studio. Bobby's interview appeared just after an Alpo dog food commercial.[88]

Bobby spoke for fifteen minutes with anchor Hugh Downs and Washington correspondent Ray Scherer. Downs asked, "What about the charge that the Communists have tended to dominate any government in which they were invited to participate on a 'coalition' basis?"

"Well, let me say," Bobby said. "If there was a choice, I would obviously be against having any of the Communists in. If there were just a choice, I would be obviously in favor of not having the war there. But I think the choice is really that we suppress them or we turn the country over to them or we try to have elections and we reach an accommodation of some kind.

"I would think that just from the statements in the last twenty-four hours by representatives of the executive branch of the government on various sides of this that there is some confusion within our own government as to what we want to accomplish, what our political objectives are."

When Scherer pressed him on this charge of "confusion" in the administration, Bobby responded, "First we said there would be no preconditions, and evidently from what they have said, there are preconditions. And one of the preconditions is that there's not going to be any representation under any circumstances of the Communists within the government of Vietnam even if they win elections. That's a precondition. We should make that known, therefore, and the American people should understand that, if that's our policy.

"We have to deal with the realities of the situation in Vietnam. I'm in favor of not having them in at all if that was a possibility, but I think that the alternative to that is a bloody, bloody war, and I'd like to move off and discuss things in real terms. If this isn't our policy, if we think that this is a mistake, then we should know it and realize what's in store for us as far as the future."

Policy objectives mattered, Bobby insisted. "If I could just take—I'm going back to October of 1962 again. Our objective regarding the missiles in Cuba was limited. It wasn't the destruction of Castro. Maybe some people thought it should be. It wasn't the destruction of Cuba. It wasn't the humiliation of Mr. Khrushchev. It wasn't the destruction of the Soviet Union. It was to try to get the missiles out of Cuba . . . No effort, force, was used to try to accomplish something beyond that political objective. Therefore I think that if we have our own political objectives clearly in mind in Vietnam and have it understood we are not going to use any force beyond that to accomplish that political objective, I think that there will be more confidence within our own country and around the world and that we will have a better opportunity of finding a peaceful solution to this very, very unfortunate struggle."[89]

Kempton wrote that Bobby's tone "aimed at surprise; but most of what emerged sounded like confirmed mistrust . . . The most reckless and romantic of the Kennedys seemed as though deliberately reshaping himself according to his memory of the coolest and most detached of them." Bobby and Kempton repaired to a coffee shop on Manhattan's Madison Avenue, where he reflected on the missiles of October 1962 and "that room" where they had talked it through until they found "an alternative."

Then Bobby stopped, Kempton wrote, and suddenly "seemed miles away," as if the grief were brimming his throat.[90]

The *Today* show was just the beginning of Bobby's damage control. He spent the morning and afternoon working the phones with reporters and columnists, conferred with Maxwell Taylor and Bill Moyers, and concluded with a follow-up press conference. "I am not suggesting that the Communists automatically should be brought into the interim government," Bobby told the reassembled group of reporters. "This should be left open to those carrying on the discussions . . . but I would hold out to the Communists the possibility that they will have some say in the arrangements ultimately to be made to establish a permanent government in Vietnam." Bobby said he was surprised that his position was met with such vehemence from the administration after Rusk said in the Fulbright hearings that America would accept the outcome of elections.

He tried to assuage concerns of a policy break with the administration. "In discussing with Mr. Moyers," Bobby said, "I find no disagreement between what Mr. Moyers said and what I have said."

Moyers, too, said they were in agreement "if Senator Kennedy did not propose a coalition government with Communist participation before elections are held." He bristled at Bobby's saying there is "some confusion" within the executive branch over its objectives. "I don't think it is the administration that is confused," Moyers said in a dig at Bobby's doubling back.[91]

As mightily as he tried, Bobby lost the argument. One bemused reporter left the press conference called to explain his first press conference saying, "He didn't exactly back away from it, but he tried to fuzz it up." The very critics the White House feared would rally to Bobby's side did just the opposite, beginning with James Reston, who called for "unconditional negotiations . . . between the Senator and his speechwriters." Mary McGrory wrote, "When Bobby Kennedy disappeared from Camp Johnson last Saturday, he left a note on his bunk. The trouble was nobody could read his writing." Robert Novak and Bobby's friend Rowland Evans labeled it a "major miscalculation with long-range ramifications." Reston surmised that Kennedy was trading "the considerable influence of his family name against the President's negotiating position" to win favor "with the voters of New York and the disenchanted liberals and intellectuals elsewhere."[92]

Bobby had said what he had been holding in for months, if not longer, with the hope it might lead somewhere, only to have his position reduced to half-baked political posturing.

WHILE PRESIDENT JOHNSON genuinely worried about enemies questioning America's resolve, Congress questioning his finances was the bigger concern.

Johnson met with congressional leaders for two and a half hours on February 22, lobbying them to get behind his $4.8 billion in emergency war funds. Senator George Smathers of Florida emerged with a call for the Senate to end the debate and support "our brave fighting men in Vietnam." Senator Fulbright came away concerned that another funding vote would be a de facto endorsement of Vietnam policy. Mississippi's John Stennis, the Southern powerhouse at the axis of the Senate Armed Services and Appropriations committees, knew the United States would have to pour even more resources into the war. In January, Stennis had given a speech on the Senate floor saying that current troop levels in Vietnam were insufficient to destroy the enemy. He was certain that a tripling was necessary—"to commit six hundred thousand men to battle." The Stennis force estimate continued to appear in the news as the Senate debated funding.[93]

While the meeting notes of the President's discussions with top national security advisers at this time show that Bobby was mentioned, Johnson said the "real source of our trouble is Stennis . . . The wild figures in the papers come from him." Only thing was, Stennis was right. "The problem is that he gets our figures," the President said. McNamara reminded the President the administration had not yet indicated its plans. Johnson replied, "The real plans do get to Stennis and let's try to prevent it."[94]

The President's dissembling at this pivotal moment went much, much further. When war estimates surfaced, officials planned for the fighting to last at least another three, if not seven, more years. Yet the Johnson budget planned for the war to end within just sixteen months. While the President had said that the situation would change along with the one on the ground, others would conclude he was burying the war's true cost to shield the Great Society.[95]

Guns or butter. Johnson knew that Congress would give him the war, but not his social programs. On March 1, Bobby was among the senators voting in favor of the supplemental spending bill to fund the war. Backing the administration didn't stop others from branding him a hypocritical opportunist for putting forth a provocative argument on Vietnam that seemed to contradict old views. Drew Pearson wrote there was "a lot of irony" in Bobby's being the messenger for a power-sharing agreement, as his old boss Joe McCarthy had persecuted State Department officials for considering similar arrangements with China. "Bobby never spoke out against the persecution of State Department officials," Pearson wrote.[96]

And while Bobby's stance might have won a few admirers in Washington, it was decidedly unpopular in statehouses across the nation. A survey of governors found near-uniform rejection of antiwar sentiments. Iowa governor Harold Hughes, a Democrat, said that if the Fulbright hearings were "helpful to anyone, they were helpful to the Vietcong . . . I feel the same way about the Kennedy proposal."[97]

The *Chicago Tribune* ran a dispatch from Saigon, reporting "astonished" reactions to Bobby's call for inclusion, listing the civilian atrocities of the enemy. It included the story of "three little girls whose father had refused to collaborate with the Viet Cong. The nose and one ear of each child had been cut off. Their bellies had been ripped open, and they were alive." The reporter invited "apologists for the Communists" to witness the "dismembered and mutilated corpses and others hanging from tree limbs or lamp poles."[98]

The State Department had cabled assurances to South Vietnamese prime minister Nguyen Cao Ky that despite "the statement of Senator Robert Kennedy," the American government's position had not changed. Questioned about it in an interview with the *Washington Post*, Ky showed he had no doubts.

"When is the American election?" Ky asked the American reporter in English.

"Nineteen sixty-eight."

"I think now is too soon to begin the campaign," Ky said of Bobby and his proposal. "It is not good if you use the destiny of twenty million people as an issue in the campaign." Ky then told the reporter he would continue reforming the South Vietnamese government. His plan included the executions of allegedly corrupt officials.[99]

WITHIN DAYS OF Bobby's drubbing over Vietnam, Vice President Humphrey returned from his trip rallying allies in the Pacific, where he had faced vicious protests. In Wellington, New Zealand, anti-American demonstrators rushed his car, chanting, "Sieg Heil!" Four chained themselves to the pillars of parliament in protest. Outside the U.S. embassy, a demonstrator hollered, "When are your sons going to Vietnam, Mr. Humphrey?" Another: "The threat to world peace is American imperialism."[100] Unlike Bobby, Humphrey never stopped to speak with his foreign hecklers.

Also unlike Bobby, Humphrey was welcomed back at the White House with open arms and incredible fanfare. President Johnson, his dogs, and daughter Luci waited for him on the South Lawn with a throng of cameras standing by. The Vice President's chopper hovered an extra ten minutes in the winter air to land precisely at five thirty P.M., so that the President's hug could be broadcast live on the evening news.[101]

President Johnson had a speech in New York City that night accepting an award from Freedom House, a benefit that Bobby was also invited to. To prove there were no hard feelings, Johnson offered the junior senator a ride on Air Force One. Seeing Bobby board the plane, Moyers quipped, "The fox in the chicken coop." Senator Kennedy was booed when his name was announced inside the Waldorf-Astoria ballroom, and he sat there glumly as the President received an oversize bronze bust of himself.[102]

"Some people ask if we are caught in a blind escalation of force that is pulling us headlong toward a wider war that no one wants," Johnson said. "The answer, again, is a simple no . . . This is prudent firmness under what I believe is careful control. There is not, and there will not be, a mindless escalation."

Near the end of his speech, Johnson read a minute-long quote from JFK's inaugural, beginning with "Let the word go forth . . . that the torch has been passed" and concluding with "we shall pay any price, bear any burden, meet any hardship, support any friend, oppose any foe, to assure the survival and the success of liberty."[103]

The CBS News cameraman turned his lens on Bobby, whose eyes spoke sadness as he looked straight ahead, folded his arms during the applause, and chewed on a cigar.[104]

The next morning's newspapers featured the President's words in big bold banners: "'No Mindless Escalation' of War—LBJ," in the *Washington Post*, and "Lyndon Won't Widen War," atop the *Chicago Tribune*. Beneath were photos from the White House lawn of Humphrey and Johnson locked in an embrace.[105] The President had managed the Vietnam debate expertly.

Yet like the telltale heart, its beat kept drumming beneath the floorboards.

As Johnson had approached the podium at the Waldorf, a man had bolted up onto his chair and torn off his dinner jacket to reveal PEACE IN VIETNAM written on both sides of his shirt. He screamed his plea—"Peace in Vietnam! Peace in Vietnam!"—until security pulled him down and dragged him away, gashing his lip by stuffing a napkin in his mouth to silence him. Johnson kept on as if he didn't hear. Behind police cordons on Park Avenue, four thousand demonstrators gathered—some with Vietcong flags, one with a sign that said IMPEACH LYNDON JOHNSON—as they marched to a loud, jarring chant:

"Hey, hey, LBJ,
How many kids
You kill today?"[106]

RIPPLE

March 1966–June 1966

IT DID NOT TAKE LONG for Bobby to realize his attempt to single-handedly dial back the United States' escalation in Vietnam was a mistake. "I made the speech because I thought there was something that was worth saying," he told a writer that March. The reports that followed gave him pause—especially hearing that the harshest critics of the Johnson administration were rallying to his side. "Those are the people with picket signs and beards, aren't they?" he asked *U.S. News & World Report* in an unpublished portion of a damage-control interview. "I'm not their Wayne Morse."[1]

Bobby's hair had grown in these months; a forelock swooped across his brow with ends that stood up, going in all directions. Rides in his open convertible completed the windswept look, with his policy of having the top down "always . . . unless something is falling," his driver would say.[2] It was an untamed expression atop an otherwise conventional-looking politician entering middle age. A signal, conscious or not, that conveyed the spirit sweeping the generation of Americans that had entered maturity as the New Frontier reached its shocking, violent end.

Bobby didn't want to be their Wayne Morse in part because he knew Wayne Morse couldn't get the job done. Adam Walinsky said that Bobby believed Senator Fulbright's Vietnam hearings had been "terribly ineffectual" because "they weren't ready to really do anything . . . There was some talk of a Senate resolution" after Bobby's speech on giving the Vietcong a share of power and responsibility in Saigon, "and there was some talk back and forth with Fulbright, but it just sort of drifted away. It went to smoke."[3]

In one of the many follow-up interviews to the speech, Bobby outlined some of the concessions he wanted the Vietcong to make, such as opening up the areas they controlled to the central government—necessary trades that would let them "be brought into the political structure" of the country. But as he said later, "We hadn't really discussed with any completeness or thoroughness the heart of what our policy should be. I made some mistakes in handling it. I think it was unpopular politically. But I would do it all over again if I had to."[4]

His taking a stand had forced a contradiction of the Johnson administration's policy out into the open, as Vice President Humphrey soon admitted that the United States would never support a government role for the Vietcong. "Why suggest that the South Vietnamese invite into their house their assassins?" Humphrey asked.[5]

Bobby responded on another Sunday show, "I think statements that are made that we will never deal with assassins and we will never deal with murderers makes it difficult for them to believe that they are being asked to come to the negotiating table other than to surrender."[6] Bobby's assessment of the administration's position was simple: the United States wasn't asking for negotiations, it was demanding surrender.

Bobby and Humphrey, the two heirs to the Democratic banner, had reached an uneasy peace. Bobby knew he had leaped before he truly looked. And Humphrey knew he had gone too far in his rhetoric criticizing Bobby's suggestion, as the *Washington Post* reported from administration insiders. Bobby had to rethink how he voiced his concerns. On St. Patrick's Day, he marched up Fifth Avenue alongside the New York City Council. "They're the only ones who wanted me," he quipped.[7]

The people seemed to feel differently, as the controversy didn't hurt his standing in presidential polling. *Gallup* asked voters if they would support him or Nixon for the presidency. Bobby won, 54–41 percent, while Humphrey and Nixon were effectively tied, 47–45. Bobby left the St. Patrick's Day parade and met privately that evening with war skeptic George Kennan at the Century Club. Humphrey continued to plead with liberals to support the war, soon telling an Americans for Democratic Action gathering, "Saigon is as close to this ballroom tonight as London was in 1940."[8]

While some saw evolution in Bobby's scrape with the White House, conservative columnist William F. Buckley saw calculation. "Senator Kennedy has an aversion to unpopular causes," Buckley wrote, "and inasmuch as he is a superb politician . . . one must, if not exactly deduce, at least concede the possibility that the appeasement cause will be very popular in the foreseeable future."[9]

The future was a long way off. Bobby had positioned himself in favor of the funding resolutions in early March rather than cast his lot with a dozen or so like Morse. Whatever cause Bobby would lead, it would be on his own. He had eased off the careful work of incurring goodwill with his fellow senators. At the start of the year, his secretary, Angie Novello, sent him a note with yearly totals of time presiding from the rostrum, a duty of new members. In 1965, fellow freshmen Walter Mondale and Fred Harris logged 107 and 138 hours each. Bobby had put in 75 hours and 47 minutes. "I didn't do too well, did I," Bobby scrawled at the bottom of the note. "NOPE!" Novello replied. His numbers plummeted in the first five months of 1966: Harris with twenty-six and half hours, and Bobby with less than seven.[10]

Bobby was too impatient for the Senate. He disliked the formalities and cared even less for debate. In one instance, two senior senators argued over a point for what Bobby felt was an interminable time. He waited fifteen minutes, tossed his statement into the air, and stalked out. In a Labor Committee hearing on a July afternoon, two members went back and forth on the wording of a sentence. "Oh, hell, why don't you just flip a coin?" Bobby said as he stood up and left. The senators were his New York colleague Jacob Javits and Wayne Morse.[11]

He was far from the only senator to cut corners or lose his patience at a hearing. Nevertheless, he commanded his colleagues' respect because the Senate respected attention, and Bobby possessed an endless supply. The correspondent for the *Christian Science Monitor* noted in late March that when visitors came to the chamber, they were invariably heard asking, "Is Bobby here?" One liberal Democratic senator told Mary McGrory, "If you care about the issue, you have to be glad that a Kennedy is for it." In one instance that spring, Teddy and George McGovern teamed up for a statement on China, but when the senator named Kennedy spoke first and concluded, the galleries emptied out, leaving the South Dakotan to an empty chamber. "It's a little painful, of course," McGovern said, "but I thank God the Kennedys are so far out in front on controversial issues."[12]

Without a doubt, Bobby worked hard on his legislation. But he preferred to shape it away from Capitol Hill. "It takes longer to get things done in the Senate than I like to see things done," he complained to a reporter that year. To another: "They only take about one vote a week here, and they never can tell you in advance when it is going to be so you can schedule other things. If I am not going to be working here, I want to go somewhere I can do something."[13]

And so in the spring of 1966, Bobby went. First across the country, to Senate field hearings on migratory farm labor in the rural communities of Visalia and Delano, California. A Labor subcommittee on the subject was considering legislation to extend collective bargaining rights and federal minimum-wage standards to farm workers, but the room was bustling with atypically youthful faces for a Senate hearing. "I see a large number of young people here in the audience," said Chairman Harrison Williams of New Jersey, "and I know that you're here for a variety of reasons."

"I was just going to say," Republican senator George Murphy of California joked, "that Senator Kennedy would not appreciate being called 'a variety.'"[14]

The farmworkers had a burgeoning movement, one that labor allies in the United Auto Workers were encouraging Bobby's office to take note of. Peter Edelman first read about Cesar Chavez that January, while he was leading an improbable strike of mostly Latin grape pickers. Bobby's aide quickly learned about how labor standards were rarely if ever enforced in the fields, how the growers sprayed the picket lines with insecticide and fertilizer, and the unique challenges of effective protest at a farm—"like striking an industrial plant that has a thousand entrance gates and is 400 square miles long," as the *New Republic* put it.[15]

What's more, the strikers had to deal with harassment from law enforcement, who were on the side of the region's major employers: the growers. Bobby asked one of the witnesses, the Reverend David Havens, about his arrest in Delano during a picket: "What were you arrested for?"

"Reading a definition of a strikebreaker by Jack London."

"That's illegal in Delano?" Bobby asked.

"The police thought it was," Reverend Havens said.

When the county sheriff and the district attorney who handled the arrest came before the panel, Bobby asked them about similar arrests. The district attorney said the noise had grown "beyond normal, peaceful picketing," and "some of the things that were being said caused [the sheriff] to feel that perhaps a riot might be imminent."

Bobby said he understood their "difficult responsibility" as a law enforcement veteran himself. "But I think that those who have a difficult time, they deserve our help." He directed his attention toward the sheriff. "Have you taken pictures of the people that are picketing? Sheriff, have you been taking pictures?"

"Oh, yes, there have been pictures taken at various times."

"Why do you take pictures of them?"

"Well, you have people who come in from other places that we don't know, and we keep in touch, find out who they are, why they're here." The district attorney again interjected, saying they had learned lessons from melees with the Hells Angels motorcycle club that they had to have other means of identifying people during riots.

"Yes," Bobby said, "but let me ask, have there been riots?"

"No, there have been potential riots on occasion."

"I'll tell you this, I've never heard of police departments in other communities that have been going around taking pictures of people walking around with picket signs." Bobby got down to basics. "You're a law enforcement official. It is in some way an act of intimidation to go around and be taking their pictures."

"I've got to identify those people through my district attorney. I've got to identify that is the man."

" 'That is the man' that what?" Bobby asked.

"That caused this trouble," the sheriff said.

Bobby finally got to ask why the sheriff had rounded up and arrested some forty people for picketing.

The sheriff replied, "Well, if I have reason to believe there's going to be a riot started, and somebody tells me that there's going to be trouble if you don't stop them, it's my duty to stop them."

"Then do you go out and arrest them?"

"Yes," the sheriff said.

"And charge them?"

"Charge them."

"What do you charge them with?"

"Violation of—unlawful assembly."

"I think that's most interesting. Who told you that they're going to riot?"

"The men right out in the field"—strikebreakers—"that they were talking to said, 'If you don't get them out of here, we're going to cut their hearts out.' So," the sheriff said, "rather than let them get cut, we removed the cause."

Senator Murphy butted in, defending the officials' "precautionary moves," until Bobby continued. "This is the most interesting concept, I think, that you suddenly hear or you talk about the fact that somebody makes a report about somebody going to get out of order—perhaps violate the law—and you go and arrest them, and they haven't done anything wrong. How can you go arrest somebody if they haven't violated the law?"

"They're ready to violate the law."

Senator Murphy tried again: "I think it's a shame you weren't there before the Watts riots."

As chairman, Senator Williams tried to put an end to it. "We will recess—"

But Bobby broke in again. "Could I just suggest that the district attorney and sheriff reconsider their procedures," he said. "Can I suggest in the interim period of time, the luncheon period of time, that the sheriff and the district attorney read the Constitution of the United States?"[16]

The farmworkers were up against a lot. The area's congressman, Democrat Harlan Hagen, questioned Cesar Chavez on suspected ties to Communists. Chavez denied them. Hagen continued in his questioning before Senator Williams cut him off: "This committee does not work this way."[17]

Bobby came away impressed with Chavez, his commitment to nonviolence, and his being a brown leader in a labor movement whose top ranks remained largely white. "What I'm hoping for," Chavez said to the senators, "is that we, the farmworkers, will not have to fight very much longer to prove that we are ready for our freedom."[18]

When a witness said a system for collective bargaining for farmworkers was impossible, Bobby replied, "If we can put a man on the moon by the end of the 1960s, it seems we should be able to work out such a simple problem for farmworkers after thirty years of talking about it."[19]

IN HIS QUEST for action, Bobby continued to push—heading right into the cauldron of racial politics in the Kennedy administration: the campuses of the University of Mississippi in Oxford, and the University of Alabama in Tuscaloosa. The Ole Miss appearance was especially controversial since it had been the site of the most serious confrontation between the federal government and the State of Mississippi since the Civil War. In September of 1962, U.S. marshals overseeing the registration of the institution's first Negro student, James Meredith, were confronted by an angry mob. Rioting and violence followed. In all, twenty-eight marshals were shot—including one in the throat. Canisters of tear gas and, later, the army were deployed. Two people died, and some held Bobby responsible.[20]

So when he accepted the university students' invitation to speak there four years later, resistance was instantaneous. One state legislator compared Bobby to a murderer returning to the scene of his crime. Another member of the state legislature introduced a resolution to "deplore and protest" Bobby's visit, gaining the support of several members. "The soil of Mississippi is too good for his feet," said the head of Women for Constitutional Government. Americans for the Preservation of the White Race said they would hold a "ride-in." The Klan was reportedly meeting in secret, discussing what they ought to do.[21]

His assassination was openly discussed.

"There are men in our state who might take fantastic risks to 'get even' for the 1962 military occupation of Oxford by federal troops," a columnist for the *Jackson Clarion-Ledger* wrote. "There is no sure way of knowing what high-powered weapons are in whose fanatical hands these days . . ." The president of a racist group told the *New York Times* that the senator's visit "could well be another planned assassination" to "give the revolutionists of the world the excuse they want to liquidate the white race out of the South."[22]

The university was planning a special guard for the visit. Dozens of FBI agents arrived in town early that week, followed by security men from the Justice Department, and the event was moved from a chapel with fourteen hundred seats to the campus Coliseum, which could accommodate over eight thousand.[23]

On the morning of the speech, Bobby and Ethel flew into Memphis, on their way to catch a smaller plane to fly to Oxford. Sensing that Bobby was nervous, the driver turned on the radio. Suddenly, the musical program was interrupted: "We have a special treat for you today. Here in full—without condensation, censorship, abridgment, or exaggeration—is the speech that Senator Robert F. Kennedy will deliver later today in Mississippi." An announcer began reading the prepared text.[24]

In the end, the protesters were on the periphery—signs in the distance said GO HOME, LITTLE ROBERT and IF THE NIGGERS OF MISSISSIPPI DON'T LIKE OUR STATE THEY CAN GO NORTH WITH NIGGER LOVER BOBBY KENNEDY.[25]

During the '62 riots, students had chanted, "Ask us what we say, it's to hell with Bobby K." Southern conservative columnist James J. Kilpatrick made the trip to Oxford, remembering that the last time he had been in the state "the campus reeked of tear gas, a cotton-stuffed dummy dangled in effigy from an overpass on the road to Jackson . . . labeled BOBBY K." This time, Kilpatrick found five thousand people greeting Bobby like "Little Leaguers come to welcome Mickey Mantle."[26]

There was shoving and pulling and yelling and stamping as he and Ethel made their way inside the auditorium. "They clapped and they whooped; there wasn't a boo or a hiss or a heckle in the crowd," Kilpatrick wrote. The *Baltimore Sun*'s Adam Clymer heard "a handful of sour remarks, mainly about his bushy hair."[27]

"I know there was some controversy about my being invited here," Bobby said with a smile. "Some compared it with inviting a fox into a henhouse. But some of my friends thought it more like putting a chicken in a fox house." The students laughed.[28]

The university still had a long way to go. Fourteen Negro students were enrolled by the spring of 1966: eleven men and three women. Billie Joyce Ware, a sophomore, said that when the other two Negro women went home on the weekend, "It's like getting sick on a desert island and nobody to help you." She said that few of her white roommates in the dormitory spoke to her, and even less so in public. "It will be a long time before the ice is broken around campus for us. However, it is becoming ever so slightly cracked." She was part of the thaw that began in protest and violence four years earlier.[29]

"I know we have many differences of view and opinion," Bobby began his remarks, but he looked to cast their condition in the same light as the rest of the United States. "Racial injustice and poverty, ignorance and hope for world peace, are to be found in the streets of New York and Chicago and Los Angeles, as well as in the towns and farmlands of Mississippi." He continued directly, "You have no problem the nation does not have. You share no hope that is not shared by your fellow students and young people across this country." It was a "New South," he spoke of—"the modern Southern revolution."[30]

"Your generation," Bobby said, "cannot afford to waste its substance and its hopes in the struggles of the past . . . when beyond these walls there is a world to help."[31]

Just as he had with young people around the world, he welcomed their questions. Students wanted to know about the view from his end as their campus had plunged into chaos in 1962. He recounted the events in a soft voice. "We had to decide whether orders of a federal court would be followed," he said. "It was not a question of whether you did or did not like Negroes. I do not believe anybody here would have done any different than we did."[32]

Comically, he laid bare just how silly the reality of politics could be, describing how then-Governor Ross Barnett had demanded that the attorney general instruct the federal marshals to have their pistols drawn so that Barnett could claim they were being overpowered by federal force. "I said I would have the chief marshal pull his gun," Bobby told the students. "He called back in a little while and said he had talked with his advisers in Jackson, and *all* the marshals would have to pull their guns." The students laughed.

The state had gone 88 percent for Goldwater in 1964, and a student asked Bobby how the national Democrats might win given Mississippi's hard right turn toward Republicans. "I think it's going to be damned tough," he said to more laughter. "I think I made the major contribution to that difficulty." With all the police and FBI agents during his four hours in Oxford, Bobby was the most heavily guarded person in America with the exception of the President. Yet hundreds of students surrounded him and Ethel, hoping for autographs or a touch. With every step he took, they urged him, "Come back."[33]

In Tuscaloosa, Bobby spoke at Foster Auditorium, where Governor George Wallace had made his symbolic school-door stand. Adam Clymer wrote that the extra security forces "had little to do except direct traffic." Four thousand students awaited Bobby in a racially mixed crowd on a Friday night, hardly the time when most students went to see a political speech.[34] Just as he had with students in Latin America and elsewhere, Bobby had to connect his message with the Alabama students' history and culture. And so he told them what they knew in their hearts and needed to hear pass his Yankee lips: that bringing the necessary racial progress would create strife in the North as it had in the South. Nevertheless, they had to continue. The students applauded.

But the questions in Tuscaloosa that evening turned to and focused on Vietnam. An icy silence came across the auditorium as Bobby repeated his position that negotiations might involve concessions. He told them that the Chinese had built airfields along their border with North Vietnam, and that if the United States bombed Hanoi and Haiphong, the North might appeal to

China for air support from those bases. Then America would be presented with the question of bombing targets in China. Bobby asked for a show of hands about admitting Communist China to the United Nations, and another for giving them diplomatic recognition from the United States. He thought the split was about even. A student asked about political reshuffling in the State Department to bolster Secretary Dean Rusk's hawks. Bobby deflected with a joke that he would get right to the bottom of it. "I'm a very important senator. I'm ninety-sixth in the order of seniority."

A Negro student asked Bobby if he and President Johnson ever differed on civil rights. Bobby said he only had admiration for Johnson in that regard.

A reporter in Oxford heard some students say they might vote for him to become president one day. Someone had even asked if he would accept the nomination in 1972.

"I haven't been offered it by anyone yet," Bobby quipped.[35]

Edward Ellington, an Ole Miss law student and head of the speakers' bureau that had invited Bobby, reminded the audience that the day's event was a political statement in itself. Noting that Governor Wallace's invitation to speak at Yale had been rescinded due to protests, Ellington said, "Never again let it be uttered that this is a closed society." The comment received a standing ovation.[36]

LESS THAN A week after Bobby's trip into the heart of Southern resistance, a representative of another land trying to prove it was an open society crossed the threshold of his Senate office. South African minister Johann Botha handed Kennedy a letter granting his requested visa to enter the country.[37]

However, the letter said the date of his invitation from the leading antiapartheid student group to give the Day of Affirmation address conflicted with the state's preparations for its national independence celebration. He was not permitted to be in the country that day or for the entire week around it, but could visit any other time he liked.[38]

Bobby immediately replied in a telephone interview with the *New York Times*, saying he and the students would reschedule to April or June. "I am very pleased and look forward toward going," he said. "I appreciate the courtesy of the South Africa government and am looking forward to visiting the country."[39]

The *Los Angeles Times* reported, "U.S. officials were expecting further roadblocks to be raised by the South African government to the senator's planned speech." For more than a month, Bobby and the students would keep the new date of his appearance a closely guarded secret, ultimately settling on June 6, 1966.[40]

As if by fate, the South African government's attempt to silence Bobby put his address exactly two years to the day before an assassin's bullets did what their government could not.

OTHERS WERE MONITORING Bobby closely as he triumphed in his visit with Southern students. From Minneapolis that weekend, a political associate of Hubert Humphrey's watched the scenes from Mississippi on television and exclaimed, "Bolt the doors, boys! Here they come again!"[41]

Bobby was constantly in the news, tied to candidates for statewide offices supposedly locked in battle with Humphrey-aligned candidates. RFK dismissed the chatter. "I suppose there has to be something to write about in a long spring," he told a journalist, "but it does get tiresome. Why, they've had me backing a couple of candidates that I'd never even heard of."[42]

Only the talk of intraparty warfare wasn't limited to proxy battles. Speaking before a cheering Oregon Democratic Convention in March of 1966, Senator Wayne Morse said he would support Bobby in a presumptive challenge to President Johnson in 1968. "I have no hesitancy, and I say this for the first time, in stating that if the senator from New York, Bobby Kennedy, continues to manifest as he is manifesting that he will support a change in foreign policy and the conduct of this war, then the senior senator from Oregon will be proud to support him in the Democratic nomination in 1968." Law students at the University of California in Berkeley proposed a ticket of Kennedy and Senator Fulbright, and soon ads appeared in the *New Republic* selling CITIZENS FOR KENNEDY-FULBRIGHT bumper stickers for fifty cents apiece. Someone in Baltimore paid for a billboard with Bobby's picture on it, saying BACK TO THE KENNEDY TRADITION, until his Senate office asked for it to be taken down. Even the *New York Times* captioned a photo of his trip to Mississippi with "Senator Robert F. Kennedy, shown here with students . . . has embarked on an uphill drive for the Democratic Presidential nomination."[43]

Bobby knew that he would only perpetuate the speculation by responding to it, so he shut it down by pulling Humphrey in. When Senators Kennedy and Javits sponsored a conference in Washington for mayors and municipal officials from New York to learn about the federal programs available to them, Bobby invited the vice president to speak and made light of their rivalry. He told those who would listen not to assume he and Humphrey would come into direct conflict. "My own experience in the past in these matters is that it is empty to speculate about what one is going to be doing five or six years from now—or even whether one is going to be here then."[44]

When others tried to stir trouble on more serious topics, Bobby refused to engage. Thomas Collins of *Newsday* inquired about an interview on Wayne

Morse's claim that weeks before President Kennedy's assassination, JFK told Morse that he would not send combat troops to Vietnam. Joe Dolan sent Bobby a memo that said, "Collins still wants to do a 'no attribution' or background interview on this subject." Bobby scrawled back, "I will not discuss it. I do not discuss P. Kennedy's views on any matter."[45]

Morse's mission was not his. The fight Bobby took on that spring was protecting the Great Society from its author. War spending had ballooned the federal deficit from earlier estimates, and fiscal hawks demanded cuts. Senator Richard Russell cautioned the President against trying to fight "this so-called War on Poverty" while a military war was on, and to "abandon some of the less pressing new programs, however desirable their objectives might be." Republicans said the issue was "rifles vs. ruffles"—suggesting the Great Society was ornamental rather than fundamental. The real enemy was inflation and too much economic expansion. The Republicans felt the War on Poverty could withstand a pause. And so the Johnson administration proposed $1.1 billion in domestic cuts to its 1967 budget.[46]

Bobby fought back.

He had already mingled guns and butter, helping to narrowly pass a Republican-sponsored amendment to a Vietnam War tax bill that expanded Social Security benefits for 1.8 million senior citizens. Its surprise victory prompted the administration's floor manager, Russell Long of Louisiana, to declare, "We might just as well stand up on the top of the Washington Monument and throw the money to the winds."[47]

While Johnson huddled with his cabinet, Bobby went to a Senate education subcommittee hearing to denounce a major reduction in new education spending primarily benefiting low-income families, including school milk and lunch programs.[48] Bobby questioned officials from Johnson's Department of Health, Education, and Welfare how their department filed a $1.3 billion budget request in December, then slashed it by $230 million—an 18 percent reduction—by April 1. "It would appear to me, from the request that they made of the Bureau of Budget," Bobby said, "that HEW felt they could use this money." He added that although he supported the much larger appropriations being requested to fight in Vietnam, "the country suffers" from cuts to education.

"Furthermore, much of this money is being used for the deprived . . . obviously, in areas where there are minority groups, including the Negroes. We have seen figures that the Negroes in Vietnam are 15 percent of our fighting force, as compared to 10 percent of the population. The casualties among Negroes in Vietnam are a higher percentage than among whites. It is also clear that the lower economic groups are being taken and fighting in Vietnam to a higher degree—a higher percentage of them than those from the higher economic groups in the United States. And the education program was aimed at the lower economic groups. So not only are they sacrificing—doing more than their part in the effort, in the struggle in Vietnam—but they are also suffering, if we are cutting back on programs which would help them and help their families. When we think that probably two hundred million dollars that is being cut is what it costs to send B-52s over Vietnam for perhaps a week, it is a matter of great concern to me."

The commissioner of education, Harold Howe, told Bobby and the subcommittee that since the aid program was new—approved in 1965—their formula had been "at a higher degree" than what was necessary. "So there is at least the possibility that these funds will do the job," Howe said.

"I am sure there is a possibility," Bobby replied. "There is a possibility of anything." But he asked that if an overcalculation in the formula explained the reduction, why didn't HEW know about it when they submitted their budget in December?

Howe couldn't answer.

"I am not married to any of these programs," Bobby said, "but what is of concern to me is . . . there are cuts made in educational programs we anticipated would be in effect this year. And we talk about the fact that it is a tight budget, but we are spending twelve billion dollars each year extra in Vietnam, and most that is dealing with killing people, and it doesn't seem to me—I think it is shortsighted at the same time not to be doing what we have to do in our own country to educate people."[49]

Bobby continued his broadside against the rollback at home for the war abroad with a speech before a civic dinner in upstate New York on April 19: "Time after time," he said, "the cuts will be felt most by those least able to afford them—the disadvantaged, particularly the disadvantaged children, who live in the vast urban ghettos, and the rural hollows of the nation."[50]

Johnson was not mentioned by name. This was a conscious choice—RFK edited out stronger attacks in Edelman's draft. Bobby repeated that the United States ought to keep its commitment in Vietnam, while also remaining remain committed to "what needs to be done at home."

"We shall fail as a society if we do not do both. And the fact is that we can do both."[51]

A stern rebuke came from Democratic congressman Joseph Resnick, a Johnson ally whose district Bobby had spoken in. Resnick accused Bobby of "talking like a demagogue" about the cuts, saying, "President Johnson got these programs passed. President Kennedy tried to and failed."[52]

In Johnson's press conference three days later, he was asked about Bobby's criticism and talked about increasing spending under his watch, but avoided a direct response.[53] In a speech later that day, Johnson spoke of his priorities and said, "We will make mistakes—many of them. You will read about most of them. Few ever escape the poison pens. Our yearly budgets will never seem sufficient . . . But we shall not be stampeded into unwise programs."[54]

It was in those last weeks of April that Senator Fulbright said, "Congress as a whole has lost interest in the Great Society; it has become politically and psychologically a 'war Congress.' "[55]

THE SKIES OVER North Vietnam posed a new risk for the United States. As Bobby discussed with the students in Tuscaloosa, the Chinese had constructed air bases across their border with the North, and high-speed aerial battles were heating up. Seventy miles from the Chinese border, Soviet-made jets and American fighter pilots were engaging in their first bouts of combat in the war. Jet fighters had clashed three times above North Vietnam in late April, with the Sidewinder missile of a U.S. Air Force Phantom blowing the tail off a Soviet-designed MiG-21 sixty-five miles northeast of Hanoi. The question that Bobby had posed to the students—whether these battles would cross the border into China and threaten wider war—was answered by the administration when Secretary Rusk said the United States would not recognize the principle of "sanctuary" for attacking forces in Vietnam as it had in Korea. Jets engaged in combat could make hot pursuit over borders, striking enemy aircraft and their bases, if necessary. Senate Republican leader Everett Dirksen defended the position, as did Democratic senator Henry Jackson, who said it was acceptable and reasonable to warn the Chinese of such actions.[56]

Bobby took to the Senate floor. "What will be the Chinese response," he said, "if her territory is bombed or her airspace invaded? Will the Chinese seek to strike at our air bases—in Vietnam or Thailand or aboard our aircraft carriers? And if they do, what then will our response be? Further bombing? And if the scale of bombing increases, will China confine herself to air fighting—or will it send its troops to engage ours on the ground in South Vietnam?"[57]

Bobby quoted Scotty Reston's column in that morning's New York Times, which said administration officials didn't view spilling over into China as a major risk since "the men running the war . . . have gradually come to believe that China and the Soviet Union will tolerate military defeats the United States clearly would not tolerate itself."[58]

Bobby said, "Such assumptions are not a sound basis for policy. Similar assumptions about the Vietcong and North Vietnam have been proven wrong time and time again in this war." Moreover, he said this was only a hindrance— a distraction—from the underlying problem that kept the United States in

Vietnam, the one he had addressed in his February speech and the one he had been highlighting for years. "Without a viable political structure in South Vietnam, the efforts and sacrifice of our fighting men will be wasted. But no military action in North Vietnam or China can create or contribute to the creation of such a political structure in South Vietnam. The extension of the war into China will not, in my judgment, give us success in South Vietnam."[59]

Within another day, administration officials clarified that President Johnson alone would decide whether to authorize "hot pursuit," a subtle acknowledgment that Rusk's declaration put too much power in the hands of a single fighter pilot.[60] A number of senators had risen in objection to the policy, but Bobby's message rose above them all.

He continued to fight to ease tensions. When the State Department acknowledged that the United States had rejected a Chinese pact not to use nuclear weapons against each other, Bobby again took the Senate floor to urge the administration to invite China to the Geneva nuclear disarmament talks, or to engage in "direct, high-level discussions for just this purpose anywhere in the world . . . The time to move is immediately." Rusk countered that the Chinese had shown no interest in talks, so what was the point?[61] Bobby pressed for initiative.

Something was happening—a pull in the minds of many on Vietnam. People looked toward Bobby for leadership. In Allen Park, Michigan, a thirty-four-year-old man found himself reclassified 1-A in the draft despite being the father of eight children. And though he was not a constituent of New York, when he brought his story to the press, he said he would seek help from Robert Kennedy. His was a name, as Murray Kempton had written, "at which lonely men grasp in their loneliness."[62]

"Long ago," an anonymous Washington politician told the *New Republic*, "Robert Kennedy discovered that no one was going to like him, in the sense that people liked Roosevelt, or Stevenson, or Jack Kennedy. So he decided to make people follow him because of the power of his ideas, or the rightness of his positions."[63]

William F. Buckley offered the backhanded compliment that Bobby had finally pulled himself into a real position of political leadership "and is no longer thought of purely as a political technician, useful only for organizing the armies, or poisoning the rivals' soup."[64]

Bobby punctuated his foreign-policy focus with a Senate speech on Latin America. The State Department did not ask for a report on his findings, so he made his assessment public in fifty-four pages of single-spaced typewritten copy on long legal folio sheets. The first half alone took two and a half hours to read and had to be delivered over two days. He spoke of a place where hope was lacking, where 90 percent of the land belonged to less than 10 percent of those who owned any. He urged the United States to align itself with "peaceful revolutionary change," against its current direction.

"There are still those who believe," he said, "that stability can be maintained and Communism defeated, by force of arms; that those who have waited three centuries for justice can wait for another so that old privileges may be preserved; that the economic machinery of the twentieth century can be developed and managed by social structures which were outmoded in the eighteenth." In all, he felt that large-scale land redistribution—a tenet of the Alliance for Progress— would bring the countries "away from the oligarchy and privilege, toward more popular government."[65]

In the *New York Times*, Scotty Reston saw it fitting into a pattern of Bobby's speeches. "He differs with the administration just enough to establish an independent position that strengthens him where the President is weak, but praises the President just enough to avoid an open break."[66] In the second day of his speech, the former aide to Joseph McCarthy spoke of the danger of approaching the world with the sole mission of rooting out Communists.

"If we allow ourselves to become allied with those to whom the cry of 'Communism' is only an excuse for the perpetuation of privilege . . . if we assist, with military materials and other aid to prevent reform for the people, then we will give the Communists a strength which they cannot attain by anything they themselves might do." All action—even military actions—had to be in line with the hopes of the impoverished. "Counterinsurgency," he said, "might best be described as social reform under pressure."[67]

IN SOUTH AFRICA, where Bobby would next take his revolutionary message, the avowedly anti-Communist government was at its height. White South African voters had delivered a near-total victory to the apartheid policies of Prime Minister Hendrik F. Verwoerd's Nationalist Party. The Progressive Party, which shared the ideals of the National Union of South African Students, won just a single representative in the 166-seat Parliament. *New York Times* correspondent Joseph Lelyveld stopped by an illegal drinking spot in a black township, where many nonwhites had been forcibly relocated, to report the patrons' laments.[68]

Before the next month was out, Lelyveld and his family would be expelled from the country with no reason given. Just a week before Bobby's visit, forty print and television journalists who had applied to get into the country to cover the trip were denied entry. The South African Information Department defended the ban by calling the reporters Mr. Kennedy's "publicity teams," complicit in providing footage for Kennedy's "buildup for a future presidential election." The government said that the country already had enough foreign news outlets—ones that had the added pressure of staying on the good side of the ruling party or finding themselves like Lelyveld, or worse.[69]

Under the Suppression of Communism Act, the state of South Africa designated Ian Robertson, the twenty-one-year-old president of NUSAS who had invited Bobby to the country, a banned person. Sentenced to a term of five years, he could not partake in public events. His movements were closely monitored and restricted. He was forbidden to be in a room with more than one other person at a time, to be quoted in the press in any way, or to take part in political or social life. A law student, he was now prohibited from entering a courtroom. To add to the indignity, Robertson was notified of his banning by a form letter, his basic freedoms erased without even the attempt at justification. He was a nonperson . . . as some would call them, "the walking dead."[70]

Bobby kept a close watch on events, but waited to make his statements until he was in the country. A contact at Harvard passed on a letter from Robertson, who wrote, "The gremlins are watching every move I make in the hope of catching me breaking the order. It was quite amusing giving them the slip for the first few days but it is becoming quite a bind now." Robertson described the banning's coming before the Day of Affirmation as "a blow," though he remained hopeful, writing, "In a way it has been a good thing, because it has galvanized NUSAS in so staggering a way."[71]

Robertson's courage was just another example of what Bobby found all over the world. "There's a sharp difference between this generation and the last," he said that spring. "Young people today have that motivation—idealism and dissatisfaction." An empty chair would be left next to Bobby's at his address in Cape Town, a silent acknowledgment of Robertson's absence.[72]

Bobby arrived in South Africa late on a Saturday night to a chaotic reception. A massive crowd had gathered at Jan Smuts Airport, a long way outside Johannesburg with no public transportation. He and Ethel made their way through a thousand shouting and pushing onlookers, many greeting him, a few heckling him.[73] He stepped up to the news microphones, placed at the nonwhite gate, and said he was glad for the reception. Over the cheering, a man from a distance shouted, "Go home!"

"I'm particularly delighted," Bobby said, "that, as in my own country, that there is a divergent point of view." The crowd cheered. "I'm particularly delighted—" and someone from behind interrupted by tossing a large wreath of flowers over his head and onto his neck and shoulders. Bobby eyebrows danced amid the camera flashes. He took the wreath and handed it to Ethel and redirected his attention to the protester. "I'm delighted that we're able to express it, and I'm delighted that you had the chance and the opportunity to write the sign YANKEE GO HOME."[74]

Four American newsmen tried to sneak into the country, flying in from Nairobi, but they were discovered by authorities and put on a plane for Rhodesia. The South African press welcomed the ban on foreign journalists for self-interested reasons. They inundated the U.S. Information Service in Africa with requests for spots on the press plane and Kennedy's schedule, which Bobby's aide Tom Johnston held closely until five minutes before the morning newspaper deadlines. Some of the leading editors met with Bobby on the first day of his visit at the home of an American embassy official. As de facto representatives of the ruling party, they were the most prominent officials that Bobby would speak with. Prime Minister Verwoerd and others were said to have turned down his invitation to meet as "not convenient."[75]

In his notes, Bobby would remember speaking with "the editors of the papers who supported the government" about how they classified people, since there were eleven million black South Africans, three million white South Africans, and two million "colored" people, who were classified with the blacks. "Who were these two million people?" Bobby asked. "They were quiet for a moment," he wrote, "but finally their spokesman said, a 'bastard.' But if a white woman has a child out of wedlock with a white man, is the baby a 'colored' person? They replied, 'No.'" They told him that a colored person "is a person who is not white or black. A South American, an Indian, a Chinaman, yes. A Japanese—no. He is considered white. 'Why?' I asked. There are not many of them, they replied." But Bobby soon discovered that the Japanese did a lot of business with South Africa, therefore received a preferable classification.[76]

The system of segregation was similar to the codes the United States was working to change in the South. Unlike in America, South Africans did not have the Bill of Rights. Protest was dangerous. Mere associations led to banishment. Joseph Lelyveld sent RFK a ten-page memo before his trip, underlining only one sentence: "Merely shaking hands with a black man in South Africa is a fantastic gesture." But after that handshake, black South Africans still had to live in South Africa. Reuters reported how some blacks moved away when Bobby and Ethel approached, rather than be seen with him. In one photograph, published in the *New York Times*, Bobby is seen leaning in for the hand of a visibly uncomfortable black man, who stands back, only slightly extending his arm. Behind them in the photo was a white man holding up a camera, a possible agent of the government, which was documenting Kennedy's every move.[77]

The surveillance was on his mind in the hours before the Day of Affirmation address when his car diverted onto an otherwise quiet street in Cape Town to visit the garden apartment of NUSAS president Ian Robertson.[78] It was just the two of them, for that was all the government would allow.

"One of the first things he asked me was 'Is this place bugged?'" Robertson revealed later. "I said I would think it is."

"Do you know how to disturb a bugging mechanism?" Bobby asked.

Robertson said he didn't. Bobby told him to stamp his foot on the floor, and that would throw it off for a few minutes. "Well, how do you know that?"

"I used to be attorney general," Bobby grinned.

Robertson would remember decades later how they had a deep discussion about politics—in South Africa and the world. "He wanted to know about my welfare. He wanted to know what I thought about South Africa. He wanted to know what I and other students thought about the United States. He asked about Vietnam." Bobby told Robertson that he was sorry about what had happened to him. As a token of their bond, he gave the twenty-one-year-old a copy of *Profiles in Courage*, with an inscription from Jacqueline Kennedy.[79]

The steps to Jameson Hall at the University of Cape Town were crowded that evening as Bobby made his way into the auditorium to give his address to the all-white audience permitted inside.[80] Many had input into what Bobby would say that night, with some urging him to be bolder, and Bobby concerned about not getting any more students into a fix with the government. The words he decided to deliver were a call to the younger generation, like the ones he had spoken at universities in New York and Mississippi, Latin America and Europe, and even the words he had written for his brother and himself in the darkest time of his life. That evening, Robert Kennedy defined change.

"I came here," he began, "because of my deep interest and affection for a land settled by the Dutch in the mid-seventeenth century, then taken over by the British, and at last independent; a land in which the native inhabitants were at first subdued, but relations with whom remain a problem to this day; a land which defined itself on a hostile frontier; a land which has tamed rich natural resources through the energetic application of modern technology; a land which once imported slaves, and now must struggle to wipe out the last traces of that former bondage . . . I refer, of course, to the United States of America." A smile broke across his face and the room erupted in applause.

He spoke of individual liberty as their inheritance—"the power to be heard"—and government as its means of protection. "Everything that makes men's lives worthwhile—family, work, education, a place to rear one's children and a place to rest one's head—all this depends on the decisions of government. All can be swept away by a government which does not heed the demands of its people"—here Bobby emphasized, just as he had when speaking about the problems of ghettos in the United States—"and I mean *all* of its people."

He talked about those who denied freedom, "those in every land who would label as 'Communist' every threat to their people," and he spoke of the prejudice within the United States, reminding the South Africans, just as he did in a rooms of white men in Scranton, Pennsylvania, and upstate New York, how the Irish faced discrimination. He invoked Martin Luther King Jr.— whose visa had been denied by the South African government—and his Nobel Peace Prize, an unmistakable nod to the president of the African National Congress, Chief Albert Luthuli, who had also been banned by the Suppression of Communism Act.

As Bobby had at colleges in New York one year earlier, he asked the students to consider the pace of change, and what it meant. "In a few hours, the plane that brought me to this country crossed over oceans and countries which have been a crucible of human history," he said. "In minutes we traced the migration of men over thousands of years; seconds, the briefest glimpse, and we passed battlefields on which millions of men once struggled and died." Boundaries were erased. Only nature and works of man remained. "If we would lead outside our borders, if we would help those who need our assistance, if we would meet our responsibilities to mankind, we must first—all of us— demolish the borders which history has erected between men within our own nations—barriers of race and religion, social class and ignorance."

This, he said, was a job that required "the qualities of youth . . . not a time of life but a state of mind, a temper of the will, a quality of the imagination, a predominance of courage over timidity, of the appetite for adventure over the love of ease."

"It is a revolutionary world we live in," Bobby said, "and thus, as I have said in Latin America and Asia, in Europe and in the United States, it is young people who must take the lead." Once again and in yet another land, he recounted the young men and women who had marked their names in the history books, who had taken change into their own hands. It was not the destiny for all, but it was their responsibility to try. "Few will have the great- ness to bend history itself, but each of us can work to change a small portion of events, and in the total of all those acts will be written the history of this generation . . . It is from numberless diverse acts of courage and belief that human history is shaped.

"Each time a man stands up for an ideal or acts to improve the lot of others or strikes out against injustice, he sends forth a tiny ripple of hope, and crossing each other from a million different centers of energy and daring those ripples build a current which can sweep down the mightiest walls of oppression and resistance."

Bobby would conclude his speech in a familiar fashion: quoting from his brother's inaugural address, whose words he had carried to a mountaintop. But they were his words, spoken for the first time that night, that would ring off the walls, out of the hall, and go forever.

He left them that night declaring, "Each of us have our own work to do," asking "if a man of forty" can claim membership in "the world's largest younger generation."[81] He had carried his brother's torch deeper into a decade that had changed in ways neither could have expected and would change further still.

MEMORIAL

June 8, 1968

IN KENYA A FEW days after departing South Africa, Robert Kennedy walked up to within twenty feet of a rhinoceros despite Ethel's shouting for him to come back. The rhino looked at him, snorted, and ran away. Bobby put his hands on his knees and laughed. Asked what he would have done had the beast charged, he said, "I'd have thought about that then."[1]

His address on the Day of Affirmation contained some fine words, but as he always did, he was looking for more of a challenge. So he spent the rest of his time in South Africa seeking out and engaging critics: conservative university students and supporters of the apartheid regime. He went to the sprawling relocation area Soweto—"a dreary concentration camp," he called it—to meet those living in extreme poverty in the place where the government confined them. Bobby hoped his very presence, walking openly with nothing to fear, would send a message and inspire others to visit.

At the University of Natal in Durban, he was told that the church taught apartheid as biblical truth—the will of God. "But suppose God is black," Bobby replied. "What if we go to heaven, and we, all our lives, have treated the Negro as inferior, and God is there, and we look up and he is not white? What then is our response?"[2]

When leaving the university, he hopped onto the top of a car and led the crowd that had gathered in singing the American protest hymn "We Shall Overcome."[3]

"If he had known ahead of time," his aide Tom Johnston would later say, "that he'd be singing 'We Shall Overcome' with a lot of students in South Africa, he probably wouldn't believe that. But, that was, I think, revealing, both about him and also about the conditions in those countries and the fact the police and the police state can really move you to do things that you don't think you're capable of under normal circumstances."[4] It wasn't just the conditions of the police state—it was all the conditions Bobby had experienced.

His whole life had become doing the things that he had not dreamed of three years earlier.

He and Ethel boarded a tiny helicopter and paid a visit to Chief Albert Luthuli, the Nobel Peace Prize winner banned by the South African government and restricted to his rural homestead. Bobby brought along a portable record player for the chief to listen to recordings of President Kennedy's speeches, and together with Luthuli's daughters and two government minders, they sat quietly and listened to President Kennedy's civil rights address, given just three years earlier on June 11, 1963.

There was darkness on the horizon. The elation of Bobby's visit—and his recent reception in Mississippi—was bloodied when news came that James Meredith had been shot and grievously wounded as he marched for freedom along a Southern highway. And still unknown to the Kennedys was that lurking among the thousands of South Africans who took to the streets to greet them was a man named Dimitri Tsafendas. Less than three months later, Tsafendas would murder apartheid's chief proponent, Prime Minister Hendrik Verwoerd. "Violence," Bobby would say of the assassination, "is not an answer to problems which must be worked out between people with compassion and understanding on both sides."[5] As he had quoted the Greek poet Aeschylus at the ceremony upon his leaving the Justice Department in 1964, they must "tame the savageness of man, and make gentle the life of this world."

Those words would find RFK again while he was running for president in April 1968, hours after the assassination of Dr. Martin Luther King Jr. Bobby arrived late to his speech before a black audience gathered on an outdoor basketball court in Indianapolis. A reporter saw him walking with his eyes cast down and lips moving "almost as if he were saying a silent prayer."[6] Others believed in those moments that he was talking to Jack.

Bobby's brother was on his mind that night. People cried out in horror when he said Dr. King had been shot and killed, a shriek sweeping across the basketball court. Bobby spoke of King's dedication to love and justice and addressed those "tempted to be filled with hatred and distrust at the injustice of such an act against all white people.

"I would only say that I can also feel in my own heart the same kind of feeling. I had a member of my family killed, but he was killed by a white man. But we have to make the effort in the United States, we have to make an effort to understand, to get beyond or go beyond these rather difficult times." He recited his favorite poem about "the pain which cannot forget" that "falls drop by drop upon the heart," until "wisdom through the awful grace of God." He told them, "What we need in the United States is not division. What we need in the United States is not hatred. What we need in the United States is not violence and lawlessness, but is love and wisdom and compassion toward one another—a feeling of justice toward those who still suffer within our country, whether they be white or whether they be black." A few began to clap, and then the sound of children rose, and the audience cheered for the first time. He asked those gathered there to dedicate themselves to those ideals, to "return home and to say a prayer for the family of Martin Luther King . . . and say a prayer for our country, and for our people."[7]

LATE IN 1966, Bobby and his new press secretary, Frank Mankiewicz— the Peace Corps official he had bonded with at the briefing on Latin America— went by Arlington National Cemetery to see President Kennedy's new gravesite as it was being completed. The stonework was nearly done, the words were being cut on the front wall, and the landscaping was under way. Bobby asked Mankiewicz what he thought. "I don't really like it," Mankiewicz said, later telling Ethel in a letter he thought it was "too *permanent*" and could have been the grave of any American president. "It could, for instance, have been Rutherford B. Hayes, or anyone else rewarded late in his career by his party with one term in the Presidency, and who had died of pleurisy at the age of 84." There was nothing there "to speak of the unfulfilled promise, or of the sudden raw emotions his death brought forth, or of the terrible national wound."

Mankiewicz told Bobby that he missed what had been JFK's temporary gravesite. Smaller, more modest—as if it had happened without planning.

"I think you're right," Bobby said.[8]

He was still concerned, just as he had been in those dark weeks of December 1963, with how the country would remember his brother. RFK complained to Dick Goodwin about Lyndon Johnson late one evening, "All those things he's doing . . . poverty, civil rights, they're things we had just begun. We just didn't have the time." Dick walked over to the bookshelf in Bobby's apartment and grabbed a volume of Shakespeare off the wall.

"Look at this," Dick said. "Julius Caesar is an immortal, and he was only emperor of Rome for a little more than three years."

The senator smiled. "Yes . . . but it helps if you have Shakespeare to write about you."

Bobby cared greatly about President Kennedy's reputation—Dick thought him "obsessed."[9] And he was still puzzled by his own.

Sipping a vodka tonic on a New York–bound shuttle after a long day of work at the Senate in 1966, Bobby turned to a reporter he had just met and asked, "Why do you think so many people dislike me?"

The reporter responded with the same reasons Bobby himself had given in the past: his involvement in divisive issues and polarizing effect on people. Bobby didn't like the answer. "Why do you have to theorize like that? Why can't you just say what you see? I know what you're going to write—a critical piece like all the others. I don't think you're thinking about me at all. I think you're just reading yourself into me."[10]

And yet he would keep going back for more. "All I can say is that I like this kind of life better than basking on the beach at Acapulco," he said shortly after entering the Senate in 1965. "I am not giving up anything by leading this life . . . I might say it is the only life worth living for me . . . My reason for being alive."[11]

He continued to change. His positions grew bolder. His risk taking increased. His hair grew longer—what one reporter called "a wig-like mop."

"Grab me some of his hair and give me some!" a teenage girl cried to her friend during a campaign stop that October of 1966.[12]

Bobby didn't have enough time. But in the choices he made with what was left to him, he was a bridge for a country that was tearing apart. David Halberstam would write that Robert Kennedy "was at the exact median point of American idealism and American power." He used American idealism to advocate for unsettling progress, and understood how American power could make that change a reality. "The correlation was such," Halberstam wrote, "that his speeches could be written by young radicals like Adam Walinsky and Peter Edelman, and yet his children named after [establishment figures] Douglas Dillon and Maxwell Taylor."[13]

As Bobby had shown in committee hearings when weighing air raids above Vietnam against cuts to school lunch programs, he understood what the Gross National Product counted, but most importantly what it did not. "It measures everything," he told students in Kansas two days after announcing his presidential candidacy in March of 1968, "except that which makes life worthwhile. And it can tell us everything about America except why we are proud that we are Americans."[14]

The campaign was tragically brief, but it was full of old friends. Fred Dutton and Steve Smith helped keep it organized, and even Paul Corbin showed up— under an assumed name. Bobby was accused of ruthlessness and opportunism until its final day, though that was par for the course. While the power rested with the delegates to the 1968 Democratic National Convention, his triumph in the June 4 California presidential primary indicated that rank-and-file voters were with him. Then, minutes after his victory speech, he was shot repeatedly while exiting through the pantry of the Ambassador Hotel in Los Angeles.[15]

"If you ask me," Bobby once said, "whether I would like to see one or all of

my sons in politics someday, the answer is yes. I would do nothing to influence or push them into it, but I would be pleased if it happened. Politics can
hurt badly, but there are lots of other ways of getting hurt in life."[16]

WHEN IT CAME time to bury him, Jack's words from a decade earlier rang
out again: "Just as I went into politics because Joe died, if anything happened
to me tomorrow, my brother Bobby would run for my seat in the Senate. And
if Bobby died, Teddy would take over for him."[17]

And as Bobby had memorialized Jack in the foreword to *Profiles in
Courage*, it was left to Teddy to memorialize Bobby.

"This is the way he lived," the youngest brother said before a grand cathedral on June 8, 1968. "That is what he leaves us."

Their mother, Rose, sat in a front pew. She refused to show the depth of her
pain. "If I had broken down in grief," she would later write, "I would only have
added to the misery of the others and possibly could have set off a chain reaction of tearfulness."[18] Kennedys didn't cry so that others might not cry, too.

"My brother need not be idealized," Teddy said, "or enlarged in death
beyond what he was in life. To be remembered simply as a good and decent
man, who saw wrong and tried to right it . . . saw suffering and tried to heal
it . . . saw war, and tried to stop it."

It is the best biography of Robert Kennedy ever written. And it is the
description of a politician.

Bobby's grave would be a simple white cross sticking out of the ground just
a few yards from where his brother lay, the two of them close once again.
Along a wall, carved in stone, are the words he spoke that day in South Africa,
about a man standing up for an ideal, and sending forth a ripple of hope.

In the scale of world events, there was nothing particularly remarkable
about what he did there, giving a speech about protest to students in Cape
Town. He did not save the world from annihilation or set a new policy or start
a revolution. Rather, his words and gestures had altered some lives and given
some hope and comfort to those who desperately needed it. As much could
be said for him when he left the world exactly two years later, on June 6, 1968.
His words, however, were a unique event. History is inclined to remember the
call to arms, the transfer of power, the turn of phrase upon some barrier-
breaking achievement or agreement. This moment contained none of that
glory. In this speech—this simple speech to children about to inherit what
every generation before them had built upon—Bobby said the tiniest movement was the center from which the world shakes. In it, he had offered his
definition of politics, and understanding of change.

This was the lesson he had learned in the years after JFK. It was the way he lived, the way he never stopped living, until the day he traveled to a distant coast and spent his last seconds of consciousness. In those final moments, lying on a pantry floor, his head bleeding and his sighs falling shallow, his wife would press her ear to his chest and find the smallest comfort amid the chaos, that his heart was still beating.[19]

ACKNOWLEDGMENTS

To Joan and Richard Cramer, for everything . . .

To Adam Goodheart and Ted Widmer for the desk in the attic; to Matt DeFilippis, for the spark; to Paul Swibinski, for the front-row seat; to Matt Bai, for showing how it's done; to Birch and Kitty Bayh, for the ongoing colloquy; to Michael Weisman, for wit and will; to Andrew Oros, Steve Clemons, Dan Premo, Melissa Deckman, Janet Kaufman, Harold Heinz, Leslie Breese, Robert Lynch, Christine Wade, and Donald McColl, for making me think . . .

To the New York Public Library, its Frederick Lewis Allen Room, and Jay Barksdale, for the shelf and the quiet; to the JFK Library, its research staff and the Theodore C. Sorensen Fellowship, for letting us touch history; and to Washington College's C.V. Starr Center for the Study of the American Experience, for opening the door to the past . . .

To all the archivists and librarians, and sources who spoke to me, for their time—especially Peter Edelman, Adam and Jane Walinsky, and Frank Mankiewicz, for talking to a kid; and to Nancy Dutton, for the best interviews . . .

To agent Robert Guinsler, for direction and humor; to Flip Brophy, for curiosity and honesty; to my first editor, Pete Beatty, for the crack at it; to editor George Gibson, for his warm guidance; to assistant editor Grace McNamee for keeping the train on the tracks; to publicists Beth Parker and Lauren Hill, for liftoff; to Jackie Johnson, Callie Garnett, Sara Kitchen, Jennifer Kelaher, and the team at Bloomsbury, for seeing it through . . .

To Brendan Cunningham, for the best advice; to Bob Bennett, for the guide to gardening and life; to Steve Kornacki, for a few hundred editing tutorials and many more laughs; to Joe Scarborough, Mika Brzezinski, and Willie Geist, for making waves; to Casey Schaeffer, Eelin Reily, and Alex Korson, for their supportive leadership . . .

To friends and colleagues—Josephine Bathan, Sterling Brown, Mike Buczkiewicz, Louis Burgdorf, Laura Chamberlain, Jayme Cohen, Stephanie

Cunningham, Jason Driscoll, Brian Duffy, Pam Granda, Eric Greenberg, Maureen Hanna, Miller Hawkins, Dan Hollis, Sasha Issenberg, Drew Katchen, Marc Katz, Laura Kim, Colleen King, Eric Kleefeld, Steve Lima, Russell Lovelady, Alex Lupica, Jack Manning, Henry Melcher, Jonathan Martin, Ben Mayer, Merrick Nelson, Adam Noboa, Areej Noor, Patrick O'Neill, Dom Palumbo, Camila Perez, Amitai Perline, Daniela Pierre-Bravo, Scott Rocco, Yadira Rodriguez, Andy Salsman, Lauren Schweitzer, Jason Squitieri, Anthony Scutro, Amy Shuster, Ben Smith, Austin Stone, Monica Suarez, Luna Szoke, Jesse Rodriguez, Yadira Rodriguez, Brittany Terrell, Anne Thompson, Adam Tzanis, Morgan Walker, Jeremiah Wilcox, and Corey Yow—for making life easier . . .

To Teresa Gianotti, for filling up my heart and home—and Tux's bowl; to Rita Ciolli, for making coffee; Peter Gianotti and Claire Gianotti, for pasta and cannoli . . .

To Josephine Richards, for her love of storytelling; Belle Richards and Michael Bokar, for a well of confidence; to Marilyn and Tuck Cach, the Infante famiglia, the O'Donnells, the Williams clan, Jim Bohrer and his brood, for helping make my story . . .

To Gerald Edward, for being my first role model; to Jerry Bohrer, for always doing the right thing; and to Joanne Bohrer, my best girl, and to whom this book is dedicated . . .

I thank you from the bottom of my heart.

NOTES

A GUIDE TO ABBREVIATIONS AND SELECT SOURCES

NEWSPAPERS, PERIODICALS, AND WIRE SERVICES

AC	*Atlanta Constitution*	NW	*Newsweek*
ADW	*Atlanta Daily World*	NYDN	*New York Daily News*
AP	Associated Press	NYHT	*New York Herald Tribune*
AS	*Austin Statesman*	NYP	*New York Post*
BG	*Boston Globe*	NYT	*New York Times*
BS	*Baltimore Sun*	SEP	*Saturday Evening Post*
CDD	*Chicago Daily Defender*	SPS	*Syracuse Post-Standard*
CDM	*Concord Daily Monitor*	ST	*Scranton Times*
CSM	*Christian Science Monitor*	TDN	*The Detroit News*
CT	*Chicago Tribune*	TNR	*The New Republic*
GDN	*The Guardian* (U.K.)	TNY	*The New Yorker*
HC	*Hartford Courant*	TS	*The Spectator* (U.K.)
HST	*Hampden-Sydney Tiger*	UPI	United Press International
LAT	*Los Angeles Times*	WP	*Washington Post*
ND	*Newsday*	WSJ	*Wall Street Journal*
NEN	*Newark Evening News*		

JOHN F. KENNEDY LIBRARY (JFKL), BOSTON, MASSACHUSETTS

AWP	Adam Walinsky Personal Papers	RFKOH	Robert F. Kennedy Oral History Collection
EGP	Edwin O. Guthman Personal Papers	RFKSCP	Robert F. Kennedy Senate Papers: Correspondence— Personal File, 1964–68
JDP	Joseph F. Dolan Personal Papers	RFKSSPR	Robert F. Kennedy Senate Papers: Speeches and Press Releases, 1964–68
JFKOH	John F. Kennedy Oral History Collection		
JRP	Jacob "Jack" Rosenthal Personal Papers	RFKST	Robert F. Kennedy Senate Papers: Trips, 1964–66
RFKAG	Robert F. Kennedy Attorney General Papers	WDP	William L. Dunfey Personal Papers

New York Public Library (NYPL), New York, New York

ASNYPL   Arthur M. Schlesinger Jr.
          Papers

U.S. Department of Justice (DOJ), Washington, D.C.

Robert Kennedy's Attorney General
Speeches: justice.gov/ag/speeches-25

Lyndon Baines Johnson Library (LBJL), Austin, Texas

Daily Diary Entries: lbjlibrary.net   LBJOH   LBJ Library Oral History
/collections/daily-diary.html   Collection

The Miller Center of the University of Virginia (TMC), Charlottesville, Virginia

LBJ Phone-Call Recordings: millercenter
.org/scripps/archive/presidentialrecord
ings/johnson

Books

ATD	Arthur M. Schlesinger Jr., *A Thousand Days*	*RA*	Richard N. Goodwin, *Remembering America*
TDOAP	William Manchester, *The Death of a President*	*RKA40*	Nick Thimmesch, *Robert Kennedy at 40*
FRUS	*Foreign Relations of the United States*	*RK&HT*	Arthur M. Schlesinger Jr., *Robert Kennedy and His Times*
MC	Jeff Shesol, *Mutual Contempt*	*WBOB*	Edwin O. Guthman, *We Band of Brothers*

People

AMS	Arthur M. Schlesinger Jr.	LBJ	Lyndon B. Johnson
AW	Adam Walinsky	PBE	Peter B. Edelman
EOG	Edwin O. Guthman	RK	Robert F. Kennedy

INTRODUCTION: MEMORIAL (PGS. 1 TO 8)

1. Alexander M. Bickel, "Robert Kennedy as History," *TNR*, July 5, 1969.
2. "Segregation March Precedes Robert Kennedy's Ala. Visit," *ND*, April 26, 1963; "Pickets Seized Before Speech by Robert Kennedy," *NYT*, October 6, 1963.
3. *Robert Kennedy: In His Own Words*, ed. Edwin O. Guthman and Jeffrey

Shulman (Toronto: Bantam Books, 1988), 330.

4. John Douglas, RFKOH, June 16, 1969, 10; Ramsey Clark, RFKOH, July 20, 1970.

5. Peter Maas, "What Will R.F.K. Do Next?," *SEP*, March 28, 1964, 18.

6. "Kennedy Airport Law Is Signed; Idlewild Name Changes Tuesday," *NYT*, December 19, 1963; AP, "Kennedy Half Dollar Approved," *NYT*, December 19, 1963.

7. Evan Thomas to RK, December 16, 1963, RFKAG, Box 93: "Books: Profiles in Courage; Correspondence RF Foreword Memorial Edition."

8. Paul O'Neil, "The No. 2 Man in Washington," *Life*, January 26, 1962, 76.

9. Gloria to Angie Novello, December 17, 1963, and Gertrude Ball to Angie Novello, January 6, 1964, RFKAG, Box 93: "Books: Profiles in Courage; Correspondence RF Foreword Memorial Edition."

10. Jack Rosenthal to EOG, December 20, 1963, JRP, Box 3: "Memoranda 1963: November–December."

11. RK, "Tribute to JFK," *Look*, February 25, 1964, 38.

12. Rose Fitzgerald Kennedy, *Times to Remember* (New York: Doubleday, 1974), 144–45.

13. RK, "Tribute to JFK," 42.

14. RK, "Day of Affirmation Address, University of Capetown," June 6, 1966, JFKL.

15. David Nasaw, *The Patriarch: The Remarkable Life and Turbulent Times of Joseph P. Kennedy* (New York: Penguin, 2012), 664.

16. AMS, *Robert Kennedy and His Times* (Boston: Houghton Mifflin, 1978), 133–34.

17. "Democrats: Little Brother Is Watching," *Time*, October 10, 1960.

18. Charles Bartlett, "Can Robert Soften His 'Bark'?," *BG*, August 27, 1964.

19. Fletcher Knebel, "The Unknown JFK," *Look*, November 17, 1964, 46.

20. Drew Pearson, "Kennedy Plans N.Y. Senate Bid," *WP*, August 10, 1964.

21. Arthur Edson, "Has J.F.K.'s Popularity Brushed Off on Bobby?," *BS*, December 12, 1965.

22. O'Neil, "No. 2 Man in Washington," 90.

23. Guthman and Shulman, *Robert Kennedy*, 44.

24. AP, "Secretary Quotes Kennedy Putting Aside Talk of Peril," *BS*, August 17, 1965.

25. Fred A. Forbes, JFKOH, March 4, 1966, 32.

26. "Democrats: Little Brother Is Watching."

27. David Nasaw, author interview.

28. Kennedy, *Times to Remember*, 102.

29. *RK&HT*, 97.

30. O'Neil, "No. 2 Man in Washington," 92.

31. "Kennedy Stamina Cited by Brother," *NYT*, February 11, 1964; David Wise, "The Kennedy Dynasty and the Future," *NYHT*, December 15, 1963, 8; Douglas Kiker, "President to Bobby—Stay On," *NYHT*, December 1, 1963, 15; Ted Lewis, "Capitol Stuff," *NYDN*, December 4, 1963, 4.

32. Joe McCarthy, *The Remarkable Kennedys* (New York: Popular Library, 1960), 89.

33. RK, "Tribute to JFK," 40; *RK&HT*, 95.

34. "University College of Buffalo—Commencement," June 5, 1965, RFKSSPR, Box 1: "June 1, 1965–June 10, 1965."

35. "Before Peruvian Students," November 10, 1965, RFKSSPR, Box 1: "November 1, 1965–November 10, 1965."

36. RK, "Tribute to JFK," 42.

1. THE FUTURE QUESTION (PGS. 11 TO 27)

1. William Manchester, *TDOAP: November 20–November 25, 1963* (New York: Harper & Row, 1967), 146, 196–97, 256–57.

2. *RK&HT*, 608.

3. Manchester, *Death of a President*, 196–97, 256–59.

4. Robert A. Caro, *The Years of Lyndon Johnson: The Passage of Power* (New York: Alfred A. Knopf, 2012), 327–28.

5. Manchester, *Death of a President*, 196–97, 256–59.

6. Edwin Guthman, *We Band of Brothers* (New York: Harper & Row, 1971), 244.

7. Monroe W. Kamin, "Hopeful Air Pervades Capital as Officials Buckle Down to Jobs," *WSJ*, November 27, 1963, 1.

8. Jack Rosenthal, author interview, January 24, 2013.

9. Jeff Shesol, *MC* (New York: W. W. Norton, 1997), 122–23; Manchester, *TDOAP*, 639; LBJ Daily Diary, November 27, 1963, LBJL.

10. *RK&HT*, 628.

11. Anthony Lewis, "From Johnson, the Homely Touch," *NYT*, November 28, 1963.

12. John L. Seigenthaler, RFKOH, June 5, 1970, 3–4, 7.

13. Walter Sheridan, RFKOH, May 1, 1970, 2–4.

14. Kennedy, *Times to Remember*, 458; Homer Bigart, "Kennedys Gathering for Sad Thanksgiving Reunion at Hyannis Port," *NYT*, November 28, 1963; *RK&HT*, 613.

15. AP, "Robert Kennedy Back at Office," *WP*, December 5, 1963.

16. Nasaw, *Patriarch*, 759.

17. Shesol, *MC*, 124.

18. LBJ in conversation with Clark Clifford, December 4, 1963, TMC.

19. AP, "Assassination Sparks Killing, Threat, Tragedy," *WP*, November 26, 1963; UPI, "Hoffa Tells Union Parley Robert Kennedy 'Is Out,'" *NYT*, December 2, 1963.

20. AMS, *Journals: 1952–2000*, ed. Andrew Schlesinger and Stephen Schlesinger (New York: Penguin, 2007), 212; Tim Weiner, *Enemies: A History of the FBI* (New York: Random House, 2012), 236, 240–41; Manchester, *Death of a President*, 257; *RK&HT*, 629; Guthman and Shulman, *Robert Kennedy*, 128.

21. Dean Markham to RK, November 28, 1963, RFKAG, Box 90: "1963, Marin-Murphy"; Angie Novello to RK, December 12, 1963, RFKAG, Box 94: "Christmas 1964, Cuff Links"; Rosenthal, author interview.

22. James Reston, "Kennedy Babies Reburied with Father in Arlington," *NYT*, December 5, 1963; *RK&HT*, 133; Winzola McLendon, "Sen. Kennedy on Mediterranean Trip Unaware His Wife Has Lost Baby," *WP*, August 25, 1956.

23. Manchester, *Death of a President*, 391–92, 619; AP, "Mrs. Kennedy Puts Flowers on Grave in Nighttime Visit," *NYT*, November 26, 1963.

24. Peter Lisagor, "Portrait of a Man Emerging from Shadows," *NYT*, July 19, 1964; Marguerite Higgins, "Q. What Now for Bobby?," *ND*, December 4, 1963; Helen Fuller, *Year of Trial: Kennedy's Crucial Decisions* (New York: Harcourt, Brace & World, 1962), 44.

25. Ruth Hagy Brod, "'More Than New Political Career,'" *Toledo Blade*, November 5, 1964.

26. Joseph Wershba, "Bobby Kennedy Today," *NYP*, March 27, 1964, 25.

27. Warren Weaver Jr., "Parties' Outlook for '64 Confused," *NYT*, November 23, 1963.

28. AMS, *Journals*, 211–12.

29. Dorothy Schiff to Dorothy Schiff, "Meeting with President Kennedy, Saturday, May 25, 1963, 10:30 a.m., White House," May 27, 1963, Dorothy Schiff Papers, NYPL, Box 256.

30. AMS, *Journals*, 212.

31. Manchester, *Death of a President*, 359; AMS, November 28, 1963, December 9, 1963, ASNYPL, Series II: Journals, Box 313: "5," 1214, 1223.

32. James A. Wechsler, "Plane Drama," *NYP*, December 10, 1963, 30.

33. *RK&HT*, 148; Edwin A. Lahey, "Bobby Kennedy: What's Next," *NYP*, December 13, 1963, 1, 5; Nasaw, *Patriarch*, 776–77, 781.

34. Lahey, "Bobby Kennedy," 1, 5; Rowland Evans Jr., RFKOH, July 30, 1970, 15.

35. Murray Kempton, "Robert F. Kennedy: Pure Irish," *TNR*, February 15, 1964, 9.

36. Hugh Sidey, "Journey out of Grief: R.F.K.'s Mission to Asia," *Life*, January 31, 1964, 32–33.

37. LBJ in conversation with George Smathers, August 1, 1964, TMC; AMS, December 13, 1963, ASNYPL, Series II: Journals, Box 313: "5," 1234; AMS, *Journals*, 213.

38. *RK&HT*, 630–31; Richard N. Goodwin, "The Structure Itself Must Change," *Rolling Stone*, June 6, 1974, 30–31; AMS, *Journals*, 214–15. This is drawn from Schlesinger's and Goodwin's memories, taking guidance from Schlesinger's composite of the conversation in *RK&HT*, while consulting Goodwin's original article and Schlesinger's fuller account in his unpublished journal at the New York Public Library.

39. Samuel Lubell, "Robert Kennedy Stirs Strong Voter Reaction," *LAT*, December 13, 1963.

40. AMS to RK, December 15, 1963, ASNYPL, Series II: Journals, Box 313: "5."

41. AP, "Bobby Keeps Date with 700 Children," *BG*, December 21, 1963; Gerald Grant, "Justice Dept. Is Santa to School Children," *WP*, December 21, 1963; Ralph Blumenfeld, "Robert Kennedy Keeps a Date for Christmas," *NYP*, December 22, 1963, 5; *WBOB*, 247; "Good to See Our Man Smile Again," *CDD*, December 23, 1963; Maas, "What Will R.F.K. Do Next?," 19.

42. AP, "Mrs. Kennedy Draws Crowd in Palm Beach Store Tour," *NYT*, December 23, 1963; Philip Benjamin, "Idlewild Is Rededicated as John F. Kennedy Airport," December 25, 1963; UPI, "Robert Kennedys at Ski Resort," *HC*, December 25, 1963; Maas, "What Will R.F.K. Do Next?," 18; UPI, "Bob Kennedy's Team Beats Ted's on Skis," *CT*, January 3, 1964; Sidey, "Journey out of Grief," 32–33.

43. AP, "Mobs Protesting Malaysia Raid Embassies in Jakarta," *NYT*, September 17, 1963; Reuters, "10 Indonesians Killed in Sabah Encounter," *WP*, January 8, 1964; *Foreign Relations of the United States, 1964–1968*, vol. 26, *Indonesia; Malaysia-Singapore; Philippines* (Washington, DC: Government Printing Office, 2001), Document 8.

44. Sidey, "Journey out of Grief," 32–33; *FRUS, 1964–1968*, vol. 26, Documents 8, 13; *RK&HT*, 569; Roger Hilsman, *To Move a Nation: The Politics of Foreign Policy in the Administration of John F. Kennedy* (New York: Delta, 1967), 408.

45. "Bobby's Back," *NW*, January 20, 1964, 14; Anthony Lewis, "Robert Kennedy Defeats Despair," *NYT*,

January 9, 1964; UPI, "Attorney General Kennedy to Remain in Job Till After Election, He Says," *WP*, January 10, 1964; AP, "Kennedy Gave World Confidence, Robert Says," *HC*, January 10, 1964.

46. Warren Unna, "LBJ May Use Robert Kennedy as Foreign 'Trouble-Shooter,'" *WP*, January 13, 1964; Warren Unna, author interview, June 11, 2013; *WBOB*, 247; McGeorge Bundy, RFKOH, January/December 1972, 10; UPI, "Robert F. Kennedy Talks with Johnson," *NYT*, January 15, 1964; *FRUS, 1964–1968*, vol. 26, Document 16.

47. "Filipino Crowd Cheers Him," *NYT*, January 20, 1964; *WBOB*, 251; UPI, "Kennedy Asks Sukarno Halt Malaysia Row," *CT*, January 18, 1964.

48. *RK&HT*, 634; UPI Telephoto, January 17, 1964.

49. Maas, "What Will R.F.K. Do Next?," 19; Seth S. King, "Direct Diplomacy," *NYT*, January 25, 1964; "Kennedy's Accord Limited," *NYT*, January 24, 1964; "On Bobby Kennedy's Assignment," *NYP*, January 16, 1964, 28; J. D. Legge, *Sukarno: A Political Biography* (New York: Praeger, 1972), 369–70; "The Kennedy Touch," *NW*, February 3, 1964, 36, 38.

50. King, "Direct Diplomacy"; Maas, "What Will R.F.K. Do Next?," 19; UPI, "Kennedy Asks Sukarno Halt"; *RK&HT*, 564–65, 634.

51. *WBOB*, 249; UPI, "Kennedy Asks Sukarno Halt"; "Memories at Kuala Lumpur," *NW*, February 3, 1964, 38; UPI, "Bobby Kennedy Flies to Visit

Korea GIs," *HC*, January 19, 1964; UPI, "Kennedy at Korea Line Looks Across to North," *NYT*, January 19, 1964; EGP, Box 4: "Trip: Korea Jan 1964"; "Filipino Crowd Cheers Him."

52. Maas, "What Will R.F.K. Do Next?," 19.

53. Kempton, "Robert F. Kennedy."

54. Telegram from the Department of State to the attorney general, January 20, 1964, RFKAG, Box 274: "January 64: Far East Trip: Telegrams, Department of State"; Maas, "What Will R.F.K. Do Next?," 19–20; Lawrence Fellows, "Britain Bids U.S. Consider Sending Troops to Cyprus," *NYT*, January 27, 1964; "Graveside Visit," *NYT*, January 27, 1964; Sydney Gruson, "Stand Reported Easing," *NYT*, January 28, 1964; Robert Ajemian, "A Man's Week to Reckon," *Life*, July 3, 1964, 28; *WBOB*, 251; "Robert F. Kennedy Ends Malaysia Trip," *NYT*, January 28, 1964.

55. *WBOB*, 251, 253.

56. Kempton, "Robert F. Kennedy."

57. Maas, "What Will R.F.K. Do Next?," 29.

58. Seigenthaler, RFKOH, June 5, 1970, 13–14; Wershba, "Bobby Kennedy Today," *NYP*, March 23, 1964, 25; Maas, "What Will R.F.K. Do Next?," 17; "Memories at Kuala Lumpur," 38; Lisagor, "Portrait of a Man"; Don Smith, "A Family Bears Up in Time of Sorrow," *ND*, May 20, 1964; Kempton, "Robert F. Kennedy," 9.

59. Maas, "What Will R.F.K. Do Next?," 17, 20.

60. Wershba, "Bobby Kennedy Today," 25.

2. A JOB FOR BOBBY (PGS. 28 TO 48)

1. John Douglas to RK, January 6, 1964, RFKAG, Box 91: "1964, Capell-Dutton."

2. John W. Douglas, RFKOH, June 11, 1970, 45–46; "January 8, 1964," RFKAG, Box 146: "1964 Book 1."

3. Paul Corbin, JFKOH, November 27, 1967, 64–65.

4. AMS, *Journals*, 217; "Buffalo Democrats Want Robert Kennedy on Ticket," *NYT*, January 27, 1964; Clayton Knowles, "Democrats Score Stand by Buffalo," *NYT*, January 28, 1964.

5. Peter Crotty to RK, February 13, 1964, ASNYPL, Series IV: Research files, Box 501: "Vice Presidential Nomination 1964."

6. Stan Hinden, "Boom for Bobby Is Dud at Dem Dinner," *ND*, January 29, 1964; Joseph Alsop, "Matter of Fact," *WP*, January 29, 1964; Edward O'Neill, "City Hall," *NYDN*, February 3, 1964, 4.

7. Barbara J. Coleman, RFKOH, December 8, 1969, 4, 8.

8. Director, FBI, to the attorney general, January 31, 1961, FBI, Paul Corbin Bureau File, 161-HQ-166; Miles McMillin, "Curious Lack of Publicity About Paul Corbin," January 2, 1961, FBI, Paul Corbin Bureau File, 100-HQ-328876; Doris Fleeson, "New Hampshire Aftermath," *Sarasota Journal*, March 16, 1964; A. H. Belmont to D. M. Ladd, June 2, 1951, FBI, Paul Corbin Bureau File, 100-HQ-328876.

9. SAC Milwaukee to director, April 9, 1959, FBI, Paul Corbin Bureau File, 100-HQ-328876; Corbin, JFKOH, November 18, 1965, 15.

10. Corbin, JFKOH, November 27, 1967, 25, 29, 45–46; Kenneth P. O'Donnell and David F. Powers with Joe McCarthy, *Johnny We Hardly Knew Ye* (Boston: Little, Brown, 1970), 178; *RK&HT*, 94; McMillin, "Curious Lack of Publicity."

11. Corbin, JFKOH, November 27, 1967, 42–43, 46, 54, 74–75; Mr. Parsons to A. Rosen, January 11, 1961, FBI, Paul Corbin Bureau File, 161-HQ-166;

Belmont, "Re: Paul Corbin," February 1, 1962, FBI, Paul Corbin Bureau File, 161-HQ-166.

12. James W. Hilty, *Robert Kennedy: Brother Protector* (Philadelphia: Temple University Press, 1997), 477; Barbara Coleman, RFKOH, December 8, 1969, 4.

13. ASNYPL, Series IV: Research files, Box 494: "Corbin, Paul."

14. Seigenthaler, RFKOH, June 5, 1970, 5–6; Guthman and Shulman, *Robert Kennedy*, 406–7; Corbin, JFKOH, November 27, 1967, 28, 38, 65; Sheridan, RFKOH, May 1, 1970, 46–49; Seymour Hersh, *The Dark Side of Camelot* (Boston: Little, Brown, 1997), 443–45; LBJ in conversation with Cliff Carter, February 11, 1964, TMC.

15. Bill Dunfey to Governor King, January 28, 1964, WDP, Box 15; Bernard L. Boutin to William L. Dunfey, December 9, 1963, and Bill Dunfey to Bernie Boutin, January 3, 1964, WDP, Box 11; "Democrats Foil Chiefs, Write RFK," *CDM*, January 31, 1964, 1; "Governor Comments on Write-in for Kennedy," *CDM*, February 3, 1964, 1; Charles Bartlett, "Is Lid Off on RFK?," *BG*, February 2, 1964.

16. John F. English, RFKOH, November 25, 1969, 60.

17. Rowland Evans and Robert Novak, "The Write-in Dangers," *WP*, March 8, 1964; Robert Shaine and Josh Shaine, author interview, April 2, 2013; Corbin, JFKOH, November 18, 1965, 2–4; Corbin, JFKOH, November 27, 1967, 65; "Paul Corbin," January 17, 1961, FBI, Paul Corbin Bureau File, 161-HQ-166; Nasaw, *Patriarch*, 733; Sheridan, RFKOH, May 1, 1970, 51.

18. "Democrats: Bobby for Veep?," *Time*, March 20, 1964; *RK&HT*, 651; UPI, "'You Don't Decide Until You're Asked,'" *BG*, February 7, 1964.

19. Thomas Collins, "Johnson Herd Blends Two Breeds," *ND*, August 22, 1964; Cabell Phillips, "'Kennedy Men' Aid Johnson Campaign," *NYT*, August 19, 1964; LBJ in conversation with Cliff Carter, February 10, 1964, TMC.

20. LBJ in conversation with RK, February 10, 1964, TMC; LBJ Daily Diary, February 11, 1964, LBJL; LBJ in conversation with Carter, February 10, 1964.

21. Guthman and Shulman, *Robert Kennedy*, 406–7.

22. LBJ in conversation with John Bailey, February 11, 1964, TMC.

23. LBJ in conversation with Cliff Carter, February 11, 1964, TMC; Clifton C. Carter, LBJOH, October 30, 1968, 6.

24. Guthman and Shulman, *Robert Kennedy*, 407.

25. February 11, 1964, RFKAG, Box 258: "Telephone Messages January 1964–May 1964."

26. February 12, 1964, RFKAG, Box 258: "Telephone Messages January 1964–May 1964"; "Tel. Msgs. Wednesday, February 19, 1964," RFKAG, Box 258: "Telephone Messages, January 1964–May 1964"; William L. Dunfey, RFKOH, December 15, 1971, 26.

27. RFKAG, Box 257: "February 11, 1964–March 13, 1964"; RFKAG, Box 146: "Desk Diary: 1964 Book 1"; RFKAG, Box 258: "Telephone Messages, January 1964–May 1964"; Sheridan, May 1, 1970, 46; "The Choice of Humphrey, Step by Step," *NYT*, August 27, 1964.

28. LBJ in conversation with Carter, February 11, 1964.

29. Guthman and Shulman, *Robert Kennedy*, 406–7.

30. LBJ in conversation with Carter, February 11, 1964.

31. Guthman and Shulman, *Robert Kennedy*, 406; *WBOB*, 254.

32. LBJ in conversation with Carter, February 11, 1964; Jack Valenti, *A Very Human President* (New York: Norton, 1975), 130–31.

33. Office talk before LBJ in conversation with McGeorge Bundy, February 12, 1964, TMC.

34. Patrick J. Sloyan, *The Politics of Deception: JFK's Secret Decisions on Vietnam, Civil Rights, and Cuba* (New York: Thomas Dunne Books, 2015), 157–58; J. Edgar Hoover confidential memorandum, February 5, 1964, FBI, Robert Kennedy Bureau File 77-51387.

35. SAC, Los Angeles to director, December 27, 1963, FBI, Robert Kennedy Bureau File 77-51387; Taylor Branch, *Pillar of Fire: America in the King Years, 1963–65* (New York: Simon & Schuster, 1998), 243–47.

36. *WBOB*, 257.

37. Branch, *Pillar of Fire*, 246–47.

38. Weiner, *Enemies*, 294.

39. "U.A.W. Gives Robert Kennedy Warm Welcome at Convention," *NYT*, February 20, 1964; "Robt. Kennedy Thanks UAW for Support," *CT*, February 20, 1964.

40. Maas, "What Will R.F.K. Do Next?," 19.

41. George Gallup, "Robert for V.P.," *BG*, March 6, 1964.

42. Bernard L. Boutin to William L. Dunfey, December 9, 1963, Bill Dunfey to Bernie Boutin, January 3, 1964, WDP, Box 11; Robert Healy, "N.H. Democrats Want RFK on Slate," *BG*, March 4, 1964; Leon W. Anderson, "The State's My Beat," *CDM*, March 3, 1964, 4.

43. *WBOB*, 256; "The Pattern Is Set," March 5, 1964, *CDM*, 4.

44. Robert Healy, "Kennedy NH Boom Irks LBJ," *BG*, March 7, 1964; *WBOB*, 254–55; "Democrats: Bobby for Veep?"

45. *WBOB*, 254–55.

46. Don Henderson, "Wisconsin Group to Boost Kennedy Envisions Committee in Each State," *WP*, March 12, 1964; Healy, "Kennedy NH Boom Irks LBJ"; "Kennedy," *CDM*, March 6, 1964, 1, 8; Jack Valenti in conversation with Ben Bradlee, March 7, 1964, TMC.

47. LBJ in conversation with John McCormack, March 7, 1964, TMC.

48. Robert Healy, "Now—All Out Push for LBJ," *BG*, March 9, 1964.

49. LBJ in conversation with George Reedy, July 20, 1964, TMC; LBJ in conversation with Edwin Weisl Sr., March 9, 1964, TMC; RFKAG, "March 9, 1964," Box 146: "1964 Book 1"; "President Johnson, as Well as His Wife, Appears to Hold Big Personal Fortune," *WSJ*, March 23, 1964; Louis M. Kohlmeier, "The Johnson Wealth," *WSJ*, March 23, 1964.

50. LBJ in conversation with Weisl, March 9, 1964.

51. Larry Berman, *Planning a Tragedy: The Americanization of the War in Vietnam* (New York: W. W. Norton, 1982), 4.

52. LBJ in conversation with Bill Moyers, March 9, 1964, 2439, LBJL.

53. Leon W. Anderson, "Democrats Would Link LBJ-RFK," *CDM*, March 5, 1964, 1; "Bob Kennedy Votes Boost Johnson Too," *BG*, March 11, 1964; WDP, Box 15: "Kennedy, Robert F. & Staff—Corresp. & Newsclips 1964–66."

54. Healy, "Now—All Out Push for LBJ."

55. UPI, "New Hampshire Vote Count Is Completed," *WP*, March 15, 1964.

56. Henderson, "Wisconsin Group to Boost Kennedy."

57. February 28, 1964, March 3, 1964, March 11, 1964, March 12, 1964, RFKAG, Box 257: "February 11, 1964–March 13, 1964"; March 2, 1964, March 11, 1964, RFKAG, Box 146: "1964 Book 1."

58. Joseph A. Loftus, "'Draft Kennedy' Unit Files in Wisconsin," *NYT*, March 11, 1964; Edward T. Folliard, "Power Struggle Talk Has Kennedy Puzzled," *WP*, March 12, 1964.

59. March 12, 1964, RFKAG, Box 257: "February 11, 1964–March 13, 1964"; UPI, "Wisconsin Drive for Kennedy 'Won't Stop,'" *LAT*, March 13, 1964; George Armour, "Wisconsin's Kennedy Committee Crumbling," *WP*, March 17, 1964.

60. "Tel. Msgs. Thursday, March 19, 1964," RFKAG, Box 258: "Telephone Messages, January 1964–May 1964."

61. Anthony Lewis, "Kennedy Denies a Johnson Feud," *NYT*, March 13, 1964; AP, "Aides Discount Reports of LBJ-Kennedy Feud," *HC*, March 12, 1964; Robert E. Thompson, "Johnson-Kennedy Coolness Hinted," *LAT*, March 12, 1964.

62. Edward T. Folliard, "R. F. Kennedy Wants Write-in Bid Halted," *WP*, March 13, 1964; Robert Young, "Baker Is Not My Protégé, Johnson Says," *CT*, March 16, 1964.

63. Robert Thompson, "Kennedy Denies Feud with Johnson on Primary Votes," *LAT*, March 13, 1964; "Democrats: Bobby for Veep?"

3. SEEING GHOSTS (PGS. 48 TO 67)

1. February 25, 1964, RFKAG, Box 258: "Telephone Messages, January 1964–May 1964"; *WBOB*, 267.

2. Joseph P. Lash, *A World of Love: Eleanor Roosevelt and Her Friends, 1943–1963* (Garden City, NY:

Doubleday, 1984), 406n; Maxeda von Hesse, "I Teach Famous Men to talk," *McCall's*, February 1965, 98, 179; The von Hesse Studios, RFKAG, Box 92: "Bills Receipted 1964."

3. March 16, 1964, RFKAG, Box 146: "1964 Book 1."

4. RK, "To the Friendly Sons of St. Patrick of Lackawanna County," March 17, 1964, DOJ.

5. *WBOB*, 269.

6. Joseph X. Flannery, "Bobby Mobbed on Arrival," *ST*, March 18, 1964, 3–5.

7. *WBOB*, 267; "Choice for VP," *ST*, March 18, 1964, 1; "RFK on VP Show Here: I Think It's Out of Place," *ST*, March 18, 1964, 1, 42; "Magical Power Still Exists," *ST*, March 18, 1964, 3–5; William G. Loftus, "RFK Urges Irish to Help Others Be Free," *ST*, March 18, 1964, 3, 42; Rowland Evans and Robert Novak, "Inside Report," *WP*, March 25, 1964.

8. "Robt. Kennedy Urges Irish to Help Negroes," *CT*, March 18, 1964.

9. "RFK on VP Show," 1, 42; *RK&HT*, 617; William G. Loftus, "RFK Urges Irish to Help Others," March 18, 1964, 3, 42.

10. Doris Fleeson, "The Silent Kingmaker," *BG*, April 15, 1964; George Gallup, "Robert Kennedy Shows Big Gain for 2d Spot," *WP*, April 12, 1964; Earl Mazo, "Robert Kennedy Favored in Polls," *NYT*, April 30, 1964; *WBOB*, 269.

11. November 16, 1966, ASNYPL, Series II: Journals, Box 313: "14," 1421–22; "Brown Names Ex-Aide Dutton Regent of UC," *LAT*, March 22, 1962; January 10, 1961, "Frederick Gary Dutton," FBI, Frederick Dutton Bureau File, 1321474-0; "The 'New' Pat Brown," *WSJ*, June 2, 1959; "Brown Aide Quits Post for Kennedy," *LAT*, August 11, 1960; Frederick A. Dutton, JFKOH, May 3, 1965, 27–30, 37–38;

"Dutton, Kennedy Aide, Tells of New Problems," *LAT*, February 9, 1961.

12. W. V. Cleveland to Courtney Evans, "[Subject Redacted]," March 2, 1961, FBI, Frederick Dutton Bureau File, 1321474-0; Courtney Evans to Mr. Parsons, "[Subject Redacted]," March 3, 1961, FBI, Frederick Dutton Bureau File, 1321474-0; Nancy Dutton, author interview, June 24, 2016.

13. Don Shannon, "Rusk Looms as Victor in Kennedy's Shakeup," *LAT*, November 27, 1961; Nancy Dutton, author interviews; FBI, Frederick Dutton Bureau File, 1321474-0.

14. Fred Dutton, "How Vice Presidential Nominees Are Chosen: The Historical Record," RFKAG, Box 90: "1963, Danzig-Dutton."

15. Carroll Kilpatrick, "JFK Intimates Tape Their Memories," *WP*, April 19, 1964.

16. Fred Dutton to RK, April 3, 1964, RFKAG, Box 91: "1964, Capell-Dutton."

17. April 21, 1964, RFKAG, Box 146: "1964 Book 1"; Fred Dutton to RK, April 22, 1964, RFKAG, Box 91: "1964, Capell-Dutton."

18. Ajemian, "Man's Week to Reckon," 26; Private papers of Fred Dutton; SAC, Charlotte, to Director Hoover, May 26, 1964, FBI, Robert Kennedy Bureau File, 77-51387; Mr. Belmont to Mr. Evans, "Travel of the Attorney General," May 25, 1964, FBI, Robert Kennedy Bureau File, 77-51387; Fred Dutton, "Memorandum to the Attorney General, Re: July 6–August 15," July 1, 1964, EGP, Box 13: "JFK Death 1964 to NY camp"; July 25, 1964, RFKAG, Box 146: "Desk Diary, 1964 Book 1."

19. Wershba, "Bobby Kennedy Today," 25; Guthman and Shulman, *Robert Kennedy*, 66; Wesley Barthelmes,

RFKOH, May 20, 1969, 36; Sheridan, RFKOH, June 12, 1970, 126–27.

20. *WBOB*, 219–21; *RK&HT*, 332–33; Branch, *Pillar of Fire*, 89.

21. Layhmond Robinson, "Robert Kennedy Fails to Sway Negroes at Secret Talks Here," *NYT*, May 26, 1963.

22. Wershba, "Bobby Kennedy Today," 25; Al Kuettner, "Kennedy's Backing Cheered," *ADW*, May 27, 1964.

23. Anthony Lewis, "The Strategy of Closure," *NYT*, June 11, 1964; Robert C. Albright, "GOP Leader Gives Southern Senators One Week's Notice," *WP*, April 29, 1964; "Seek Accord on 40 Changes in Rights Bill," *CT*, May 6, 1964; Joseph Hearst, "Senate Rights Fight Reverts to Talkathon," *CT*, May 8, 1964; Andrew J. Glass, "Key Deal on Rights," *BG*, May 13, 1964; E. W. Kenworthy, "Rights Plan Goes to Senate Today," *NYT*, May 26, 1964; Joseph Hearst, "Revised Civil Rights Bill Introduced in Senate," *CT*, May 27, 1964; Robert C. Albright, "Draft of Rights Bill Approved, 76 to 18," *WP*, June 18, 1964.

24. Robert J. Donovan, "Racial Conflict Building to a Climax," *LAT*, April 19, 1964; Anthony Lewis, "Civil Rights Campaigns: The Moderates vs. the Extremists," *NYT*, April 19, 1964; Percy Shain, "Kennedy Outlines Integration," *BG*, May 14, 1964.

25. AP, "RFK Says Poverty War Started with JFK," *BG*, April 8, 1964.

26. Marjorie Hunter, "Kennedy Defends Antipoverty Bill," *NYT*, April 8, 1964.

27. "Kennedy in West Virginia," *NYT*, April 30, 1964; Arthur Edson, "The Kennedys, 6 Months Later," *HC*, May 17, 1964; *WBOB*, 271; "Notes on Attorney General's Trip to West Virginia," April 29, 1964, EGP, Box 13: "JFK Death 1964 to NY camp."

28. Edson, "Kennedys, 6 Months."

29. AP, "Bob Kennedy Receives Pupils' Library Gift," *HC*, May 12, 1964; Jean M. White, "Farmville Children Thank RFK," *WP*, May 12, 1964; Charlie, "RFK Visits Hill," *HST*, May 15, 1964, 2.

30. "Robert F. Kennedy Challenges H-S Students to Debate Issue," *HST*, May 15, 1964, 1.

31. White, "Farmville Children Thank RFK"; "Robert F. Kennedy Challenges H-S Students," 1; John Harvey, "Crises in Viet Nam America Must Decide," *HST*, May 15, 1964, 2.

32. Charlie, "RFK Visits Hill," 2; "Kennedy Draws Virginian Cheers," *NYT*, May 12, 1964.

33. John Herbers, "Georgia Campus Cheers Kennedy," *NYT*, May 27, 1964; Eugene Patterson, "The Young Are Not Buying," *AC*, May 28, 1964, 4; Reg Murphy, "Kennedy Gets Fantastic Reception," *AC*, May 27, 1964, 20.

34. Reg Murphy, "Kennedy Defends Help for Negroes," *AC*, May 27, 1964, 1, 24; Herbers, "Georgia Campus Cheers Kennedy"; AP, "Robert Kennedy Cheered in Georgia Rights Talk," *HC*, May 27, 1964.

35. Kuettner, "Kennedy's Backing Cheered."

36. Murphy, "Kennedy Gets Fantastic Reception," 20; Patterson, "Young Are Not Buying," 4; "Robert Kennedy Wins Admiration of W.G.C. Students During Visit," *West Georgian*, May 29, 1964, 1.

37. Angelo Baglivo, "Wallace Vote Seen No Rights Brake," *NEN*, May 21, 1964, 1, 15; Don Irwin, "Bob Kennedy's Plans? Even He Isn't Sure," *LAT*, May 1, 1964.

38. Rowland Evans and Robert Novak, "Inside Report," *WP*, May 15, 1964.

39. Peter Maas, " 'I'd Study N.Y. Offer,' Says RFK," *BG*, May 17, 1964; James Reston, "Washington: 'Tired of

Chasing People'—Robert Kennedy," *NYT*, May 6, 1964.

40. Guthman and Shulman, *Robert Kennedy*, 413–18.

41. AP, "Red Sox Down White Sox, 4–1, in Game Dedicated to Kennedy," *NYT*, April 18, 1964.

42. "RFK Governor in '66, Ted Hints," *BG*, April 27, 1964; UPI, "Teddy Touts Bobby for V.P. Choice," *CT*, April 27, 1964.

43. "Democratic Delegates Elected," *BG*, April 29, 1964; UPI, "Robert Kennedy Bypasses Primary," *BG*, April 29, 1964; C. R. Owens, "Ted, Ed Out-Poll D.C. Kin," *BG*, May 3, 1964; "Ted Undisputed State Party Leader," *BG*, April 30, 1964.

44. Shesol, *MC*, 179–80; " 'What's Bobby Going to Do?'—an Informal Talk with RFK," *NW*, July 6, 1964, 24–25.

45. Robert Healy, "What's Ahead for Robert Kennedy: VP or Bay State?," *BG*, June 28, 1964; Murray Kempton, "Stephen E. Smith," *TNR*, March 9, 1963, 17; English, RFKOH, November 3, 1969, 22; Dick Zander, "Profile: John F. English," *ND*, May 19, 1964; English, RFKOH, November 3, 1969, 22–23, 28.

46. Dorothy McCardle, "Race for Senate in New York Is Studied for R. F. Kennedy," *WP*, May 5, 1964; "Keating vs. Kennedy?," *NYT*, May 17, 1964.

47. Stan Hinden, "Dem Chiefs Boost RFK for Senate," *ND*, May 15, 1964; "Another Senator Kennedy?," *NYT*, May 16, 1964; "Bobby? No Thanks," *ND*, May 16, 1964.

48. Warren Weaver Jr., "Decision Due Soon on Kennedy Race," *NYT*, May 23, 1964; Homer Bigart, "Kennedy Makes 4 Speeches in Metropolitan Area," *NYT*, May 21, 1964.

49. Baglivo, "Wallace Vote Seen No Rights Brake," 1, 15.

50. AP, "Robt. Kennedy Doubts He'll Run for Senate," *BG*, May 20, 1964.

51. Clayton Knowles, "Kennedy Says Resident of State Would Be Preferable for Senate," *NYT*, May 20, 1964.

52. Gertrude Ball to RK, June 10, 1964, RFKAG, Box 92: "Family 1964."

53. Ronald Sullivan, "Bingham Attacked by '62 Buckley Foe," *NYT*, May 21, 1964; Marquis Childs, "David and Goliath Clash in the Bronx," *WP*, May 25, 1964.

54. Guy Savino, "Kennedy Boosts Buckley," *NEN*, May 21, 1964, 15.

55. "The 'Outstanding' Mr. Buckley," *NYT*, May 23, 1964; Kevin Kelly, "Vidal Levels His Wit on RFK, Arthur Miller," *BG*, June 16, 1964; Henry J. Taylor, "New York's Mayor Wagner Sees Robert Kennedy Zeroing In on Him," *LAT*, May 22, 1964; Douglas Dales, "Keating Neutral on an Opponent," *NYT*, May 24, 1964; Clayton Knowles, "Johnson to Speak at Rally Tonight," *NYT*, May 28, 1964.

56. McCarthy, *Johnny We Hardly Knew Ye*, 25; David Nasaw, author interview.

57. Wershba, "Bobby Kennedy Today," 25.

58. Lisagor, "Portrait of a Man."

59. Ajemian, "Man's Week to Reckon," 29.

60. Lisagor, "Portrait of a Man"; Manchester, *Death of a President*, 642; photo caption, *Life*, July 3, 1964, 29.

61. Lisagor, "Portrait of a Man"; photo caption, *Life*, 29; Wershba, "Bobby Kennedy Today," 25; D. C. Morrell to Mr. DeLoach, February 24, 1964, FBI, Robert Kennedy Bureau File, 77-51387.

62. Frances Lewine, "Mrs. Kennedy Her Smiling Self Again," *CT*, May 10, 1964; Edith Hamilton, *The Greek Way* (New York: W. W. Norton, 1964), 28, 52; *RK&HT*, 618.

63. Lisagor, "Portrait of a Man."

64. Lester David, *Ethel: The Story of Mrs. Robert F. Kennedy* (New York: World Publishing, 1971), 168.

65. Victor Riesel, "Labor, Kennedy and New York," *LAT*, May 27, 1964; Nasaw, *Patriarch*, 268–69.

66. Knowles, "Johnson to Speak at Rally"; AP, "RFK Still Unsure on Senate Post," *HC*, June 3, 1964.

67. AP, "'Mind Not Made Up on V.P. Bid'—RFK," *BG*, June 8, 1964.

68. John F. Kraft to Stephen Smith, June 7, 1964, RFKAG, Box 91: "1964, Jackson-Lisagor"; *WBOB*, 285.

69. Stephen A. Rogers, "Kennedy Looks Like Man on Way to Senate," *SPS*, June 3, 1964, 5; Miriam Ottenberg, "President Rules Out Post for Kennedy in Viet Nam," *Washington Evening Star*, June 18, 1964, A-1; Murray Kempton, "Will Bobby Kennedy Run in New York?," *TNR*, June 6, 1964, 7–8.

70. Ajemian, "Man's Week to Reckon," 25; Clayton Knowles, "Wagner Confers with Liberals as Kennedy Ponders Decision," *NYT*, June 12, 1964.

71. Jack Anderson, "Bobby Tells Johnson He'll Bid for Senate," *SPS*, June 10, 1964, 1; Victor Riesel, "Bobby Ready to Run for Senate," *SPS*, June 10, 1964, 17; "A Democratic Opportunity," *NYT*, June 12, 1964.

4. DISTRACTIONS (PGS. 68 TO 86)

1. "'What's Bobby Going to Do?,'" 25.

2. LBJ Daily Diary, June 10, 1964, LBJL.

3. "'What's Bobby Going to Do?,'" 25–26; Lisagor, "Portrait of a Man"; Ajemian, "Man's Week to Reckon," 26.

4. Wershba, "Bobby Kennedy Today," 25.

5. Robert Healy, "Why Lodge Took the Job," *BG*, March 18, 1964.

6. Bundy, RFKOH, January–December 1972, 3–4; Kempton, "Robert F. Kennedy," 9; Berman, *Planning a Tragedy*, 29; Baglivo, "Wallace Vote Seen No Rights Brake," 1, 15.

7. LBJ in conversation with RK, May 28, 1964, TMC.

8. Clark Clifford with Richard Holbrooke, *Counsel to the President: A Memoir* (New York: Random House, 1991), 395; Lisagor, "Portrait of a Man"; *RK&HT*, 761.

9. Shesol, *MC*, 199.

10. *FRUS, 1964–1968*, vol. 1, *Vietnam, 1964*, ed. Edward C. Keefer and Charles S. Sampson (Washington, DC: Government Printing Office, 1992), Document 204.

11. June 16, 1964, ASNYPL, Series II: Journals, Box 313: "7," 1286–87; Seigenthaler, RFKOH, June 5, 1970, 31; Shesol, *MC*, 199.

12. Clifford with Holbrooke, *Counsel to the President*, 395.

13. LBJ in conversation with RK, June 11, 1964, TMC.

14. James Reston, "Johnson Declines an Offer of Kennedy Aid in Saigon," *NYT*, July 18, 1964.

15. Valenti, *Very Human President*, 141.

16. Jack Rosenthal to EOG, July 31, 1964, JRP, Box 3: "Memoranda, 1964: July–December"; James Reston, "Washington: The Latest Capital Rumor: Kennedy to Saigon," *NYT*, June 17, 1964; Reston, "Johnson Declines an Offer."

17. ASNYPL, Box 313, 1289.

18. LBJ in conversation with Richard Russell, June 11, 1964, TMC; LBJ in conversation with RK, June 12, 1964, TMC; LBJ in conversation with Robert McNamara, June 12, 1964, TMC.

19. *RK&HT*, 748–49.

20. "Robert F. Kennedy on Luncheon with Ambassador Anatoly Dobrynin," July 7, 1964, RFKAG, Box 97: "Kennedy, Robert F.; 1961–1964."

21. Ajemian, "Man's Week to Reckon," 27; AP, "Ted Kennedy Hurt in Plane Crash," *ND*, June 20, 1964; John H. Fenton, "Senator Kennedy Is Recovering; Party Back Him for Full Term," *NYT*, June 21, 1964.

22. "Jacqueline, Children at Cape," *BG*, June 20, 1964; Jimmy Breslin, "A November Chill Fills a Visit to Ted," *TDN*, June 21, 1964, 1; AP, "Ted Kennedy Hurt"; Nick Thimmesch and William Johnson, *RKA40* (New York: W. W. Norton, 1965), 167; "The Nurses' Story—So Sudden . . . So Grim . . . A Never-Ending Night," *BG*, June 23, 1964.

23. Ajemian, "Man's Week to Reckon," 25–26; Lewis, "Robert Kennedy Defeats Despair"; Bruce Galphin, "Ted Kennedy: Glimpses of Past, Future," *AC*, May 6, 1964; Lisagor, "Portrait of a Man."

24. "Dead Pilot's Son Student at Air Force Academy," *BG*, June 21, 1964; Herbert Black, "Bobby Reassures LBJ," *BG*, June 21, 1964; LBJ in conversation with RK, June 20, 1964, TMC.

25. Sheridan, RFKOH, May 1, 1970, 12.

26. Breslin, "November Chill Fills a Visit," 1.

27. UPI, "Ted Kennedy Picked Again for Senate," *CT*, June 21, 1964; *WBOB*, 286; Douglas S. Crocket, "Ted Due for Several Months in Hospital," *BG*, June 21, 1964,

28. Lisagor, "Portrait of a Man."

29. Anthony Lewis, "Robert Kennedy Rules Out Race for Senate Seat," *NYT*, June 24, 1964.

30. *WBOB*, 286.

31. Lisagor, "Portrait of a Man"; James L. Jones, "Dulles to Head Rights Trio Hunt," *BG*, June 24, 1964.

32. Robert E. Baker, "Kennedy Greets NAACP March," *WP*, June 25, 1964; AP, "2,000 Stage NAACP March on

Justice Dept.," *LAT*, June 25, 1964; John H. Fenton, "29 Jurists, Disputing Kennedy, Say U.S. Can Act in Mississippi," *NYT*, July 1, 1964.

33. Larry Rue, "Bob Kennedy Fears Rights Strife Spread," *CT*, June 26, 1964.

34. Baker, "Kennedy Greets NAACP March"; AP, "2,000 Stage NAACP March."

35. LBJ in conversation with Bill Moyers, April 23, 1964, TMC; Marquis Childs, "Why Kennedy Went to Warsaw," *WP*, July 8, 1964; private papers of Fred Dutton.

36. LBJ in conversation with RK, July 18, 1964, TMC; LBJ in conversation with Moyers, April 23, 1964.

37. Private papers of Jack Rosenthal; AMS to RFK, June 18, 1964, ASNYPL, Series IV: Research Files, Box 404: "4"; Nancy Dutton, author interview, March 31, 2014.

38. Susan N. Wilson, "A Guide to Travelling with the Robert F. Kennedys," ASNYPL, Series IV: Research Files, Box 501: "RFK Trips: Poland, Germany, 1964."

39. UPI, "Chant of 'Bobby, Bobby' Greets RFK in Germany," *BG*, June 26, 1964; "West German Press Reaction to Visit of Robert F. Kennedy," private papers of Jack Rosenthal.

40. Arthur J. Olsen, "Kennedy Renews Pledge to Berlin," *NYT*, June 27, 1964; Larry Rue, "Berliners Hail 2d Kennedy," *CT*, June 27, 1964; RK, "West Berlin, Excerpts from Remarks at the Dedication of the John F. Kennedy Platz," June 26, 1964, DOJ; *Look*, August 25, 1964, 25; RK, "Free University of Berlin," June 26, 1964, DOJ.

41. Vincent Buist, "Poles Go Wild over Kennedys," *BG*, June 28, 1964; "Address by Attorney General Robert

F. Kennedy at Heidelberg University, Heidelberg, Germany, June 27, 1964," DOJ; UPI, "GIs Dying for You: Kennedy to Germany," *CT*, June 28, 1964.

42. Buist, "Poles Go Wild over Kennedys"; Calvin Aarons, "Varied Receptions Greet RFK, Tito, K in Poland," *HC*, August 30, 1964; Arthur J. Olsen, "Kennedy Reminds Poles of U.S. Ties," *NYT*, June 28, 1964.

43. *Look*, August 25, 1964, 26, 28, 30; Arthur J. Olsen, "Warsaw Throngs Engulf Kennedys," *NYT*, June 29, 1964; "Kennedys Hailed on Cracow Visit," *NYT*, June 30, 1964; Joseph Y. Smith, "A World Apart—Cheers for Lodge, RFK," *BG*, June 29, 1964; UPI, "Polish Eyes Are Smiling for Kennedy," *ND*, June 29, 1964.

44. Vincent Buist, "Poles Throw Bouquets at Robt. Kennedy," *CT*, June 29, 1964.

45. John Herlin, "Five Kennedys Atop a Car," *BG*, July 8, 1964; John Moors Cabot, JFKOH, January 27, 1971, 22; *Look*, August 25, 1964, 22–23, 28.

46. *Look*, August 25, 1964, 30.

47. UPI, "RFK Describes Oswald as Anti-Social 'Loner,'" *BG*, June 30, 1964; *Look*, August 25, 1964, 30; AP, "Oswald Acted Alone, Says Kennedy," *WP*, June 30, 1964; AP, "'Misfit Killed Brother,' Kennedy Says in Poland," *HC*, June 30, 1964; Ajemian, "Man's Week to Reckon," 29; "Kennedys Hailed on Cracow Visit."

48. UPI, "RFK Describes Oswald"; Arthur J. Olsen, "Kennedy's Visit Jolts Regime in Poland," *NYT*, July 5, 1964.

49. Olsen, "Kennedy's Visit Jolts Regime"; *Look*, August 25, 1964, 26, 28; Arthur J. Olsen, "Kennedy Meets Polish Cardinal," *NYT*, July 1, 1964; AP, "Robert Kennedy Given Big Play in Polish Press," *CT*, July 3, 1964; Reuters, "Polish Officials Join U.S.

Holiday Party," *WP*, July 4, 1964; Arthur J. Olsen, "Kennedy Exhorts the Poles to Further U.S.-Soviet Friendship," *NYT*, July 2, 1964; John Moors Cabot, JFKOH, January 27, 1971, 22.

50. Olsen, "Kennedy's Visit Jolts Regime."

51. Cabot, JFKOH, January 27, 1971, 22.; Buist, "Poles Throw Bouquets"; Olsen, "Kennedy Meets Polish Cardinal"; Olsen, "Kennedy's Visit Jolts Regime."

52. RFK's notes on discussion with deputy foreign minister Jozef Winiewicz at Cabot's, June 29, 1964, ASNYPL, Series IV: Research Files, Box 501: "RFK Trips: Poland, Germany, 1964"; Olsen, "Kennedy's Visit Jolts Regime."

53. RFK's notes on discussion with Deputy Foreign Minister Winiewicz and RFK's notes on his conversation with Foreign Minister Adam Rapacki at Jablonna, Poland, on Sunday, June 28, 1964, ASNYPL, Series IV: Research Files, Box 501: "RFK Trips: Poland, Germany, 1964"; Cabot, JFKOH, January 27, 1971, 23; Ajemian, "Man's Week to Reckon," 28.

54. RFK's notes on discussion with Deputy Foreign Minister Winiewicz.

55. Olsen, "Kennedy Meets Polish Cardinal"; Buist, "Poles Throw Bouquets."

56. Cabot to State, July 1, 1964, ASNYPL, Box 501: "RFK Trips: Poland, Germany, 1964"; *Look*, August 25, 1964, 25, 28.

57. Olsen, "Kennedy Meets Polish Cardinal"; Reuters, "R. Kennedy Meets with Wysznski [*sic*]," *WP*, July 1, 1964; RFK's notes on meeting Cardinal Wyszynski, June 30, 1964, ASNYPL, Series IV: Research Files, Box 501: "RFK Trips: Poland, Germany, 1964."

58. ASNYPL, Series IV: Research Files, Box 501: "RFK Trips: Poland, Germany, 1964."

59. RFK's notes on meeting Cardinal Wyszynski.

60. Cabot to State, July 1, 1964, ASNYPL, Series IV: Research Files, Box 501: "RFK Trips: Poland, Germany, 1964."

61. Olsen, "Kennedy Exhorts the Poles"; AP, "Poles Warm Toward U.S.; Top Officials Are Cool," HC, July 2, 1964.

62. Olsen, "Kennedy's Visit Jolts Regime."

63. LBJ in conversation with RK, July 2, 1964, TMC, 4117.

5. LOYALTY ABOVE ALL (PGS. 87 TO 108)

1. Ajemian, "Man's Week to Reckon," 28.

2. George P. Hunt, "A Reunion of Two Classmates," Life, July 3, 1964, 3.

3. Marguerite Higgins, "On the Spot," ND, July 6, 1964.

4. Drew Pearson, "Making Time in Justice Dept.," LAT, July 6, 1964.

5. June 15, 1964, RFKAG, Box 146: "Desk Diary, 1964 Book 1."

6. "'What's Bobby Going to Do?,'" 24–25.

7. UPI, "R. Kennedy on Vice Presidency: 'I'm Last Man LBJ Would Pick,'" BG, June 30, 1964; Mary McGrory, "Bobby Bent on Political Suicide?," BG, July 6, 1964; Arthur Krock, "The Kennedy Interview," NYT, July 5, 1964; "President's News Parley on Domestic and Foreign Affairs," NYT, July 11, 1964.

8. LBJ in conversation with RK, July 2, 1964.

9. LBJ Daily Diary, July 2, 1964, LBJL; David Kraslow, "Bob Kennedy Gets Rights Bill Pen Souvenirs," LAT, July 3, 1964; Tom Wicker, "Johnson Bestows Pens Used on Bill," NYT, July 3, 1964; "President Johnson's Remarks on the Signing of the Civil Rights Bill, July 2, 1964," LBJL, https://www.youtube.com/watch?v=sQsVVYpY6pI; Harris Wofford, Of Kennedys and Kings: Making Sense of the Sixties (New York: Farrar, Straus and Giroux, 1980), 288; Beverly Gage, "What an Uncensored Letter to M.L.K. Reveals," NYT, November 11, 2014.

10. "Robert F. Kennedy on Luncheon with Ambassador Anatoly Dobrynin."

11. Cabell Phillips, "Thurmond Critical of Views of Floridian, Named to Head Agency Under New Act," NYT, July 8, 1964; Jack Raymond, "Johnson and Kennedy Exchange Words of Praise," NYT, July 9, 1964.

12. LBJ in conversation with RK, July 6, 1964, TMC.

13. "Robert F. Kennedy on Luncheon with Ambassador Anatoly Dobrynin."

14. Mary McGrory, "Democrats Harried by Too Many Stars," BG, July 22, 1964.

15. LBJ in conversation with Cliff Carter, July 23, 1964, TMC.

16. "Choice of Humphrey"; Doris Kearns, Lyndon Johnson and the American Dream (New York: Harper & Row, 1976), 199–200; Louis Harris, "Humphrey Is Favorite of Democrats Since President Eliminated Kennedy," WP, August 3, 1964; Carroll Kilpatrick, "Running-Mate Suspense Had Touch of Old Drama," WP, August 27, 1964.

17. Kearns, Lyndon Johnson, 199–200; "Bob Kennedy Saddened at Exhibit Here," CT, July 23, 1964; "Poignant Pause," ND, July 24, 1964; July 22, 1964, RFKAG, Box 146: "Desk Diary, 1964 Book 1."

18. LBJ in conversation with John Connally, July 23, 1964, TMC.

19. Clifton C. Carter, LBJOH, October 30, 1968, 6; Shesol, *MC*, 204.

20. LBJ in conversation with Connally.

21. LBJ in conversation with RK, July 27, 1964, TMC; *WBOB*, 280.

22. July 27, 1964, RFKAG, Box 257: "Telephone Logs, June 21, 1964–August 19, 1964"; LBJ Daily Diary, July 27, 1964, LBJL; LBJ in conversation with RK, July 27, 1964; July 28, 1964, RFKAG, Box 146: "Desk Diary, 1964 Book 1."

23. Louis Harris, author interviews, April 2014, May 23, 2014; July 28, 1964, RFKAG, Box 146: "Desk Diary, 1964 Book 1."

24. A. H. Raskin, "Alex Rose of Liberal Party, a Power in Politics, Is Dead," *NYT*, December 29, 1976; Richard Reeves, "Kennedy: 2 Years After His Election," *NYT*, November 14, 1966.

25. LBJ in conversation with Alex Rose, August 1, 1964, TMC.

26. LBJ in conversation with RK, July 21, 1964, TMC.

27. "Memo for Joe Dolan," July 27, 1964, JRP, Box 3: "Memoranda, 1964: July–December."

28. "Mrs. Kennedy Buys 5th Ave. Apartment," *NYT*, July 29, 1964; RK to McGeorge Bundy, March 13, 1964, McGeorge Bundy Personal Papers, JFKL, Box 36: "RFK correspondence, December 1965–December 1962."

29. Bundy, RFKOH, January 12, 1972, 11–12.

30. LBJ in conversation with McGeorge Bundy, July 29, 1964, TMC.

31. James Doyle, "O'Donnell Subs for Ted as Delegate—Manager for RFK," *BG*, July 30, 1964; "Mrs. Kennedy Celebrates 35th Birthday," *BG*, July 29, 1964; LBJ in conversation with Clark Clifford, July 29, 1964, TMC.

32. LBJ in conversation with Bundy, July 29, 1964.

33. *RK&HT*, 689.

34. Lyndon B. Johnson, *The Vantage Point: Perspectives of the Presidency, 1963–1969* (New York: Holt, Rinehart & Winston, 1971), 100, 576–77.

35. Theodore H. White, *The Making of the President: 1964* (New York: Atheneum, 1965), 265; *RK&HT*, 661; LBJ Daily Diary, July 29, 1964, LBJL; LBJ in conversation with Bundy, July 29, 1964; LBJ in conversation with Clifford, July 29, 1964.

36. *RK&HT*, 659.

37. EOG, July 29, 1964, EGP, Box 13: "JFK Death, 1964 to NY camp."

38. Shesol, *MC*, 204; Johnson, *Vantage Point*, 100, 576–77; AP, "Offer Being Considered: Johnson Is Said to Have Asked Kennedy to Manage Campaign," *NYT*, August 1, 1964; Rowland Evans and Robert Novak, "Inside Report: The Unprepared Campaign," *WP*, July 30, 1964; LBJ in conversation with Alex Rose, August 1, 1964.

39. *RK&HT*, 659–61; LBJ in conversation with Clifford, July 29, 1964.

40. Jean Stein, *American Journey*, ed. George Plimpton (New York: Harcourt Brace Jovanovich, 1970), 178–79.

41. Guthman and Shulman, *Robert Kennedy*, 417.

42. *RK&HT*, 660; LBJ in conversation with Clifford, July 29, 1964.

43. LBJ in conversation with Clifford, July 29, 1964.

44. Robert Thompson, "Two Vivid Versions," *LAT*, August 16, 1964; Chalmers M. Roberts, "Fadeout of Kennedy in 3-Act VP Drama," *WP*, August 16, 1964.

45. EOG, July 29, 1964, EGP, Box 13: "JFK Death, 1964 to NY camp"; Bundy, RFKOH, January 12, 1972, 11.

46. *WBOB*, 282; Mary McGrory, "RFK Buildup Nipped in Bud," *BG*, July 31, 1964.

47. Robert David Johnson, *All the Way with LBJ: The 1964 Presidential Election* (New York: Cambridge University Press, 2009), 149.

48. LBJ in conversation with Clifford, July 29, 1964; LBJ in conversation with David Lawrence, July 29, 1964, TMC; LBJ in conversation with Richard Daley, July 29, 1964, TMC; LBJ in conversation with Robert Wagner, July 30, 1964, TMC.

49. "Thicker Than Water," *BG*, July 30, 1964.

50. LBJ in conversation with Dean Rusk, July 30, 1964, TMC.

51. July 27, 1964, RFKAG, Box 257: "June 21, 1964–August 19, 1964"; Robert Thompson, "It's Kennedy, Humphrey or McNamara," *LAT*, June 14, 1964; LBJ in conversation with McGeorge Bundy, July 30, 1964, TMC.

52. Robert Healy, "Bobby's Reaction: 'All the Hurt Went in November,'" *BG*, August 2, 1964.

53. LBJ in conversation with Robert McNamara, July 30, 1964, TMC; LBJ in conversation with Dean Rusk, July 30, 1964.

54. Edward T. Folliard, "Johnson Bars Cabinet, Aides as Vice President," *WP*, July 31, 1964; LBJ Daily Diary, July 30, 1964, LBJL; Robert Thompson, "Johnson Shocker," *LAT*, July 31, 1964; "Bobby Is Out" (photo) *HC*, July 31, 1964; AP, "LBJ Rules Kennedy Out as VP," *BG*, July 31, 1964; LBJ Daily Diary, July 30, 1964, LBJL.

55. Johnson, *All the Way*, 150.

56. "LBJ Bars Bobby, Top Aides as VP," *ND*, July 31, 1964; AP, "LBJ Rules Kennedy Out as VP."

57. Johnson, *All the Way*, 151; "Bobby Keeps Them Laughing," *ND*, August 7, 1964; AP, "Kennedy Voices a Wry Regret," *NYT*, August 7, 1964; Paul A. Schuette, "Kennedy Gives Campaign Cram Course," *WP*, August 7, 1964.

58. Merle Miller, *Lyndon: An Oral Biography* (New York: G. P. Putnam's Sons, 1980), 389; Robert A. Caro, *The Years of Lyndon Johnson: Means of Ascent* (New York: Vintage, 1990), 399.

59. LBJ in conversation with Bill Moyers, July 31, 1964, TMC.

60. Robert J. Donovan, "The Last Frontier for the New Frontier?," *BG*, July 31, 1964; Anthony Ramirez, "Robert J. Donovan, 90, the Author of 'PT-109,'" *NYT*, August 10, 2003.

61. "Democrats: The Problems of Being Bobby," *Time*, August 14, 1964.

62. Robert Healy, "It's a One Man Rule in Atlantic City," *BG*, August 21, 1964.

63. Laurence Stern, "Candidate Kennedy Mobbed on Boardwalk," *WP*, August 26, 1964; Robert Healy, "RFK Jumps In, a Bit Hesitant," *BG*, August 26, 1964.

64. AP, "Crashes Window to See Mrs. JFK," *BG*, August 28, 1964; Maxine Cheshire, "They'll Shake Hands with 5,000 Friends," *WP*, August 26, 1964; Maureen O'Neill, "Jackie Kennedy: So Well Remembered," *ND*, August 28, 1964; Jimmy Breslin, "Many Memories but Few Words," *BG*, August 28, 1964; UPI, "Mrs. Kennedy Steps Back into Spotlight at 5-Hour Reception," *LAT*, August 28, 1964.

65. UPI, "Mrs. Kennedy Steps Back into Spotlight"; Laurence Stern, "Ebullient Humphrey Is Campaigning Hard," *WP*, August 28, 1964; AP, "Crashes Window to See Mrs. JFK"; R. W. Apple Jr., "Kennedy Gets an Ovation; Recalls Ideals of Brother," *NYT*, August 28, 1964; Cheshire, "They'll Shake Hands with 5,000."

66. Apple, "Kennedy Gets an Ovation"; Jack Vanderberg, "Kennedy Plugs

Ticket Before 8 State Groups," *WP*, August 28, 1964; Robert Healy, "They Still Adore the Magnificent Kennedy Style," *BG*, August 28, 1964.

67. *WBOB*, 291.

68. Joseph Hearst, "Attorney General Cheered Wildly by Delegates," *CT*, August 28, 1964; "Tears, Pride Greet '1,000 Days' of JFK," *BG*, August 28, 1964; Apple, "Kennedy Gets an Ovation"; Richard Reston, "Bob Kennedy Given Thunderous Ovation," *LAT*, August 28, 1964; White, *Making*

of the President: 1964, 292; Dick Zander, "Poignant Minutes Rekindle a Flame," *ND*, August 28, 1964.

69. Dunfey, RFKOH, December 15, 1971, 27.

70. "Dictated over phone by RFK— August 26, 1964," RFKAG, Box 255: "Democratic National Convention, August 27, 1964 Drafts."

71. White, *Making of the President: 1964*, 292; Arnold Abrams, "Weekly Review," *ND*, August 29, 1964; "The Kennedy Legacy," *WP*, August 29, 1964; Johnson, *All the Way*, 196.

6. A NEWER WORLD (PGS. 109 TO 133)

1. Tom Wicker, "The Name Is Smith," *NYT*, July 28, 1963; Alan L. Otten and Charles B. Seib, "The Kennedy Clansman Nobody Knows," *SEP*, September 7, 1963; Richard Reeves, "Says Campaign Chairman Steve Smith . . ." *NYT*, June 14, 1970.

2. Otten and Seib, "Kennedy Clansman"; Murray Kempton, "Stephen E. Smith," *TNR*, March 9, 1963; "Alter Ego of Kennedys," *NYT*, August 26, 1964; Reeves, "Says Campaign Chairman Steve Smith . . ."; Wicker, "Name Is Smith."

3. R. W. Apple Jr., "How Kennedy Did It: 27 Days of Hard Politicking," *NYT*, August 26, 1964.

4. R. W. Apple Jr., "Stratton Assails Race by Kennedy," *NYT*, August 27, 1964; R. W. Apple Jr., "Kennedy Weighs Race for Senate; He Sees Wagner," *NYT*, August 8, 1964; Milton S. Gwirtzman, RFKOH, December 23, 1971, 23.

5. "Democrats: Little Brother Is Watching."

6. *RK&HT*, 667; R. W. Apple Jr., "McKeon to Urge Kennedy to Make Race for Senate," *NYT*, August 11, 1964; R. W. Apple Jr., "Mayor

Endorses Race by Kennedy; Cites 'Eminence,'" *NYT*, August 22, 1964; C. R. Owens, "Bobby Resigns as Delegate," *BG*, August 24, 1964; UPI, "Kennedy Entry Set for Today," *WP*, August 25, 1964; "The Kennedy Steamroller," *NYT*, August 15, 1964.

7. Julius Duscha, "N.Y. Senate Race Entered by Kennedy," *WP*, August 26, 1964; Healy, "RFK Jumps In"; "Kennedy Enters Race for Senate," *NYT*, August 26, 1964.

8. Martin Arnold, "Democratic State Convention Has National Floor," *NYT*, September 2, 1964; William Fulton, "Pick Kennedy for New York Senate Race," *CT*, September 2, 1964; Stan Hinden, "Dems Tell Bobby: Your Ball, Run," *ND*, September 2, 1964.

9. R. W. Apple Jr., "Kennedy Swamps Stratton to Win State Nomination," *NYT*, September 2, 1964; Gerald Gardner, *Robert Kennedy in New York* (New York: Random House, 1965), 18–19.

10. Robert Mayer and Myron S. Waldman, "He's Off at Dawn, Fishes for Votes," *ND*, September 2, 1964.

11. James Reston, "New York," *NYT*, September 25, 1964.

12. Robert Healy, "6:25 A.M. . . . Time to Go Fishing . . . for Votes at Fulton Market," *BG*, September 3, 1964.

13. Mayer and Waldman, "He's Off at Dawn"; Dick Zander, "Bobby Leaving His U.S. Post Today," *ND*, September 3, 1964; R. W. Apple Jr., "Kennedy Opens His Campaign at Fulton Fish Market," *NYT*, September 3, 1964.

14. Myron S. Waldman, *Forgive Us Our Press Passes: The Memoirs of a Veteran Washington Reporter* (New York: St. Martin's Press, 1991), 23.

15. RK to David Powers, September 2, 1964, RFKAG, Box 44: "Justice Department: Farewell Letters from RFK."

16. R. W. Apple Jr., "Kennedy Quits Post in Cabinet to Wage Campaign in State," *NYT*, September 4, 1964; Phil Casey, "RFK Goodby Sounds Like 'I'll Be Back,'" *BG*, September 4, 1964; Phil Casey, "Students Steal Show as Kennedy Resigns," *WP*, September 4, 1964.

17. R. W. Apple Jr., "Kennedy Decides Not to Vote Nov. 3," *NYT*, September 5, 1964.

18. "Keating vs. Kennedy: High Stakes in New York," *NW*, October 12, 1964, 38; Warren Weaver Jr., "Kennedy and Keating: Senate Race in New York Expected to Offer a Study in Contrasts," *NYT*, August 22, 1964; Homer Bigart, "Keating vs. Kennedy: A Campaign Marked by Sharp Contrasts," *NYT*, October 9, 1964; "Keating Offers Bobby Some Left-hand Help," *ND*, August 26, 1964.

19. "'What's Bobby Going to Do?,'" 25; Bigart, "Keating vs. Kennedy"; Stein, *American Journey*, 181.

20. Apple, "Kennedy Decides Not to Vote"; UPI, "N.Y. Labor Leaders Endorse Bob Kennedy," *LAT*, September 3, 1964; Bigart, "Keating vs. Kennedy."

21. R. W. Apple Jr., "Throngs Mob Kennedy at Beach," *NYT*, September 7, 1964.

22. Ken Byerly and Robert Mayer, "Bobby Pulls the Crowds but Will He Pull Votes?," *ND*, September 10, 1964.

23. Apple, "Throngs Mob Kennedy"; UPI, "RFK Mobbed on Long Island," *BG*, September 7, 1964.

24. "Weigh Extra Pay for RFK Cop Detail," *ND*, October 27, 1964.

25. Martin Arnold, "Kennedy Mobbed in Grand Central," *NYT*, September 5, 1964.

26. "Dean P. Markham," *NYT*, September 25, 1966; Waldman, *Forgive Us Our Press Passes*, 24; Myron S. Waldman, "You Might Call Him RFK's Chief Hanger-on," *ND*, October 1, 1964.

27. Waldman, *Forgive Us Our Press Passes*, 23; R. W. Apple Jr., "Kennedy Cheered by Throngs Here," *NYT*, September 13, 1964.

28. Homer Bigart, "Kennedy Tames Bearish Crowd," *NYT*, October 3, 1964; Peter J. Kumpa, "Senate Race Is About Even Between Kennedy, Keating," *BS*, September 28, 1964; Martin Arnold, "Kennedy Cheered at Reform Dance," *NYT*, September 28, 1964; Byerly and Mayer, "Bobby Pulls the Crowds."

29. *WBOB*, 295.

30. Peter Maas, "Can Kennedy Take New York?," *SEP*, October 31, 1964.

31. *WBOB*, 295; Martin Arnold, "Kennedy Spends Day in Glen Cove," *NYT*, September 12, 1964; R. W. Apple Jr., "Kennedy Enlisting a Diversified Staff; Raising $1 Million," *NYT*, September 18, 1964.

32. Maas, "Can Kennedy Take New York?"; "Campaigning," *TNY*, October 24, 1964, 50–51; Relman Morin, "'An Astonishing Human Storm,'" *BG*, September 13, 1964.

33. Oriana Fallaci, "Robert Kennedy Answers Some Blunt Questions," *Look*, March 9, 1965, 62.

34. *WBOB*, 294.

35. Maas, "Can Kennedy Take New York?"

36. "Democrats: Little Brother Is Watching"; R. W. Apple, Jr., "Rochester, Keating Home Town, Gives Kennedy Rousing Welcome," *NYT*, September 10, 1964; Justin N. Feldman, RFKOH, November 26, 1969, 33; Gwirtzman, RFKOH, December 23, 1971, 32.

37. Feldman, RFKOH, November 26, 1969, 34.

38. Layhmond Robinson, "Democrats Form a Keating Group," *NYT*, September 29, 1964; "Why I Would Not Vote for Bobby Kennedy," *I. F. Stone's Weekly*, October 19, 1964.

39. Wershba, "Bobby Kennedy Today," 25.

40. Gwirtzman, RFKOH, December 23, 1971, 27.

41. *WBOB*, 296; Murray Kempton, "The Kennedy Squeal," *TS*, September 11, 1964; Gwirtzman, RFKOH, December 23, 1971, 31–32; Homer Bigart, "Johnson to Seek Votes Here Today," *NYT*, October 14, 1964.

42. Maureen O'Neill, "'John-John' Gives Uncle's Drive a Boost," *ND*, October 8, 1964; "Kennedy Visits Childhood Home," *NYT*, October 8, 1964.

43. Dorothy McCardle, "Bells Are Ringing in Her Campaigns," *WP*, October 2, 1964.

44. AP, "Jean Ascends Request List by Substitution," *WP*, October 2, 1964.

45. Martin Tolchin, "Kennedy's Wife Joins Campaign," *NYT*, September 11, 1964.

46. Jimmy Breslin, "Robert Doesn't Need Reminder," *BG*, September 28, 1964.

47. Anthony Lewis, "Panel Unanimous," *NYT*, September 28, 1964; Breslin, "Robert Doesn't Need Reminder."

48. Richard D. Mahoney, *Sons & Brothers: The Days of Jack and Bobby Kennedy* (New York: Arcade, 1999), 302; Myron S. Waldman, "In a Hectic Race, Time Out for Jackie," *ND*, September 29, 1964; Homer Bigart, "Kennedy, Disturbed by Memory of Tragedy, Cancels Rally Here," *NYT*, September 29, 1964; Waldman, *Forgive Us Our Press Passes*, 23; Relman Morin, "'An Astonishing Human Storm,'" *BG*, September 13, 1964.

49. Evan Thomas, *Robert Kennedy: His Life* (New York: Touchstone, 2000), 298.

50. Mahoney, *Sons & Brothers*, 302; Bigart, "Kennedy, Disturbed by Memory."

51. Feldman, RFKOH, November 26, 1969, 34.

52. Dick Zander, "Keating Hits RFK on Aniline Sale," *ND*, September 24, 1964; Bigart, "Keating vs. Kennedy."

53. David Halberstam, "Keating Assails Rival on Rights," *NYT*, September 20, 1964; Jackie Robinson, "Kennedy & Keating," *New York Amsterdam News*, September 19, 1964.

54. *WBOB*, 264–65; "RFK Admits He's Trailing," *BG*, October 12, 1964; John Cummings and Robert A. Caro, "Ken Makes Valachi a Key Vote Issue," *ND*, October 12, 1964.

55. David Halberstam, "Cites Suit on Aniline," *NYT*, September 21, 1964; *WBOB*, 102.

56. Halberstam, "Cites Suit on Aniline"; Art Bergmann, "Keating Says RFK Aided 'Nazi Cartel,'" *ND*, September 21, 1964; Gwirtzman, RFKOH, December 23, 1971, 28.

57. "Nonsense for New Yorkers," *NYT*, September 25, 1964.

58. Alice Murray, "Kennedy Defended in Aniline Deal," *ND*, September 22, 1964; Homer Bigart, "Kennedy Assails Keating Tactics," *NYT*, September 23, 1964.

59. Myron S. Waldman, "Kennedy," *ND*, September 23, 1964.

60. R. W. Apple Jr., "The Kennedy Strategy," *NYT*, September 21, 1964; "RFK Admits He's Trailing."

61. PBE, RFKOH, November 12, 1969, 90–93; PBE, author interview, February 5, 2009.

62. Thimmesch and Johnson, *RKA40*, 218–19.

63. Jerry Bruno and Jeff Greenfield, *The Advance Man* (New York: William Morrow, 1971), 104–5; David Halberstam, "Kennedy Fighting 'Ruthless' Image," *NYT*, October 27, 1964.

64. Terry Smith, "Bobby's Image," *Esquire*, April 1965; Bruno and Greenfield, *Advance Man*, 104–5.

65. Myron S. Waldman, "RFK Ponders *the* Question," *ND*, September 30, 1964; Feldman, RFKOH, November 26, 1969, 34; *WBOB*, 234; "Campaigning," 50–51; Frederic S. Papert, author interview, September 2, 2010.

66. Martin Arnold, "Kennedy Assails Immigration Curb," *NYT*, October 6, 1964.

67. 1964 campaign footage of Frederic S. Papert.

68. John Seigenthaler, "Robert F. Kennedy Conference," JFKL, moderated by John Seigenthaler, November 18, 2000, 21; "Untitled notes on RFK's speeches and press conferences," Ken J. Lupino Personal Papers, JFKL, Box 1: "RFK Speech Schedule September 1964–October 1964 and Research Report on Keating."

69. ASNYPL, Series IV: Research Files, Box 490: "1964 RFK Speeches"; Jimmy Breslin, "Nobody but Kennedy Could Have Invaded New York," *BG*, October 25, 1964.

70. "Kennedy Visits Childhood Home."

71. Terry Smith, "Kennedy, Keating Spent Millions in Senate Race," *WP*, December 6, 1964; advertisement, *NYT*, October 8, 1964, 86; advertisement, *ND*, October 8, 1964, 4C; Bigart, "Keating vs. Kennedy."

72. Byerly and Mayer, "Bobby Pulls the Crowds."

73. Peter Edelman, *Searching for America's Heart: RFK and the Renewal of Hope* (Boston: Houghton Mifflin, 2001), 32–33; PBE, RFKOH, December 12, 1969, 77–78, 100–101; PBE, author interview.

74. William vanden Heuvel and Milton Gwirtzman, *On His Own: Robert F. Kennedy, 1964–1968* (Garden City, NY: Doubleday, 1970), 49; Ted Sorensen, "Robert F. Kennedy Conference," JFKL, November 18, 2000; Philippe Y. Sanborne, "B'klyn Hails Conquering Heroes," *ND*, October 16, 1964; "Kennedy and Johnson Lead in *Daily News* Straw Poll," *NYT*, October 15, 1964.

75. "Campaigning," 50–51; John Cummings, "RFK 'Distorts' Voting Record, Keating Says," *ND*, October 14, 1964.

76. David Halberstam, "Kennedy Explains Refusal of Brother to Bomb Cuba," *NYT*, October 14, 1964; Cummings, "RFK 'Distorts' Voting Record."

77. R. W. Apple Jr., "'Unfair' Assertion Laid to Kennedy," *NYT*, 1964; Robert A. Caro, "Keating Pushes Bid to Label RFK 'Liar,'" *ND*, October 27, 1964.

78. Apple, "'Unfair' Assertion"; Halberstam, "Kennedy Fighting 'Ruthless' Image"; "Smear!," *ND*, October 29, 1964.

79. Halberstam, "Kennedy Fighting 'Ruthless' Image."

80. Bernie Bookbinder, "The Making of Senator Bobby," *ND*, November 7, 1964.

81. R. W. Apple Jr., "Group Retracts Kennedy Rebuke," *NYT*, October 28, 1964.

82. *RK&HT*, 675, 671; William E. Farrell, "Kennedy, Keating Agree to 2 Debates," *NYT*, October 9, 1964; Ronald Sullivan, "Keating Advised to Avoid Debate," *NYT*, October 13, 1964.

83. "Keating Says He'll Debate Kennedy or Empty Chair," *NYT*, October 27, 1964; Homer Bigart, "Kennedy vs. Keating: A Near Debate," *NYT*, October 28, 1964; Gardner, *Robert Kennedy in New York*, 146–48.

84. PBE, RFKOH, December 12, 1969, 103–5.

85. AW, RFKOH, November 29, 1969, 12–13; Thimmesch and Johnson, *RKA40*, 217–18.

86. Myron S. Waldman and Robert A. Caro, "The Great Debate: RFK, Ken, Don't Meet," *ND*, October 28, 1964; Homer Bigart, "Keating vs. Kennedy: A Near-Debate," *NYT*, October 28, 1964; Waldman, *Forgive Us Our Press Passes*, 28–30.

87. R. W. Apple Jr., "Kennedy Reports Gains on Keating," *NYT*, October 29, 1964; Robert A. Caro, "Keating Feels Low After the TV Show," *ND*, October 29, 1964; William C. Selover, "Polls Cling to Forecasts," *CSM*, November 3, 1964.

88. R. W. Apple Jr., "Kennedy, Keating Close Campaigns," *NYT*, November 3, 1964.

89. R. W. Apple Jr., "Kennedy Edge 6–5," *NYT*, November 4, 1964; "Just a Day at the Zoo for Bobby Kennedy," *BG*, November 4, 1964; Edward Jenner, "Kennedys Waited in Hospital, N.Y.C.," *BG*, November 4, 1964.

90. Bernie Bookbinder and Jack Schwartz, "Early Keating Optimism Turned Sour Fast," *ND*, November 4, 1964; Peter Kihss, "Kennedy Greeted by Adulation of Screaming, Youthful Crowd," *NYT*, November 4, 1964; *WBOB*, 311; Apple, "Kennedy Edge 6–5."

91. LBJ in phone conversation with Bill Moyers, November 4, 1964, TMC; *Guide to U.S. Elections*, 6th ed. (Washington, DC: CQ Press, 2010); Shesol, *MC*, 213.

92. "Ties with Kennedy Predicted by Javits," *NYT*, November 7, 1964.

93. LBJ in phone conversation with RK, November 3, 1964, TMC.

94. Bookbinder, "Making of Senator Bobby."

95. Margaret Laing, *The Next Kennedy* (New York: Coward-McCann, 1968), 31.

96. Bookbinder, "Making of Senator Bobby."

97. William V. Shannon, *The Heir Apparent: Robert Kennedy and the Struggle for Power* (New York: Macmillan, 1967), 7.

7. THE SIXTIES BREAKING OPEN
(PGS. 137 TO 153)

1. LBJ in phone conversation with Bill Moyers, November 3, 1964, TMC.

2. *FRUS, 1964–1968*, vol. 1, Documents 393–395, 398.

3. Robert S. McNamara, *In Retrospect: The Tragedy and Lessons of Vietnam* (New York: Times Books, 1995), 128–39; "The President's Address," *NYT*, August 5, 1964.

4. John H. Averill, "Goldwater Hints Politics in Viet Raid," *LAT*, November 2, 1964; AP, "U.S. Got Warning of Raid, Nixon Says," *AC*, November 2, 1964; "Thurmond Says Casualties at Bienhoa Were About 300," *NYT*, November 3, 1964; *FRUS, 1964–1968*, vol. 1, Document 395.

5. David Halberstam, *The Unfinished Odyssey of Robert Kennedy* (New York: Bantam Books, 1969), 22, 24.

6. Michael Forrestal, LBJOH, November 3, 1969, 36; Jack Raymond, "Taylor Denies Threat to Quit over Vietnam War," *NYT*, November 27, 1964; Philippe Y. Sanborne, "Weekly Review," *ND*, January 9, 1965.

7. Martin Tolchin, "Bitterness Shows at Navy Yard Despite a Guarantee of Job Opportunities for All," *NYT*, November 20, 1964.

8. David Wise, "McNamara Dooms 95 Bases, Protests Pour in," *BG*, November 20, 1964; Tolchin, "Bitterness Shows at Navy Yard."

9. AW, RFKOH, November 29, 1969, 1, 24–25; AW, author interview, January 2, 2009.

10. U.S. Congress, House, *To Amend the Immigration and Nationality Act: Hearings Before Subcommittee No. 1 of the Committee on the Judiciary*, 88th Cong., 2nd sess., 1964, 409–10, 435–36; C. P. Trussell, "New Alien Quotas Urged by Kennedy," *NYT*, July 22, 1964.

11. AW, RFKOH, November 29, 1969, 2, 7–9, 15–16, 23; Adam and Jane Walinsky, author interview, January 2, 2009.

12. Adam Walinsky to David M. Trubek, February 19, 1965, 1–2, AWP, Box 2: "Campaign 1968, September 1967–March 1968"; Shesol, *MC*, 122.

13. Adam Walinsky to RK, "Legislative Programs and Strategy for New Session," November 7, 1964, AWP, Box 24: "Kennedy, Robert F.: Campaign Proposals, 1968."

14. AW, author interview.

15. Joseph Alsop, "Matter of Fact: The Baffled Republicans," *WP*, January 8, 1965.

16. Milt Gwirtzman to RK, "Organization of and Personnel Needs for a Senate Office," November

3, 1964, Milton S. Gwirtzman Personal Papers, Box 5.

17. AW, RFKOH, November 29, 1969, 25–26; PBE, RFKOH, December 12, 1969, 112–16; Edelman, *Searching for America's Heart*, 33.

18. Jack Newfield, *RFK: A Memoir* (New York: Thunder's Mouth Press/Nation Books, 2003), 53; AW, RFKOH, November 29, 1969, 31; *RK&HT*, 677.

19. Warren Weaver, "Will the Real Robert Kennedy Stand Up?," *NYT*, June 20, 1965; Dick Hildreth, "RFK Draws Laughs of Collegians," *SPS*, December 16, 1964, 6; AW, RFKOH, November 29, 1969, 29–30; Ronald Sullivan, "Kennedy Winds Up an Upstate Tour," *NYT*, December 12, 1964; PBE, RFKOH, December 12, 1969, 117–21; Murray Kempton, "Robert Kennedy— Provincial New Yorker," *TNR*, January 2, 1965; Dick Hildreth, "Kennedy Told of Unemployment," *SPS*, December 16, 1964, 6; Fred Powledge, "Upstate Leaders Ask Kennedy Aid," *NYT*, December 16, 1964; Dick Hildreth, "Welfare Report Revealing," *SPS*, December 16, 1964, 6.

20. Warren Weaver Jr., "Senator Kennedy (D., N.Y.) Settles in New Job," *NYT*, February 21, 1965.

21. Kempton, "Robert Kennedy— Provincial New Yorker."

22. Warren Weaver Jr., "Old Hands to Run Kennedy's Office," *NYT*, January 10, 1965; Shesol, *MC*, 231–32; John Seigenthaler, author interview, July 28, 2009; Wesley Barthelmes, RFKOH, May 20, 1969, 4–5.

23. Joe Dolan to RK, December 9, 1964, JDP, Box 1, "Memoranda December 5, 1964–April 15, 1965"; Cabell Phillips, "6 New Democrats Get Senate Posts," *NYT*, January 9, 1965.

24. Phillips, "6 New Democrats Get"; Warren Weaver Jr., "Kennedy Seeking

2 Posts in Senate," *NYT*, December 20, 1964; Dolan to RK, December 9, 1964; Thomas Collins, "RFK Joins Ted and a Memory in Senate Duty," *ND*, January 9, 1965.

25. Richard L. Lyons, "Democrats Put 3 Liberals in Key Senate Positions," *WP*, January 9, 1965.

26. Weaver, "Will the Real Robert Kennedy Stand Up?"

27. Robert Healy, "Kennedys Make Senate History," *BG*, January 5, 1964; AP, "Kennedys Celebrate Seating of Brothers," *HC*, January 5, 1965; Bonnie Angelo, "Senate Embraces Kennedy Brothers," *SPS*, January 5, 1965; Warren Weaver Jr., "Kennedy (D.-N.Y.) Gets a Back Seat," *NYT*, January 5, 1965; Thimmesch and Johnson, *RKA40*, 250; vanden Heuvel and Gwirtzman, *On His Own*, 56; *RK&HT*, 681; RK, "Women's National Press Club," January 6, 1965, RFKSSPR, Box 1, January 1, 1965–January 15, 1965.

28. AP, "Kennedys Celebrate Seating"; Thomas Collins, "Bobby Joins 'Club,' Has Seat with a View," *ND*, January 5, 1965.

29. Mary McGrory, "Sizeups Begin: Ted Bests Bob," *BG*, January 6, 1965; Adam Clymer, *Edward M. Kennedy: A Biography* (New York: William Morrow, 1999), 18, 44, 63; AMS, *Journals*, 236.

30. Dan Cordtz, "White House Prospects of Senators Bob, Ted Stir New Speculation," *WSJ*, January 7, 1965; Thimmesch and Johnson, *RKA40*, 286.

31. Richard L. Strout, "Kennedy Tandem Moves Forward on Political Stage," *CSM*, May 13, 1965.

32. Edward M. Kennedy, *True Compass: A Memoir* (New York: Twelve, 2009), 17; Thimmesch and Johnson, *RKA40*, 254, 274; Clymer, *Edward M. Kennedy*, 104–5.

33. Warren Weaver Jr., "At Inaugural Moment, Some Stand by Kennedy's Grave," *NYT*, January 21, 1965; AP, "Kennedy Brothers Take Different Role This Time," *WP*, January 21, 1965; Thomas Collins, "Memories Were Louder Here," *ND*, January 21, 1965; AP photo, *WP*, January 21, 1965; Thimmesch and Johnson, *RKA40*, 253.

34. AP, "Robert Kennedy Visits Grave of His Brother," *CT*, November 6, 1964; Nan Robertson, "Robert Kennedy Leads the Family as 40,000 Pay Tribute at Arlington," *NYT*, November 23, 1964; Thomas, *Robert Kennedy*, 302.

35. AW, RFKOH, November 29, 1969, 30–31.

36. UPI, "V.A. to Shut 14 Hospitals in Economy Move, Including 3 Upstate," *NYT*, January 13, 1965, 21; PBE, author interview, February 2, 2009; PBE, RFKOH, December 12, 1969, 129–32; Weaver, "Senator Kennedy (D., N.Y.) Settles In."

37. U.S. Congress, Senate, *Proposed Closings of Veterans' Hospitals: Hearings Before the Subcommittee on Veterans' Affairs of the Committee on Labor and Public Welfare*, 89th Cong., 1st sess., 1965, 263, 273, 275–81, 434.

38. William Moore, "Bob Kennedy Blasts VA's Acting Chief," *CT*, January 29, 1965; Laurence Stern, "Sens. Kennedy Grill VA Officials in Hearing on Closing of Hospitals," *WP*, January 29, 1965.

39. AP, "Johnson Adamant on V.A. Closings," *NYT*, February 5, 1965, 15; Tom Wicker, "Johnson and Congress," *NYT*, February 7, 1965; "Change Is Urged on V.A. Closings," *NYT*, May 12, 1965, 47.

40. AW, RFKOH, November 5, 1973, 228–29; U.S. Congress, Senate, *Elementary and Secondary Education*

Act of 1965: Hearings Before the Subcommittee on Education of the Committee on Labor and Public Welfare, 89th Cong., 1st sess., 1965, 263–66; Joseph Alsop, "Matter of Fact," *WP*, March 3, 1965.

41. Robert C. Albright, "Senate Authorizes $1.09 Billion in Aid for Appalachia Area," *WP*, February 2, 1965; Douglas Robinson, "13 Upstate Counties Welcome U.S. Aid Plan," *NYT*, February 23, 1965; Warren Weaver Jr., "Senator vs. Governor," *NYT*, February 16, 1965; AW, RFKOH, November 30, 1969, 43; Majorie Hunter, "Senate Approves $1.1 Billion in Aid for Appalachia," *NYT*, February 2, 1965; Thimmesch and Johnson, *RKA40*, 256–57; Robert C. Albright, "Others Want in on Appalachia Bill," *WP*, January 22, 1965; PBE, RFKOH, January 3, 1970, 33, 43–44; AW, RFKOH, November 5, 1973, 234, 247; John Harris, "Kennedy Differs with Saltonstall on Tidelands Oil," *BG*, April 21, 1953; Wilfrid C. Rodgers, "Senator's 1st Speech—a Lasting Impact," *BG*, April 10, 1964.

42. U.S. Senate, *Congressional Record*, 89th Cong., 1st sess., February 1, 1965, 1695; Hunter, "Senate Approves $1.1 Billion."

43. U.S. Senate, *Congressional Record*, 89th Cong., 1st sess., February 1, 1965, 1695; Warren Weaver Jr., "Paradox of Jacob Javits," *NYT*, April 25, 1965; AW, RFKOH, October 5, 1973, 285.

44. Hunter, "Senate Approves $1.1 Billion"; "'The Senator from Mass.' Scores a Point for NY," *ND*, February 2, 1965; William Moore, "Appalachia Aid Bill OK'd," *CT*, February 2, 1965.

45. *FRUS, 1964–1968*, vol. 2, *Vietnam*, January–June 1965, ed. David C. Humphrey, Ronald D. Landa, and Louis J. Smith (Washington, DC:

Government Printing Office, 1996), Document 87; William E. Farrell, "Kennedy Baby Is Named in Honor of Maxwell Taylor," *NYT*, January 18, 1965.

46. John M. Taylor, *General Maxwell Taylor: The Sword and the Pen* (New York: Doubleday, 1989), 311, 360.

47. *WBOB*, 318; Chalmers M. Roberts, "Our 25 Years in Vietnam," *WP*, June 2, 1968; *FRUS, 1964–1968*, vol. 2, Document 145; David Kraslow and Stuart H. Loory, *The Secret Search for Peace in Vietnam* (New York: Vintage Books, 1968), 100–101.

48. *WBOB*, 318–19; "Viet Nam," EGP, Box 5: "Correspondence 1964–1968."

49. "U.S. Aides Praise Pleiku Defenders," *NYT*, February 9, 1965; *FRUS, 1964–1968*, vol. 2, Document 92.

50. *FRUS, 1964–1968*, vol. 2, Document 84.

51. McGeorge Bundy, LBJOH, February 17, 1969, 11.

52. *FRUS, 1964–1968*, vol. 2, Document 88.

53. Johnson, *Vantage Point*, 125.

54. *FRUS, 1964–1968*, vol. 2, Documents 95–96.

55. Johnson, *Vantage Point*, 130–31; Tom Wicker, "Mann Is Appointed to Harriman Post as No. 2 Rusk Aide," *NYT*, February 13, 1965.

56. Halberstam, *Unfinished Odyssey*, 21.

57. *FRUS, 1964–1968*, vol. 2, Documents 175, 267.

58. *WBOB*, 319; "Kennedy Opposes Withdrawal," *NYT*, February 24, 1965.

59. *FRUS, 1964–1968*, vol. 2, Document 187; Jack Raymond, "3,500 U.S. Marines Going to Vietnam to Bolster Base," *NYT*, March 7, 1965; Jack Languth, "Force 'Strictly Defensive'— Arrival Is Protested by Hanoi and Peking," *NYT*, March 8, 1965.

60. Maxwell Taylor, LBJOH, January 9, 1969, 18.

8. RUTHLESS (PGS. 154 TO 176)

1. UPI, "Kennedy Puts Aside Presidency Question," *WP*, February 22, 1965; Fallaci, "Robert Kennedy Answers," 60–63; Drew Pearson, "Robert Kennedy out of Politics?," *LAT*, May 14, 1964.

2. Fallaci, "Robert Kennedy Answers," 61.

3. AP, "Hoffa Assails Kennedy," *NYT*, December 15, 1964.

4. R. W. Apple Jr., "A Shadow over Albany," *NYT*, January 8, 1965; Ken Byerly, "Kennedy's Foes Rap Intervention in Setup at Albany," *ND*, February 12, 1965; R. W. Apple Jr., "Kennedy Shunning Speakership Battle," *NYT*, December 8, 1964; Warren Weaver Jr., "Kennedy Views Battle as Warm-up for Campaign Against Mayor in '66," *NYT*, January 9, 1964; Newfield, *RFK*, 146–47; Thimmesch and Johnson, *RKA40*, 231; Robert Wagner in conversation with LBJ, December 2, 1964, TMC; Thomas P. Ronan, "Maneuver in Albany Stuns Wagner's Opponents," *NYT*, February 4, 1965; Douglas Dales, "Kennedy Asserts Democrats 'Fail,'" *NYT*, February 5, 1965; Stan Hinden, "Bobby Jumps into NY Dem Feud," *ND*, February 11, 1965; "The Text of Kennedy's Letter to Albany," *NYT*, February 11, 1965.

5. Patrick Anderson, "Robert's Character," *Esquire*, April 1965, 142.

6. *RK&HT*, 105; U.P., "Cohn, in 'Hate' Clash, Comes Near to Blows," *NYDN*, June 12, 1954, C2, C8.

7. U.S. Congress, Senate, *Invasions of Privacy (Government Agencies): Hearings Before the Subcommittee on Administrative Practice and Procedure of the Committee on the Judiciary*, 89th Cong., 1st sess., 1965, 243–44.

8. James Cary, "Kennedy Denies Exposé Charge and Challenges Committee Action," *WP*, March 4, 1965; U.S. Congress, Senate, *Invasions of Privacy*, 272; Sam Baron, "A Top Teamster Hits Back at Hoffa," *Life*, July 20, 1962; Willard Edwards, "Bob Kennedy Blasts Long in Hoffa Case," *CT*, March 4, 1965.

9. U.S. Congress, Senate, *Invasions of Privacy*, 274, 276–77.

10. Edwards, "Bob Kennedy Blasts Long"; Thimmesch and Johnson, *RKA40*, 263; Weaver, "Will the Real Robert Kennedy Stand Up?"

11. "Scott Hits RFK; Backs Viet Raids," *BG*, March 6, 1965; "Long of Missouri Tied to Payments," *NYT*, May 21, 1967; Alfonso A. Narvaez, "Bernard Fensterwald, 69, Lawyer for James Ray and Watergate Spy," *NYT*, April 4, 1991.

12. Roscoe Drummond, "RFK Moves In," *WP*, February 8, 1965; AP, "Bobby Kennedy, Sen. Byrd Meet; Find Common Ground in Dog Talk," *HC*, May 12, 1965; Maxine Cheshire, "Oriental Art Brands Those Wealthy Texans," *WP*, February 14, 1965; Warren Weaver, Jr., "Senator Kennedy (D., N.Y.) Settles In." *NYT*, February 21, 1965.

13. Warren Weaver Jr., "Mail to Kennedy Swamps Offices," *NYT*, March 14, 1965; PBE, author interview, August 4, 2008; Weaver, "Will the Real Robert Kennedy Stand Up?"; Laing, *Next Kennedy*, 35–36; Charles Dancey, "The Open Door Policy Fools the Tourists," *Peoria Journal Star*, March 19, 1967, C-5; Joe Dolan to RK, March 11, 1965, JDP, Box 1: "Memoranda December 5, 1964–April 15, 1965."

14. Weaver, "Mail to Kennedy Swamps Offices"; Dancey, "Open Door Policy

Fools"; Joe Dolan to RK, December 5, 1964, JDP, Box 1: "Memoranda December 5, 1964–April 15, 1965"; PBE, RFKOH, December 12, 1969, 126.

15. Thimmesch and Johnson, *RKA40*, 280; Laing, *Next Kennedy*, 35–36; Andrew J. Glass, "Why Bobby Wanted to Be V.P.," *BG*, April 18, 1965.

16. Marquis Childs, "Bobby and Teddy, or a View of 1972," *WP*, June 25, 1965.

17. Tom Wicker, "Johnson and Congress," *NYT*, February 7, 1965, E5; William Shannon, "The President and Congress," *NYT*, February 15, 1965.

18. "The Central Points," *Time*, March 19, 1965; Taylor Branch, *At Canaan's Edge: America in the King Years, 1965–68* (New York: Simon & Schuster, 2006), 50–56, 80–85, 94–101; Andrew Beck Grace, "A Call from Selma," *NYT*, March 6, 2015; Nicholas deB. Katzenbach, *Some of It Was Fun: Working with RFK and LBJ* (New York: W. W. Norton, 2008), 166.

19. Richard N. Goodwin, *Remembering America: A Voice from the Sixties* (Boston: Little, Brown, 1988), 326–36.

20. Seigenthaler, RFKOH, June 5, 1970, 22; AMS, *Journals*, 237; Stanley Meisler, "Negro Can Be U.S. President, Atty.-Gen. Says," *WP*, May 27, 1961; "Mr Baldwin Versus Mr Buckley," *GDN*, February 19, 1965.

21. Dolan to RK, December 9, 1964; David K. Willis, "Capital Menaced," *CSM*, March 2, 1965; Thimmesch and Johnson, *RKA40*, 252; "Kennedy Broadside on Crime Came as No Surprise," *WP*, May 3, 1965; Elsie Carper, "Race Issue Is Linked to Home Rule," *WP*, March 10, 1965; "Bob Kennedy Spurs Better-Schools Rally," *WP*, March 29, 1965.

22. Godfrey Sperling Jr., "Kennedy Views 'Rights' Tasks," *CSM*, March 22, 1965;

"Bob Kennedy Spurs Better-Schools Rally."

23. Sperling, "Kennedy Views 'Rights' Tasks."

24. Emanuel Perlmutter, "Suspect Gives Up in IND Killing; Sister Calls Him Black Extremist," *NYT*, March 18, 1965; Joseph Egelhof, "10 See Killing on Subway, but Remain Silent," *CT*, March 14, 1965; Sperling, "Kennedy Views 'Rights' Tasks."

25. Paul Schuette, "Welfare Job Candidate, Byrd Clash," *WP*, May 8, 1963; "The Man in the House," *WP*, May 7, 1965; Elsie Carpenter, "Justice Dept. Urges Delay on Crime Bill, Plans New Proposals," *WP*, April 28, 1965.

26. Robert Kennedy, "Our Climb up Mt. Kennedy," *Life*, April 9, 1965, 27.

27. "Bobby's Next Boost: By Pitons, Not Politics," *ND*, March 22, 1965; AP, "'Copter Carries RFK to Kennedy Mountain," *BG*, March 23, 1965.

28. AP, "RFK to Climb Kennedy Peak," *BG*, March 19, 1965; Martin Arnold, "Kennedy Party Continues Climb Despite Loss of Its Transmitter," *NYT*, March 24, 1965; Warren Weaver Jr., "Kennedy Will Join Mt. Kennedy Climb," *NYT*, March 19, 1965.

29. Arnold, "Kennedy Party Continues Climb"; "Bobby on Way to the Top," *ND*, March 24, 1965.

30. Martin Arnold, "Kennedy Puts Flag atop Mt. Kennedy," *NYT*, March 25, 1965.

31. Martin Arnold, "Senator Is Praised by Teammates on Homeward Trip," *NYT*, March 26, 1965; Arnold, "Kennedy Party Continues Climb"; "Kennedy Is Aiding Sherpa Education," *NYT*, April 8, 1965.

32. Kennedy, "Our Climb up Mt. Kennedy," 27.

33. UPI, "Slipped into Peak Crevice, Kennedy Says," *CT*, March 26, 1965;

UPI, "Bobby Fell Through Crevasse in Climb," *AC*, March 26, 1965; Kennedy, "Our Climb up Mt. Kennedy," 22, 27; Arnold, "Senator Is Praised by Teammates."

34. Kennedy, "Our Climb up Mt. Kennedy," 27; Arnold, "Senator Is Praised by Teammates."

35. Kennedy, "Our Climb up Mt. Kennedy," 27; UPI, "Bobby Fell Through Crevasse"; Arnold, "Kennedy Puts Flag atop Mt. Kennedy."

36. "RFK Plants Family Flag at Peak of Mt. Kennedy," *BG*, March 25, 1965; Kennedy, "Our Climb up Mt. Kennedy," 27.

37. AP, "Tired and Happy Kennedy Calls Mountain Marvelous," *BS*, March 26, 1965; Paul Gardner, "Channel 5 to Present Shaw's 'Don Juan' Sequence," *NYT*, April 5, 1965; "Kennedy Is Aiding Sherpa Education."

38. Fred Dutton to Robert F. Kennedy, April 6, 1966, RFKSCP, Box 3: "Dutton, Frederick, 1965–1966."

39. Shannon, *Heir Apparent*, 255.

40. UPI, "New Selma Killing," *LAT*, March 26, 1965.

41. Walter Trohan, "Washington Scrapbook," *CT*, April 18, 1965.

42. PBE, RFKOH, January 3, 1970, 52–56, 64; John Chadwick, "Kennedy Move on Poll Tax Hit as Peril to Bill," *WP*, May 8, 1965; UPI, "Ted Leads Campaign for Fast Poll Tax Ban," *BG*, May 4, 1965; Andrew J. Glass, "Ted Kennedy 'Comes of Age,'" *BG*, May 5, 1965; Thomas Collins, "Teddy Wins Praise in Defeat," *ND*, May 12, 1965; Weaver, "Will the Real Robert Kennedy Stand Up?"; Katzenbach, *Some of It Was Fun*, 173.

43. Mary McGrory, "Senate Dims Lindsay Hope," *BG*, May 21, 1965.

44. AW, RFKOH, November 30, 1969, 42–43.

45. Allen L. Otten, "Lyndon the Lobbyist," *WSJ*, April 9, 1965; Charles Bartlett, "LBJ Formula for Success," *BG*, April 11, 1965; Arthur Krock, "In the Nation: At Breakneck Speed," *NYT*, April 11, 1965.

46. *RK&HT*, 687–88.

47. "President Johnson's Remarks on Vietnam at Johns Hopkins University, April 7, 1965, MP549," LBJL, youtube.com/watch?v=NSWQztZPMdg; *FRUS, 1964–1968*, vol. 2, Document 267; Jack Raymond, "3,500 U.S. Marines Going to Vietnam to Bolster Base," *NYT*, March 7, 1965; " 'We Still Seek No Wider War,' " *ND*, August 5, 1964.

48. Glass, "Why Bobby Wanted to Be V.P."; Weaver, "Mail to Kennedy Swamps Offices"; AW, author interview.

49. *FRUS, 1964–1968*, vol. 2, Documents 266, 269.

50. Ted Lippman, "Senate Argues Vote Bill; Ellender Sees Long Duel," *WP*, April 23, 1965; Nan Robertson, "A White House Garden Is Named for Mrs. Kennedy," *NYT*, April 23, 1965; LBJ Daily Diary, April 22, 1965, LBJL; Andrew Glass, "Bobby, LBJ Split on Policy," *BG*, May 9, 1965; LBJ, LBJOH, August 12, 1969, 20.

51. LBJ, *Vantage Point*, 136; LBJ, LBJOH, August 12, 1969, 18.

52. Walter LaFeber, "Latin American Policy," in *The Johnson Years, Volume One: Foreign Policy, the Great Society, and the White House* (Lawrence: University of Kansas Press, 1987), 64; President John F. Kennedy, "Address at a White House Reception for Members of Congress and for the Diplomatic Corps of the Latin American Republics," March 13, 1961, JFKL.

53. Thomas C. Mann, LBJOH, November 4, 1968, 9; LaFeber, *Johnson Years*, 64; Wicker, "Mann Is Appointed to Harriman Post."

54. AP, "Dominican Rising Said to Collapse," *NYT*, April 25, 1965; Tad Szulc, "Bosch Says He'll Return," *NYT*, April 26, 1965.

55. *FRUS, 1964–1968*, vol. 32, *Dominican Republic; Cuba; Haiti; Guyana*, ed. Daniel Lawler and Carolyn Yee (Washington, DC: Government Printing Office, 2005), Document 22.

56. Tad Szulc, "U.S. to Evacuate Nationals Today in Dominican Crisis," *NYT*, April 27, 1965; Tad Szulc, "Dominican Revolt Fails After a Day of Savage Battle," *NYT*, April 28, 1965.

57. *FRUS, 1964–1968*, vol. 32, Document 23.

58. Ibid., Documents 28–29, 31.

59. Charles Mohr, "President Sends Marines to Rescue Citizens of U.S. from Dominican Fighting," *NYT*, April 29, 1965; Charles Mohr, "Johnson's Action on Troops Swift," *NYT*, May 1, 1965.

60. *FRUS, 1964–1968*, vol. 32, Document 42.

61. Tad Szulc, "2,500 Men Fly In," *NYT*, April 30, 1965; *FRUS, 1964–1968*, vol. 32, Document 43; Peter Kihss, "G.I.'s Advance in Santo Domingo; Johnson Sends 2,000 More Troops; U.N. Talks Set at Soviet Behest," *NYT*, May 2, 1965.

62. "President Johnson's Remarks on the Dominican Crisis, May 2, 1965, MP546," LBJL, youtube.com /watch?v=qiI3jqOwa4c.

63. John D. Onis, "$3 Million Spent by U.S. So Far to Pay Dominican Civil Service," *NYT*, May 23, 1965.

64. "Dominican Web," *NYT*, May 16, 1965.

65. Max Frankel, "Johnson Reiterates Warning on Reds," *NYT*, May 4, 1965; "Ford Says Johnson Implied Criticism of Predecessor," *NYT*, May 5, 1965; *RA*, 406–7; AMS to Moyers, Bundy, Goodwin, "Dominican Situation," May 2, 1965, AMS Papers, JFKL, Box P-2: "Dominican Republic (1965) Correspondence."

66. Frankel, "Johnson Reiterates Warning on Reds"; AW, RFKOH, November 29, 1969, 21–22.

67. Robert Donovan, "LBJ Determined to Avoid 2d 'Cuba,'" *BG*, May 2, 1965.

68. Charles Mohr, "House Panel Acts," *NYT*, May 5, 1965.

69. Edward T. Folliard, "LBJ Asks Congress to Back Policy with $700 Million More Viet Funds," *WP*, May 5, 1965.

70. David Halberstam, *The Best and The Brightest* (New York: Penguin Books, 1972), 88-9.

71. Weaver, "Will the Real Robert Kennedy Stand Up?"; Edwin O. Guthman and C. Richard Allen, eds., *RFK: Collected Speeches* (New York: Viking, 1993), 272.

72. AW, RFKOH, May 22, 1972, 112; AW, RFKOH, November 29, 1969, 21–22; AW, author interview.

73. AW to RK, May 5, 1965, AWP, Box 16: "Files: Foreign Policy, Vietnam April 1965–May 1965."

74. AW, RFKOH, May 22, 1972, 97–98.

75. PBE, RFKOH, January 3, 1970, 166; RK, "Vietnam & the Dominican Republic," RFKSSPR, Box 1: "May 1, 1965–May 10, 1965."

76. Mary McGrory, "Senate Uneasy, Unhappy in Voting Viet Funds," *BG*, May 7, 1965.

77. Guthman and Allen, *RFK: Collected Speeches*, 271–73; U.S. Senate, *Congressional Record*, 89th Cong., 1st sess., May 6, 1965, 9760–62.

78. McGrory, "Senate Uneasy."

79. Howard Margolis, "$700-Million Viet Bill Passes Senate, 88–3," *WP*, May 7, 1965.

80. Robert Barkdoll, "Senate Gives Final OK to War Fund Bill," *LAT*, May 7, 1965; UPI, "Senate Votes 88–3 for Viet Fund Boost amid Sharp Criticism," *BG*, May 7, 1965.

81. John D. Morris, "Kennedy Critical of Johnson Move," *NYT*, May 8, 1965.
82. PBE, RFKOH, December 12, 1969, 199–202.
83. Ted Knap, "What Would JFK Have Done?," *New York World-Telegram and the Sun*, May 8, 1965, 1.
84. PBE, RFKOH, December 12, 1969, 199–202.
85. Glass, "Bobby, LBJ Split on Policy."
86. Eugene Patterson, "Johnson, Sí; Kennedy, No," *AC*, May 10, 1965.
87. James Wechsler, "RFK's Muted Challenge Unheard," *BG*, May 15, 1965.
88. Tom Wicker, "U.S. Raids North Vietnam After 6-Day Lull Brings No Overture from Hanoi," *NYT*, May 19, 1965.
89. LBJ, LBJOH, August 12, 1969, 20–21.

9. THE REVOLUTION NOW IN PROGRESS
(PGS. 177 TO 197)

1. James K. Galbraith, "Exit Strategy: In 1963, JFK Ordered a Complete Withdrawal from Vietnam," *Boston Review*, September 1, 2003.
2. RK, "Tribute to JFK," 42.
3. Nan Robertson, "Throng at Grave Salutes Kennedy," *NYT*, November 23, 1966.
4. RK, "Dedication of John F. Kennedy Center; Fort Bragg, NC," May 29, 1965, RFKSSPR, Box 1: "May 21, 1965–May 31, 1965."
5. "University College of Buffalo—Commencement"; "Economic Unrest Cited by Kennedy," *NYT*, June 6, 1965.
6. Claude Sitton, "Graves at a Dam," *NYT*, August 5, 1964.
7. RK, "Queens College—Commencement," June 15, 1965, RFKSSPR, Box 1: "June 11, 1965–June 20, 1965."
8. E. W. Kenworthy, "Debate over Vietnam Policy—and Views of Key Senators," *NYT*, June 6, 1965.
9. Richard Critchfield, "U.S. Resigned to Widen War," *Washington Evening Star*, June 8, 1965, 1; AP, "The Story of War's Escalation Since '59 in Words, Actions," *ND*, June 11, 1965.
10. Victor Wilson, "Day Calls RFK Postal Job Boss," *BG*, June 28, 1965; E. C. Hallbeck, "The Book Ain't Sexy, but It's Funny—and Sheds Light," *WP*, July 10, 1965.
11. Theodore H. White, *The Making of the President: 1960* (New York: Atheneum Publishers, 1962), 176.
12. Theodore H. White, "A Go-between's Memo on the Wild Day L.B.J. Was Named Vice President," *Life*, July 18, 1965, 90.
13. David Wise, "In New White Book—Bobby Claims LBJ Didn't Tell Truth," *BG*, June 22, 1965; AP, "Bare Bobby Kennedy Spat with Johnson," *CT*, June 23, 1965; David Kraslow, "Book Recites Johnson Eagerness for Page 1," *LAT*, June 23, 1965.
14. Warren Weaver Jr., "Far-Reaching Decision," *NYT*, June 11, 1965; Pearson, "R. Kennedy Refused Bow"; RFK, "The Kennedy-Javits Amendment," *TNR*, June 12, 1965; AP, "RFK Decries Mail Order Guns," *BG*, May 21, 1965; Elsie Carper, "Gun Control Bill Backed by Kennedy," *WP*, May 21, 1965.
15. Rowland Evans and Robert Novak, "Humphrey vs. the Super-Liberals," *LAT*, June 4, 1965.
16. Alan L. Otten, "Kennedys vs. Administration?," *WSJ*, June 17, 1965.
17. AW, RFKOH, December 4, 1974, 511–13.

18. Gwen Gibson, "Kennedy Fiesta Bests Perle Mesta," *BG*, June 27, 1965; Michael Posner, "Capital Party Crisis—Ted vs. Perle," *BG*, June 26, 1965; AP, "Mansfield Spreads Oil on Capital Social Waters," *HC*, June 27, 1965.

19. AP, "Kennedys Not Political Foes—Humphrey," *CT*, June 5, 1965.

20. Robert Healy, "Kennedy Bros. Filling Vacuum," *BG*, June 28, 1965.

21. Kempton, "Robert F. Kennedy."

22. AW, author interview.

23. AMS, *A Thousand Days: John F. Kennedy in the White House* (Boston: Houghton Mifflin, 1965), 902.

24. Shesol, *MC*, 269–70; Frederick Dutton to RK, May 12, 1965, RFKSCP, Box 3, "Dutton, Frederick: 1965–1966."

25. Guthman and Allen, *RFK: Collected Speeches*, 217–18.

26. AW, RFKOH, October 5, 1973, 258–59; Guthman and Allen, *RFK: Collected Speeches*, 218; Eric Pace, "Roswell L. Gilpatric, Lawyer and Kennedy Aide, Dies at 89," *NYT*, March 17, 1996; James Reston, "Washington: Kennedy's Maiden Speech," *NYT*, June 25, 1965.

27. AW, RFKOH, October 5, 1973, 259; Guthman and Allen, *RFK: Collected Speeches*, 218.

28. AW, RFKOH, May 2, 1972, 171–73.

29. U.S. Senate, *Congressional Record*, 89th Cong., 1st sess., June 23, 1965, 14566-68.

30. "Statement by Senator Robert F. Kennedy on Senate Floor," June 23, 1965, RFKSSPR, Box 1: "June 21, 1965–June 30, 1965"; Guthman and Allen, *RFK: Collected Speeches*, 218–22; E. W. Kenworthy, "Kennedy Proposes Treaty to Check Nuclear Spread," *NYT*, June 24, 1965.

31. U.S. Senate, *Congressional Record*, 89th Cong., 1st sess., June 23, 1965,

14568–76; "The Nation: Johnson and Kennedy," *NYT*, June 27, 1965.

32. Kenworthy, "Kennedy Proposes Treaty."

33. AW, RFKOH, October 5, 1973, 261.

34. Ibid., 261–62; Howard Margolis, "R. Kennedy Urges U.S. Slow Spread of Nuclear Arms," *WP*, June 24, 1965.

35. Margolis, "R. Kennedy Urges U.S. Slow"; Tom Wicker, "Emerging as Party Independents," *NYT*, June 24, 1965.

36. Kenworthy, "Kennedy Proposes Treaty."

37. Reston, "Washington: Kennedy's Maiden Speech."

38. *RA*, 397; Robert A. Divine, "Lyndon Johnson and Strategic Arms Limitation," in *The Johnson Years, Volume Three: LBJ at Home and Abroad* (Lawrence: University Press of Kansas, 1994), 273–74; LBJ, *Vantage Point*, 469–70, 479.

39. Richard L. Stout, "Johnson: Each Mood a Debate," *CSM*, July 9, 1965; Pearson, "R. Kennedy Refused Bow."

40. AW, RFKOH, October 5, 1973, 262–65.

41. Joseph Alsop, "The State of LBJ," *WP*, July 5, 1965; Richard Wilson, "Johnson Reaction to Criticism May Be His Greatest Weakness," *LAT*, July 13, 1965; Stout, "Johnson: Each Mood a Debate"; Robert E. Thompson, "LBJ vs. LBJ: The Image Crisis," *BG*, July 11, 1965.

42. "Kennedy Speaks Out," *NYT*, June 25, 1965.

43. "Kennedys Change Plans," *NYT*, June 30, 1965; AP, "RFK Clan Plans Weekend Venture Shooting Rapids," *WP*, July 2, 1965; AP, "Kennedy Leads 83-Mile Raft Trip," *NYT*, July 3, 1965; AP, "Kennedy Trip Ends as Senator Shoots River Rapids in One-Man Kayak," *NYT*, July 5, 1965.

44. Bill Hogan, "Weekly Review," *ND*, June 26, 1965; Ted Sell, "War Losses Grow," *LAT*, June 24, 1965.

45. "Still Vietnam," *NYT*, July 11, 1965.

46. "Joe Dolan to the Senator," June 23, 1965, JDP, Box 1, "Memoranda May 11, 1965–May 27, 1965"; Andrew J. Glass, "RFK Alters Caustic Talk on Viet Nam," *BG*, July 10, 1965.

47. AW, RFKOH, October 30, 1973, 287–88; "Joe Dolan to the Senator," June 23, 1965; RK, "The Opening to the Future," California Institute of Technology, June 8, 1964, DOJ.

48. AP, "Rob't Kennedy Sees Need for De-escalation," *ND*, July 9, 1965; AP, "Political Appeal Seen as Key to Winning War," *LAT*, July 10, 1965.

49. AW, RFKOH, May 2, 1972, 99–101.

50. "Address by Senator Robert F. Kennedy, International Police Academy Commencement," July 9, 1965, 4, RFKSSPR, Box 1: "July 1, 1965–July 10, 1965."

51. W. Marvin Watson with Sherwin Markman, *Chief of Staff: Lyndon Johnson and His Presidency* (New York: St. Martin's Press, 2004), 124–25; David E. Bell, JFKOH, July 6, 1964, 41.

52. Watson with Sherwin, *Chief of Staff*, 125–26; Shesol, *MC*, 275.

53. Julius Duscha, "Bob Kennedy Deletes Possible LBJ Criticism," *WP*, July 10, 1965.

54. "Address by Senator Robert F. Kennedy, International Police Academy Commencement," 2–3.

55. Ibid., 5.

56. Glass, "RFK Alters Caustic Talk"; "Kennedy Urges Political Stance," *NYT*, July 10, 1965.

57. Watson with Sherwin, *Chief of Staff*, 127; Phillip Potter, "Robert Kennedy Alters Talk, Avoids U.S. Policy Criticism," *BS*, July 10, 1965.

58. "Kennedy Urges Political Stance"; Potter, "Robert Kennedy Alters Talk"; Glass, "RFK Alters Caustic Talk"; Joseph Alsop, "Vital Insight on RFK Speech," *BG*, July 13, 1965.

59. Potter, "Robert Kennedy Alters Talk."

60. Robert B. Semple, "Moyers' First Day in New Job Brings Twin News Conferences," *NYT*, July 10, 1965.

61. "The President's News Conference," July 9, 1965, American Presidency Project, http://www.presidency.ucsb.edu/ws/index.php?pid=27071; Potter, "Robert Kennedy Alters Talk"; AP, "Lodge to Resume Old Post in Saigon," *ND*, July 9, 1965; "Still Vietnam."

62. Potter, "Robert Kennedy Alters Talk."

63. Shesol, *MC*, 275; Watson with Sherwin, *Chief of Staff*, 127.

64. David Wise, "Schlesinger Says JFK Didn't Want Johnson," *BG*, July 13, 1965.

65. AMS, "Author's View on How Johnson Was Chosen," *Life*, July 16, 1965, 69.

66. *ATD*, 54–56.

67. Tom Wicker, "'60 Days Depicted by Schlesinger," *NYT*, July 13, 1965.

68. Wise, "Schlesinger Says JFK Didn't Want Johnson."

69. Berman, *Planning a Tragedy*, 5.

70. Shesol, *MC*, 320–21.

71. AP, "LBJ Gives Version of VP Bid," *HC*, July 14, 1965.

72. Manchester, *Death of a President*, 475.

73. AP, "JFK Saw LBJ as Best Successor: Bobby," *ND*, August 16, 1965.

74. Ward Just, "Kennedy Left a Wordy Crew," *WP*, September 5, 1965.

75. James Wechsler, "The Bay of Pigs and Viet Nam," *BG*, July 29, 1965.

76. AW, RFKOH, November 30, 1969, 42; Marguerite Higgins, "The Kennedy Irritant," *ND*, July 16, 1965; Roscoe

Drummond, "Heir Un-Apparent," *CSM*, July 26, 1965.

77. "Johnson Stresses Stand on Vietnam," *NYT*, July 26, 1965; Walter Mears, "Johnson Sending 50,000 More Troops to Viet Nam and Doubling Draft," *AC*, July 29, 1965; John D.

Pomfret, "No Reserve Call," *NYT*, July 29, 1965.

78. "S. Africans to Invite Mr Kennedy," *GDN*, July 13, 1965; Joseph Lelyveld, "Robert Kennedy to Visit South Africa," *NYT*, October 24, 1965.

10. SLOW BOIL (PGS. 198 TO 227)

1. "Hourly Poll Shows a Shift on Vietnam," *NYT*, July 30, 1965.
2. "An Interview with LBJ," *NW*, August 2, 1965, 20–21.
3. Pomfret, "No Reserve Call"; Dan Cordtz, "Lyndon's Legislation," *WSJ*, August 11, 1965.
4. E. W. Kenworthy, "Most in Congress Relieved by the President's Course," *NYT*, July 29, 1965; Godfrey Sperling Jr., "Thurmond Calls for 'Win' Policy in Vietnam Struggle," *CSM*, July 28, 1965; John Herbers, "Johnson Rebukes Rioters as Destroyers of Rights," *NYT*, August 21, 1965.
5. Kenworthy, "Most in Congress Relieved"; Sperling, "Thurmond Calls for 'Win' Policy"; E. W. Kenworthy, "Johnson's Policy in Vietnam—Four Positions in Congress," *NYT*, July 25, 1965.
6. "President Denies Substantial Split in U.S. on Vietnam," *NYT*, August 10, 1965.
7. Joseph R. L. Sterne, "E. M. Kennedy Airs Concern on Refugees," *BS*, July 16, 1965.
8. Robert Healy, "The Kennedys and Johnson," *BG*, July 18, 1965.
9. Richard L. Strout, "Safety Standards," *CSM*, July 24, 1965; David R. Jones, "U.S. Agency Spurs Car Safety Drive," *NYT*, January 27, 1965.
10. Morton Mintz, "Senate Safety Quiz Jolts Top Car Men," *WP*, July 14, 1965; "GM to Back $1 Million Road-Safety

Study; Sen. Robert Kennedy Calls Sum Inadequate," *WSJ*, July 14, 1965.
11. U.S. Congress, Senate, *Federal Role in Traffic Safety: Hearings Before the Subcommittee on Executive Reorganization of the Committee on Government Operations*, 89th Cong., 1st sess., 1965, 777–81.
12. Mintz, "Senate Safety Quiz Jolts"; Dan Cordtz, "Auto Executives Hurt Own Cause," *WSJ*, July 20, 1965.
13. "Ford to Put GSA-Asked Safety Devices on All Cars, Completing Plan in '67 Model," *WSJ*, July 22, 1965; "GM Says It Spent $193 Million in 1964 on Automobile Safety," *WSJ*, July 19, 1965; AP, "Chrysler Tells of $76 Million for Car Safety," *LAT*, July 26, 1965.
14. Elizabeth Brenner Drew, "The Quiet Victory of the Cigarette Lobby: How It Found the Best Filter Yet—Congress," *Atlantic Monthly*, September 1965.
15. PBE, RFKOH, July 15, 1969, 8–9, 11; Robert Wald, e-mail to author, May 21, 2009.
16. U.S. Senate, *Congressional Record*, 89th Cong., 1st sess., June 16, 1965, 13903, 13908–9.
17. E. W. Kenworthy, "Cigarette Warning Favored by Senate," *NYT*, June 17, 1965.
18. Guthman and Shulman, *Robert Kennedy*, 204–5.
19. Willard Edwards, "Senate Gets Work Law Repeal Bill," *CT*, September 2, 1965; "Kennedy Criticizes Banking

Bill," *NYT*, August 25, 1965; AP, "Senate Sharpens Criminal Laws in Washington," *HC*, September 1, 1965; Stein, *American Journey*, 168–69.

20. Stewart Alsop, "Robert Kennedy and the Liberals," *SEP*, August 28, 1965.

21. Fred Powledge, "Kennedy Aids Start of Harlem Poverty Project," *NYT*, June 12, 1965; "$1 Million Granted to Help Youth Here," *NYT*, August 13, 1965; "City Gets $236,802 Grant for Training of Dropouts," *NYT*, August 17, 1965.

22. Barthelmes, RFKOH, May 20, 1969, 43–44; "Kennedy Coming Here for VISTA Block Party," *NYT*, August 10, 1965, 14; Douglas Robinson, "Kennedy, at Rally Here, Urges All to Join in Fight on Poverty," *NYT*, August 13, 1965.

23. "National Council of Christians and Jews," April 28, 1965, RFKSSPR, Box 1: "April 21, 1965–April 30, 1965."

24. "Hot Summer of Negro Discontent," *NYT*, August 15, 1965; Peter Bart, "Watts Riot Panel Warns on Danger of New Violence," *NYT*, December 7, 1965.

25. Lawrence E. Davies, "California Issue for '66 Emerges," *NYT*, August 16, 1965.

26. Andrew J. Glass, "'They Have Made Conditions Worse,'" *BG*, August 18, 1965; David S. Broder, "Yorty and Shriver Disagree on Riots," *NYT*, August 18, 1965.

27. "State Convention—Independent Order of Odd Fellows," Spring Valley, NY, August 18, 1965, RFKSSPR, Box 1: "August 11, 1965–August 20, 1965."

28. "Respect for Law," *CSM*, August 21, 1965; Tom Wicker, "The South: The Second Secession," *NYT*, September 5, 1965; "Los Angeles: The Far Country," *Time*, September 24, 1965.

29. UPI, "RFK: 'More Leadership Must Come from Negroes,'" *Chicago*

Defender, September 4, 1965; UPI, "Kennedy Asks Action in North Racial Crisis," *WP*, September 4, 1965; AW, RFKOH, November 30, 1969, 93.

30. AP, "Not Seeking No. 2, Says Bob Kennedy," *AC*, August 26, 1965.

31. Jack Bell, "Bob Kennedy Says He Had No Disagreement with Brother over Johnson," *CT*, August 26, 1965; AP, "RFK 'Enthusiastic' on LBJ—Sorensen," *BG*, August 18, 1965.

32. "Kennedy Rejects a National Race," *NYT*, August 26, 1965.

33. Rowland Evans and Robert Novak, "LBJ and Bobby Kennedy," *WP*, August 19, 1965; Mary McGrory, "Mrs. Lincoln Has Faster Typewriter," *AC*, August 4, 1965; UPI, "Memoirs Reportedly Upset Mrs. Kennedy," *CT*, August 28, 1965; Vera Glaser, "Is the Sun Breaking Through?," *BG*, September 26, 1965; UPI, "No, That Isn't Jackie on Frankie's Yacht," *AC*, August 10, 1965.

34. UPI, "Third Child of Kennedy Is Injured," *WP*, August 30, 1965; UPI, "Kennedy Daughter Hurt as Horse Falls," *AC*, August 30, 1965; Ward Just, "RFK Goes Overboard in High Sea," *WP*, September 2, 1965; UPI, "Heavy Seas Failed to Stop Bob Kennedy," *LAT*, September 3, 1965.

35. *RK&HT*, 812.

36. UPI, "Tells of JFK's Retarded Sister," *ND*, September 18, 1965; McCarthy, *Johnny We Hardly Knew Ye*, 12; Nasaw, *Patriarch*, 90, 532–36, 628–31.

37. AW, RFKOH, November 30, 1969, 55; McCandlish Phillips, "Hospitals' Wards: A Study in Misery," *NYT*, September 10, 1965; John Sibley, "Kennedy Charges Neglect in State Care of Retarded," *NYT*, September 10, 1965; Homer Bigart, "Willowbrook Seeks to End Crowding and Add to Staff," *NYT*, October 14, 1965;

"Excerpts from Statement by Kennedy," *NYT*, September 10, 1965; Homer Bigart, "Willowbrook Doctor Is Striving to End 2 Snake Pits," *NYT*, September 13, 1965.

38. AW, RFKOH, November 30, 1969, 55.
39. Bigart, "Willowbrook Doctor Is Striving."
40. Phillips, "Hospitals' Wards"; "Before the Joint Legislative Committee on Mental Retardation," Concourse Plaza Hotel, September 9, 1965, 1, RFKSSPR, Box 1: "September 1, 1965–September 10, 1965."
41. Sibley, "Kennedy Charges Neglect"; Bigart, "Willowbrook Doctor Is Striving."
42. AW, RFKOH, November 30, 1969, 55–58.
43. "Before the Joint Legislative Committee on Mental Retardation," 1–2, 5; Maureen O'Neill, "2 NY Mental Schools Worse Than Zoo: RFK," *ND*, September 10, 1965.
44. "Before the Joint Legislative Committee on Mental Retardation," 10–11.
45. Sibley, "Kennedy Charges Neglect."
46. John Sibley, "Kennedy Backed by Secret Report on Mental Homes," *NYT*, September 11, 1965; John Sibley, "State Study Asks 150 Local Centers for Mentally Ill," *NYT*, September 13, 1965; John Sibley, "State Speeds Aid to Mental School," *NYT*, October 13, 1965; John Sibley, "State Unit Urged for the Retarded," *NYT*, October 18, 1965.
47. AW, RFKOH, October 5, 1973, 245–46; "Governor to Push Aid to Retarded," *NYT*, December 2, 1965.
48. Warren Weaver Jr., "Kennedy Accuses Rockefeller Again," *NYT*, December 21, 1965; Emanuel Perlmutter, "Kennedy Clashes with Rockefeller on Mental Funds," *NYT*, December 19,

1965; AW, RFKOH, November 30, 1969, 58–59.
49. McCarthy, *Johnny We Hardly Knew Ye*, 93; John H. Fenton, "Massachusetts Legislators Back Judge Morrissey for Federal Bench," *NYT*, October 1, 1965.
50. *RA*, 25–26.
51. Jeremiah V. Murphy, "Morrissey Called 'Unqualified,'" *BG*, September 27, 1965; James S. Doyle, "U.S. Judgeship for Morrissey?," *BG*, August 27, 1965; L. Dana Gatlin, "Bar Opposes Judge for U. S. Bench," *CSM*, September 8, 1965.
52. Gwirtzman, RFKOH, February 10, 1972, 62; Kennedy, *True Compass*, 234.
53. AW, RFKOH, October 30, 1973, 280; Gwirtzman, RFKOH, February 10, 1972, 69; Tom Wicker, "The Morrissey Affair," *NYT*, October 22, 1965; Clymer, *Edward M. Kennedy*, 73–74.
54. Gwirtzman, RFKOH, February 10, 1972, 64; James S. Doyle, "Bar Assn., Morrissey Conflict," *BG*, October 13, 1965; Martin Nolan, "Hearing an Education for Morrissey Jr.," *BG*, October 13, 1965.
55. Doyle, "Bar Assn., Morrissey Conflict."
56. Fred P. Graham, "Morrissey Admits Using a 'Quickie' Law Diploma," *NYT*, October 13, 1965; James S. Doyle and Martin F. Nolan, "Ted Vows Push for Morrissey," *BG*, October 16, 1965; Clymer, *Edward M. Kennedy*, 74–75.
57. "Judge Coleman?," *TNR*, May 29, 1965; "Senate Backs Coleman 76 to 8, for Judgeship on Appeals Court," *NYT*, July 27, 1965, 16; "Jackie Robinson Says: Hypocrisy," *CD*, August 14, 1965; John Herbers, "Coleman Backed by Senate Panel," *NYT*, July 14, 1965; PBE, RFKOH, January 3, 1970, 208–9; Clymer, *Edward M. Kennedy*, 74; David Wise, "Ted Can Win and Still

Lose," *BG*, October 20, 1965; "Morrissey Backed by Robert Kennedy," *NYT*, October 15, 1965.

58. Robert Healy, "Morrissey Hurting Ted Kennedy," *BG*, October 18, 1965; Gwirtzman, RFKOH, February 10, 1972, 68; Adam Clymer, "Close Senate Vote Seen on Morrissey," *BS*, October 21, 1965; Fred P. Graham, "Edward Kennedy Drops His Fight for Morrissey," *NYT*, October 22, 1965; Clymer, *Edward M. Kennedy*, 75–76.

59. James S. Doyle and Martin F. Nolan, "Ted Yields; Morrissey Appointment Shelved," *BG*, October 22, 1965.

60. Rowland Evans and Robert Novak, "Kennedy Bloc Strained," *WP*, October 24, 1965; Doyle and Nolan, "Ted Yields."

61. Gwirtzman, RFKOH, February 10, 1972, 69.

62. Clymer, *Edward M. Kennedy*, 76; Robert Healy, "There Was Only One Path Left for Kennedy: He Took It," *BG*, October 22, 1965; "Kennedy Ends Battle for Morrissey," *BS*, October 22, 1965; Doyle and Nolan, "Ted Yields."

63. Healy, "There Was Only One Path Left"; *ATD*, 31; PBE, RFKOH, January 3, 1970, 178–79.

64. Thomas, *Robert Kennedy*, 285.

65. Arthur Edson, "Bobby Working Hard to Get New Image," *Reading Eagle*, December 12, 1965.

66. "Immigration, Aid Bills Top Senate Calendar," *WP*, September 20, 1965; U.S. Senate, *Congressional Record*, 89th Cong., 1st sess., September 22, 1965, 24776–78.

67. William Moore, "Senate Votes New Plan on Immigration," *CT*, September 23, 1965; Douglas Kiker, "Johnson Signs Immigration Bill," *BG*, October 4, 1965; AP, "R. F. Kennedy Credited with Blockade Decision," *HC*, August 19, 1965.

68. Fred Dutton to RK, July 29, 1965, RFKSCP, Box 3: "Dutton, Frederick, 1965–1966"; AW, RFKOH, October 30, 1973, 288–89, 298–99.

69. AP, "Kennedy Would Invite Red China to A-Ban Talks," *ND*, October 13, 1965.

70. John W. Finney, "Kennedy Proposes U.S. Invite Peking to Parley on Arms," *NYT*, October 14, 1965; Stuart S. Smith, "Greater A-Ban Efforts Asked by Robert Kennedy," *BS*, October 14, 1965; "Prevention of Spread of Nuclear Weapons," October 13, 1965, RFKSSPR, Box 1: "October 11, 1965–October 20, 1965"; Norman Runnion, "RFK: Get China to Nuclear Talks," *BG*, October 14, 1965; Reuters, "China Is Silent on Geneva Bid," *WP*, October 16, 1965.

71. AP, "U.S. Names 58 Battle Dead; Vietnam Total Now at 831," *NYT*, October 15, 1965; Douglas Robinson, "Policy in Vietnam Scored in Rallies Throughout U.S.," *NYT*, October 16, 1965; "They March, Doubting They Will Overcome," *TNR*, October 30, 1965, 9.

72. Ronald Sullivan, "Kennedy Defends Academic Liberty," *NYT*, October 15, 1965; Thomas O'Neill, "Politics and People," *BS*, October 27, 1965; George H. Favre, "Genovese Case Flares," *CSM*, October 29, 1965.

73. Ronald Sullivan, "Nixon, Backing Dumont, Urges Ouster of Genovese," *NYT*, October 25, 1965; Richard M. Nixon, "Nixon Explains Stand on Ousting Genovese," *NYT*, October 29, 1965.

74. Rowland Evans and Robert Novak, "Inside Report: Humphrey & Boss Smith," *WP*, October 20, 1965; AP, "Kennedy Backs Lee in New Haven Visit," *HC*, October 24, 1965.

75. Shannon, *Heir Apparent*, 161.

76. Clayton Knowles, "Democrats List 2,354,989 Voters," *NYT*, August 5, 1965.

77. Shannon, *Heir Apparent*, 206; Warren Weaver Jr., "Big Gamble of John Vliet Lindsay," *NYT*, May 23, 1965; James Reston, "New York: A New Show Comes to Town," *NYT*, May 23, 1965; Charles Bartlett, "N.Y.'s Fragmentized Democrats Watch Lindsay's Blazing Star," *LAT*, July 16, 1965.

78. Newfield, *RFK*, 148; Rowland Evans and Robert Novak, "Wagner Eradicated," *WP*, September 19, 1965; Warren Weaver Jr., "Kennedy Declares Lindsay Leads Now but Can Be Beaten," *NYT*, July 23, 1965; RK to Tony Lewis, July 19, 1965, RFKSCP, Box 20: "Kennedy, Robert F.: Handwritten Notes."

79. Richard Witkin, "Lindsay Chooses Liberals' Leader as Running Mate," *NYT*, June 30, 1965; Thomas P. Ronan, "Lindsay Planning Party on 3d Line," *NYT*, August 8, 1965; Martin F. Nolan, "Mirror, Mirror, Who's Most Faithful?," *BG*, November 7, 1965; Richard Witkin, "William Buckley Jr. Is Reported Considering Running for Mayor," *NYT*, June 4, 1965.

80. Tom Collins and Si Radiloff, "Kennedy Is Leaving LI, Buys Co-op Apt. in City," *ND*, June 18, 1965; Phil Ryan to Angie Novella [*sic*], July 6, 1965, RFKSCP, Box 21: "Park Ave, 200, July 1965–January 1966"; "Kennedy's First Vote as Resident Cast Here," *NYT*, September 15, 1965.

81. Richard Witkin, "Lindsay Defeats Beame in Close Mayoral Contest," *NYT*, November 3, 1965; Sam Tanenhaus, "The Buckley Effect," *NYT*, October 2, 2005; "The Nation: Leaders Line Up," *NYT*, August 1, 1965; Martin Tolchin, "Democrats Assay Liberals' Action," *NYT*, June 29, 1965; Thomas P. Ronan, "Costikyan Yields Democratic Post," *NYT*, November 6, 1964, 22; Richard Witkin, "Beame Charts Campaign, Seeks to Reunify Party," *NYT*, September 16, 1965.

82. Joe Dolan to RK, "Memo," September 15, 1965, JDP, Box 1: "Memoranda, September 3, 1965–September 15, 1965"; vanden Heuvel and Gwirtzman, *On His Own*, 128–29; Richard Witkin, "Seesaw Contest," *NYT*, November 3, 1965; Rowland Evans and Robert Novak, "Democratic Chaos," *WP*, October 29, 1965; Thomas P. Ronan, "Beame Supported by Baptist Group," *NYT*, October 29, 1965; Richard Witkin, "City Will Elect a Mayor Today; Heavy Vote Due," *NYT*, November 2, 1965.

83. PBE, RFKOH, January 3, 1970, 174–76; Murray Kempton, "Running Against Buckley, Lindsay Beats Beame," *TNR*, November 13, 1965.

84. Martin Arnold, "'Squad' Attacks Lindsay Record," *NYT*, October 26, 1965.

85. Abraham D. Beame, RFKOH, June 27, 1978, 2–3, 6–7.

86. John J. Burns, "That Shining Hour," ed. Patricia Kennedy Lawford (not published, 1969), 87–88, JFKL.

87. William S. White, "Lindsay and Kennedy," *WP*, November 8, 1965; Arnold, "'Squad' Attacks Lindsay Record"; Mary McGrory, "In NYC . . . Pow! Crash! . . . Out Climbs Bobby Without a Scratch," *BG*, November 8, 1965.

88. Shannon, *Heir Apparent*, 166; Murray Kempton, "Kennedy and Lindsay," *TS*, November 5, 1965.

89. Warren Weaver Jr., "Camps Are Wary," *NYT*, November 1, 1965.

90. Witkin, "Seesaw Contest."

91. AP, "Polls Challenge Fails to Block Kennedys," *LAT*, November 3, 1965.

92. Lyn Shepard, "New York Win Pushes Lindsay Up Front in GOP," *CSM*, November 4, 1965.

93. Ronald Sullivan, "A Sweep in Jersey," *NYT*, November 3, 1965; "Talk to Be Preceded by Doheny Ceremonies," *Daily Trojan*, November 5, 1965; Carl Greenberg, "Kennedy Backs Dissent If It's Knowledgeable," *LAT*, November 6, 1965.

94. "University of Southern California Convocation," November 5, 1965, RFKSSPR, Box 1: "November 1, 1965–November 10, 1965"; Greenberg, "Kennedy Backs Dissent."

95. "University of Southern California Convocation."

96. Stan Metzler, "Senator Emphasizes Youth Responsibility," *Daily Trojan*, November 9, 1965.

97. "Tentative Schedule," RFKSCP, Box 21: "February 1965–November 1965."

98. AP, "Blood Drive Is Defended by Kennedy," *BS*, November 6, 1965; "Hysteria on the Hill," *WP*, August 23, 1965.

99. PBE, RFKOH, January 3, 1970, 181; "Portion of RFK Press Conference, November 5, 1965, a.m., regarding donation of blood to North Vietnamese," RFKSSPR, Box 1: "November 1, 1965–November 10, 1965."

100. AP, "Campus Gets 'Blood Fight,'" *BS*, November 3, 1965; UPI, "Blood for Reds Sought," *NYT*, November 2, 1965.

101. PBE, RFKOH, January 3, 1970, 181; "Portion of RFK Press Conference, November 5, 1965, a.m."; "Kennedy Voices Concern," *NYT*, November 6, 1965.

102. "Portion of RFK Press Conference, November 5, 1965, a.m."

103. AP, "Blood Drive Is Defended by Kennedy"; *CT*, November 10, 1965; Marguerite Higgins, "On the Spot: The New RFK," *ND*, November 12, 1965; Rowland Evans and Robert Novak, "RFK Trapped on Blood Issue," *BG*, December 5, 1965.

104. UPI, "Goldwater Lashes Radical Left," *WP*, November 7, 1965; Seymour Korman, "Barry Rips Bobby Blood-to-Enemy Remark," *CT*, November 7, 1965.

105. Peter Bart, "Goldwater Regrets That G.O.P. Didn't Attack Extremism in '64," *NYT*, October 15, 1965; R. W. Apple Jr. to RK, October 15, 1965, RFKSCP, Box 6: "Kennedy, Edward M. 1965"; "Vietnam Assessment: 'Difficult Times Ahead,'" *ND*, November 6, 1965.

106. PBE, RFKOH, January 3, 1970; "Kennedy Visits *Sentinel*; Talks at Testimonial," *Los Angeles Sentinel*, November 11, 1965.

107. "S. Africans to Invite Mr Kennedy"; Lelyveld, "Robert Kennedy to Visit South Africa"; Joseph Lelyveld, "Kennedy a Trial for South Africa," *NYT*, October 31, 1965.

108. "S. Africans to Invite Mr Kennedy."

109. Lelyveld, "Robert Kennedy to Visit South Africa"; Lelyveld, "Kennedy a Trial for South Africa"; Joseph Lelyveld, "Robert Kennedy's Plan Assailed in Johannesburg," *NYT*, October 27, 1965; Jaap Boekkool, "South Africa Plans Bar to Kennedy, King Visits," *WP*, November 23, 1965.

110. Kempton, "Kennedy and Lindsay."

11. *REVOLUCIÓN* (PGS. 228 TO 249)

1. Fred Dutton to Robert Kennedy, July 27, 1965, RFKSCP, "Dutton Frederick 1965–1966"; *ATD*, 194.

2. Philip Potter, "Mann Plugs Latin Policy," *BS*, October 13, 1965.

3. AW, RFKOH, May 22, 1972, 118.

4. John M. Goshko, "Vaughn Riding Alliance Trail," *WP*, August 29, 1965.

5. Mankiewicz, RFKOH, June 26, 1969, 5–6, 17; *RK&HT*, 693; vanden Heuvel and Gwirtzman, *On His Own*, 164–65.

6. AW, RFKOH, May 22, 1972, 119–20.

7. Mankiewicz, RFKOH, June 26, 1969, 6, 17–18.

8. Vanden Heuvel and Gwirtzman, *On His Own*, 165; Stein, *American Journey*, 152; *ATD*, 194.

9. Stein, *American Journey*, 152; *RK&HT*, 693.

10. Juan de Onis, "Democracy Brazilian Style," *NYT*, November 28, 1965.

11. Mankiewicz, RFKOH, June 26, 1969, 2–4, 7–8; Margie Bonnet, "Frank Mankiewicz," *People*, May 24, 1982.

12. Mankiewicz, author interview, June 19, 2008; Shesol, *MC*, 282.

13. Mankiewicz, RFKOH, June 26, 1969, 7–8; *An Honorable Profession: A Tribute to Robert F. Kennedy*, ed. Pierre Salinger, Edwin Guthman, Frank Mankiewicz, and John Seigenthaler (New York: Doubleday, 1968), 23.

14. Mankiewicz, RFKOH, June 26, 1969, 8–9; Victor Lasky, *Robert F. Kennedy: The Myth and the Man* (New York: Trident Press, 1968), 265.

15. Rowland Evans and Robert Novak, "Inside Report: Bobby & the Latins," *WP*, November 9, 1965; "R. F. Kennedy Starts Latin Trip Wednesday," *WP*, November 9, 1965.

16. Vanden Heuvel and Gwirtzman, *On His Own*, 165.

17. Evans and Novak, "Inside Report: Bobby & the Latins."

18. Branch, *Pillar of Fire*, 100–101; *RA*, 326–27, 406, 419–24, 433–34; Philip Dodd, "2 Special Assistants Quit White House Jobs," *CT*, September 16, 1965.

19. UPI, "Peruvians Greet Robert Kennedy as Tour Opens," *HC*, November 11, 1965; Andrew Glass, "The Compulsive Candidate," *SEP*, April 23, 1966, 36.

20. Dan Kurzman, "Robt. Kennedy's Tour Is Successful in Peru," *WP*, November 13, 1965; Glass, "Compulsive Candidate," 36; "Peruvians Welcome Kennedy," *CDD*, November 11, 1965; UPI, "Peruvians Greet Robert Kennedy."

21. AW, RFKOH, May 22, 1972, 124; AW, author interview.

22. "Statement by Robert F. Kennedy Before Peruvian Students," November 10, 1965, RFKSSPR; AW, RFKOH, May 22, 1972, 121–24, 136; Martin Arnold, "Robert Kennedy for President, Some Latins Say," *NYT*, November 18, 1965.

23. Martin Arnold, "Robert Kennedy Ends Peru Tour," *NYT*, November 14, 1965.

24. Lasky, *Robert F. Kennedy*, 268; "Text of Senator Robert F. Kennedy Speech to Students at Estadio Nataniel," November 15, 1965, RFKSSPR, Box 1: "November 11, 1965–November 20, 1965"; "Remarks of Senator Robert F. Kennedy to Students, Buenos Aires, Argentina," November 19, 1965, RFKSSPR, Box 1: "November 11, 1965–November 20, 1965."

25. Jules Dubois, "Bobby Bumps Yanks from Plane in Peru," *CT*, November 11, 1965; Kurzman, "Robt. Kennedy's Tour Is Successful"; Glass, "Compulsive Candidate," 37; "Children Cry Viva as Robert Kennedy Visits Peru's Cuzco," *NYT*, November 12, 1965.

26. Glass, "Compulsive Candidate," 37.

27. Thomas M. C. Johnston, RFKOH, October 27, 1969, 227, 234; Arnold, "Robert Kennedy Ends Peru Tour"; "Children Cry Viva"; Shannon, *Heir Apparent*, 126; Kurzman, "Robt. Kennedy's Tour Is Successful"; *RK&HT*, 695; *RA*, 438; Lasky, *Robert*

F. Kennedy, 266–67; AW, RFKOH, May 22, 1972, 168; UPI, "Kennedy Flying to Chile," *HC*, November 14, 1965.

28. Stein, *American Journey*, 152; AW, RFKOH, May 22, 1972, 129–30.

29. Stein, *American Journey*, 152–53; AW, RFKOH, May 22, 1972, 130–31; vanden Heuvel and Gwirtzman, *On His Own*, 166; *RA*, 438–39.

30. Martin Arnold, "Kennedy Winning Latins' Acclaim," *NYT*, November 22, 1965; AW, RFKOH, May 2, 1972, 131–33.

31. Arnold, "Kennedy Winning Latins' Acclaim"; Dan Kurzman, "Chilean Throngs Cheer Robert Kennedy," *WP*, November 16, 1965; Stein, *American Journey*, 153.

32. Glass, "Compulsive Candidate," 37.

33. "Chileans Cheer R. F. Kennedy," *BS*, November 14, 1965; Reuters, ". . . Chileans Weep as They See RFK," *BG*, November 15, 1965; Nathan Miller, "Frei Reviews Reform Plan for Kennedy," *BS*, November 15, 1965; Glass, "Compulsive Candidate."

34. "Chileans Cheer R. F. Kennedy"; "Kennedy, in Chile, Confers with Frei," *NYT*, November 15, 1965; *RK&HT*, 695; Kurzman, "Chilean Throngs Cheer Robert Kennedy"; Glass, "Compulsive Candidate."

35. Vanden Heuvel and Gwirtzman, *On His Own*, 167–68; Glass, "Compulsive Candidate"; *RK&HT*, 695–96.

36. Richard Reeves, "The People Around Bobby," *NYT*, February 12, 1967.

37. Glass, "Compulsive Candidate"; AP, "Robert Kennedy, Visiting Chile, Is Target of Abuse by Students," *NYT*, November 17, 1965; vanden Heuvel and Gwirtzman, *On His Own*, 168; *RK&HT*, 696; AP, "Bobby Jeered at Chilean Rally," *CT*, November 16, 1965; Stein, *American Journey*, 154; AP, "Rusk Gets Spat At in Uruguay,

and Robert Kennedy in Chile," *NYT*, November 17, 1965.

38. Glass, "Compulsive Candidate."

39. *WP*, November 17, 1965, A23; AW, RFKOH, May 2, 1972, 178–79; AW, RFKOH, June 11, 2009.

40. Glass, "Compulsive Candidate."

41. "Kennedys Visit a Boy Hurt by Buenos Aires Motorcade," *NYT*, November 20, 1965; Martin Arnold, "Kennedy to the Latins: 'I Have Come to Learn,'" *NYT*, November 28, 1965.

42. Arnold, "Robert Kennedy for President."

43. Glass, "Compulsive Candidate"; vanden Heuvel and Gwirtzman, *On His Own*, 169; Laing, *Next Kennedy*, 291–92.

44. Glass, "Compulsive Candidate."

45. Dan Cordtz, "Sen. Kennedy Defends Johnson's Policies on South American Visit," *WSJ*, November 18, 1965.

46. Glass, "Compulsive Candidate"; Kurzman, "Chilean Throngs Cheer Robert Kennedy."

47. AP, "Argentines Hail Robert Kennedy," *BS*, November 19, 1965; "Robert Kennedy Is Cheered by Thousands in Argentina," *NYT*, November 19, 1965.

48. Glass, "Compulsive Candidate"; AW, RFKOH, May 22, 1972, 136–37.

49. AP, "Argentines Hail Robert Kennedy."

50. Nathan Miller, "Kennedy Denies Latin Policy Rift," *BS*, November 22, 1965.

51. Glass, "Compulsive Candidate."

52. Arnold, "Kennedy Winning Latins' Acclaim."

53. Cordtz, "Sen. Kennedy Defends Johnson's Policies"; Miller, "Kennedy Denies Latin Policy Rift."

54. "Robert Kennedy Says He Won't Run in 1968," *NYT*, November 16, 1965; *RA*, 438, 435.

55. Thimmesch and Johnson, *RKA40*, 288.
56. James Reston, "Washington: The Education of Robert Kennedy," *NYT*, November 10, 1965.
57. Glass, "Compulsive Candidate"; *RK&HT*, 697; vanden Heuvel and Gwirtzman, *On His Own*, 171.
58. AW, RFKOH, November 30, 1969, 92.
59. Jules Dubois, "Bob Kennedy Skips Rio Date with Rusk," *CT*, November 22, 1965; "Brother Prays in Brazil," *NYT*, November 23, 1965; Glass, "Compulsive Candidate."
60. Reuters, "Boy Makes a Try," *WP*, December 2, 1965.
61. "Brother Prays in Brazil"; *RK&HT*, 697; vanden Heuvel and Gwirtzman, *On His Own*, 171; Glass, "Compulsive Candidate."
62. "RFK Tells Latins: You Have an Amigo," *ND*, November 24, 1965; "Nip Brazil Acid Plot Against RFK," *ND*, November 23, 1965; UPI, "3 Held in Plot to Hurl Acid at Kennedy," *WP*, November 24, 1965.
63. Francis B. Kent, "Act and Criticize Freely, Brazilian Youths Told," *LAT*, November 26, 1965.
64. Arnold, "Kennedy to the Latins."
65. "Remarks of Senator Robert F. Kennedy, Catholic University, Rio de Janeiro," November 25, 1965, RFKSSPR, Box 2: "November 21, 1965–November 30, 1965"; UPI, "Robert Kennedy Challenges Rio Students to Aid Needy," *NYT*, November 26, 1965; Kent, "Act and Criticize Freely."
66. Arnold, "Kennedy to the Latins."
67. "Remarks of Senator Robert F. Kennedy, Recife, Brazil," November 23, 1965, RFKSSPR, Box 2: "November 21, 1965–November 30, 1965."
68. "RFK Tells Latins."
69. "Remarks of Senator Robert F. Kennedy, Catholic University, Rio de Janeiro."
70. Dan Kurzman, "Conference Seeks More OAS Power, Prestige," *WP*, November 25, 1965.
71. Glass, "Compulsive Candidate," 44.
72. Johnston, RFKOH, October 27, 1969, 228, 235–36; de Onis, "Democracy Brazilian Style"; Kurzman, "Conference Seeks More OAS Power."
73. *RA*, 440–41; Glass, "Compulsive Candidate."
74. UPI, "Robert Kennedy Challenges Rio Students"; "RFK Sails into Brazil's 'Green Hell,'" *CDD*, November 25, 1965; James Nelson Goodsell, "Dear Editor," *CSM*, December 17, 1965; Glass, "Compulsive Candidate."
75. James Nelson Goodsell, "Kennedy Hailed Along Amazon," *CSM*, December 1, 1965; Goodsell, "Dear Editor"; Glass, "Compulsive Candidate."
76. Goodsell, "Dear Editor"; Glass, "Compulsive Candidate"; *RA*, 441–42.
77. Martin Arnold, "Robert Kennedy Exhorts Latins Toward Role in Asia and Africa," *NYT*, December 1, 1965; Glass, "Compulsive Candidate."
78. Arnold, "Robert Kennedy Exhorts Latin"; AW, RFKOH, May 2, 1972, 101–3.
79. Stein, *American Journey*, 154–55.
80. David Kraslow, "U.S. Explains Rejection of Peace Feeler," *LAT*, November 27, 1965; Charles Mohr, "M'Namara Finds Hanoi's Build-up Means Long War," *NYT*, November 30, 1965.
81. *Meet the Press*, NBC Universal archives, December 5, 1965; AWP, Box 24: "Kennedy, Robert F.: General."
82. *Meet the Press*, December 5, 1965.
83. Richard Eder, "Kennedy Asks Talks on G.I. Build-up," *NYT*, December 6, 1965.

84. *Meet the Press*, December 5, 1965; AWP, Box 24: "Kennedy, Robert F.: General.

85. Joseph Kraft, RFKOH, March 7, 1970, 23.

86. George Gallup, "Robert Kennedy Building Strength for Presidency," *HC*, November 28, 1965.

87. Martin F. Nolan, "Kennedy (D-N.Y.)," *BG*, November 28, 1965.

88. Gallup, "Robert Kennedy Building Strength."

89. Arthur Edson, "Has J.F.K.'s Popularity Brushed Off on Bobby?," *BS*, December 12, 1965.

12. POWER AND RESPONSIBILITY
(PGS. 250 TO 277)

1. *ND*, February 28, 1966, 67.

2. *NYT*, July 15, 1965.

3. *FRUS, 1964–1968*, vol. 3, *Vietnam, June–December 1965*, ed. David C. Humphrey, Edward C. Keefer, and Louis J. Smith (Washington, D.C.: Government Printing Office, 1996), Document 203.

4. John D. Pomfret, " 'Overture' Relayed by Italian Visitors," *NYT*, December 18, 1965; *FRUS, 1964–1968*, vol. 3, Documents 205–7; *RK&HT*, 733.

5. Kraslow and Loory, *Secret Search for Peace*, 133–34.

6. *RK&HT*, 733–74.

7. Kraft, RFKOH, March 7, 1970, 22, 37–38.

8. *RK&HT*, 733–34; Kraslow and Loory, *Secret Search for Peace*, 133–34.

9. McGeorge Bundy, LBJOH #2, February 17, 1969; *FRUS, 1964–1968*, vol. 3, Document 208.

10. Tom Wicker, "Now Congress Takes a Hard Look at Vietnam Policy," *NYT*, December 26, 1965; *FRUS, 1964–1968*, vol. 3, Document 208; Tom Wicker, "Johnson Is Beset by Tax Rise Issue," *NYT*, December 20, 1965.

11. "Long Island University, Metcalf Hall, Brooklyn Center," December 16, 1965, RFKSSPR. Box 2: "December 11, 1965–December 20, 1965."

12. Peter Bart, "Watts Riots Panel Warns on Danger of New Violence," *NYT*, December 7, 1965; Philip Geyelin, "U.S. Studies Coupling Bold Show of Firmness with a Push for Talks," *WSJ*, December 23, 1965; Arthur Krock, "In the Nation: 'Seatbelt' Tax Strategy," *NYT*, December 19, 1965.

13. Kraslow and Loory, *Secret Search for Peace*, 113, 138; "Kennedy Urges U.S. Try to Extend Truce Offered by Vietnam," *NYT*, December 10, 1965; Tom Lambert, "RFK to Rusk: Push Yule Truce," *BG*, December 10, 1965.

14. Martin F. Nolan, "Viet Policy Clash," *BG*, December 26, 1965.

15. "Truman, on Walk, Chides 2 Kennedys," *NYT*, December 24, 1965.

16. Nolan, "Viet Policy Clash"; *FRUS, 1964–1968*, vol. 3, Document 208.

17. Tom Lambert, "U.S. Restudies Idea of Christmas Cease-fire," *LAT*, December 22, 1965; *FRUS, 1964–1968*, vol. 3, Document 208.

18. Philip Dodd, "Month Truce in Viet Urged by Mansfield," *CT*, December 25, 1965; Murrey Marder, "If Truce Stands Up, U.S. May Extend It," *BG*, December 25, 1965.

19. "Brief Truce but No Talks," *NYT*, December 26, 1965; Kraslow and Loory, *Secret Search for Peace*, 138–43.

20. AP, "Bobby, Jackie Go Caroling," *CT*, December 18, 1965.

21. AP, "Kennedy Urges Racial Board in Each U.S. City," *LAT*, December 17,

1965; "Long Island University, Metcalf Hall, Brooklyn Center."

22. PBE, RFKOH, January 3, 1970; "Press Release," January 20, 1966, RFKSSPR, Box 2: "January 11, 1966–January 20, 1966."

23. "Luncheon of the Federation of Jewish Philanthropies of New York, Americana Hotel, New York City," January 20, 1966, RFKSSPR, Box 2: "January 11, 1966–January 20, 1966"; Guthman and Allen, *RFK: Collected Speeches*, 166–69.

24. PBE, RFKOH, January 3, 1970, 94; Richard J. H. Johnston, "Kennedy Warns of Negro Revolt," *NYT*, January 21, 1966.

25. Steven V. Roberts, "More Jobs Urged to Relieve Ghettos," *NYT*, January 22, 1966.

26. RK, "January 21, 1966—3:30 p.m.," January 21, 1966, RFKSSPR, Box 2: "January 21, 1966–January 31, 1966."

27. AW, RFKOH, July 3, 1974, 498; AW, RFKOH, November 30, 1969, 91–92.

28. Adam Walinsky, "Keeping the Poor in Their Place," *TNR*, July 4, 1964.

29. "Joint Conference Regions 9 and 9a, United Auto Workers," January 22, 1966, RFKSSPR, Box 2: "January 21, 1966–January 31, 1966."

30. David S. Broder, "Kennedys Join a Salute to O'Donnell," *NYT*, January 23, 1966; James S. Doyle, "Amidst Joking: Kennedys Join New 'Campaign,'" *BG*, January 23, 1966.

31. "Real Estate Notes," *NYT*, October 27, 1965.

32. Ralph Blumenthal, "Brooklyn Negroes Harass Kennedy," *NYT*, February 5, 1966.

33. "Wagner to Be Honored at Roosevelt Day Dinner," *NYT*, January 21, 1966; Martin F. Nolan, "RFK Invades ADA with Hubert's Help," *BG*, January 28, 1966; Frederick G. Dutton to RK,

November 29, 1966, RFKSCP, Box 3: "Dutton, Frederick, 1965–1966."

34. George Gallup, "Johnson Rated 'Most Admired Man of '65,'" *LAT*, January 2, 1966; Rowland Evans and Robert Novak, "Poll Results Jolt Humphrey Staff," *LAT*, December 21, 1965.

35. Marquis Childs, "How Much Press for Bob and Ted?," *WP*, January 19, 1966; Evans and Novak, "Poll Results Jolt Humphrey Staff"; Mary McGrory, "How Tough Can HHH Be?," *BG*, January 9, 1966.

36. Nolan, "RFK Invades ADA."

37. AW, RFKOH, November 30, 1969, 61; AW, author interview.

38. "ADA National Roosevelt Day Dinner," New York, NY, January 27, 1966, RFKSSPR, Box 2: "January 21, 1966–January 31, 1966."

39. "New York State Society of Newspaper Editors," Utica, NY, February 7, 1966, RFKSSPR, Box 2: "February 1, 1966–February 10, 1966."

40. AW, RFKOH, October 5, 1973, 236.

41. Bill Henry, "LBJ Believes in Full Treatment," *LAT*, January 4, 1966.

42. *FRUS, 1964–1968*, vol. 4, *Vietnam, 1966*, ed. David C. Humphrey (Washington, DC: Government Printing Office, 1998), Documents 3, 6.

43. Ibid., Document 3.

44. Ibid., Document 14.

45. Ibid., Document 24.

46. Ibid., Document 43.

47. Jack Bell, "Bombing: Senators' Opinions Vary Widely," *AS*, January 26, 1966.

48. Thomas Collins, "LBJ's Vietnam Quandary: What Next," *ND*, January 24, 1966.

49. Shesol, *MC*, 285–86, 520n.

50. *FRUS, 1964–1968*, vol. 4, Document 50.

51. *BG*, February 1, 1966, 1; LBJ, "Statement on the Resumption of

Bombing in North Vietnam," TMC, January 31, 1966.

52. E. W. Kenworthy, "Senators Reluctantly Back President on Air Strikes," *NYT*, February 1, 1966; Martin F. Nolan, "Ted, Bobby Differ on Bombing," *BG*, February 1, 1966.

53. "The President's Decision on the Tragic War in Vietnam," January 31, 1966, RFKSSPR, Box 2: "January 21, 1966–January 31, 1966."

54. Kenworthy, "Senators Reluctantly Back President."

55. William Borders, "Kennedy Spends a Day in Suburbs," *NYT*, January 18, 1966; Warren Weaver Jr., "Promises of Aid Given by Kennedy," *NYT*, January 20, 1966.

56. E. W. Kenworthy, "Senate Panel Will Conduct Broad Inquiry on Vietnam," *NYT*, February 4, 1966.

57. E. W. Kenworthy, "M'Namara Balks at Public Inquiry," *NYT*, February 5, 1966; Douglas Kiker, "Viet War: A Test in Congress . . . a Papal Proposal," *BG*, January 30, 1966.

58. *FRUS, 1964–1968*, vol. 4, Documents 64, 84; Kenworthy, "M'Namara Balks."

59. *FRUS, 1964–1968*, vol. 4, Document 63; Tom Wicker, "Johnson Arrives for Hawaii Talks with Saigon Aides," *NYT*, February 6, 1966; "Pressures on Hanoi," *NYT*, February 6, 1966.

60. "1,500 Women Peace Marchers Picket and Lobby in the Capital," *NYT*, February 10, 1966.

61. Neil Sheehan, "Edward Kennedy Tours in Vietnam," *NYT*, October 25, 1965.

62. Frederick G. Dutton to RK, "Re: Suggested South Viet Nam Trip," February 8, 1966, RFKSCP, Box 3: "Dutton, Frederick, 1965–1966."

63. AP, "Collegians Differ on Viet War," *AS*, February 7, 1966.

64. Homer Bigart, "Divorce Law Called 'Unfair' by Kennedy," *NYT*, February 8, 1966.

65. UPI, "Kennedy Attacks Draft as Unfair," *NYT*, February 12, 1966.

66. *RA*, 453–55; Dick Goodwin to RK, February 2, 1966, RFKSCP, Box 4: "Goodwin, Richard, 1965–1966."

67. James J. Kilpatrick, "Somehow, the Vietnam Hearings Seemed Unreal," *LAT*, February 24, 1966; Marvin Kalb, "The Vital Interests of Mr. Kennan," *NYT*, March 27, 1966.

68. *FRUS, 1964–1968*, vol. 4, Document 78.

69. David S. Broder, "Democrats Fear Midterm Losses," *NYT*, February 17, 1966; Jack Bell, "Liberals—Miffed at LBJ—Say 'He Won't Run Again,'" *BG*, February 13, 1966; *FRUS, 1964–1968*, vol. 4, Document 6.

70. *FRUS, 1964–1968*, vol. 4, Document 24.

71. U.S. Congress, Senate, *Supplemental Foreign Assistance Fiscal Year 1966—Vietnam: Hearings Before the Committee on Foreign Relations*, 89th Cong., 1966, 661–65; E. W. Kenworthy, "Rusk Says Peace of World Is Issue in Vietnam War," *NYT*, February 19, 1966; Max Frankel, "A Calm Rusk Holds Stage for 7 Hours," *NYT*, February 19, 1966.

72. *RA*, 453–55; Richard Goodwin to RK, February 17, 1966, RFKSCP, Box 4: "Goodwin, Richard, 1965–1966"; "Goodwinisms," *WP*, January 26, 1966.

73. E. W. Kenworthy, "Kennedy Bids U.S. Offer Vietcong a Role in Saigon," *NYT*, February 20, 1966.

74. Barthelmes, RFKOH, May 20, 1969, 31, 33; Shesol, *MC*, 289.

75. Robert E. Thompson, "Bob Kennedy Urges Share for Reds in Saigon Regime," *LAT*, February 20, 1966; Kenworthy, "Kennedy Bids U.S. Offer"; Fred Farrar, "Let Reds Help

Run S. Viet, Bobby Urges," *CT*, February 20, 1966; Murrey Marder, "Viet Coalition Rule Urged by Kennedy," *WP*, February 20, 1966.

76. James S. Doyle, "RFK Would Let Cong Share Viet Nam Rule," *BG*, February 20, 1966; AP, "Kennedys Ski Stowe Slopes," *BG*, February 19, 1966; UPI, "Kennedys Enjoy Day on Slopes," *BG*, February 22, 1966; "Nation: A Fox in a Chicken Coop," *Time*, March 4, 1966.

77. Sheldon M. Stern, *The Cuban Missile Crisis in American Memory: Myths Versus Reality* (Stanford, CA: Stanford University Press, 2012), 141.

78. Kenworthy, "Kennedy Bids U.S. Offer."

79. RK to McGeorge Bundy, February 24, 1966, ASNYPL, Box 501: "Background Materials, Vietnam, RFK Correspondence."

80. Thompson, "Bob Kennedy Urges Share for Reds"; "White House Stands on View on Vietcong," *NYT*, February 20, 1966.

81. Carl T. Rowan, "Why Humphrey Slammed RFK," *BG*, March 6, 1966; Don Smith and Edward G. Smith, "President's Men Attack Kennedy's Ideas on Cong," *ND*, February 21, 1966; Robert J. Donovan, "Humphrey Raps Viet Coalition Proposal of Robert Kennedy," *LAT*, February 21, 1966.

82. AP, "New Viet Shuffle," *LAT*, February 21, 1966; Ferenc Nagy, "Urges Caution in Coalition Plan for Viet," *CT*, February 21, 1966.

83. "Ho Chi Kennedy," *CT*, February 21, 1966; Eugene Patterson, "The President Is Challenged," *AC*, February 23, 1966; "Peace and Principle," *WP*, February 21, 1966.

84. David S. Broder, "Kennedy's Vietnam Plea Spurs Popularity on Democratic Left," *NYT*, February 21, 1966; Mary

McGrory, "RFK Creates New Role," *BG*, February 22, 1966; John Maffre, "Bundy and Ball Denounce Idea; Some Support It," *WP*, February 21, 1966.

85. Tom Wicker, "The Job After Bundy," *NYT*, December 9, 1965.

86. Richard Eder, "Ball and Bundy Score Idea," *NYT*, February 21, 1966; Arthur Krock, "In the Nation: Robert Kennedy's Proposal," *NYT*, February 22, 1966.

87. *RK&HT*, 736–37.

88. Murray Kempton, "The King over the Water," *TS*, March 4, 1966.

89. AP, "RFK Clarifies Plan on Cong," *AS*, February 22, 1966; "RFK Explains His Case," *BG*, February 23, 1966.

90. Kempton, "King over the Water."

91. E. W. Kenworthy, "Kennedy Agrees with White House on Vietnam Point," *NYT*, February 23, 1966; Joseph R. L. Sterne, "Johnson, Kennedy Narrow Viet Policy Differences," *BS*, February 23, 1966.

92. Warren Weaver Jr., "Kennedy vs. Humphrey—the Race Is On," *NYT*, February 27, 1966; James Reston, "Washington: Who Will Count the Ballots?," *NYT*, February 23, 1966; Mary McGrory, "RFK Returns to Camp LBJ," *BG*, February 24, 1966; Rowland Evans and Robert Novak, "Kennedy and Vietnam," *WP*, February 23, 1966.

93. "Kennedy and LBJ Draw Near Accord on Viet Cong Role," *ND*, February 23, 1966; E. W. Kenworthy, "15 in Senate Urge President Extend Pause in Bombing," *NYT*, January 28, 1966; John M. Hightower, "Viet Debate: LBJ Sees Solons' Stalemated; His Policies Standing," *AS*, February 24, 1966.

94. *FRUS, 1964–1968*, vol. 4, Document 79.

95. Seymour Topping, "U.S. and Vietnam Draw War Plans for 3 to 7 Years,"

NYT, February 26, 1966; Donald F. Kettl, "The Economic Education of Lyndon Johnson: Guns, Butter, and Taxes," in *Johnson Years, Volume Two*, 54–55, 62.

96. "Congress Passes Viet War Fund Bill," *WP*, March 2, 1966; Drew Pearson, "Looking Back at RFK," *WP*, February 27, 1966.

97. Godfrey Sperling Jr., "Governors' Poll Shows Viet Policy Ferment: Proposal 'Shocking,'" *CSM*, February 25, 1966.

98. Chesly Manly, "Assert S. Viet Reds Proven Unfit to Rule," *CT*, March 7, 1966.

99. *FRUS, 1964–1968*, vol. 4, Document 80; Ward Just, "Ky Vows Execution of Corrupt Officials," *WP*, February 26, 1966.

100. Reuters, "Humphrey Meets Rougher Pickets in Wellington," *Jerusalem Post*, February 21, 1966; Robert J. Donovan, "Humphrey Raps Viet Coalition Proposal of Robert Kennedy," *LAT*, February 21, 1966.

101. E. W. Kenworthy, "Humphrey Home from Asian Trip," *NYT*, February 24, 1966.

102. John D. Pomfret, "Johnson Denies 'Blind Escalation' in Vietnam War," *NYT*, February 24, 1966; Joseph S. Dineen Jr., "Across the City Desk," *BG*, March 6, 1966; Jimmy Breslin, "Must We Be Stupid?," *NYHT*, February 24, 1966; *RK&HT*, 737.

103. LBJ, "Remarks on Receiving the National Freedom Award," February 23, 1966, TMC.

104. Martin Nolan, "LBJ Offers TV Drama," *BG*, February 28, 1966.

105. *WP*, *CT*, February 24, 1966.

106. James Peck, *Upperdogs vs. Underdogs* (Canterbury, NH: Greenleaf Books, 1969), 102; Breslin, "Must We Be Stupid?"; Pomfret, "Johnson Denies 'Blind Escalation.'"

13. RIPPLE (PGS. 278 TO 297)

1. Andrew Kopkind, "Robert Kennedy's Road to Somewhere," *TNR*, April 2, 1966; Shesol, *MC*, 293.

2. Thomas Collins, "Kennedys Inc.," *ND*, November 13, 1965.

3. AW, RFKOH, October 30, 1973, 282–83.

4. "Kennedy on Kennedy," *WP*, March 2, 1966; Kopkind, "Robert Kennedy's Road."

5. UPI, "Humphrey Reports on Viet Nam Trip," *CDD*, February 26, 1966.

6. Richard Eder, "Humphrey Scores Vietcong as Unfit to Share in Rule," *NYT*, February 28, 1966.

7. Julius Duscha, "Humphrey Firm on War, Saddened at Liberal Split," *WP*, March 6, 1966; Paul L. Montgomery, "Irish Parade, and Politicians Beam," *NYT*, March 18, 1966.

8. George Gallup, "Kennedy Outpolls Nixon," *LAT*, March 11, 1966; March 17, 1966, RFKSCP, Box 21: "Schedules: January 1966–October 1966 + undated"; William Chapman, "Humphrey Urges ADA War Support," *WP*, April 24, 1966.

9. William F. Buckley Jr., "Dissecting Kennedy's Proposal Is Revealing," *LAT*, March 2, 1966.

10. Drew Pearson, "Democratic 'Doves' vs. Johnson," *WP*, March 10, 1966; Angie Novello to RK, "Your Presiding Score 1965," January 14, 1966, RFKSCP, Box 20: "Memoranda: Inter-Office, 1966"; Joe Dolan to RK, "Voting Percentage," May 18, 1966,

JDP, Box 1: "Memoranda, May 3, 1966—May 31, 1966."

11. Collins, "Kennedys Inc."; Richard Reeves, "Kennedy 2 Years After His Election," *NYT*, November 14, 1966.

12. Richard L. Strout, "Washington Watches Political Power Play," *CSM*, March 28, 1966; Mary McGrory, "Kennedys Lead Liberal Opposition," *BG*, May 8, 1966.

13. Reeves, "Kennedy 2 Years After"; Shannon, *Heir Apparent*, 89.

14. Harry Bernstein, "Surplus of Farm Hands in State, Tieburg Reports," *LAT*, March 14, 1966; U.S. Congress, Senate, *Amending Migratory Labor Laws: Hearings Before the Subcommittee on Migratory Labor of the Committee on Labor and Public Welfare*, 89th Cong., 2nd sess., 1966, 429–30.

15. PBE, RFKOH, July 15, 1969, 125–26; Andrew Kopkind, "The Grape Pickers' Strike," *TNR*, January 29, 1966, 12–14.

16. U.S. Congress, Senate, Subcommittee, *Amending Migratory Labor Laws*, 548, 626–30.

17. Harlan Trott, "Senate Probes Farm Wage: $1.20 Minimum Sought," *CSM*, March 29, 1966.

18. PBE, RFKOH, July 15, 1969, 127–30; Trott, "Senate Probes Farm Wage."

19. Harry Bernstein, "2 Senators Term Farm Housing in Tulare 'Shameful,'" *LAT*, March 16, 1966.

20. AP, "RFK to Be Guarded on Visit to Ole Miss," *BG*, March 4, 1966; *RK&HT*, 320–25; Victor S. Navasky, *Kennedy Justice* (New York: Atheneum, 1971), 236.

21. "Mississippi Split on Kennedy Visit," *NYT*, February 20, 1966; AP, "RFK to Be Guarded"; UPI, "Segregationists to Protest Kennedy Mississippi Speech," *NYT*, February 15, 1966; "Mississippi Is Urged to Stay Calm Today as Kennedy Visits," *NYT*, March 8, 1966.

22. Jack Nelson, "Bob Kennedy Warned of Visit to Mississippi," *LAT*, February 20, 1966; "A Kennedy Protest Dropped in Jackson," *NYT*, March 16, 1966.

23. AP, "RFK to Be Guarded"; "Mississippi Is Urged to Stay Calm."

24. Barrett Prettyman Jr., undated, AWP, Box 24: "Kennedy, Robert F.: Mississippi-Alabama Trip, March 1966."

25. AP, "Bobby Lays Ole Miss Riot to Gov. Barnett," *CT*, March 19, 1966; *WP*, March 19, 1966, A2.

26. Robert E. Baker, "Bobby Charms Ole Miss Despite '62," *WP*, March 19, 1966; James J. Kilpatrick, "Turnabout in Dixie," *ND*, March 25, 1966.

27. Barrett Prettyman Jr., undated, AWP, Box 24; Kilpatrick, "Turnabout in Dixie"; Adam Clymer, "A Kennedy Penetrates the South," *BS*, March 24, 1966.

28. "AP, "Bobby Lays Ole Miss Riot to Gov. Barnett."

29. "14 Negroes Attend Changed Ole Miss," *ND*, March 11, 1966.

30. "University of Mississippi Law School Forum," March 18, 1966, RFKSSPR, Box 2: "March 11, 1966–March 20, 1966."

31. "Bobby in Ole Miss with Rights Plea," *ND*, March 18, 1966.

32. UPI, "Kennedy Blames Barnett at Ole Miss," *AC*, March 19, 1966.

33. Roy Reed, "Kennedy Cheered in Ole Miss Talk by Crowd of 5,500," *NYT*, March 19, 1966; Mary McGrory, "Kennedy Charm Erodes Resistance," *BG*, March 23, 1966.

34. Baker, "Bobby Charms Ole Miss"; Clymer, "A Kennedy Penetrates the South"; Jim Bennett, "Bobby Is Cheered in Miss., Ala.," *ND*, March 19, 1966.

35. Clymer, "A Kennedy Penetrates the South"; "Mary McGrory on Robert

Kennedy's Trip Through the Deep South," *BG*, April 13, 1966.

36. Adam Clymer, "R. F. Kennedy at Ole Miss," *BS*, March 19, 1966.

37. Andrew J. Glass, "RFK Plans Controversial South Africa Visit in June," *BG*, March 25, 1966.

38. AP, "Sen. Kennedy Gets Visa to Visit S. Africa," *CT*, March 23, 1966.

39. "Robert Kennedy Gets Visa to Visit South Africa," *NYT*, March 23, 1966.

40. "Kennedy Trip to Africa Set for Summer," *LAT*, March 24, 1966; "RFK to Speak at Cape Town," *WP*, May 12, 1966.

41. David S. Broder, "Democrats Start to Form '72 Lines," *NYT*, March 24, 1966.

42. Warren Weaver Jr., "One of Them Will Probably Be Next in the White House," *NYT*, May 22, 1966.

43. AP, "Morse May Back Kennedy in 1968," *BS*, March 27, 1966; Daryl E. Lembke, "Morse May Back Bob Kennedy in '68 Presidential Race," *LAT*, March 27, 1966; "Student Group Pushes RFK for Presidency," *WP*, April 3, 1966; *TNR*, April 9, 1966, 30; "Kennedy Billboard Coming Down," *WP*, May 2, 1966; "The Nation: They're Off! For 1972," *NYT*, March 27, 1966.

44. "3 Boys from D.C. Frolic," *ND*, April 23, 1966; "Senator Robert Kennedy Explains His Position," *U.S. News & World Report*, March 14, 1966, 49.

45. Philip Dodd, "Raps Foreign Military Aid and Makes Hit," *CT*, April 26, 1966; Joe Dolan to RK, April 28, 1966, JDP, Box 1: "Memoranda, April 1, 1966–April 10, 1966."

46. AP, "LBJ Asks Cut in Outlay of $1.1 Billion," *ND*, April 2, 1966; Dick Herbert, "Viet Cong Peace Role Backers Denounced in Russell Speech Here," *AC*, March 5, 1966; Majorie Hunter, "President Wins Key House Tests; $2.5 Billion Voted," *NYT*, March 30, 1966.

47. AP, "Senate OKs Cash for Those over 70," *ND*, March 9, 1966.

48. AP, "LBJ Asks Cut in Outlay."

49. U.S. Congress, Senate, *Elementary and Secondary Education Act of 1966: Hearings Before the Subcommittee on Education of the Committee on Labor and Public Welfare*, 89th Cong., 2nd sess., 1966, 343–44, 349.

50. Warren Weaver Jr., "Kennedy Assails Johnson's Plans for Budget Cuts," *NYT*, April 20, 1966.

51. PBE, RFKOH, February 21, 1970, 220; Weaver, "Kennedy Assails Johnson's Plans."

52. Warren Weaver Jr., "Johnson Defended on Kennedy Budget Charges," *NYT*, April 21, 1966.

53. "Partial Transcript of President's News Conference on Vietnam and Other Subjects," *NYT*, April 23, 1966.

54. Roland J. Ostrow, "Johnson Hits Critics of Health, Poverty Efforts," *LAT*, April 23, 1966; LBJ, "Remarks in Baltimore at the Celebration of the Bicentennial of American Methodism," April 22, 1966, TMC.

55. "The World: Johnson and Critics," *NYT*, May 1, 1966.

56. "The World: Whose MiG's in Vietnam?," *NYT*, May 1, 1966; "U.S. Jet Shoots Down Enemy's Best Plane," *HC*, May 1, 1966; Murrey Marder, "LBJ Alone to Decide on Viet 'Hot Pursuit,'" *WP*, April 29, 1966.

57. "Text of Kennedy Statement on Bombing in Vietnam," *NYT*, April 28, 1966.

58. E. W. Kenworthy, "Kennedy Assails Sanctuary Policy," *NYT*, April 28, 1966; James Reston, "Washington: 'There Is No Sanctuary,'" *NYT*, April 27, 1966.

59. "Text of Kennedy Statement on Bombing in Vietnam."

60. "President Alone to Decide on Pursuit of Red Planes," *NYT*, April 29, 1966.

61. Philip Potter, "Kennedy Has More Advice for Johnson on Red China," *BS*, May 13, 1966; Robert C. Albright, "RFK Urges Red China Be Invited to A-Talks," *WP*, May 13, 1966; John W. Finney, "Senate Supports Treaty to Curb Spread of Atomic Weapons," *NYT*, May 18, 1966.

62. "1-A Father of 8 Asks Help," *NYT*, April 13, 1966; Kempton, "Kennedy and Lindsay."

63. Kopkind, "Robert Kennedy's Road."

64. William F. Buckley, "The Inevitability of Bobby Kennedy," *BG*, April 8, 1966.

65. James A. Wechsler, "Did RFK Really Travel South?," *BG*, December 10, 1965; Richard Eder, "Kennedy Bids U.S. Aid Latin Change," *NYT*, May 10, 1966; Dan Kurzman, "RFK Urges Latin Aid Be Reform Spur," *WP*, May 10, 1966.

66. James Reston, "New York: The Mounting Kennedy Campaign," *NYT*, May 11, 1966.

67. Richard Eder, "Kennedy Cautions on U.S. Policy of Opposing Latin 'Communists,'" *NYT*, May 11, 1966.

68. Joseph Lelyveld, "Verwoerd's Party Scores Heavy Election Gains," *NYT*, March 31, 1966.

69. AP, "Times Man in South Africa Leaves at Regime's Order," *NYT*, April 28, 1966; UPI, "South Africa Bars Foreign Reporters on Kennedy's Tour," *NYT*, May 25, 1966.

70. "South Africa Curbs a Student Leader," *NYT*, May 12, 1966; Robert F. Kennedy, "Suppose God Is Black," *Look*, August 23, 1966; *RFK in the Land of Apartheid: A Ripple of Hope* (Shoreline Productions, 2009), DVD.

71. Trevor Coombe to AW, May 31, 1966, RFKST, Box 13: "South Africa, May 25, 1966–May 31, 1966."

72. Kopkind, "Robert Kennedy's Road"; "Bobby Kennedy: A Political Safari," *WP*, June 5, 1966.

73. "South African Trip Begun by Kennedy; 1,000 Welcome Him," *NYT*, June 5, 1966.

74. *RFK in the Land of Apartheid.*

75. UPI, "Kennedy Begins Trip to 4 African Lands," *NYT*, June 2, 1966; USIS Pretoria to USIA Washington, June 10, 1966, RFKST, Box 13: "South Africa, June 1966"; "Kennedy Gets Book on Apartheid, Gives One on U.S. Negroes," *NYT*, June 6, 1966.

76. "RFK's handwritten notes," July 8, 1966, RFKST, Box 19: "*Look* Article, RFK Notes, July 8, 1966."

77. Joseph Lelyveld to RK, undated memo, AWP, Box 15: "Foreign Policy: Africa, undated memoranda"; Reuters, "R. Kennedy Reports South African Rebuff," *WP*, June 6, 1966; "Excerpts from Robert Kennedy's Address in South Africa Assailing Apartheid," *NYT*, June 7, 1966.

78. "Kennedy and Robertson Chat in Flat," *Cape Times*, June 7, 1966; RFKST, Box 13: "South Africa, June 7, 1966."

79. Ian Robertson interview, private papers of Larry Shore; "S. Africans Hail Talk by Kennedy," *WP*, June 7, 1966.

80. *RFK in the Land of Apartheid.*

81. RK, "Day of Affirmation Address, University of Capetown."

EPILOGUE: MEMORIAL (PGS. 298 TO 303)

1. Penn Kimball, "He Builds His Own Kennedy Identity and the Power Flows Freely to Him," *Life*, November 18, 1966.
2. Kennedy, "Suppose God Is Black."
3. "Kennedy Invited Back to South Africa," *NYT*, June 8, 1966.
4. Johnston, RFKOH, October 27, 1969, 236.
5. Kennedy, "Suppose God Is Black"; Stanley Uys, "Assassin Tried to Sue U.S. Government," *WP*, September 12, 1966; "Johnson Decries Assassination; Rights Leaders Echo Dismay," *NYT*, September 7, 1966.
6. Frank Maier, "'So I Ask You to Return Home and Say a Prayer,'" *BG*, April 5, 1968.
7. RK, "Statement on the Death of Martin Luther King, Jr.," April 4, 1968, JFKL.
8. Frank Mankiewicz to Ethel Kennedy, November 25, 1968, Frank Mankiewicz Personal Papers, JFKL.
9. *RA*, 450–51.
10. Laing, *Next Kennedy*, 40–41.
11. Fallaci, "Robert Kennedy Answers," 62.
12. Richard Stout, "What's Ahead for Robert Kennedy?," *CSM*, November 2, 1966.
13. Halberstam, *Unfinished Odyssey*, 31.
14. RK, "Remarks at the University of Kansas," March 18, 1968, JFKL.
15. *RK&HT*, 908, 914.
16. Fallaci, "Robert Kennedy Answers," 61.
17. McCarthy, *Johnny We Hardly Knew Ye*, 89.
18. Kennedy, *Times to Remember*, 477.
19. Paul Houston, "Wife Was Reassured by Heartbeat Sounds," *LAT*, June 6, 1968.

INDEX

A Note on the Author

John R. Bohrer is a reporter, historian, and television news producer. He has prepared news anchors for high-profile interviews, and his research has been cited by the *New York Times*, the *Washington Post*, and the *Boston Globe*. His writing has appeared in *New York* magazine, the *New Republic*, *Politico*, and *USA Today*, among other publications. *The Revolution of Robert Kennedy* is his first book. A New Jersey native and graduate of Washington College in Chestertown, Maryland, he currently resides in Brooklyn, New York.